MacBook For Dummies, 2nd Edition

W9-BOM-057

Cheat Sheet

Finder Keyboard Shortcuts

Key	Function	Key	Function
⌘+A	Selects all items in the active window	⌘+↑ (up arrow)	Shows enclosing folder
⌘+C	Copies selected items	⌘+`	Cycles through windows
⌘+D	Duplicates the selected items	⌘+Shift+?	Displays the Mac OS X Help Viewer
⌘+E	Ejects the selected volume	⌘+Shift+A	Takes you to your Applications folder
⌘+F	Displays the Find dialog box		
⌘+H	Hides All Finder windows	⌘+Shift+C	Takes you to the top-level computer location
⌘+I	Shows info for selected items	⌘+Shift+G	Takes you to a folder that you specify
⌘+J	Shows the view options for the active window	⌘+Shift+H	Takes you to your Home folder
⌘+K	Displays the Connect to Server dialog box	⌘+Shift+I	Connects you to your iDisk
		⌘+Shift+Q	Logs you out
⌘+L	Creates an alias for the selected item	⌘+Shift+N	Opens a new untitled folder in the active window
⌘+M	Minimizes the active window		
⌘+N	Opens a new Finder window	⌘+Shift+U	Takes you to your Utilities folder
⌘+O	Opens (or launches) the selected item	⌘+Shift+Del	Deletes the contents of the Trash
⌘+R	Shows the original for the selected alias	⌘+Option+ Esc	Displays the Force Quit Applications dialog
⌘+T	Adds the selected item to the Sidebar	⌘+Option+H	Hides all windows except the Finder window
⌘+V	Pastes an item from the Clipboard		
⌘+W	Closes the active window	⌘+Option+N	Opens a new Smart Folder
⌘+X	Cuts the selected items	⌘+Option+T	Hides the Finder window toolbar
⌘+Z	Undoes the last action (if possible)	⌘+Ctrl+ Power	Restarts your laptop if it locks up
⌘+,	Displays Finder Preferences		
⌘+1	Shows the active window in icon mode	F9 (or fn+F9)	Uses Exposé to show all open windows
⌘+2	Shows the active window in list mode		
⌘+3	Shows the active window in column mode	F10 (or fn+F10)	Uses Exposé to show all open windows for the current application
⌘+[	Moves back to the previous Finder location		
		F11	Uses Exposé to hide all windows and display the Desktop
⌘+]	Moves forward to the next Finder location		
⌘+Del	Moves selected items to the Trash	F12	Displays your Dashboard widgets

MacBook For Dummies, 2nd Edition

Cheat Sheet

Strange-Looking Menu Keys

Symbol	Action	What It Does
⏏	Media Eject	Ejects a CD or DVD from your optical drive
◀	Audio Mute	Mutes (and restores) all sound produced by your MacBook
☀	Keyboard Illumination	Increases, decreases, or turns off the brightness of your keyboard backlighting (MacBook Air and MacBook Pro only)
◀)))	Volume Up	Increases the sound volume
◀)	Volume Down	Decreases the sound volume
⌘	Command	Primary modification for menus and keyboard shortcuts
⌃	Control	Displays the right-click/Control-click menu
⌥	Option	Modifier for keyboard shortcuts
⌦	Del	Deletes the selected text

Startup Keys You Should Memorize Eventually

Key	Effect on Your Mac
C	Boots from the CD or DVD loaded in your optical drive (if you have one)
Media Eject	Ejects the CD or DVD in your optical drive (again, if you have one)
Option	Displays a menu allowing you to choose the boot volume
Shift	Prevents your login Items from running
T	Starts your laptop in FireWire Target Disk mode (not available on MacBook Air)
⌘+V	Show Mac OS X console messages
⌘+S	Starts your laptop in single-user mode
⌘+Option+P+R	Resets Parameter RAM (PRAM)

For Dummies: Bestselling Book Series for Beginners

MacBook®

FOR

DUMMIES®

2ND EDITION

by Mark L. Chambers

Wiley Publishing, Inc.

MacBook® For Dummies®, 2nd Edition

Published by
Wiley Publishing, Inc.
111 River Street
Hoboken, NJ 07030-5774

www.wiley.com

Copyright © 2008 by Wiley Publishing, Inc., Indianapolis, Indiana

Published by Wiley Publishing, Inc., Indianapolis, Indiana

Published simultaneously in Canada

For general information on our other products and services, please contact our Customer Care Department within the U.S. at 800-762-2974, outside the U.S. at 317-572-3993, or fax 317-572-4002.

For technical support, please visit www.wiley.com/techsupport.

Wiley also publishes its books in a variety of electronic formats. Some content that appears in print may not be available in electronic books.

Library of Congress Control Number: 2008930523

ISBN: 978-0-470-27816-1

Manufactured in the United States of America

10 9 8 7 6 5 4 3 2 1

WILEY

About the Author

Mark L. Chambers has been an author, computer consultant, BBS sysop, programmer, and hardware technician for 25 years — pushing computers and their uses far beyond "normal" performance limits for decades now. His first love affair with a computer peripheral blossomed in 1984 when he bought his lightning-fast 300 BPS modem for his Atari 400. Now he spends entirely too much time on the Internet and drinks far too much caffeine-laden soda.

With a degree in journalism and creative writing from Louisiana State University, Mark took the logical career choice: programming computers. After five years as a COBOL programmer for a hospital system, however, he decided there must be a better way to earn a living — and he became the Documentation Manager for Datastorm Technologies, a well-known communications software developer. Somewhere in between designing and writing software manuals, Mark began writing computer how-to books. His first book, *Running a Perfect BBS,* was published in 1994 — and after a short decade or so of fun (disguised as hard work), Mark is one of the most productive and best-selling technology authors on the planet.

Along with writing several books a year and editing whatever his publishers throw at him, Mark has also branched out into Web-based education, designing and teaching a number of online classes — called *WebClinics* — for Hewlett-Packard.

His favorite pastimes include collecting gargoyles, watching St. Louis Cardinals baseball, playing his three pinball machines and the latest computer games, supercharging computers, and rendering 3-D flights of fancy with TrueSpace — and during all that, he listens to just about every type of music imaginable. Mark's worldwide Internet radio station, *MLC Radio* (at www.mlcbooks.com), plays only CD-quality classics from 1970 to 1979, including everything from Rush to Billy Joel to the Rocky Horror Picture Show.

Mark's rapidly expanding list of books includes *iMac For Dummies,* 5th Edition; *Mac OS X Leopard All-In-One Desk Reference For Dummies; Building a PC For Dummies,* 5th Edition; *Scanners For Dummies,* 2nd Edition; *CD & DVD Recording For Dummies,* 2nd Edition; *PCs All-In-One Desk Reference For Dummies,* 3rd Edition; *Mac OS X Tiger: Top 100 Simplified Tips & Tricks; Microsoft Office v. X Power User's Guide; BURN IT! Creating Your Own Great DVDs and CDs; The Hewlett-Packard Official Printer Handbook; The Hewlett-Packard Official Recordable CD Handbook; The Hewlett-Packard Official Digital Photography Handbook; Computer Gamer's Bible; Recordable CD Bible; Teach Yourself the iMac Visually; Running a Perfect BBS; Official Netscape Guide to Web Animation;* and the *Windows 98 Troubleshooting and Optimizing Little Black Book.*

His books have been translated into 16 languages so far — his favorites are German, Polish, Dutch, and French. Although he can't read them, he enjoys the pictures a great deal.

Mark welcomes all comments about his books. You can reach him at mark@mlcbooks.com, or visit MLC Books Online, his Web site, at www.mlcbooks.com.

Dedication

This book is dedicated to Jody Cooper, a true friend who just won't quit —
whether he's elbow-deep in a computer chassis or dancing the Time Warp in
front of the Silver Goddess. May our friendship last another 20 years . . . and
longer!

Author's Acknowledgments

It hit me right in the middle of this project — while writing a book about
Apple's well-designed Macintosh laptops and software, I had the "best-
designed" people in the technology publishing business working alongside
me! These folks made sure that what you read is accurate, funny, and easy to
understand.

Coincidence? I think not. That's the Wiley Way.

First, I'd like to thank my technical editor, Greg Willmore, whose expert
knowledge of Apple hardware and software ensured that I didn't get FireWire
400 mixed up with FireWire 800. I owe a huge debt of gratitude as well to my
hardworking senior copy editor, Teresa Artman, who once again provided
the perfect combination of an eagle eye and a welcome sense of humor!

As with every book I've written, I'd like to thank my wife, Anne; and my children, Erin, Chelsea, and Rose; for their support and love — and for letting me
follow my dream!

Finally, I need to send my heartfelt thanks — once *again* — to two wonderful
editors at Wiley: my project editor, Mark Enochs, and my acquisitions editor,
Bob Woerner. A book like this wouldn't be possible without the patience,
guidance, and hard work that Mark and Bob provide . . . and they're great
friends as well. It's win-win!

Publisher's Acknowledgments

We're proud of this book; please send us your comments through our online registration form located at www.dummies.com/register/.

Some of the people who helped bring this book to market include the following:

Acquisitions and Editorial

Senior Project Editor: Mark Enochs

Executive Editor: Bob Woerner

Senior Copy Editor: Teresa Artman

Technical Editor: Greg Willmore

Editorial Manager: Leah Cameron

Editorial Assistant: Amanda Foxworth

Senior Editorial Assistant: Cherie Case

Cartoons: Rich Tennant (www.the5thwave.com)

Composition Services

Project Coordinator: Katie Key

Layout and Graphics: Stephanie D. Jumper, Christine Williams

Proofreaders: Caitie Kelly, Bonnie Mikkelson

Indexer: Potomac Indexing, LLC

Publishing and Editorial for Technology Dummies

Richard Swadley, Vice President and Executive Group Publisher

Andy Cummings, Vice President and Publisher

Mary Bednarek, Executive Acquisitions Director

Mary C. Corder, Editorial Director

Publishing for Consumer Dummies

Diane Graves Steele, Vice President and Publisher

Composition Services

Gerry Fahey, Vice President of Production Services

Debbie Stailey, Director of Composition Services

Contents at a Glance

Introduction 1

Part I: Tie Myself Down with a Desktop? Preposterous!... 7

Chapter 1: Hey, It Really Does Have Everything I Need 9

Chapter 2: Turning On Your Portable Powerhouse 31

Chapter 3: The Laptop Owner's Introduction to Mac OS X 43

Part II: Shaking Hands with Mac OS X 53

Chapter 4: Opening and Closing and Clicking and Such 55

Chapter 5: Getting to the Heart of the Leopard 77

Chapter 6: A Nerd's Guide to System Preferences 93

Chapter 7: Sifting through Your Stuff 109

Part III: Connecting and Communicating 119

Chapter 8: Taking Your Laptop on Safari! 121

Chapter 9: .Mac Is .Made for Mac Laptops 137

Chapter 10: Spiffy Connections for the Road Warrior 149

Part IV: Living the iLife 161

Chapter 11: The Multimedia Joy of iTunes 163

Chapter 12: That Masterpiece That Is iPhoto 185

Chapter 13: Making Film History with iMovie 205

Chapter 14: Creating DVDs on the Road with iDVD 221

Chapter 15: GarageBand on the Go 241

Part V: Sharing Access and Information 261

Chapter 16: Your Laptop Goes Multiuser 263

Chapter 17: Working Well with Networks 281

Chapter 18: Communicating with That Bluetooth Guy 301

Part VI: Necessary Evils: Troubleshooting, Upgrading, Maintaining 309

Chapter 19: When Good Mac Laptops Go Bad 311
Chapter 20: Adding New Stuff to Your Laptop 325
Chapter 21: Tackling the Housekeeping 337

Part VII: The Part of Tens 349

Chapter 22: Top Ten Laptop Rules to Follow...351
Chapter 23: Ten Things to Avoid Like the Plague..357

Index 365

Table of Contents

Introduction *1*

What's Really Required..1
About This Book 2
Conventions Used in This Book..3
    Stuff you type 3
    Menu commands 3
    Web addresses 3
How This Book Is Organized 4
    Part I: Tie Myself Down with a Desktop? Preposterous!...................4
    Part II: Shaking Hands with Mac OS X 4
    Part III: Connecting and Communicating 4
    Part IV: Living the iLife 4
    Part V: Sharing Access and Information 5
    Part VI: Necessary Evils: Troubleshooting,
       Upgrading, Maintaining 5
    Part VII: The Part of Tens..5
Icons Used in This Book 5
Where to Go from Here...6
A Final Word...6

Part 1: Tie Myself Down with a Desktop? Preposterous! ... 7

Chapter 1: Hey, It Really Does Have Everything I Need 9

An Overview of Your Mac Laptop 10
    The parts you probably recognize 10
    The holes called ports..14
    Don't forget the parts you can't see 15
Meet the New MacBook Air 17
    Comparing 'twixt MacBooks...17
    Look, Ma, no moving parts! 20
    What if I need that pesky optical drive? 21
Location, Location, Location!..22
Unpacking and Connecting Your Laptop...................................23
    Unpacking for the road warrior 23
    Connecting cables 101..24
Great, a Lecture about Handling My Laptop..............................25
An Overview of Mac Software Goodness....................................26
    What comes with my laptop? 26
    Connecting to the Internet from your lap..............................26

Applications that rock...27
Boot Camp For Dummies 28
Other Stuff That Nearly Everyone Wants 28

Chapter 2: Turning On Your Portable Powerhouse **31**

Tales of the On Button...31
Mark's Favorite Signs of a Healthy Laptop.........................32
You're Not Going to Lecture about Batteries, Are You?..........33
Setting Up and Registering Your Laptop 35
Setting up Mac OS X Leopard...............................36
Registering your MacBook...................................37
Importing Stuff from Another Mac 37
Importing Stuff from Windows (If You Must)........................40

Chapter 3: The Laptop Owner's Introduction to Mac OS X **43**

Your Own Personal Operating System 44
The Leopard Desktop..44
Why get so excited by Leopard?.............................48
Like Windows done right 49
And Just in Case You Need Help 50
The Leopard built-in Help system 51
The Apple Web-based support center 51
Magazines 51
Mac support Web sites 51
Mac newsgroups on Usenet.................................52
Local Mac user groups 52

Part II: Shaking Hands with Mac OS X *53*

Chapter 4: Opening and Closing and Clicking and Such **55**

Using the All-Powerful Finder 55
Wait a Second: Where the Heck Is the Right Mouse Button?...................58
Clicking and right-clicking magic 60
It's okay to scroll with your fingers 60
Doing the Multi-Touch thing................................61
Launching and Quitting Applications with Aplomb..............61
Juggling Folders and Icons 64
A field observer's guide to icons 64
Selecting items 66
Copying items...68
Moving things from place to place 69
Duplicating in a jiffy..69

Keys and Keyboard Shortcuts to Fame and Fortune 70
   Special keys on the keyboard 70
   Using Finder and application keyboard shortcuts 71
Performing Tricks with Finder Windows 72
   Scrolling in and resizing windows 72
   Minimizing and restoring windows 73
   Moving and zooming windows 74
   Closing windows 75

Chapter 5: Getting to the Heart of the Leopard 77
Home, Sweet Home Folder 77
Personalizing Your Desktop 80
Customizing the Dock Just So 82
   Adding Dock icons 82
   Removing Dock icons 83
   Using Dock icon menus 83
What's with the Trash? 84
Working Magic with Dashboard, Exposé, and Spaces 86
   Using Dashboard 86
   Switching between apps with Exposé 87
   Switching between desktops with Spaces 88
Printing within Mac OS X 90

Chapter 6: A Nerd's Guide to System Preferences 93
An Explanation (In English, No Less) 93
Locating That Certain Special Setting 95
Popular Preference Panes Explained 96
   The Displays pane 97
   The Desktop & Screen Saver pane 98
   The Exposé & Spaces pane 99
   The Appearance pane 102
   The Energy Saver pane 103
   The Dock pane 105
   The Sharing pane 106
   The Time Machine pane 106

Chapter 7: Sifting through Your Stuff 109
A Not-So-Confusing Introduction to Spotlight 109
   Searching with Spotlight 111
   Working with matching stuff 113
   Tweaking Spotlight in System Preferences 114
Other Search Tools Are Available, Too 116
With Widgets, the Internet Is Your Resource 117

Part III: Connecting and Communicating.................... 119

Chapter 8: Taking Your Laptop on Safari! 121
It's Not Just Another Web Browser... 121
Visiting Web Sites 123
Basic Navigation While on Safari 124
Putting Down Roots with a New Home Page........................... 126
Adding and Using Bookmarks 128
Downloading Files 129
Using Subscriptions and History 130
Tabs Are Your Browsing Friends.. 131
Saving Web Pages 132
Protecting Your Privacy 133
    Yes, there are such things as bad cookies 134
    Cleaning your cache 135
    Handling ancient history... 136
    Avoiding those @*!^%$ pop-up ads 136

Chapter 9: .Mac Is .Made for Mac Laptops 137
Where Exactly Is My .Mac Stuff Stored? 137
Opening a .Mac Account.. 139
Using Your iDisk on the iRoad 141
    It's all in the folders 141
    Mirror, mirror, on your drive 143
    Monitoring and configuring your iDisk 144
Backing Up Your Treasured Laptop Stuff............................... 145
    Installing Backup... 146
    Saving your stuff 146
Publishing a Web Site with HomePage 147

Chapter 10: Spiffy Connections for the Road Warrior 149
Connecting Printers 149
    USB printers... 150
    Networked printers 152
Connecting Scanners.. 153
Using Photo Booth and Front Row 154
    Capturing the moment with Photo Booth 154
    Controlling your laptop remotely with Front Row 156
    Using iSight with iChat AV 159
Turning Your MacBook into a TV — And More........................ 159

Part IV: Living the iLife 161

Chapter 11: The Multimedia Joy of iTunes 163

What Can I Play on iTunes?.. 163
Playing an Audio CD.. 165
Playing Digital Audio and Video 166
    Browsing the Library... 169
    Finding songs in your Music Library.............................. 170
    Removing old music from the Library 170
    Watching video 170
Keeping Slim Whitman and Slim Shady Apart:
    Organizing with Playlists 171
Know Your Songs.. 173
    Setting the song information automatically 173
    Setting or changing the song information manually 174
Ripping Audio Files.. 175
Tweaking the Audio for Your Ears 177
A New Kind of Radio Station 177
    iTunes Radio... 178
    Tuning in your own stations... 178
    Radio stations in your Playlists 179
Burning Like a True Techno.. 180
    Visualization: Music for your eyes................................. 182
    Buying Billie Holiday from the Apple Music Store 182

Chapter 12: That Masterpiece That Is iPhoto 185

Delving into iPhoto.. 185
Working with Images in iPhoto... 187
    Import Images 101... 188
    Organize mode: Organizing and sorting your images 189
    Edit mode: Removing and fixing stuff the right way........ 196
Producing Your Own Coffee-Table Masterpiece 199
Introducing Web Gallery!.. 202

Chapter 13: Making Film History with iMovie 205

Shaking Hands with the iMovie Window 206
A Bird's-Eye View of Moviemaking.. 208
Importing the Building Blocks 209
    Pulling in video clips 209
    Making use of still images... 211
    Importing and adding audio from all sorts of places 212

Building the Cinematic Basics 215
    Adding clips to your movie 215
    Removing clips from your movie 217
    Reordering clips in your movie 217
    Editing clips in iMovie 217
    Transitions for the masses 218
    Even Gone with the Wind had titles 219
Sharing Your Finished Classic with Others 220

Chapter 14: Creating DVDs on the Road with iDVD **221**
Hey, Where's the Complex Window? 222
Starting a New DVD Project 224
    Creating a new project 225
    Opening an existing project 225
    Automating the whole darn process 226
Creating a DVD from Scratch 226
    Choosing just the right theme 227
    Adding movies 228
    Great! Now my audience demands a slideshow! 230
    Now for the music 232
Giving Your DVD the Personal Touch 233
    Using Uncle Morty for your DVD Menu background 233
    Adding your own titles 234
    Changing buttons like a highly paid professional 234
    Give my creation motion! 235
Previewing Your Masterpiece 236
A Word about Automation 237
    One-click paradise with OneStep DVD 237
    Exercising control with Magic iDVD 238
Recording a Finished Project to a Shiny Disc 239

Chapter 15: GarageBand on the Go **241**
Shaking Hands with Your Band 242
Composing and Podcasting Made Easy 244
    Adding tracks 245
    Choosing loops 248
    Resizing, repeating, and moving loops 251
    Using an Arrange track 254
    Tweaking the settings for a track 255
Automatic Composition with Magic GarageBand 256
Sharing Your Songs and Podcasts 257
    Creating MP3 and AAC files 258
    Sending a podcast to iWeb or iTunes 258
    Burning an audio CD 259

Part V: Sharing Access and Information 261

Chapter 16: Your Laptop Goes Multiuser .... .263
Once Upon a Time (An Access Fairy Tale)................................264
Big-Shot Administrator Stuff 265
Deciding who needs what access 265
Adding users...266
Modifying user accounts...268
I banish thee, Mischievous User! 270
Setting up Login Items and Parental Controls.............271
Mundane Chores for the Multiuser Laptop............................276
Logging on and off in Leopard For Dummies 276
Interesting stuff about sharing stuff............................279
Encrypting your Home folder can be fun......................279

Chapter 17: Working Well with Networks .... .281
What Exactly Is the Network Advantage?...............................281
Should You Go Wired or Wireless? 282
Be a Pal — Share Your Internet! 284
Using your MacBook as a sharing device 284
Using a dedicated Internet-sharing device 285
What Do I Need to Connect? 285
Wireless connections 286
Wired connections...291
Connecting to the Network 294
Verifying that the contraption works...........................295
Sharing stuff nicely with others 296
USE YOUR FIREWALL! 298

Chapter 18: Communicating with That Bluetooth Guy. 301
Bluetooth: What a Silly Name for Such Cool Technology 302
A little Danish history..302
Is your MacBook Bluetooth-ready? 302
Leopard and Bluetooth, together forever......................303
Adding Wireless Keyboards and Mice to Your Laptop 305
Getting Everything in iSync 307
The Magic of Wireless Printing...308

Part VI: Necessary Evils: Troubleshooting, Upgrading, Maintaining 309

Chapter 19: When Good Mac Laptops Go Bad 311
Repeat After Me: Yes, I Am a Tech! 311
Step-by-Step Laptop Troubleshooting 312
    The Number One Rule: Reboot! 312
    Special keys that can come in handy 314
    All hail Disk Utility, the troubleshooter's friend 315
    Mark's MacBook Troubleshooting Tree 319
Okay, I Kicked It, and It Still Won't Work 323
    Apple Help Online 323
    Local service, at your service 324

Chapter 20: Adding New Stuff to Your Laptop 325
More Memory Will Help 325
    Figuring out how much memory you have 326
    Installing memory modules 327
Considering a Hard Drive Upgrade? 331
    Consider your external options 332
    Gotta have internal 334
A List of Dreamy Laptop Add-Ons 335
    Game controllers 335
    Video controllers 335
    Audio hardware 335

Chapter 21: Tackling the Housekeeping 337
Cleaning Unseemly Data Deposits 337
    Getting dirty (Or, cleaning things the manual way) 338
    Using a commercial cleanup tool 340
Backing Up Your Treasure 340
    Saving files 341
    Putting things right with Time Machine 342
Maintaining Hard Drive Health 344
Automating Those Mundane Chores 344
Updating Mac OS X Automatically 347

Part VII: The Part of Tens 349

Chapter 22: Top Ten Laptop Rules to Follow 351
Keep Your Laptop in a Bag 351
Maximize Your RAM 352

Install a Tracker Application...353
Keepest Thy Home Folder Encrypted.....................................353
Brand Your MacBook..354
Disable Your Wireless...354
Bring a Surge Protector with You..355
Use Leopard Power-Saving Features......................................355
Use an External Keyboard and Mouse....................................356
Not Again! What Is It with You and Backing Up? 356

Chapter 23: Ten Things to Avoid Like the Plague.................357
USB 1.1 Storage Devices 358
Phishing Operations..358
Oddly Shaped Optical Discs..359
Submerged Keyboards..360
Antiquated Utility Software...360
Software Piracy...360
The Forbidden Account..361
Unsecured Wireless Connections...361
Refurbished Hardware..362
Dirty Laptops 363

Index.. *365*

Introduction

*L*aptop owners are special people.

You see, a laptop owner demands everything from a computer that a desktop owner does: reliability, performance, expandability, and ease of use. Owners of Mac Pro or iMac desktop computers can draw the line right there because their computers are designed for a stationary existence. But, you and I are laptop owners. We also need that same computer to be an inch thick (or less). We demand that it run for hours on a single battery charge. We require that it be light as a feather.

Today's Apple laptops deliver all that, and more! If you've bought one of these modern masterpieces — or you're thinking about it right now — I applaud your good taste, common sense, and discerning eye. Apple laptops have everything: super performance, a top-shelf LCD screen, rugged reliability, and a trouble-free, powerful operating system. Heck, your Intel-based Apple laptop can even run . . . wait for it . . . Windows XP or Vista. (If you absolutely have to, the option is there.)

I wrote this book for myself — and for every other Apple laptop owner who desires to become a laptop techno-wizard. In these pages, you find a guide to both your laptop's hardware and Mac OS X Leopard, the latest version of Apple's superb operating system. After I cover the basics that every laptop owner should know, you find out how to accomplish all sorts of cutting-edge audio, visual, and Internet projects. (Oh, and if you already have another of my books, you know that I don't skimp on the power user tips and tricks that save you time, effort, *and* money.)

Like my dozen-or-so other *For Dummies* titles, I respect and use the same English language you learned in school, avoiding jargon, ridiculous computer acronyms, and confusing techno-babble whenever possible. (Plus, I try to bring out the humor that's hidden inside every computer. Finding out how to use your Mac should be fun, and not a chore!)

What's Really Required

If you're *not* an engineer with a degree in Advanced Thakamology — imagine that — there's no need to worry! Here's a reasonably complete list of what's *not* required to use this book.

✔ I make no assumptions about your previous knowledge of computers — laptop or otherwise — and software. I start at the beginning, which is where every book should start.

✔ Still considering buying a MacBook, MacBook Air, or MacBook Pro? Heck, you don't even need the computer! If you're evaluating whether a Mac laptop is right for you, this book is a great choice. I introduce you to both the hardware and software you'll get, so you can easily determine whether a Mac is the machine for you. (It is. Trust me.)

✔ Upgrading from the monster that is Windows? I have tips, tricks, and entire sections devoted to the hardy pioneers called *Switchers!* You discover the similarities and differences between the two operating systems, how you can make the switch as easy and quick as possible, and how to run Windows on your new laptop, if you absolutely must.

✔ If your friends and family have told you that you're going to spend half your savings on software — or that there's no decent software available for Mac computers — just smile quietly to yourself! These are two persistent myths about Mac computers, and those same folks are going to be blown away by the images, music, movies, and documents you produce. (Oh, by the way, your Mac laptop comes complete with a ton more software than any other PC or laptop, and the iLife suite of applications is better than anything available on a PC!) To sum up: *You can do virtually everything in this book with the software that came with your Mac!*

So what *is* required? Only your Mac laptop and the desire to become a power user — someone who produces the best work in the least amount of time and has the most fun doing it!

This book was written using the latest MacBook Pro computer, so owners of older Mac laptops who aren't running Intel processors might not be able to follow along with everything I cover. However, if you've upgraded an older G4 laptop with Mac OS X Leopard and the iLife '08 application suite, you should be able to use most of the book with no problem.

About This Book

Each chapter in this book is written as a reference on a specific hardware or software topic. As fruit of the hard work of my editors, you can begin reading anywhere you like because each chapter is self-contained. However, if you want to get the most out of this tome (and your MacBook experience), nothing's wrong with reading this book from front to back. I warn you, however, that Tom Clancy and Stephen King have nothing to fear from my "no-frills" prose.

Conventions Used in This Book

Even with a minimum of techno-speak, this book needs to cover the special keys you have to press or menu commands you have to choose to make things work. Hence, this short list of conventions.

Stuff you type

I may ask you to type a command in Mac OS X. That text often appears like this:

Type me.

You usually have to press the Return key before anything happens.

Menu commands

I list menu commands, using this format:

Edit⇨Copy

This example of shorthand menu instruction indicates that you should click the Edit menu and then choose the Copy menu item.

Web addresses

No up-to-date book on a computer is complete without a bag full of Web addresses for you to check out. When you see these in the text, they look like this — www.mlcbooks.com — or like this:

www.mlcbooks.com

(By the way, that Web site does exist. You're always welcome to check out my little acre of Web space!)

For the technically curious

Your MacBook is an elegant and sophisticated machine — and as easy to use as a computer can be — but from time to time, you may be curious about the technical details surrounding your hardware and software. (You probably disassembled alarm clocks as a kid, like I did.) Techie stuff is formatted as a sidebar, like this one, and you don't have to read it unless you want to know what makes things tick. (Pun by sheer accident.)

How This Book Is Organized

After careful thought (read that "flipping a coin"), I divided this book into seven major parts — plus an index, just because you deserve one. For your convenience, cross-references to additional coverage of many topics are sprinkled liberally throughout the book.

The Seven Parts Shall Be As Follows.

Part 1: Tie Myself Down with a Desktop? Preposterous!

This part introduces you to the important features of your laptop — like finding out where all the cables connect — and helps you set up your system. I also introduce *Mac OS X Leopard,* which is the Apple operating system that comes preinstalled on your MacBook, MacBook Air, or MacBook Pro.

Part II: Shaking Hands with Mac OS X

Time to familiarize you with Leopard (there's much more here behind the spots). In Part II, you find out how to take care of mundane chores (such as moving your stuff) as well as how to customize and personalize your system until it fits like the proverbial glove. Switchers from the PC world will be especially interested in understanding the ins and outs of Mac OS X — and friends, *it ain't hard.* The Mac started out easier to use than a Windows PC, and **nothing** has changed.

Part III: Connecting and Communicating

In Part III, it's time to jump into the one application you're likely to use every day: your Safari Web browser! You also find out more about the Apple .Mac Internet subscriber service as well as how to connect your laptop for printing, sharing information with your PDA or cellphone, and even videoconferencing. (I told you this thing was powerful, didn't I?)

Part IV: Living the iLife

Ah, readers, you can begin humming happily to yourself right this second! Yep, Part IV provides complete coverage of the latest iLife '08 release, with the names that are the envy of the Windows crowd: iTunes, iPhoto, iMovie, iDVD, and GarageBand. You find out how to turn your mobile monster computer into the hub for all your digital media. Whether you listen to it, display it, compose it, or direct it, this part of the book will explain it.

Part V: Sharing Access and Information

In Part V, I discuss how to share your Mac laptop among a group of people and also how to connect your Mac to a network. (Wired or wireless, makes no difference to me!) I also cover how to share data among wireless devices using Bluetooth technology and iSync, and how to broadcast your music around your house like Wolfman Jack.

Part VI: Necessary Evils: Troubleshooting, Upgrading, Maintaining

In Part VI, I cover the stuff my Dad used to call the *Justin Case Guide* — that is, just in case, you want to upgrade your MacBook with more memory or new hardware. If you need to troubleshoot a problem with your hardware or software, check out my should-be-patented troubleshooting guide. Finally, I describe what you can do to help keep your Mac running as fast and as trouble-free as the day you took it out of the box!

Part VII: The Part of Tens

The two chapters here that make up the famous "Part of Tens" section contain a quick reference of tips and advice on a specific laptop or Macintosh topic. Each list has ten concise tips, and one or two readers have told me that they make excellent tattoos. (Personally, I'm not *that* much of a Mac guru.)

Icons Used in This Book

Like other technology authors, I firmly believe that important nuggets of wisdom should **stand out** on the page! With that in mind, this *For Dummies* book includes a number of margin icons for certain situations.

The most popular icon in the book, you find it next to suggestions I make that save you time and effort — and once or twice, even cash!

These are My Favorite Recommendations — in fact, I'll bet just about any laptop power user would tell you the same. Follow my Maxims, and you'll avoid the quicksand and pitfalls that I've encountered with all sorts of Macs for well over a decade!

You don't have to know this stuff, but the technologically curious love high-tech details. (Of course, we're great fun at parties, too.)

Always read the information for this icon first! I'm discussing something that could harm your hardware or throw a plumber's helper into your software.

The highlighter stuff — not quite as universally accepted (or as important to the author) as a Mark's Maxim, but a good reminder! I use these icons to reinforce That Which Should Be Remembered.

Where to Go from Here

My recommendations on how to proceed? I just happen to have three:

- ✔ If you're thinking about buying a new MacBook, MacBook Air, or MacBook Pro, the box is still unopened in your living room, or you'd like help setting things up, start with Part I.
- ✔ If you're already on the road with your laptop but you'd like guidance with running Mac OS X — Hey, you Windows Switchers! Take note! — start with Part II.
- ✔ For all other concerns, use the index or check out the table of contents to jump straight to the chapter you need.

A Final Word

I thank you for buying my book, and I hope that you find *MacBook For Dummies,* 2nd Edition invaluable! With this fearless guide in hand, I believe that you and your Mac will bond as I have with mine. (That sounds somewhat wrong, but it's really not.)

Time for the first Mark's Maxim in this book:

Take your time — after all, finding out how to use your computer isn't a race — and don't worry if you're not a graphic artist, professional photographer, or video editor. With your Mac laptop and its software, you don't have to be!™

Part I

Tie Myself Down with a Desktop? Preposterous!

In this part . . .

Your journey as a Mac Road Warrior — pun intended —
begins with a description of your laptop itself as
well as the details you need to know when unpacking and
setting up your newest family member. You'll also find an
introduction to Mac OS X Leopard, the latest version of
Apple's super-popular operating system.

I also talk about the differences between the MacBook
models as of this writing: the MacBook, MacBook Pro, and
the incredibly thin MacBook Air.

Chapter 1

Hey, It Really Does Have Everything I Need

In This Chapter

▶ Identifying the important parts of your Mac laptop

▶ Introducing the MacBook Air

▶ Locating the right home for your computer

▶ Plugging in stuff and getting hooked up

▶ Playing with your bundled software

▶ Buying additional stuff that you might need

Most action films have one scene in common: I call it the "gear up" scene, where the good guys strap on their equipment in preparation for battle. (It doesn't matter what era: You see "gear up" scenes in Gladiator, Aliens, and virtually every movie Arnold has made.) You're sure to see lots of clicking straps and equipping of offensive weapons (and sometimes even a dash of war paint. The process usually takes a minute or so, all told with whiplash camera work and stirring martial music in the background.

Well, fellow Macintosh Road Warrior, it takes only *two seconds* and *one move* for you to gear up: closing the lid. That's because your MacBook is a self-contained world, providing virtually everything you'll find on a desktop iMac or Mac Pro. This is indeed the decade of the laptop, meshing nicely with your cellphone and that wireless connection at your local coffee shop. You have selected the right companion for the open road.

Unlike some of Apple's other designs, such as the Mac Mini or the iMac, your MacBook looks similar to a PC laptop running Windows. (In fact, an Intel-based Mac laptop can run Windows, if you absolutely must.) But your laptop holds a number of pleasant surprises that no PC laptop can offer — and, in the case of the MacBook Air, you'll lose pounds and inches from your chassis! In this chapter, I introduce you to the hardware and all the major parts of the machine — and you'll even find out how to unpack and connect your computer. And, as frosting on the cake, I'll preview the software that Apple is so proud of, as well as the accessories that you should buy now instead of later.

Welcome to your Mac laptop, good reader. Gear up!

An Overview of Your Mac Laptop

Sure, your MacBook Pro might be but an inch thin (and a MacBook Air even more svelte than that — I get to that later in the chapter), but a lot of superb design lives inside, and you'll encounter the same parts that you'd find in a desktop machine. In this section, I discuss those important parts — both the stuff you can see and the stuff that's shoehorned within.

The parts you probably recognize

Every laptop requires some of the same gizmos. Figure 1-1 helps you track them down. Of course, as you'd expect, a computer has a body of sorts in which all the innards and brains are stored, a display screen, a keyboard, a trackpad or other pointing device, and ports for powering and exchanging data with outside toys.

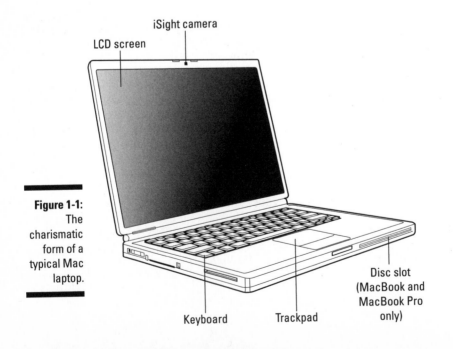

Figure 1-1: The charismatic form of a typical Mac laptop.

Feeling outdated? Never!

Are you using an older MacBook, iBook, or PowerBook? It seems that Apple's product line changes every time you tear a page from your 12-month calendar, and every new generation of laptops includes new whiz-bang features. Sometimes you can add those features separately to your older machine — such as an external iSight camera or an AirPort Extreme card — but you can't update some things, such as like your iBook motherboard. Sigh.

Here's my take on this situation: If your older laptop does what you need at a pace you can accept, there is *no need* to upgrade it.

Skeptical? Here's the proof: Before my recent upgrade to a MacBook Pro, yours truly was lugging a pristine iBook G3, which booted Mac OS X Tiger and did absolutely everything that I demanded. (A little more patience was required,

certainly, but technology authors are simply *brimming* with patience.) The moral: Avoid the upgrade fever unless you really need a new companion!

If your laptop bears the iBook or PowerBook logo, you can still enjoy this book and discover new tips and tricks from it! Unless the new breed of Intel-based Mac laptops has a feature that you absolutely can't use on your iBook (such as booting directly into Windows), you can sail on with your current computer, fiercely proud of The Bitten Apple that appears on the cover. Although this book was written with the MacBook, MacBook Air, and MacBook Pro lines in mind, virtually everything you read here still applies to your older laptop. Unless it's steam-driven, of course.

That magnificent screen

What a view you have! Today's Mac laptops feature a 13", 15", or 17" LCD display. Most displays are available in glossy or standard finish: The former is a good choice for the brightest colors and deepest blacks, and the latter is a good choice where reflections might be a problem.

LCD screens use far less electricity than their antique CRT ancestors do, and they emit practically no radiation.

Apple's laptop screens offer a *widescreen* aspect ratio (the screen is considerably wider than it is tall), which augurs well for those who enjoy watching DVD movies. (A favorite editor of mine loves it when I use the antique word *augur,* meaning *to predict or foretell.*)

That reminds me: Throw away your printed dictionary! You won't need it because Mac OS X Leopard includes the fantastic Dictionary widget, which uses the Internet to retrieve definitions from the online Oxford American Dictionary site. More on widgets in general in Chapter 5 . . . and yes, it does contain *augur.*

The keyboard and trackpad

Hey, here's something novel for your laptop. Unlike the external input devices on a standard desktop computer, your Mac has a built-in keyboard and trackpad (which does the job of a mouse). The keyboard is a particular favorite of mine for a few reasons:

- ✔ You can either control the sound volume or mute all that noise completely.
- ✔ You can use illuminated keyboards (at least on high-end Mac laptops), which are perfect for darkened dorm rooms and airplane flights.
- ✔ A handy-dandy Media Eject key lets you eject a CD or DVD.

The disc slot

You'll notice a long groove at the bottom-right corner of your MacBook or MacBook Pro. No, it's not for your credit card. This slot accepts CDs and DVDs into your optical drive. If the drive is empty, loading a disc is as simple as sliding it in an inch or so; the drive sucks in the disc automatically. (And we don't need a stinkin' floppy. Macs haven't had floppy drives for years now, and the PC types are just beginning to follow.)

A MacBook Air doesn't sport any internal optical drive (more on the MacBook Air later in this chapter). You use either the CD & DVD Sharing feature in Leopard to read discs remotely (from another Mac or PC on your network), or you can pick up an external optical drive from Apple for about $100. (Such is the price you play for super-thin and super-light.)

"Luke, the printed label side of the disc should always be *facing you* when you load a disc. Always."

Food for your ears

A machine this nice had better have great sound, and the Mac doesn't disappoint. You have a couple of options for Mac laptop audio:

- ✔ All Mac laptops sport built-in speakers (and a microphone to boot). The MacBook Air has a single speaker, and MacBook and MacBook Pro models sport stereo speakers.
- ✔ Use built-in audio Line Out jacks to connect your Mac's audio to a pair of headphones, or a more powerful (and expensive) external speaker system, or a home stereo system.

The power cable

Sorry, can't get a wireless power system . . . yet. (Apple's working hard on that one.) However, the MacBook Pro was the first major release of a laptop with a magnetic power connector; the MacBook and MacBook Air followed suit soon after. The MagSafe connector reduces the chances of your pride and joy being yanked off a desk when someone trips over the power cord, because the magnetic closure pops off under significant strain. Now that's *sassy.*

The power button

Yep, you have one of these, too. It's on the upper right, next to the keyboard, bearing the familiar "circle with a vertical line" logo.

The iSight camera

Check out that tiny square lens above your screen. That's a built-in iSight camera, which allows you to chat with others in a videoconferencing environment using Leopard's iChat feature. You can even take photos with it, using the Photo Booth software that comes with your laptop, or set up a travelin' Webcam.

The battery compartment

Owners of a MacBook or MacBook Pro can open the cover on the bottom of the laptop to switch batteries. Many road warriors who constantly use their laptops for extended periods swear by extra batteries, especially if they're on-site in the middle of nowhere and there's not an AC outlet to be found.

Of course, your laptop automatically charges the battery while it's plugged in, so you shouldn't have to remove the battery unless you're replacing it or switching it with another battery.

If you're using a MacBook Air, your battery is sealed inside the case and can't be swapped. Only an Apple technician can replace a dead battery in a MacBook Air laptop.

Hey, where's my remote?

If this isn't your first Mac laptop, you're probably looking for the Apple Remote amongst all the Styrofoam. Unfortunately, the latest crop of Mac laptops don't come with a remote. This once-standard device, which looks like an iPod Shuffle, allowed you to control your laptop wireless from across the room. Think DVD viewings, presentations, and lazy iTunes listening.

If you've picked up a used MacBook or MacBook Pro, you might have a remote already. Otherwise, you can always buy one directly from Apple for about $20. However, you can't use an Apple Remote with the MacBook Air, which doesn't have an IR (infrared) receiver.

The holes called ports

The next stop on your tour of Planet Laptop is Port Central — those rows of holes on the sides of your computer. Each port connects a different type of cable or device, allowing you to easily add all sorts of functionality to your computer.

Each of these stellar holes is identified by an icon to help you identify it. Here's a list of what you'll find, and a quick rundown on what these ports do.

Connections for external devices and networking:

- ✔ **FireWire:** These ports are the standard in the Apple universe for connecting external hard drives and DVD recorders, but they do double-duty as the connector of choice for peripherals like your digital video (DV) camcorder. (A *peripheral* is another silly techno-nerd term that means a separate device you connect to your computer.) Depending on the model of laptop you chose, you'll have one of the older FireWire 400 ports, and you may also have a much faster FireWire 800 port. (The MacBook Air doesn't have a FireWire port.)

- ✔ **USB:** Short for *Universal Serial Bus,* the familiar USB port is the jack-of-all-trades in today's world of computer add-ons. Most external devices that you want to connect to your laptop (such as portable hard drives, scanners, and digital cameras) use a USB port, including the iPod. Depending on the model of laptop, you'll have either two or three USB 2.0 ports available. USB 2.0 connections are much faster than the old USB 1.1 standard, but they still accept USB 1.1 devices running at the slower speed.

Get the lowdown on FireWire and USB ports in Chapter 20.

- ✔ **Ethernet:** Today's Mac laptops include a standard 10/100/1000 Ethernet port, so the laptop is ready to join your existing wired Ethernet network. (Alternatively, you can go wireless for your network connection; more on that in the next section and in Chapters 17 and 20.) Because the MacBook Air is designed to be completely wireless, it doesn't have a wired Ethernet port — if necessary, you can add a USB Ethernet adapter to add a wired network port to your Air.

- ✔ **ExpressCard/34:** When you need the absolute fastest performance possible from an external device, you can connect that device to your laptop by using the ExpressCard slot. These cards are the descendants of the popular PCMCIA (or PC Card) cards, which many models of older Mac PowerBooks can use. The MacBook Air doesn't have an ExpressCard slot.

Connections for external video and audio are

✔ **VGA/DVI connector:** In case that splendid screen isn't big enough, you can buy an adapter for this port that allows you to send the video signal from your laptop to another VGA or DVI monitor, or even S-Video output for your TV and VCR.

✔ **Headphone/Optical Output:** You can send the high-quality audio from your rectangular beast to a set of standard headphones or an optical digital audio device such as a high-end home theater system.

✔ **Optical Line In:** Last (but certainly not least) is the optical audio Line In jack, which allows you to pipe the signal from another audio device into your laptop. This one comes in particularly handy when you record MP3 files from your old vinyl albums or when you want to record loops in GarageBand. (The MacBook Air doesn't have an audio Line In jack.)

Don't forget the parts you can't see

When you bought your new digital pride and joy, you probably noticed a number of subtle differences between the low-end MacBook and the uber-expensive, top-end MacBook Pro and MacBook Air models. I call these differences the *Important Hidden Stuff* (or IHS, if you're addicted to acronyms already), and they're just as important as the parts and ports that you can see.

Internal storage devices:

✔ **CPU:** Today's Mac laptops feature — gasp! — Intel processors, which run faster and cooler than the old G4 processors that powered the iBook and PowerBook models. Of course, the faster the processor, the better. (Definitely *not* rocket science.)

✔ **Hard drive:** MacBook and MacBook Pro laptops use the latest in hard drive technology: namely, serial ATA hard drives, which are significantly faster than the EIDE hard drives used in previous Mac laptop models. (You don't need to worry about what ATA and EIDE mean here. Really.) As you might expect, the MacBook Pro laptop line has a larger capacity hard drive as standard equipment, but you can special order a MacBook from Apple with a larger hard drive.

The MacBook Air has two storage options: You can choose a mundane EIDE hard drive, or you can opt for the much more expensive (and much more technically impressive) solid-state drive. Hold on to your chair — there are no moving parts with a solid-state drive, and it offers better performance than a standard hard drive. Think of the solid-state drive as an internal USB flash drive, which uses RAM chips to hold your data instead of magnetic platters! Pricey, but *super-sweet*, and Apple once again introduces the latest in computer hardware.

✔ **Optical drive:** Okay, I'm cheating a little here. I mention the optical drive in an earlier section, but all you can see is the slot, so it qualifies as an IHS item. Depending on your Mac, your computer includes one of the following:

- *No built-in optical drive*

  The MacBook Air can be equipped with an external SuperDrive, or you can use another computer's drive remotely over your wireless network.

- *A DVD-R/CD-RW SuperDrive, which can play and record both CDs and DVDs*

- *A DVD/CD-RW combo drive, which can record CDs but only read DVDs*

  If your laptop can't burn DVDs with the internal drive, don't give up hope of recording your own DVD movies. Thanks to those handy FireWire ports, it's child's play to add an external DVD recorder.

Time for a plug: If you're interested in recording your own audio and data CDs, or you have an itch to burn DVD movies, I can highly recommend the bestselling *CD & DVD Recording For Dummies,* 2nd Edition (Wiley). It's written by yours truly; hence the solid recommendation. You'll find everything you need to know to use Roxio's Toast recording software. In a few minutes, you'll be burning your own shiny digital treasures.

Wireless communications devices:

✔ **Wireless Ethernet:** "Look, Ma, no wires!" As I mention earlier, you can connect your laptop to an existing wireless Ethernet network. All current Mac laptops have built-in AirPort Extreme hardware (older laptops can be upgraded with an internal AirPort or AirPort Extreme card). With wireless connectivity, you can share documents with another computer in another room, share a single high-speed Internet connection betwixt several computers, or enjoy wireless printing. Truly *sassy!*

Although Apple would want you to build your wireless wonderland with an Apple AirPort Extreme Base Station — go figure — you can use your Mac with any standard 802.11 wireless network. And yes, PCs and Macs can intermingle on the same wireless network without a hitch. (Scandalous, ain't it?)

✔ **Bluetooth:** Let's get the old "digital pirate" joke out of the way: "Arrgh, matey, I needs me a wireless parrot." (Engineers again . . . sheesh.) Although strangely named, Bluetooth is another form of wireless connectivity. This time, however, the standard was designed for accessories such as your keyboard and mouse, and devices such as a personal digital assistant (PDA) and a cellphone.

Video display device:

✔ **Video card:** If your applications rely heavily on high-speed 3-D graphics, you'll be pleased as punch to learn that today's MacBook Pro line of laptops come equipped with muscle-bound cards, such as the NVIDIA GeForce 8600M GT. This card is well suited to 3-D modeling, video editing, and well, honestly, blasting the enemy into small smoking pieces with aplomb. As of this writing, the MacBook and MacBook Air laptops use an integrated video card, so they're not a good choice for hard-core gaming or 3-D design.

Meet the New MacBook Air

Here's a corker of a conundrum: The MacBook Air is a revolutionary laptop, unique for both its size and weight (see Figure 1-2). And yet the Air is just like the MacBook and the MacBook Pro. Well, mostly.

"Hold on, Mark. How can it be so singular and yet share so much with its road warrior siblings?" That's what I'll show you in this section, which discusses the many similarities and the handful of very striking differences between the three laptops in the MacBook line. If you're considering buying an Air, this section will help you decide whether you'd like to go ultra-thin or stick with the conventional laptop crowd.

One thing's for sure — Apple *never* does things mundane!

Figure 1-2:
Behold the
MacBook
Air.

Comparing 'twixt MacBooks

Do you remember when Apple introduced those first iMacs? Although they shared the same basic components as any computer — a monitor, keyboard, ports, speakers, and cables — the iMac was revolutionary because it was completely self-contained. And it came in colors. And it didn't have a floppy drive. In fact, Apple had redesigned the common computer with the focus on *style* and *ease-of-use*, and had scrapped the floppy (and rightly so, seeing as how floppies had become practically useless and were unreliable, to boot).

I consider the MacBook Air to be an extension of the iMac revolution. With this new design, Apple has focused this time on *physical dimensions* and *weight,* and has tossed anything that isn't absolutely necessary for the lecture hall, board room, or city park. However, I'm happy to note that the Air is no toy, nor is it a bare-bones sub-notebook. You'll find the Air as powerful as the MacBook, and the Air even shares some of the features of the MacBook Pro.

What are the MacBook similarities?

Consider the similarities between the Air and the other MacBooks:

- ✔ **Widescreen display:** The Air has the same size display as the other MacBook models. Same display resolution, same gorgeous graphics. (In fact, at the time of this writing, the MacBook and MacBook Air have the same internal video hardware.)

- ✔ **Intel Core 2 Duo processor:** The Air is powered by the same type of CPU as its siblings.

- ✔ **Keyboard and trackpad:** The Air has a full-size keyboard, and it's even backlit, just like the MacBook Pro. The Air's trackpad includes support for Multi-Touch control, too. (Read more about Multi-Touch in Chapter 4.)

- ✔ **Leopard:** The Air runs the latest version of Mac OS X with aplomb.

- ✔ **iSight and microphone:** Every MacBook Air is video-ready, using the same iSight camera. You can record audio with the built-in microphone as well. (Read more about iSight and recording in Chapter 10.)

- ✔ **Wireless support:** Like the other MacBooks, the Air has both built-in AirPort Extreme hardware (802.11n) and built-in Bluetooth hardware. (Read more about these in Chapters 17 and 18.)

I think most Apple laptop owners would agree that this list covers the major features to look for in a MacBook, so we can all agree that the MacBook Air is no underpowered pushover.

So what's so flippin' radical?

I'm glad you asked! Here's the checklist of striking differences that set the Air apart from the MacBook and MacBook Pro:

- ✔ **Physical dimensions:** Apple doesn't call this machine the Air for nothing! The current Air laptop measures a mere 0.76" in height (at its tallest point) when closed, 12.8" in width, and 8.94" in depth. Oh, and hold on to your chair for this one: Our champ weighs in at a lightweight three pounds! (That's a couple of pounds you won't be carrying around all day at that convention expo. Take it from this traveler: You **will** feel the refreshing difference in just an hour or two.)

✔ **Cost:** At the time of this writing, there are two versions of the laptop. An entry-level MacBook Air will set you back $1,800, and the top-of-the-line Air is a whopping $3,100. The more expensive Air is equipped with a very pricey, solid-state drive and a faster CPU. (Don't miss the upcoming coverage on why solid-state is worth every penny.)

✔ **Ports:** The Air offers only three ports: a USB 2.0 port, an audio out jack, and a Micro-DVI for connecting an external monitor or video device. Notice I didn't mention a FireWire port, which can be a big problem for Apple old-timers like me. I have a huge collection of FireWire devices. The Air also doesn't have an infrared port, so it's not compatible with the Apple Remote. Rats.

✔ **Sealed battery:** You can't swap batteries with a MacBook Air because the battery is sealed inside the laptop. (Think iPod.)

✔ **Sealed case:** You can't add or replace RAM modules. However, a MacBook Air comes equipped with 2GB of RAM, so you should be good to go. Comparatively, the MacBook and MacBook Pro models can be upgraded to 4GB of RAM.

✔ **Speaker(s):** The MacBook Air includes but one speaker.

✔ **Solid-state drive:** Now we're talkin', Buck Rogers! I discuss the solid-state drive option in the next section.

✔ **No built-in optical drive:** *Whoa, Nellie!* This is a big one. Apple decided that a typical Air owner is likely to use a wireless connection for transferring files and media. But what if you have to reinstall Leopard or new applications? If you need to read or burn discs, a separate external USB SuperDrive is available for about $100, or you can use the Remote Disc feature and share the drive on another computer. (More on Remote Disc later in this section.)

As you can see, these striking differences make the choice between a MacBook Air and a MacBook/MacBook Pro very easy indeed. To wit: The Air is designed for the traveler who appreciates minimum weight and size, but who doesn't want to sacrifice the power, full-size screen, and full-size keyboard of a typical MacBook. These folks see the MacBook Air as a racecar: nimble, with reduced weight and no unnecessary frills. (Think of a typical NASCAR entry: Who needs an expensive stereo or air conditioning?)

If you prefer the additional versatility of a MacBook or MacBook Pro — including the standard set of ports, the ability to swap batteries, and a built-in optical drive — I highly recommend that you stick with the more conventional MacBook or MacBook Pro.

Look, Ma, no moving parts!

You're probably familiar with the common species of *usbius flashimus* — more commonly called the USB Flash drive. With one of these tiny devices, you get the equivalent of a 2–8GB hard drive that plugs into a USB 2.0 port, allowing you to pack your data with you as you jet across the continents. But have you ever asked yourself, "Self, why don't they make internal hard drives that use this same technology?"

Actually, dear reader, solid-state drives have been around for a number of years now (think iPod Shuffle). Unfortunately, however, the solid-state memory used in today's Flash drives gets pretty expensive as capacity increases. In fact, the cost has been the limiting factor, as a solid-state drive offers a number of advantages that really set it apart from a conventional magnetic hard drive:

- **No moving parts:** Unlike a typical magnetic hard drive, there's no read-write heads, no magnetic platter — just gobs of happy silicon memory chips. In effect, a solid-state drive works along the same lines as your MacBook's system RAM. Unlike your Mac's RAM, though, a solid-state drive doesn't lose the data it stores when you turn off your laptop. As you can imagine, no moving parts on a computer in motion is superior on two levels:

  - The solid-state drive never wears out or needs replacing.

  - If your laptop is accidentally abused (think, getting knocked off your desk), it's far less likely that you'll lose a hard drive's worth of priceless data when it hits the ground.

- **Speed:** Oh, my goodness, is this thing fast! Your MacBook will boot/restart/awake in far less time, and everything you do on your laptop will benefit from the speed boost. A solid-state drive can read data far faster than a conventional magnetic hard drive.

- **Power usage:** Forget your hard drive spinning up from sleep mode. The solid-state drive uses far less power than a conventional hard drive, resulting in significantly longer battery life.

- **Blessed silence:** The solid-state drive is completely silent. (No more of that gargling noise while the disk is accessed. *Sweet.*)

So do you need the solid-state drive option for your MacBook Air? The answer lies in your bank account (as well as your need for elbowroom). If you can afford the extra expense of the solid-state drive and you can fit all of your applications and data into 64GB, I heartily recommend that you consider joining Buck Rogers with the storage device of the future.

If you'd rather save that coin for something else, or you need a larger internal hard drive to hold things like digital video and a massive collection of digital images, stick with the tried-and-true magnetic hard drive.

What if I need that pesky optical drive?

Can a laptop survive in the jungle that is Real Life without a DVD drive? The terse answer is *no*. I'll be honest here: Ripping an audio CD or burning an iDVD slideshow disc without an optical drive is impossible. (Rather like a cheap tank of gas.) And the wonders of digital media are a big part of the iWorld. So what was Apple thinking?

First, a bit of explanation. Today's DVD drives are thin, but not Air thin. In order to create the stunning Air design with truly revolutionary dimensions, Apples engineers had to leave out the drive. However, if you own a MacBook Air, you have two choices when it comes to reading the contents of a CD or DVD: Go external, or find how to share.

The external USB route

This is my choice. Personally, I have no problem at all toting around an external USB DVD burner with a MacBook Air. Heck, half the time, you're likely to leave it at home because most of us don't install software every day. The folks at Cupertino want you to download your movies from the iTunes Store, so if you follow the Apple Path, you still don't need an optical drive!

A USB SuperDrive from Apple costs a mere $100, and it can read and write DVDs as well as the built-in SuperDrive you'll find in the MacBook and MacBook Pro.

You can also use any third-party USB DVD drive that's compatible with Apple's laptops and Mac OS X Leopard.

Sharing a CD or DVD drive

The other option for installing software or reading a DVD on the MacBook Air is Leopard's built-in CD/DVD Sharing feature. Sharing is an option if you have a wired or wireless network (see Chapter 17) with at least one of the following:

✔ **A Macintosh running Mac OS X Tiger or Leopard**

✔ **A PC running Windows XP or Vista**

This requires you to install a Windows application supplied by Apple with your MacBook Air.

You can ***only read from a shared optical drive.*** You can't write data to the remote drive, even if that drive is a DVD recorder.

On the Macintosh with the optical drive, open System Preferences, click the Sharing icon, and then enable the DVD or CD Sharing check box. Note that you can set whether the Mac will request your permission when another computer attempts to share the drive.

On a PC, display Control Panel, click the DVD or CD Sharing icon, and then choose the Enable DVD or CD Sharing check box. Again, you can specify that permission is required if security is a concern.

After you set up the shared drive, just load the disc, and select the Remote Disc item in any Finder sidebar. (Remote Disc appears under the Devices heading in the sidebar.) Now you can access the drive as if it were directly connected to your MacBook Air. Ah, technology!

Location, Location, Location!

If you choose the wrong spot to park your new laptop, I can **guarantee** that you'll regret it. Some domiciles and office cubicles don't offer a choice — you have one desk at work, for example, and nobody's going to hand over another one — but if you can select a home for your Mac, consider the important placement points in this section:

✔ **Keep things cool.** Your new laptop is silent, but that super-fast Intel Core 2 Duo processor generates heat. Make sure the location you choose is far from heating vents and shielded from direct sunlight. I also recommend a laptop cooling pad, which elevates the base of your laptop to allow air to circulate underneath.

✔ **Outlets are key!** Your computer needs a minimum of at least one nearby outlet, and perhaps as many as three:

   • *A standard AC outlet (using a current adapter if you're traveling abroad, if necessary)*

   • *A telephone jack (if you have an Apple modem for connecting to the Internet or sending and receiving faxes)*

   • *A nearby Ethernet jack (if you use the MacBook or MacBook Pro's built-in Ethernet port for connecting to a wired Ethernet network)*

   If you prefer to send your data over the airwaves, consider wireless networking for your Mac — I discuss everything you need to know in Chapter 17.

✔ **Don't forget the lighting.** Let me act as your Mom. (I know that's a stretch, but bear with me.) She'd say, "You can't possibly expect to work without decent lighting! You'll go blind!" She's right, you know. You need a desk or floor lamp at a minimum.

✔ **Plan to expand.** If your laptop hangs out on a desk, allow an additional foot of space on each side. That way, you have room for external peripherals, more-powerful speakers, and an external keyboard and mouse if you need one.

If you want to keep an external keyboard handy, consider using a laptop shelf. These Plexiglas or metal stands elevate your laptop several inches above the desk, putting the screen at a better ergonomic position and allowing you to park your keyboard and external mouse underneath.

Unpacking and Connecting Your Laptop

You're going to love this section. It's short and sweet because the configuration of a laptop on your desktop is a piece of cake. (Sorry about the cliché overload, but this really *is* easy.)

Unpacking for the road warrior

Follow these guidelines when unpacking your system:

✔ **Check for damage.** I've never had a box arrive from Apple with shipping damage, but I've heard horror stories from others (who claim that King Kong must have been working for That Shipping Company).

Check all sides of your box before you open it. If you find significant damage, take a photograph (just in case).

✔ **Search for all the parts.** When you're removing those chunks o' foam, make certain that you've checked all sides of each foam block for parts snuggled therein or taped for shipment.

✔ **Keep all packing materials.** Do *not* head for the trash can with the box and packing materials. Keep your box and all packing materials for at least a year, until the standard Apple warranty runs out. If you have to ship the laptop to an Apple service center, the box and the original packing is the only way for your machine to fly.

And now, a dramatic Mark's Maxim about cardboard containers:

Smart computer owners keep their boxes far longer than a year. If you sell your laptop or move across the country, for example, you'll want that box. *Trust me on this one.*™

✔ **Store the invoice for safekeeping.** Your invoice is a valuable piece of paper, indeed.

Save your original invoice in a plastic bag, along with your computer's manuals and original software, and other assorted hoo-hah. Keep the bag on your shelf or stored safely in your desk, and enjoy a little peace of mind.

✔ **Read the Mac's manual.** "Hey, wait a minute, Mark. Why do I have to read the manual from Apple along with this tome?" Good question, and here's the answer: The documentation from Apple might contain new and updated instructions that override what I tell you here. (For example, *"Never* cut the red wire. Cut the blue wire instead." Or something to that effect.) Besides, Apple manuals are rarely thicker than a restaurant menu.

You can always download the latest updated manuals for Apple computers in electronic format from Apple's Web site. (Adobe's PDF format is the standard for reading documents on your computer, and Leopard can open and display any PDF document, using the Preview application.) I always keep a copy of the PDF manual for my MacBook Pro on my hard drive, just in case.

Connecting cables 101

Your laptop makes all its connections simple, but your computer depends on you to get the outside wires and thingamabobs where they go.

The absolutely essential connection

After your new Mac is resting comfortably in its assigned spot (I assume that's a desktop), you need to make just one required connection: the power cable! Plug the cable into the corresponding socket on the Mac first, and then plug 'er into that handy AC outlet. (After your battery is completely charged, of course, you can go mobile at a moment's notice.)

Adding the Internet to the mix

If you have Internet access or a local computer network, you need to make at least one of the following connections in this section.

If you get on the Internet by dialing a standard phone number and your laptop has an external USB modem, just make two more connections:

1. **Plug one of the telephone cable's connectors into your external modem.**

2. **Plug the other telephone cable connector into your telephone line's wall jack.**

After you get your account information from your ISP, Chapter 17 has the details on configuring your modem and Internet settings for dialup access.

If you have high-speed Internet service, or if you're in an office or school with a local computer network, you can probably connect through your MacBook or MacBook Pro's built-in Ethernet port. You make two connections:

1. **Plug one end of the Ethernet cable into the Ethernet port on the Mac.**

2. **Plug the other end of the Ethernet cable into the Ethernet port from your network.**

   Your network port is probably one of the following: an Ethernet wall jack, an Ethernet hub or switch, or a cable or DSL Internet router (or sharing device).

Will you be joining a wireless network? If so, you find the information you need on configuring Leopard for wireless networking in Chapter 17.

Great, a Lecture about Handling My Laptop

Proper handling of your laptop is important, so take a moment to cover the Rules of Proper Laptop Deportment. Okay, perhaps I'm lecturing a bit, but a little common sense goes a long way when handling any computer equipment, and your laptop is no different. (Scolding mode off.)

Keep these rules in mind while opening and carrying your laptop:

- ✔ **The cover is your friend.** Open your laptop's cover slowly, without jerking or bending it.

- ✔ **Close it before you move it.** By closing your laptop, you put your Mac OS X operating system into sleep mode, and the hard drive automatically spins down (making it safer to move). The laptop is still on, and will spring back to life after you open the cover.

- ✔ **Be nice to your keyboard.** Don't press too hard on those keys! Use the same amount of pressure that you use with a desktop computer keyboard.

- ✔ **Keep food and drinks far away.** Care to turn your laptop into a very expensive doorstop? Then go ahead and park your soda next to it. (Oh, and crumbs are perfect if you're interested in buying replacement keyboards.)

- ✔ **Keep your laptop as level as possible.** Using your laptop while it's tilted too far in any direction can eventually cause problems with your hard drive. I kid you not.

An Overview of Mac Software Goodness

This section answers the most common of all novice computer questions: "What the heck will I *do* with this thing?" You find additional details and exciting factoids about the software that you get for free, software you'll want to buy, and stuff you can do on the Internet.

What comes with my laptop?

Currently, Apple laptops ship with the following major software applications installed and ready to use:

- **The iLife '08 suite:** You know you want these applications! They turn your Mac into a digital hub for practically every kind of high-tech device on the planet, including DV camcorders, digital cameras, portable music players, PDAs, and even cellphones.

  Chapters 11–15 focus on the major applications that make up iLife: iTunes, iPhoto, iMovie, iDVD, and GarageBand.

- **iWork trial version:** You can try this productivity suite from Apple, but expect to buy the full shooting match if you want to continue using the applications.

- **Photo Booth and Front Row:** You discover more about these applications in Chapter 10. For now, suffice it to say that Photo Booth works with your laptop's iSight camera, and Front Row is the remote-control software you'll use with your Apple remote (if you have one).

The installed software on your Mac might change as new programs become available.

Connecting to the Internet from your lap

What is a modern computer without the Internet? Apple gives you great tools to take full advantage of every road sign and offramp on the Information Superhighway right out of the box:

- **Web surfing:** I use Leopard's Apple Safari Web browser every single day. It's faster and better designed than Internet Explorer, with unique features such as tabbed browsing and built-in RSS feeds.

If *tabbed browsing* and *RSS feeds* sound like ancient Aztec to you, don't worry. Chapter 8 is devoted entirely to Safari.

✔ **Web searches:** Dashboard widgets can search the entire Internet for stocks, movie listings, airline schedules, dictionaries, and foreign language translations. I explain Dashboard in Chapter 5.

✔ **Chat:** *iChat* lets you use your Mac to chat with others around the world for free on the Internet — by keyboard, voice, or full-color video. This is awesome stuff straight out of Dick Tracy and Buck Rogers. If you've never seen a video chat, you'll be surprised by just how good your friends and family look!

Always wear a shirt when videoconferencing.

✔ **E-mail:** Soldier, Apple's got you covered. The Mail application is a full-featured e-mail system, complete with defenses against the torrent of junk mail awaiting you. (Imagine a hungry digital saber-toothed tiger with an appetite for spam.) Send pictures and attached files to everyone on the planet, and look doggone good doing it.

Applications that rock

Dozens of small applications are built into Mac OS X. I mention them in later chapters, but here are four good examples to whet your appetite:

✔ **Safari:** Apple's Web browser of choice — it's fast, simple and easily customized. See how to navigate the Web in style in Chapter 8.

✔ **DVD Player:** Put all that widescreen beauty to work and watch your favorite DVD movies with DVD Player! You have all the features of today's most expensive standalone DVD players, too, including a spiffy onscreen control that looks like a remote.

✔ **Address Book:** Throw away that well-thumbed collection of fading addresses. Use the Leopard Address Book to store, search, and recall just about any piece of information on your friends, family, and acquaintances.

✔ **Chess:** Ah, but this isn't the chessboard your Dad used! Play the game of kings against a tough (and configurable) opponent — your MacBook — on a beautiful 3-D board. Heck, your Mac even narrates the game by speaking the moves!

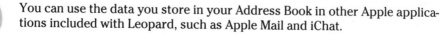

You can use the data you store in your Address Book in other Apple applications included with Leopard, such as Apple Mail and iChat.

Boot Camp For Dummies

Mac OS X Leopard introduced one particularly exciting feature for Windows switchers: You can use the Apple Boot Camp utility and your licensed copy of Windows XP to install and boot Windows on your Intel-based Mac laptop!

Boot Camp creates a Windows-friendly *partition* (or section) on your hard drive, where all your Windows files are stored. Other than the slightly strange key assignments you'll have to remember, early adopters of Boot Camp report that it's surprisingly reliable and easy to use. However, I strongly urge that you back up your laptop on a regular basis; inviting Windows to your Mac laptop also invites potential viruses as well.

Apple's Boot Camp Assistant provides step-by-step instructions, making it easy to configure your laptop for Windows. To run the Boot Camp Assistant, open your Applications folder and double-click on the Utilities folder, and then double-click on the Boot Camp Assistant application icon.

Other Stuff That Nearly Everyone Wants

No man is an island, and no computer is either. I always recommend the same set of stuff for new PC and Mac owners. These extras help keep your new computer clean and healthy (and some make sure you're happy as well):

✔ **Surge suppressor:** Even an all-in-one computer like your laptop can fall prey to a power surge. I recommend using one of these:

- *A basic surge suppressor* with a fuse can help protect your Mac from an overload.

- *A UPS (uninterruptible power supply)* costs a little more, but it does a better job of filtering your AC line voltage to prevent brownouts or line interference from reaching your computer.

  Of course, your laptop's battery immediately kicks in if you experience a blackout, so a UPS is less important for your computer. However, any computer tech will tell you that filtered AC current is far better for your laptop, and your UPS will also provide power for external devices that *don't* have a battery.

✔ **Screen wipes:** Invest in a box of premoistened screen wipes to keep your screen pristine. Your Mac's screen can pick up dirt, fingerprints, and other unmentionables faster than you think.

Make sure your wipes are especially meant for LCD or laptop computer screens.

✔ **Blank CDs and DVDs:** Depending on the type of optical drive installed in your laptop — and the type of media you're recording, such as computer data CDs, DVD movies, or audio CDs — you'll want blank discs for

- CD-R (record once)

- CD-RW (record multiple times)

- DVD-R (record once)

✔ **Cables:** Depending on the external devices and wired network connectivity you'll be using, these are

- A standard Ethernet cable (for wired networks or high-speed Internet)

- FireWire or USB cables for devices you already have

✔ **A restraining cable:** For those who are a little more security-conscious or tend to use their laptops in public places, a standard Kensington laptop lock slot is provided on the MacBook and MacBook Pro case. (Sorry, MacBook Air owners, but your case is too thin to sport a lock slot.) The principle is the same as a bicycle cable lock: If your laptop is secured by a cable to a sturdy fixture, it's nearly impossible for it to walk off with someone else.

✔ **A wrist rest:** You might have many reasons to buy a new Mac laptop, but I know that a bad case of carpal tunnel syndrome is not one of them. Take care of your wrists by carrying a keyboard wrist rest in your laptop bag.

Chapter 2

Turning On Your Portable Powerhouse

In This Chapter

▶ Turning on your laptop

▶ Checking your Mac for proper operation

▶ Monitoring your battery and heat level

▶ Setting up Mac OS X Leopard

▶ Registering your MacBook

▶ Using Migration Assistant

▶ Copying information from a Windows PC

*I*n Chapter 1, you got as far as unpacking your Mac laptop and connecting a number of cables to it, but unless you bought this computer solely as a work of modern art, it's time to turn on your Mac and begin living The Good Life. (Plus, you still get to admire that Apple design whilst using iTunes.) After you get your new beauty powered on, I show you how to run an initial checkup of your laptop's health.

I also familiarize you with the initial chores that you need to complete — such as using the Mac OS X Setup and moving the data and settings from your existing computer to your MacBook, MacBook Air, or MacBook Pro — before you settle in with your favorite applications.

In this chapter, I assume that Mac OS X Leopard was preinstalled on your Mac or that you just completed an upgrade to Leopard from an earlier version of Mac OS X.

Tales of the On Button

Your Mac's power switch is located on the right side of the keyboard. Press it now to turn on your Mac, and you will hear the pleasant startup tone that's been a hallmark of Apple computers for many years. Don't be alarmed if you don't immediately see anything onscreen because it takes a few seconds for the initial Apple logo to appear.

In my experience, sometimes a simple quick press of the power button on some Mac laptop models just doesn't do it. Rather, you actually have to hold the button down for a count of two or so before the computer turns on. However, if your Mac laptop ever locks up tight (and you can't quit an application, as I demonstrate in Chapter 4), the power button gives you another option: Hold it down for a count of five to ten (depending on your counting speed), and your Mac shuts off — even if your laptop is locked up tight.

As the Apple logo appears, you see a twirling, circular high-tech progress indicator that looks like something from a *James Bond* movie. That's the sign that your Mac is loading Leopard and checking your internal drive for problems. Sometimes the twirling circle can take a bit longer to disappear. As long as it's twirling, though, something good is happening.

Next, Leopard displays the soon-to-be-quite-familiar Aqua Blue (yup, that's its name) background while it loads certain file sharing, networking, and printing components (and such). This time, you get a more conservative progress bar, but the result is the same. Just wait patiently a bit longer.

At last, your patience of a whole 10–15 seconds is rewarded, and after a short (but neat) video, you see the Leopard Setup Assistant appear.

Mark's Favorite Signs of a Healthy Laptop

Before you jump into the fun stuff, don't forget an important step — a quick prelim check of the signs that your new mobile Mac survived shipment intact and happy.

If you can answer "yes" to each of these questions, your Mac likely made the trip without serious damage:

1. **Does the computer's chassis appear undamaged?**

   It's pretty easy to spot damage to your Mac's svelte design. Look for scratches and puncture damage.

2. **Does the LCD screen work, and is it undamaged?**

   Does the cover open smoothly? Are any individual dots (or *pixels*) on your LCD monitor obviously malfunctioning? Bad pixels appear black or in a different color than everything surrounding them. (Techs call these irritating anarchists *dead pixels*. A 13" MacBook screen has literally hundreds of thousands of pixels, and unfortunately, many new LCD screens include one or two dead ones.

3. **Do the keyboard and trackpad work?**

   Check your Mac's built-in trackpad by moving your finger across its surface; the cursor should move on your screen. To check the keyboard, press the Caps Lock key on the left and observe whether the Caps Lock light turns on and off.

If you do notice a problem with your laptop (and you can use your Safari browser and reach the Web), you can make the connection to an Apple support technician at www.apple.com. If your MacBook Pro remains dead — like an expensive paperweight — and you can't get to the Internet, you can check your phone book for a local Apple service center, or call the AppleCare toll-free number at 1-800-275-2273. Chapter 19 also offers troubleshooting information.

You're Not Going to Lecture about Batteries, Are You?

No, this is not going to be a lecture. In fact, the only lecture I put you through in this book concerns backing up (ahem, which *you should do*). Instead, consider these tips as your rules of the road for monitoring and charging your battery:

- ✔ **Recharge in sleep mode or when powered off.** Your battery recharges faster when your laptop is off or in sleep mode. (I go into more detail on sleep mode in Chapter 6.)

- ✔ **Keep your laptop plugged into an AC socket when possible.** I take every opportunity to top off my laptop's battery, and so should you.

   If you don't have much time to charge your battery before you're away from an AC socket — say, half an hour — don't use your MacBook whilst it's plugged in and charging.

- ✔ **Save your juice.** For the most juice you can scavenge, here are some easy tricks:

  - • *Turn off your laptop or leave it in sleep mode.*

  - • *Turn off unnecessary hardware.* To conserve battery power as much as possible, disconnect any USB or FireWire devices, and turn off your AirPort and Bluetooth wireless hardware if you're not connected to a network. (I cover AirPort wireless networking in Chapter 17, and Bluetooth in Chapter 18.)

- *Reduce the brightness of your display from your laptop's keyboard, using the F1 key.*

- *Remove CDs and DVDs from the optical drive. (MacBook Air owners, don't go hunting for a built-in optical drive, because your laptop doesn't have one.)*

✔ **Monitor your battery level from the Finder menu.** I love Leopard's battery-monitoring system! Your laptop's battery life can be displayed in the Finder menu in several different views — my personal favorite is as a percentage of power remaining (with a fully charged battery registering at 100%). To display the percentage, click the battery icon in the Finder menu and choose Show⇨Percentage.

Keep in mind that the percentage shown is estimated by using your current System Preference settings and power usage, so if you change your Energy Saver settings or remove a USB device that draws power from your laptop, you'll see that change reflected in the battery meter. Figure 2-1 illustrates the battery meter in Percentage view.

✔ **Calibrate your battery.** You can "train" your battery to provide the maximum charge by calibrating it, which Apple recommends doing monthly. It's a snap:

  a. *Charge your battery until the Finder menu battery meter indicates that the unit is fully charged at 100%.*

  b. *Keep your laptop connected to an AC socket for another two hours to ensure a maximum charge.*

  c. *Disconnect the power cord and use your laptop on battery power until it's fully discharged and it automatically switches to sleep mode.*

  Make sure that you close all your applications when you see the low battery warning dialog box so that you don't lose anything.

  d. *Allow your laptop to sleep (or turn it off) for a full five hours.*

  e. *Reconnect the AC cord and fully charge your battery.*

If your battery is no longer holding a charge — in other words, if you fully charge it and unplug the AC adapter, only to discover that you have only a few minutes of battery life — it's time to invest in a replacement battery. MacBook and MacBook Pro owners can buy a new battery themselves (from Apple or any one of a number of online vendors), but owners of MacBook Air laptops must bring their computers in for servicing. The Air is a sealed unit, and you can't replace the battery yourself.

Hot patootie, is my laptop steam-powered?

Laptops generate heat. And today's super-fast multicore processors can work up a head of steam — pun intended — while you're using them, and even though most MacBooks have a fan, some of that heat is simply radiated from the bottom of the computer.

What you might not realize, however, is just how *much* heat your MacBook, MacBook Air, or MacBook Pro can produce! No, you won't be scalded if you shift your MacBook from a desk to your lap (Apple dislikes lawsuits as much as the next company), but if you've been using that laptop for hours, it will be uncomfortably hot!

To avoid that burning sensation, buy a laptop stand or cooling pad for your desk. These nifty metal or Plexiglas pedestals raise your laptop up off of your desk, allowing air to flow under the bottom of the computer for better cooling. Also, a laptop stand elevates the screen to a more ergonomic position. (The keyboard might suddenly be harder to use, naturally, but that's yet another reason why I recommend an external keyboard when you're using your Mac laptop at a semipermanent desk location; it saves wear and tear on your laptop keyboard, and you get a full-size keyboard.)

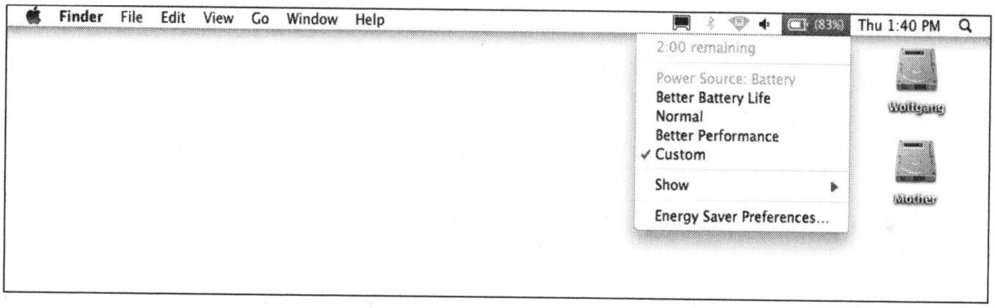

Figure 2-1: Monitor your MacBook's juice from the Finder menu.

Setting Up and Registering Your Laptop

After your Mac is running and you give it the once-over for obvious shipping damage, your next chore is to set up your laptop. Unlike other tasks in this book, I won't cover the setup process step by step. Apple contextually tweaks the questions that you see during setup on a regular basis, and the questions are very easy to answer. Everything is explained onscreen, complete with onscreen Help if you need it.

However, I do want you to know what to expect as well as what information you need to have at hand. I also want you to know about support opportunities, such as the Apple .Mac Internet services. Hence, this section: Consider it a study guide for whatever your MacBook's setup procedure has to throw at you.

Setting up Mac OS X Leopard

After you start your computer for the first time — or if you just upgraded from Mac OS 9 or an earlier version of Mac OS X — your laptop will likely launch Leopard Setup automatically. (Note that some custom install options, such as the Archive and Install option, might not launch the setup procedure.) The setup process takes care of a number of different tasks:

✔ **Setup provides Leopard with your personal information.** As I mention in Chapter 1, your Mac ships with a bathtub full of applications, and many of those use your personal data (such as your address and telephone number) to automatically fill out your documents.

If that stored personal information starts you worrying about identity theft, I congratulate you. If you're using your common sense, it *should*. However, in this case, Apple doesn't disseminate this information anywhere else, and the applications that use your personal data won't send it anywhere, either. And Safari, the Apple Web browser, fills out forms on a Web page automatically *only* if you give your permission.

✔ **Setup creates your user account.** You'll be prompted for a username and password, which Setup uses to create your administrator-level account.

✔ **Setup configures your language and keyboard choices.** Mac OS X is a truly international operating system, so you are offered a chance to configure your laptop to use a specific language and keyboard layout.

✔ **Setup configures your e-mail accounts in Apple Mail.** If you already have an e-mail account set up with your ISP, keep handy the e-mail account information that the ISP provided to answer these questions. The info should include the incoming POP3 and outgoing SMTP mail servers you'll be using, your e-mail address, and your login name and password. Leopard can even automatically configure many Web-based e-mail accounts for you (including Google Mail, Yahoo! Mail, and AOL Mail) if you supply your account ID and password. *Sweet.*

✔ **Setup allows you to open a free trial subscription with Apple's .Mac service.** A .Mac subscription provides you with online file storage, iSync capability across multiple computers, backups to your online storage, Apple e-mail accounts (through both Web mail and the Apple Mail application), photocasting, podcasting, and your own acre of iWeb site on the Internet. I go into all these in detail in Chapter 9, but for now, just sign up (or sign in, if you already have an existing account) and take the opportunity to feel smug about owning an Apple computer.

✔ **Setup sends your registration information to Apple.** As a proud owner of a Mac laptop, take advantage of the year of hardware warranty support and the free 90 days of telephone support. All you have to do is register to use 'em. Rest assured that all this info is confidential.

✔ **Setup launches Migration Assistant.** This assistant guides you through the process of *migrating* (an engineer's term for *moving*) your existing user data from your old Mac or PC to your new laptop. Naturally, if your MacBook is your first Macintosh computer, you can skip this step with a song in your heart! (Read more on Migration Assistant in the section, "Importing Stuff from Another Mac.")

Registering your MacBook

I'll be honest here: I know that many of us, myself included, don't register every piece of computer hardware we buy. For example, I didn't register my wireless Bluetooth adapter that I bought for my older iBook because the total expenditure was only around $40, the gizmo has no moving parts, and I'm never likely to need technical support to use it or get it fixed.

However, your MacBook is a different kettle of fish altogether, and I *strongly* recommend that you register your purchase with Apple during the setup process. You spent a fair amount on your computer, and it's an investment with a significant number of moving parts.

Even the hardiest of techno-wizards would agree with this important Mark's Maxim:

If you don't register your new laptop, you can't receive support.™

And rest assured that Apple is not one of those companies that constantly pesters you with e-mail advertisements and near-spam. I've registered every Apple computer I've owned, and I've never felt pestered. (And I have an extremely low tolerance for pester.)

Importing Stuff from Another Mac

If you're upgrading from an older Mac running Mac OS X to your new MacBook or MacBook Pro, I have great news for you: Apple includes *Migration Assistant,* a utility application that can help you copy (whoops, I mean, *migrate*) all sorts of data from your old Mac to your new machine, via your laptop's FireWire port.

To use Migration Assistant to copy your system from your older Mac, you need a FireWire cable to connect the computers. If you don't already have one, you can pick one up at your local Maze o' Wires electronics store or at your computer store. (This cable will probably come in handy in the future as well, so it's not a one-use wonder.)

If you're a MacBook Air owner, you might be scratching your head looking for a FireWire port on your new laptop. Let me save you the trouble: You don't have one. Therefore, you can't use the Migration Assistant in FireWire mode at the time of this writing. (I hope that Apple will fix this and add USB 2.0 support to Migration Assistant soon.) However, you *can* use a network connection between computers. Assuming that both your MacBook and your older Mac can communicate over your home or office network, just click the Use Network button on the Connect Your Computers screen to transfer data!

As I mention earlier, Setup launches Migration Assistant automatically if you indicate that you need to transfer stuff during the setup process, but you can always launch Migration Assistant manually at any time. You'll find it in the Utilities folder inside your Applications folder; just double-click the Migration Assistant icon.

The list of stuff that gets copied over includes the following:

- **User accounts:** If you set up multiple user accounts (so that more than one person can share the computer), the utility ports them all to your new Mac.

- **Network settings:** Boy, howdy, this is a real treat for those with manual network settings provided by an ISP or a network administrator! Migration Assistant can re-create the entire network environment of your old Mac on your new laptop.

- **System Preference settings:** If you're a fan of tweaking and customizing Mac OS X to fit you like a glove, rejoice. Migration Assistant actually copies over all the changes that you've made in System Preferences on your old Mac! (Insert sound of angelic chorus: *Hallelujah!*)

- **Documents:** The files in your Documents folder(s) are copied to your new Mac.

- **Applications:** Migration Assistant tries its best to copy over the third-party applications that you've installed in your Applications folder on the older Mac. I say *tries its best* because you might have to reinstall some applications, anyway. Some developers create applications that spread out all sorts of files across your hard drive, and Assistant just can't keep track of those nomadic files. And some other applications make the trek just fine, but you might have to reenter their serial numbers.

Follow these steps to use Migration Assistant:

1. **If Migration Assistant isn't already open, open the Utilities folder inside your Applications folder and then double-click the Migration Assistant icon.**

2. Click Continue on the opening screen.

Migration Assistant prompts you for the account name and password that you create during the setup procedure, as shown in Figure 2-2. Your account is an *admin account,* meaning that you have a higher security level that allows you to change things in Leopard. (See Chapter 16 for much more detail on user accounts.)

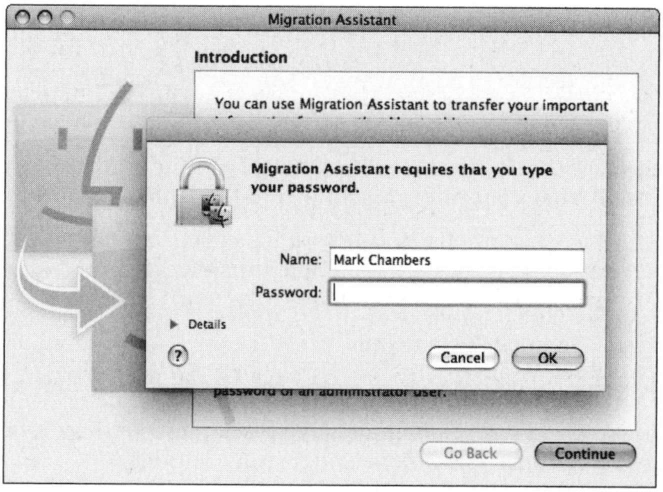

Figure 2-2:
Enter your
admin
password
to use
Migration
Assistant.

3. Type your account name and password, and then click OK.

Characters in your password are displayed as bullet characters for security. After you successfully enter your admin account name and password, this dialog disappears, and you get to play in the real Migration Assistant dialog.

4. Select the From Another Mac radio button and then click Continue.

In case you've lost the data on your hard drive (or you've upgraded your hard drive), you can also restore your MacBook's data from a Time Machine backup drive by using Migration Assistant. (You find all the details on Time Machine in Chapter 21.)

5. Connect a FireWire cable between the two computers. Then click Continue.

As I mention earlier, if you'd rather use a wired or wireless Ethernet connection between the computers, click the Use Network button and eschew the FireWire cable completely. (MacBook Air owners will also have to use a network connection because the Air doesn't have a FireWire port.)

If you take this route, skip Steps 6 and 7. Instead, run Migration Assistant on your older Mac and follow Steps 1–4, but click To Another Mac on your older machine and then click Continue. Follow the onscreen instructions to enter the passcode, and then continue with Step 8.

6. **Restart your older Mac while holding down the T key.**

   This restarts your older computer in *FireWire Target Disk mode,* in which your older Mac essentially becomes a huge external FireWire hard drive. (Neat trick.)

   You must hold down the T key until you see the FireWire symbol (which looks like a stylized Y) appears on your older machine.

7. **Click Continue.**

8. **Select the check boxes next to the user accounts that you want to transfer from your older machine and then click Continue.**

   Migration Assistant displays how much space is required to hold the selected accounts on your new laptop's hard drive.

9. **Select the check boxes next to the applications and files that you want to copy. Then click Continue.**

10. **Select the check boxes next to the settings that you want to transfer.**

    Normally, you want to migrate all three of these settings groups: Network Settings, Time Zone and Sharing Settings.

11. **Click the Migrate button.**

12. **After everything is copied, press the power button on your older Mac to shut it off. Then disconnect the FireWire cable (if necessary).**

Importing Stuff from Windows (If You Must)

If you're a Windows-to-Mac *Switcher,* you made a wise choice, especially if you're interested in the creative applications in the iLife suite! Although you could choose to start your Apple computing life anew, you probably want to migrate some of your existing documents and files from that tired PC to your bright, shiny, new MacBook.

Unfortunately, Mac OS X has no Windows Migration Assistant. However, if you're moving from a Windows PC to a Mac, you can copy your files manually from a CD or DVD, a USB Flash drive, or over a network. (Note, however, that today's Mac laptops don't come with a floppy drive. And trust me, you wouldn't want to use one to move anything that matters, anyway.)

The Mac OS X Help system contains an entire subsection on specific tricks you can use when switching from Windows to Mac, including how to connect to a Windows network and how to directly connect the two computers.

Even with *Boot Camp* — Apple's dual-boot feature that allows you to run both Leopard and Windows XP/Vista on your MacBook, MacBook Pro, or MacBook Air — manually moving existing Windows applications (such as Paint Shop Pro) to your laptop's hard drive usually won't work. That's because most Windows software installs all sorts of necessary files in several folders across your hard drive. Instead, you have to install Windows XP or Windows Vista on your Mac laptop (using Boot Camp) and then reinstall your Windows applications.

If you don't mind investing around $50, use the Move2Mac software utility, which does most of the work of Migration Assistant for those switching from a Windows PC. From Detto Technologies (www.detto.com/move2mac), Move2Mac comes complete with a special USB-to-USB cable that connects your two computers for high-speed copying. You can choose what you want to transfer to your new Mac (use Table 2-1 as a guide), and the copying is performed automatically for you. Plus, Move2Mac transfers goodies such as your home page and bookmarks from Internet Explorer, desktop backgrounds, and even your Address Book contacts and account settings from Outlook Express. Move2Mac makes switching much easier, and I can highly recommend it.

Table 2-1	Moving Media and Documents betwixt Computers		
File Type	**Windows Location**	**Mac OS X Location**	**Mac Application**
Music files	My Music folder	Music folder	iTunes
Video and movie files	My Videos folder	Movies folder	QuickTime/ DVD Player
Digital photos	My Pictures folder	Pictures folder	iPhoto
Office documents	My Documents folder	Documents folder	Mac Office/ iWork

Switching from a PC to . . . an Apple PC?

With the Leopard Boot Camp feature, you can actually create a full Windows XP or Vista system on your Intel-based Mac laptop. Yup, Windows and Leopard coexist peacefully *on the same computer*. However, you'll have to reboot your computer to use your MacBook as a Windows system.

This brings a whole new meaning to the term *Switcher* because some Mac owners are moving their stuff from Windows (running on their old PC) to . . . well, Windows (running on their new laptop) instead of Leopard. If you do decide to create a Windows system on your MacBook with Boot Camp, the files and folders on your existing PC can be copied directly by using the Files and Settings Transfer Wizard (in Windows XP) or the Windows Easy Transfer utility (in Windows Vista). In effect, you're copying your settings and data between your old PC and your new Apple-based PC! (That sounds a little skewed, but die-hard Apple apostles will have to forgive me.)

Chapter 3

The Laptop Owner's Introduction to Mac OS X

In This Chapter

▶ Introducing Mac OS X Leopard

▶ Appreciating the Unix core underneath Leopard

▶ Recognizing similarities between Windows XP and Leopard

▶ Getting help while learning about Leopard

*I*n the other books that I've written about Mac OS X Leopard, I use all sorts of somewhat understated phrases to describe my operating system of choice, such as elegantly reliable, purely powerful, and supremely user friendly.

But *why* is Leopard such a standout? To be specific, why do creative professionals and computer techno-wizards across the globe hunger for the very same Mac OS X that runs your MacBook? Why is Leopard so far ahead of Windows Vista in features and performance? Good questions, all!

In this chapter, I answer those queries and satisfy your curiosity about your new big cat. I introduce the main elements of the Leopard Desktop, and I show you the fearless Unix heart that beats underneath Leopard's sleek exterior. I also point out the most important similarities between Leopard and Windows Vista, and I outline the resources available if you need help with Mac OS X.

Oh, and I promise to use honest-to-goodness English in my explanations, with a minimum of engineer-speak and indecipherable acronyms. (Hey, you've got to boast about Leopard in turn to your family and friends. Aunt Harriet might not be as technologically savvy as we are.)

Your Own Personal Operating System

Leopard is a special type of software called an *operating system*. You know, *OS,* as in *Mac OS X?* That means that Leopard essentially runs your MacBook and also allows you to run all your other applications, such as iTunes or Photoshop. It's the most important computer application — or *software* — that you run.

Think of a pyramid, with Leopard as the foundation and other applications running on top.

You're using the OS when you aren't running a specific application, such as these actions:

- ✔ Copying files from a CD to your hard drive
- ✔ Choosing a different screensaver

Sometimes, Leopard even peeks through an application while it's running. For example, application actions like these are also controlled by Leopard:

- ✔ The Open, Save, and Save As dialogs that you see when working with files in Photoshop
- ✔ The Print dialog that appears when you print a document in Microsoft Word

In this section, I escort you personally around the most important hotspots in Leopard, and you meet the most interesting onscreen thingamabobs that you use to control your laptop. (I told you I wasn't going to talk like an engineer!)

The Leopard Desktop

This particular desktop isn't made of wood, and you can't stick your gum underneath. However, your Leopard Desktop does indeed work much like the surface of a traditional desk. You can store things there, organize things into folders, and take care of important tasks like running other applications. Heck, you've even got a clock and a trash can.

Gaze upon Figure 3-1 and follow along as you venture to your Desktop and beyond.

Finder menu   Finder Window

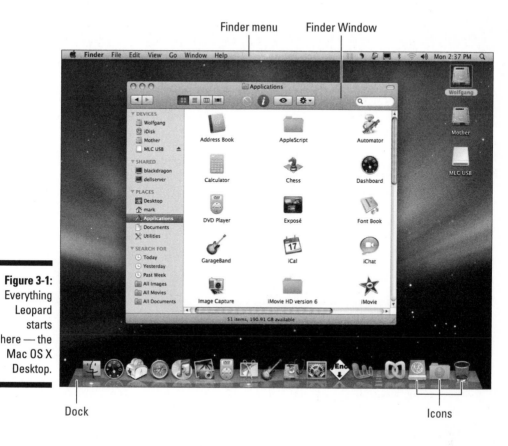

Figure 3-1:
Everything
Leopard
starts
here — the
Mac OS X
Desktop.

Dock   Icons

Meet me at the Dock

The Dock is the closest thing to the dashboard of a car that you're likely to find on a Macintosh. It's a pretty versatile combination: one part organizer, one part application launcher, and one part system monitor. From here, you can launch applications, see what's running, and display or hide the windows shown by your applications.

Each icon in the Dock represents one of the following (many of which are proudly displayed in Figure 3-2):

- ✔ An application that you can run (or is running)
- ✔ An application window that's *minimized* (shrunk)
- ✔ A Web page URL link

✔ A document or folder on your system

✔ A network server or shared folder

✔ Your Trash

I cover the Dock in more detail in Chapter 5.

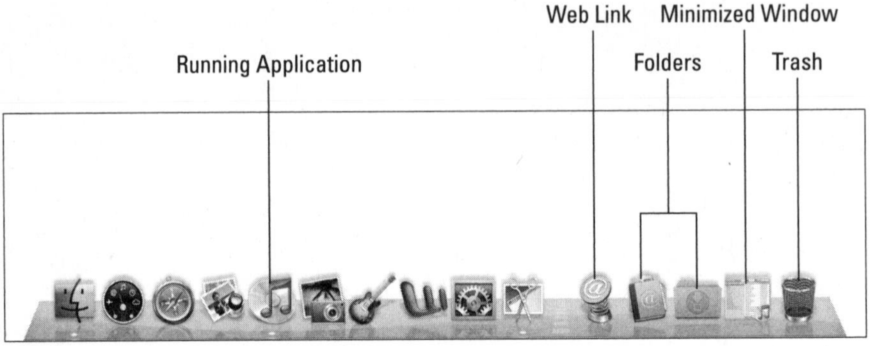

Web Link   Minimized Window

Running Application   Folders   Trash

Figure 3-2:
The Dock
can contain
all sorts of
exotic icons.

TIP

The Dock is highly configurable:

✔ It can appear at different edges of the screen.

✔ It can disappear until you move your mouse pointer to the edge to call it forth.

✔ You can resize it.

Dig those crazy icons

By default, Leopard always displays at least one icon on your Desktop: your Mac's internal hard drive. To open a hard drive and view or use the contents, you double-click the icon. Other icons that might appear on your Desktop can include

✔ CDs and DVDs

✔ An iPod

✔ External hard drives or USB Flash drives

✔ Applications, folders, and documents

✔ Files you downloaded from the Internet

✔ Your iDisk (if you have a .Mac account)

✔ Network servers you access

Chapter 4 provides the good stuff on icons and their uses within Leopard.

There's no food on this menu

The Finder menu isn't found in a restaurant. You find it at the top of the Desktop, where you can use it to control your applications. Virtually every application that you run on your laptop has a menu.

To use a menu command, follow these steps:

1. **Click the menu group (such as File or Edit).**

2. **Choose the desired command from the list that appears (see Figure 3-3).**

Virtually every Macintosh application has some menu groups, such as File, Edit, and Window. You're likely to find similar commands within these groups. However, only two menu groups are in *every* Mac OS X application:

✔ The *Apple menu* (which is identified with that jaunty Apple Corporation icon,).

✔ The *Application menu* (which always bears the name of the active application). For instance, the DVD Player menu group appears when you run the Leopard DVD Player, and the Word menu group appears when you launch Microsoft Word.

I cover these two common groups in more detail in Chapters 4 and 5.

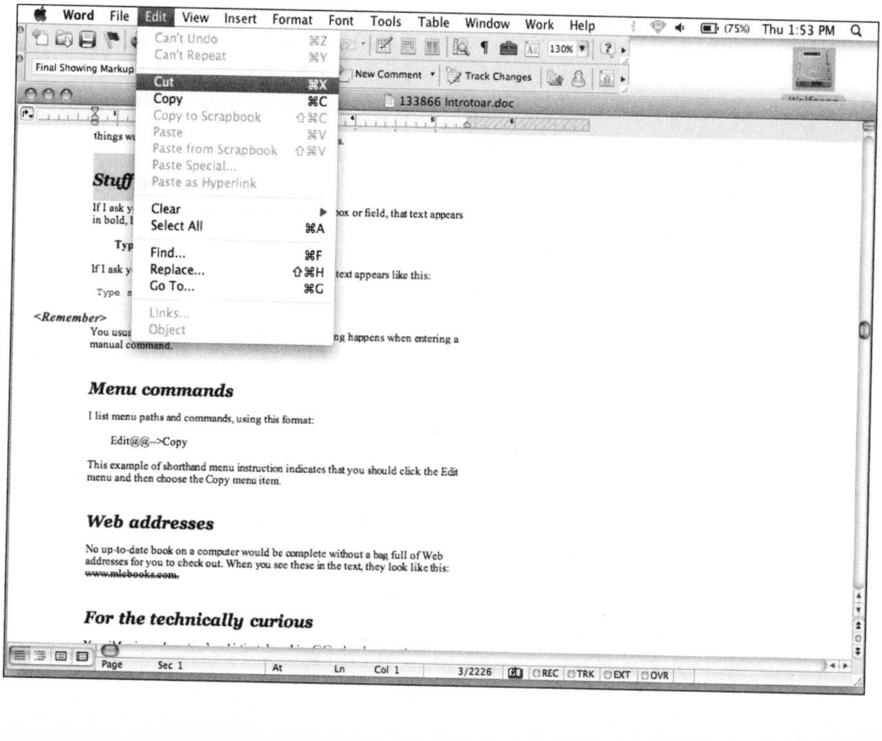

Figure 3-3:
Clicking a
menu group
displays a
list of menu
commands.

You can also display a contextual menu — which regular human beings call a *right-click menu* — by right-clicking your Leopard Desktop, or an application, a folder, or a file icon. I get into the right-click menu in detail in the next chapter. (You can also right-click by holding down the Ctrl key while clicking, or by tapping the trackpad with two fingertips.)

There's always room for one more window

You're probably already familiar with the ubiquitous window itself. Both Leopard and the applications that you run use windows to display things like

- The documents that you create
- The contents of your hard drive

For example, the window in Figure 3-1 is a Finder window, where Leopard gives you access to the applications, documents, and folders on your system.

Windows are surprisingly configurable. I cover them at length in Chapter 4.

Why get so excited by Leopard?

How the core of an operating system is designed makes more of a difference than all the visual bells and whistles, which tend to be similar between Windows Vista/XP and Mac OS X Leopard (and Linux as well, for that matter). Time for a Mark's Maxim:

Sure, Leopard's elegant exterior is a joy to use, but Mac OS X is a *better* OS than Windows because of the unique Unix muscle that lies underneath!™

So what should you and I look for in an OS? Keep in mind that today's computer techno-wizard demands three requirements for a truly high-powered software wonderland — and Mac OS X Leopard easily meets all three:

- **Reliability:** Your OS has to stay up and running reliably for as long as necessary — I'm talking *months* here — without lockups or error messages. If an application crashes, the rest of your work should remain safe, and you should be able to shut down the offending software.

- **Performance:** If your computer has advanced hardware, your OS must be able to use those resources to speed things up big-time. The OS has to be highly configurable, and it has to be updated often to keep up with the latest in computer hardware.

    "Mark, what do you mean by advanced hardware?" Well, if you're already knowledgeable about state-of-the-art hardware, examples include

    - True 64-bit computing

    - Multiple processors (like more than one Intel chip in your computer)

- A huge amount of RAM (2GB on most MacBooks, or far more on today's Mac Pro desktop computers)

- Enough hard drive space to make use of a RAID array

If all that sounds like ancient Sumerian, gleefully ignore this technical drabble and keep reading.

✔ **Ease of use:** All the speed and reliability in the world won't help an OS if it's difficult to use.

Like Windows done right

You might have heard of the *Windows Switcher:* a uniquely intelligent species that's becoming more and more common these days. Switchers are former PC owners who have abandoned Windows and bought a Macintosh, thereby joining the Apple faithful running Mac OS X. (Apple loves to document this migration on its Web site.) Because today's Macintosh computers are significantly faster than their PC counterparts — and you get neat software, such as Leopard and the iLife suite when you buy a new Mac — switching makes perfect sense.

Switchers aren't moving to totally unfamiliar waters. Windows XP, Windows Vista, and Leopard share a number of important concepts. Familiarizing yourself with Leopard takes far less time than you might think.

It's Apple to the rescue!

Unix is the established, super-reliable OS that powers most of the high-performance servers that make up the Internet. Unix has built-in support for virtually every hardware device ever wrought by the hand of Man (including all the cool stuff that came with your MacBook), and Unix is well designed and highly efficient.

Unfortunately, standard Unix looks as hideous as DOS, complete with a confusing command line, so ease-of-use for normal human beings like you and me goes out the door. Enter the genius types at Apple, who understood several years ago that all Unix needed was a state-of-the-art, novice-friendly interface! To wit: Mac OS X was developed with a Unix foundation (or *core*), so it shares the same reliability and performance as Unix. However, the software engineers at Apple (who know a thing or two about ease-of-use) made it good looking and easy to use.

If you're interested in all the details about what makes Mac OS X tick, as well as its settings and features, I can heartily recommend another of my books, the bestselling (and extremely heavy) *Mac OS X Leopard All-in-One Desk Reference For Dummies* (Wiley). It comprehensively covers everything Leopard — over 700 pages devoted entirely to Mac OS X and its companion applications!

Here's an overview of the basic similarities between the two operating systems:

✔ **The Desktop:** The Leopard Desktop is a neat representation of a real physical desktop, and Windows uses the same idea:

- You can arrange files, folders, and applications on your Desktop to help keep things handy.
- Application windows appear on the Desktop.

✔ **Drives, files, and folders:** Data is stored in files on your hard drive(s), and those files can be organized in folders. Both Leopard and Windows use the same file/folder concept.

✔ **Specific locations:** Both Windows and Leopard provide every user with a set of folders to help keep various types of files organized. For example, the My Videos folder that you can use in Windows XP corresponds to the Movies folder that you find in your Home folder within Leopard.

✔ **Running programs:** Both Leopard and Windows run programs (or applications) in the same manner:

- Double-clicking an application icon launches that application.
- Double-clicking a document runs the corresponding application and then automatically loads the document.

✔ **Window control:** Yep, both operating systems use windows, and those windows can be resized, hidden (or minimized), and closed in similar fashions. (Are you starting to see the connections here?)

✔ **Drag and drop:** One of the basics behind a GUI (a ridiculous acronym that stands for *graphical user interface*) like Windows and Leopard is the ability to drag documents and folders around to move, delete, copy, and load them. Drag-and-drop is one of the primary advantages of both of these operating systems because copying a file by dragging it from one window to another is intuitive and easy enough for a kid to accomplish.

✔ **Editing:** Along the same lines as drag-and-drop, both Leopard and Windows offer similar cut-and-paste editing features. You've likely used Cut, Copy, and Paste for years, so this is familiar stuff.

And Just in Case You Need Help . . .

You can call on these resources if you need additional help while you're discovering how to tame the Leopard.

Some of the help resources are located on the Internet, so your Web browser will come in handy.

The Leopard built-in Help system

Sometimes the help you need is as close as the Help group on the Finder menu. You can get help for either

- ✔ **A specific application:** Just click Help. Then, click in the Search box and type a short phrase that sums up your query (such as *startup keys*). You'll see a list of help topics appear on the menu. Just click a topic to display more information.

- ✔ **General topics:** Click a Finder window and then click Help on the menu. Again, you'll see the Search box, and you can enter a word or phrase to find within the Help system. To display the Help viewer window, click the Mac Help item under the Search box.

The Apple Web-based support center

Apple has online product support areas for every hardware and software product that it manufactures. Visit www.apple.com and click the Support tab at the top of the Web page.

The Search box works just like the Mac OS Help system, but the Knowledge Base that Apple provides online has a *lot* more answers.

Magazines

Many magazines (both in print and online) offer tips and tricks on using and maintaining Mac OS X Leopard.

My personal online favorites are Macworld (www.macworld.com) and MacLife (www.maclife.com).

Mac support Web sites

A number of private individuals and groups offer support forums on the Web, and you can often find help from other Mac owners on these sites within a few hours of posting a question.

I'm very fond of MacFixIt (www.macfixit.com), Mac OS X Hints (http://forums.macosxhints.com) and MacMinute (www.macminute.com).

Mac newsgroups on Usenet

If you're familiar with Usenet newsgroups, you can find lots of help (typically dispensed with a healthy dose of opinion) in newsgroups like `comp.sys.mac.system` and `comp.sys.mac.applications`. Simply post a message and then check back within a few hours to read the replies.

Local Mac user groups

I'd be remiss if I didn't mention your local Mac user group. Often, a user group maintains its own Web site and discussion forum. If you can wait until the next meeting, you can even ask your question and receive a reply from a real-live human being . . . quite a thrill in today's Web-riffic world!

Part II
Shaking Hands with Mac OS X

The 5th Wave   By Rich Tennant

AFTER INSTALLING OS X LEOPARD, NED AND LORETTA SELECT THE COMPUTER'S BACKGROUND

"Oh – I like this background much better than the basement."

In this part . . .

It's time to delve deeper into the workings of Mac OS X Leopard. Here, I show you how to perform all sorts of common tasks as well as how to customize your system, how to change settings in System Preferences, where your personal files are stored, and how to use the latest Spotlight search technology to find anything you've stored on your MacBook, MacBook Pro, or MacBook Air!

Chapter 4

Opening and Closing and Clicking and Such

In This Chapter

▶ Introducing the highlights of the Finder

▶ Coping with that missing trackpad button

▶ Launching and quitting applications

▶ Identifying and selecting icons

▶ Using keyboard shortcuts to speed things up

▶ Managing windows in Leopard

Ah, the Finder — many admire its scenic beauty, but don't ignore its unsurpassed power nor its many moods. And send a postcard while you're there.

Okay, so Leopard's Finder might not be *quite* as majestic as the mighty Mississippi River, but it's the basic toolbox that you use every single day while piloting your MacBook. The Finder includes the most common elements of Mac OS X: window controls, common menu commands, icon fun (everything from launching applications to copying files), network connections, keyboard shortcuts, and even emptying the Trash. In fact, one could say that if you master the Finder and find how to use it efficiently, you're on your way to becoming a power user! (My editor calls this the Finder "window of opportunity." She's a hoot.)

That's what this chapter is designed to do: This is your Finder tour guide, and we're ready to roll.

Using the All-Powerful Finder

This is a hands-on tour, with none of that, "On your right, you'll see the historic Go menu" for you! Time to get off the bus and start the tour with

Figure 4-1, in which I show you around the most important elements of the Finder. (In the upcoming section, "Performing Tricks with Finder Windows," I give you a close-up view of window controls.)

The popular attractions include

✔ **The Apple menu (🍎):** This is a special menu because it appears both in the Finder and within every application menu that you run. It doesn't matter whether you're in iTunes or Photoshop or Word: If you can see a menu bar, the Apple menu is there. The Apple menu contains common commands to use no matter where you are in Leopard, such as Restart, Shut Down, and System Preferences.

✔ **The Finder menu bar:** Whenever the Finder itself is ready to use (or, in Mac-speak, whenever the Finder is the *active* application, rather than another application), the Finder menu bar appears at the top of your screen. You know the Finder is active and ready when the word *Finder* appears at the left of the menu bar.

If you're brand new to computers, a *menu* is simply a list of commands. For example, you click the File menu and then choose Save to save a document. When you click a menu, it extends down so that you can see the commands it includes. While the menu is extended, you can choose any enabled menu item (just click it) to perform that action. You can tell that an item is enabled if its name appears in black. Conversely, a menu command is disabled if it is grayed out — clicking it does nothing.

When you see a menu path, like this example — File➪Save — it's just a visual shortcut that tells you to click the File menu and then choose Save from the drop-down menu that appears.

✔ **The Desktop:** Your Desktop serves the same purpose as your physical desktop: You can store stuff here (files, alias icons, and so on), and it's a solid, stable surface where you can work comfortably. Application windows appear on the Desktop, for example, as do other applications, such as your Stickies notes and your DVD player. Just double-click an application there to launch it.

Your Desktop is easily customized in many ways. For example, you can use your own images to decorate the Desktop, organize it to store new folders and documents, arrange icons how you like, or put the Dock in another location. Don't worry — I cover all this in other areas of the book — I just want you to know that you don't have to settle for what Apple gives you as a default Desktop.

✔ **All sorts of icons:** This is a Macintosh computer, after all, replete with tons of make-your-life-easier tools. Check out the plethora of icons on your Desktop as well as icons within the Finder window itself. Each icon is a shortcut of sorts to a file, folder, network connection, or device in your system, including applications that you run and documents that you create. Refer to Figure 4-1 to see the icon for my MacBook Pro's hard drive icon, labeled Wolfgang. (I'm a huge Mozart fan.) Sometimes you click an icon to watch it do its thing (like icons in the Dock, which I cover next), but usually you double-click an icon to make something happen.

✔ **The Dock:** The Dock is a launching pad for your favorite applications, documents, folders, network connections, and Web sites. You can also refer to it to see what applications are running. Click an icon there to open the item. For example, the postage stamp icon represents the Apple Mail application, and clicking the spiffy compass icon launches your Safari Web browser.

✔ **The Finder window:** Finally! The basic Finder window in Figure 4-1 displays the contents of my Applications folder. You use Finder windows to launch applications; perform disk chores, such as copying and moving files; and navigate your hard drive.

Apple menu   Finder menu bar   Icons

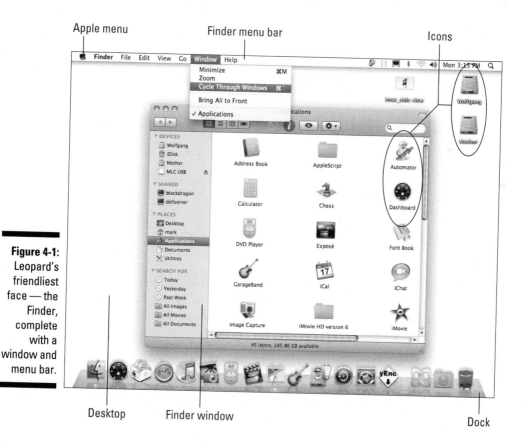

Figure 4-1:
Leopard's
friendliest
face — the
Finder,
complete
with a
window and
menu bar.

Desktop   Finder window   Dock

My, what an attractive Sidebar . . . and so useful!

Have you noticed the Sidebar that occupies the left side of every Finder window? It's a pane of links to common locations and devices that you can use to jump like a flash to a specific spot on your hard drive. For example, you can click the Applications link under the Places heading, and you're there in an instant. The Sidebar also contains a Search For heading that displays the applications, files and folders that you've accessed today, yesterday and this past week. (Heck, you can even search for all the images, movies, and documents on your system from this same Search For section!)

Here's a great example of Sidebar magic: I like as few icons on my Desktop as possible, so each book I'm working on gets its own folder. All the items for that project that might otherwise end up on my Desktop are saved into that folder instead. In fact, I make a point of adding my current book project folder to my Finder window Sidebar so that it's available immediately from any Finder window. To do this, just drag the folder into the column at the left side of the Finder window and drop it under the Places heading in the Sidebar's list.

Wait a Second: Where the Heck Is the Right Mouse Button?

Leopard takes a visual approach to everything, and what you see in Figure 4-1 is designed for point-and-click convenience because the *trackpad* is your primary navigational tool while you're using your Mac laptop. You move your finger over the surface of the trackpad, and the cursor follows like an obedient pup. The faster you move your finger, the farther the cursor goes. You click an item, it opens, you do your thing, and life is good.

Never use any object other than your finger on the trackpad! That means no pencils (no, not even the eraser end), pens, or chopsticks; they can damage your trackpad in no time at all.

If you've grazed on the other side of the fence — one of Those Who Were Once Windows Users — you're probably accustomed to using a mouse with at least two buttons. This brings up the nagging question: "Hey, Mark! Where the heck is the right button?"

In a nutshell, the right button simply ain't there. At least, if you're using your Mac laptop's trackpad, it simply ain't there. The entire bottom of the trackpad is one huge button, and you click something by pressing down anywhere on the top surface of the aforementioned bump.

Lean in closer, and I'll tell you a secret. (Dramatic pause.) This is one of the few disagreements that I have with my friends at Apple Inc. Once upon a time, Apple felt that a mouse needed but one button, and until the arrival of the Mighty Mouse on Apple's desktop models, it was the only button you got. And you liked it. And you still do, if you're using a Mac laptop's trackpad.

If you're like me, you feel that a right button is pretty doggone essential. In fact, when my laptop is on my desk at home, I plug in a Logitech optical track-ball (a really fancy mouse, in effect). This neat device has both a right mouse button and a scroll wheel. So here's a Mark's Maxim that I think you'll appreciate more and more as you use your laptop.

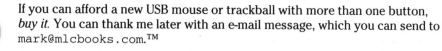

If you can afford a new USB mouse or trackball with more than one button, *buy it.* You can thank me later with an e-mail message, which you can send to mark@mlcbooks.com.™

In fact, a new industry is springing up for tiny USB mousing devices especially made for laptops. Some devices are smaller than a business card, but they still carry a full complement of two buttons and a scroll wheel. You can carry one of these mini-mice in your laptop bag and eschew your trackpad completely. In fact, in this book I'm going to refer to the pointer as the "mouse pointer," whether you're using your trackpad or a mouse.

If you have a pointing device with two buttons, you'll find that clicking the right mouse button performs the same default function in Leopard that it does in Windows. Namely, when you click the right mouse button on most items — icons, documents, even your Desktop — you get a *contextual menu* of things. That is, you get more commands specific to that item. (Boy, howdy, I hate that word *contextual,* but that's what engineers call it. I call it the right-click menu, and I promise to refer to it as such for the rest of the book.)

Figure 4-2 illustrates a typical convenient right-click menu within a Finder window. I have all sorts of cool items at my disposal on this menu because of the applications I've installed that make use of a right-click menu.

If you're using your laptop's trackpad or one-button mouse, don't despair. You can still display a right-click menu: Just hold down the Control key while you click.

Pressing an extra key, as you might imagine, can be a real downer, especially if your non-trackpad-using hand is busy doing something else. Hence my preceding Mark's Maxim. Someday, Apple will finally throw in the towel and add a second trackpad button to their laptops. Luckily, you can also configure your trackpad to recognize a tap with two fingertips as a right-click (as I mention earlier in this section).

Figure 4-2:
Well-
adjusted
folks call
this a right-
click menu.

Clicking and right-clicking magic

Here are some handy and painless workarounds: Head over to System Preferences and open the Keyboard & Mouse Pane (under Hardware). Look for the Trackpad options. Find the Clicking check box and enable it. Now, when you tap the trackpad quickly, your Mac laptop counts that as a click, and two fast taps act as a double-click. Enable the Tap Trackpad Using Two Fingers for Secondary Click check box, and suddenly a single tap with two fingers displays the right-click menu (which I cover in more detail in a paragraph or two).

It's okay to scroll with your fingers

If you move two fingers over the surface of the trackpad at once, the Finder window or application *scrolls* the contents of the window in the direction you move. (For example, you can use the scroll function to move up and down through the pages of a document or to move up and down through a long Web page.) Who needs scroll bars?

Doing the Multi-Touch thing

The latest crop of MacBooks — including the MacBook Air — have the smartest trackpads on the planet! That's because Apple recently introduced a new feature called *Multi-Touch,* which allows you to control the view of a document by using specific finger motions on the trackpad. Here's the rundown:

- ✔ **Two-finger zooming:** Pinching your thumb and first fingertip toward each on the trackpad other zooms in on a document or image. The reverse (moving your fingertips away from each other) zooms out.

- ✔ **Two-finger rotating:** Rotate your thumb and first fingertip in a circle on the trackpad to rotate an image or document in the corresponding direction.

- ✔ **Three-finger paging:** Move your thumb and first two fingertips to the left or right across your trackpad to page through a document or move to the next or previous image in a set.

Unfortunately, Multi-Touch doesn't work with every application, but support for this neat feature is rapidly being added by Apple software developers. (For now, I recommend you try out your fingertips in iPhoto and Pages!)

Visit the Keyboard & Mouse pane within System Preferences to configure your wireless mouse as well. (More on the System Preferences window in the next section.)

Launching and Quitting Applications with Aplomb

Now it's time for you to pair your newly found trackpad acumen with Leopard's Finder window. Follow along this simple exercise. Move your cursor over the iTunes icon in the Dock (this icon looks like an audio CD with musical notes on it). Then click the trackpad button (default) or tap the trackpad once with your fingertip (see the preceding section for how to set this preference). Whoosh! Leopard *launches* (or starts) the iTunes application, and you see a window much like the one in Figure 4-3.

If an application icon is already selected (which I discuss in the next section), you can simply press Ô+O to launch it. The same key shortcut works with documents, too.

Close Window button

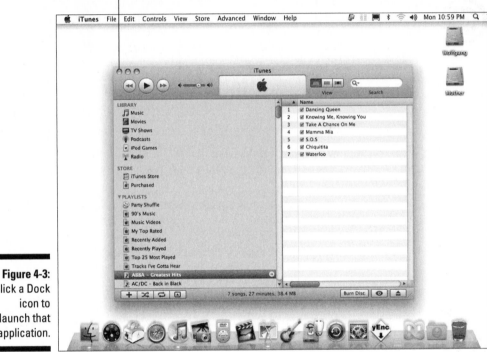

Figure 4-3:
Click a Dock
icon to
launch that
application.

Besides the Dock, you have several other ways to launch an application or open a document in Leopard:

✔ **From the Apple menu (🍎):** A number of different applications can always be launched anywhere within Leopard from the Apple menu:

- *System Preferences:* This is where you change all sorts of settings, such as your display background and how icons appear.

- *Software Update:* This uses the Internet to see whether update patches are available for your Apple software, as I discuss in Chapter 21.

- *Mac OS X Software:* This launches the Safari browser and displays software that you can download for your laptop.

✔ **From the Desktop:** If you have a document that you created or an application icon on your Desktop, you can launch or open it here by *double-clicking* that icon (clicking the trackpad button twice in rapid succession when the mouse pointer is on top of the icon). Remember that you can also configure your MacBook's trackpad to accept a single tap with one fingertip as a click.

Double-clicking a device or network connection on your Desktop opens the contents in a Finder window. This works for CDs and DVDs that you've loaded as well as external hard drives and USB Flash drives. Just double-click 'em to open them and display their contents in a Finder window. Applications and documents launch from a CD, a DVD, or an external drive just like they launch from your internal drive (the one that's typically named *Macintosh HD*), so you don't have to copy stuff from the external drive just to use it. (You can't change the contents of most CDs and DVDs; they're read only, so you can't write to them.)

✔ **From the Recent Items selection:** When you click the Apple menu and hover your mouse pointer over the Recent Items menu item, the Finder displays all the applications and documents that you used over the past few computing sessions. Click an item in this list to launch or open it.

✔ **From the Login Items list:** Login Items are applications that Leopard launches automatically each time you log in to your user account.

I cover Login Items in detail in Chapter 16.

✔ **From the Finder window:** You can also double-click an icon within the confines of a Finder window to open it (for documents), launch it (for applications), or display the contents (for a folder).

The Quick Look feature that debuted with Leopard can display the contents of just about any document or file — but without actually opening the corresponding application! *Sweet.* To use Quick Look from a Finder window, click a file to select it and then click the Quick Look button (which bears an eye icon) on the Finder window toolbar.

After you finish using an application, you can quit that application to close its window and return to the Desktop. Here are a number of different ways to quit an application:

✔ **Press ⌘+Q.** This keyboard shortcut quits virtually every Macintosh application on the planet. Just make sure that the application that you want to quit is currently active first!

✔ **Choose the Quit command from the application's menu.** To display the Quit command, click the application's name — its menu — from the menu bar. This menu is always to the immediate right of the Apple (🍎) menu. For example, Safari displays a Safari menu, and that same spot in the menu is taken up by iCal when iCal is the active application. In Figure 4-3, look for the iTunes menu, right next to 🍎.

✔ **Choose Quit from the Dock.** You can Control-click (or right-click) an application's icon on the Dock and then choose Quit from the right-click menu that appears. Alternatively, just click the icon and hold down the button to display the same menu.

A running application displays a small blue dot under its icon on the Dock.

✔ **Click the Close button on the application window; refer to Figure 4-3.** Some applications quit entirely when you close their window, like the System Preferences window or the Apple DVD Player. Other applications might continue running without any window, like Safari or iTunes; to close these applications, you have to use another method in this list.

✔ **Choose Force Quit from the Apple menu.** *This is a last-resort measure!* Use this only if an application has frozen and you can't use another method in this list to quit. Force-quitting an application doesn't save any changes to any open documents within that application!

Juggling Folders and Icons

Finder windows aren't just for launching applications and opening the files and documents that you create. You can also use the icons within a Finder window to select one or more specific items or to copy and move items from place to place within your system.

A field observer's guide to icons

Not all icons are created equal. Earlier in this chapter, I introduce you to your MacBook's hard drive icon on the Desktop, but here is a little background on the other types of icons that you might encounter during your mobile Mac travels:

✔ **Hardware:** These are your storage devices (such as your hard drive and DVD drive) as well as external peripherals (such as your iPod and printer).

✔ **Applications:** These icons represent the applications (or programs) that you can launch. Most applications have a custom icon that incorporates the company's logo or the specific application logo, so they're very easy to recognize, as you can see in Figure 4-4. Double-clicking an application usually doesn't load a document automatically; you typically get a new blank document, or an Open dialog box from which you can choose the existing file you want to open.

✔ **Documents:** Many of the files on your hard drive are documents that can be opened within the corresponding application, and the icon usually looks similar to the application's icon. Double-clicking a document automatically launches the required application (that is, as long as Mac OS X recognizes the file type).

✔ **Files:** Most of the file icons on your system are mundane things (such as preference and settings files, text files, log files, and miscellaneous data files), yet most are identified with at least some type of recognizable icon that lets you guess what purpose the file serves. You'll also come across generic file icons that look like a blank sheet of paper (used when Leopard has no earthly idea what the file type is).

Figure 4-4:
A collection
of some of
my favorite
application
icons.

✔ **Aliases:** An *alias* acts as a link to another item elsewhere on your system. For example, to launch Adobe Acrobat, you can click an Adobe Acrobat alias icon that you can create on your Desktop rather than clicking the actual Acrobat application icon. The alias essentially acts the same way as the original icon, but it doesn't take up the same space — only a few bytes for the icon itself, compared with the size of the actual application. Plus, you don't have to go digging through folders galore to find the original application icon. (Windows Switchers know an alias as a *shortcut,* and the idea is the same although Macs had it first. Harrumph.) You can always identify an alias by the small curved arrow at the base of the icon, and the icon might also sport the tag `alias` at the end of its name.

You have two ways to create an alias. Here's one:

   a. *Select the item.*

   The following section has details about selecting icons.

   b. *Choose File⇨Make Alias, or press ⌘+L.*

   Figure 4-5 illustrates a number of aliases, arranged next to their linked files.

Here's another way to create an alias:

   a. *Hold down ⌘+Option.*

   b. *Drag the original icon to the location where you want the alias.*

   Note that this funky method doesn't add the `alias` tag to the end of the alias icon name!

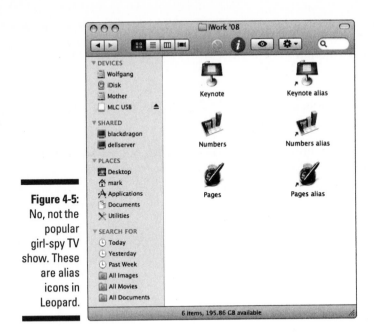

Figure 4-5:
No, not the
popular
girl-spy TV
show. These
are alias
icons in
Leopard.

So why bother to use an alias? Two good reasons:

✔ **Launch an application or open a document from anywhere on your
drive.** For example, you can start Pages directly from the folder where
you store the documents for your current Pages project. Speed, organization, and convenience . . . life is good.

✔ **Send an alias to the Trash without affecting the original item.** When
that school project is finished, you can safely delete the entire folder
without worrying about whether Keynote will run the next time you
double-click the application icon!

If you move or rename the original file, Leopard is actually smart enough to
update the alias, too! However, if the original file is deleted (or if the original
is moved to a different volume, such as an external hard drive), the alias no
longer works. (Go figure.)

Selecting items

Often, the menu commands or keyboard commands that you perform in the
Finder need to be performed on something: Perhaps you're moving an item
to the Trash, or getting more information on the item, or creating an alias for

that item. In order to identify the target of your action to the Finder, you need to select one or more items on your Desktop or in a Finder window. In this section, I show you just how to do that.

Selecting one thing

Leopard gives you a couple of options when selecting just one item for an upcoming action:

✔ **Move your mouse pointer over the item and click.** A dark border (or *highlight*) appears around the icon, indicating that it's selected.

✔ **If an icon is already highlighted on your Desktop or within a window, move the selection highlight to another icon in the same location by using the arrow keys.** To shift the selection highlight alphabetically, press Tab (to move in order) or press Shift+Tab (to move in reverse order).

Selecting items in the Finder doesn't actually *do* anything to them by itself. You have to perform an action on the selected items to make something happen.

Selecting a whole bunch of things

You can also select multiple items with aplomb by using one of these methods:

✔ **Adjacent items**

• *Drag a box around them.* If that sounds like ancient Sumerian, here's the explanation: Click a spot above and to the left of the first item; then hold down the trackpad button and drag down and to the right. (This is *dragging* in Mac-speak.) A box outline like the one in Figure 4-6 appears, indicating what you're selecting. Any icons that touch or appear within the box outline are selected when you release the button.

• *Click the first item to select it and then hold down the Shift key while you click the last item.* Leopard selects both items and everything between them.

✔ **Nonadjacent items:** Select these by holding down the ⌘ key while you click each item.

Check out the status line at the bottom of a Finder window. It tells you how much space is available on the drive you're working in as well as how many items are displayed in the current Finder window. When you select items, it shows you how many you highlighted.

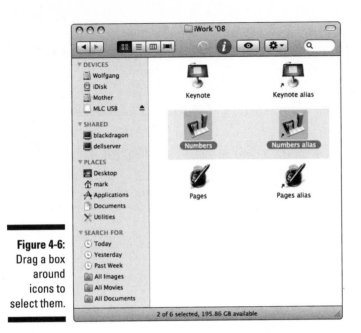

Figure 4-6:
Drag a box
around
icons to
select them.

Copying items

Want to copy items from one Finder window to another, or from one location (like a CD-ROM) to another (like your Desktop)? Très easy. Just use one of these methods:

✔ **On the same drive**

- *To copy one item to another location:* Hold down the Option key (you don't have to select the icon first) and then click and drag the item from its current home to the new location.

  To put a copy of an item within a folder, just drop the item on top of the receiving folder. If you hold the item that you're dragging over the destination folder for a second or two, Leopard opens up a new window so you can see the contents of the target. (This is called a *spring-loaded* folder. Really.)

- *To copy multiple items to another location:* Select them all first (see the earlier section, "Selecting a whole bunch of things"), hold down the Option key and then drag and drop one of the selected items where you want it. All the items that you selected follow the item you drag. (Rather like lemmings. Nice touch, don't you think?)

  To help indicate your target when you're copying files, Leopard highlights the location to show you where the items will end up. (This works whether the target location is a folder or a drive icon.) If the target location is a window, Leopard adds a highlight to the window border.

✔ **On a different drive**

- *To copy one or multiple items:* Click and drag the icon (or the selected items if you have more than one) from the original window to a window you open on the target drive. (No need to hold down the Option key whilst copying to a different drive.) You can also drag one item (or a selected group of items) and simply drop the items on top of the drive icon on your Desktop.

  The items are copied to the top level, or *root,* of the target drive.

If you try to move or copy something to a location that already has an item with the same name, you get a dialog that prompts you to decide whether to replace the file or to stop the copy/move procedure and leave the existing file alone. Good insurance, indeed.

Moving things from place to place

Moving things from one location to another location on the same drive is the easiest action you can take. Just drag the item (or selected items) to the new location. The item disappears from the original spot and reappears in the new spot.

Duplicating in a jiffy

If you need more than one copy of the same item within a folder, use the Leopard Duplicate command. I use Duplicate often when I want to edit a document but ensure that the original document stays pristine, no matter what. I just create a duplicate and edit that file instead.

To use Duplicate, you can

- ✔ **Click an item to select it and then choose File⇨Duplicate.**
- ✔ **Right-click the item and choose Duplicate from the menu.**
- ✔ **Hold down the Option key and drag the original item to another spot in the same window.** When you release the trackpad button, the duplicate file appears like magic!

The duplicate item has the word `copy` appended to its name. A second copy is named `copy2`, a third is `copy3`, and so on.

Duplicating a folder also duplicates all the contents of that folder, so creating a duplicate folder can take some time to create if the original folder was stuffed full. The duplicate folder has `copy` appended to its name, but the contents of the duplicate folder keep their original names.

Keys and Keyboard Shortcuts to Fame and Fortune

Your MacBook's keyboard might not be as glamorous as your trackpad, but any Macintosh power user will tell you that using keyboard shortcuts is usually the fastest method of performing certain tasks in the Finder, such as saving or closing a file. I recommend committing these shortcuts to memory and putting them to work as soon as you begin using your laptop so that they become second nature to you as quickly as possible.

Special keys on the keyboard

The Apple standard keyboard has a number of special keys that you might not recognize — especially if you've made the smart move and decided to migrate from the chaos that is Windows to Mac OS X! Table 4-1 lists the keys that bear strange hieroglyphics on the Apple keyboard as well as what they do.

Table 4-1		Too-Cool Key Symbols
Action	*Symbol*	*Purpose*
Media Eject	⏏	Ejects a CD or DVD from your optical drive
Audio Mute	◀	Mutes (and restores) all sound produced by your MacBook
Keyboard Illumination	☀	Increases, decreases, or turns off the brightness of your keyboard backlighting (MacBook Air and MacBook Pro only)
Volume Up	◀))	Increases the sound volume
Volume Down	◀)	Decreases the sound volume
Control	⌃	Displays right-click/Control-click menu
Command	⌘	Primary modifier for menus and keyboard shortcuts
Del	⌦	Deletes selected text
Option	⌥	Modifier for shortcuts

Using Finder and application keyboard shortcuts

The Finder is chock-full of keyboard shortcuts that you can use to take care of common tasks. Some of the handiest shortcuts are in Table 4-2.

But wait, there's more! Most of your applications also provide their own set of keyboard shortcuts. While you're working with a new application, display the application's Help file and print out a copy of the keyboard shortcuts as a handy cheat sheet.

Table 4-2	Leopard Keyboard Shortcuts of Distinction	
Key Combination	*Location*	*Action*
⌘+A	Edit menu	Selects all (works in the Finder, too)
⌘+C	Edit menu	Copies the highlighted item to the Clipboard
⌘+H	Application menu	Hides the application
⌘+M	Window menu	Minimizes the active window to the Dock (also works in the Finder)
⌘+O	File menu	Opens an existing document, file, or folder (also works in the Finder)
⌘+P	File menu	Prints the current document
⌘+Q	Application menu	Exits the application
⌘+V	Edit menu	Pastes the contents of the Clipboard at the current cursor position
⌘+X	Edit menu	Cuts the highlighted item to the Clipboard
⌘+Z	Edit menu	Reverses the effect of the last action you took
⌘+?	Help menu	Displays the Help system (works in the Finder, too)
⌘+Tab	Finder	Switches between open applications
⌘+Option+M	Finder	Minimizes all Finder windows to the Dock
⌘+Option+W	Finder	Closes all Finder windows

If you've used a PC before, you're certainly familiar with three-key shortcuts — the most infamous being Ctrl+Alt+Delete, the beloved shut-down shortcut, nicknamed the Windows Three-Finger Salute. Three-key shortcuts work the same way in Leopard (but you'll be thrilled to know you won't need to reboot by using that notorious Windows shortcut)! If you're new to computing, just hold down the first two keys simultaneously and then press the third key.

You're not limited to just the keyboard shortcuts listed above, either. Within System Preferences, visit the Keyboard & Mouse pane and then click the Keyboard Shortcuts button to change an existing shortcut or add another!

Performing Tricks with Finder Windows

In this section of your introduction to Mac OS X, I describe basic windows management within Leopard: how to move things around, how to close windows, and how to make 'em disappear and reappear like magic.

Scrolling in and resizing windows

Can you imagine what life would be like if you couldn't see more than a single window's worth of stuff? Shopping would be curtailed quite a bit — and so would the contents of the folders on your hard drives!

That's why Leopard adds *scroll bars* that you can click and drag to move through the contents of the window. You can

- Click the scroll bar and drag it.
- Click anywhere in the empty area above or below the bar to scroll pages one at a time.
- Hold down the Option key and click anywhere in the empty area above or below the bar to scroll to that spot in the window.

Of course, you can also drag two fingertips across the trackpad to scroll the contents of a window (both vertically and horizontally). To control trackpad behavior, open System Preferences, click the Keyboard & Mouse pane, and then click the Trackpad button. You can read all about this in the earlier section, "Wait a Second: Where the Heck Is the Right Mouse Button?"

Figure 4-7 illustrates both vertical and horizontal scroll bars in a typical Finder window.

Often, pressing your Page Up and Page Down keys moves you through a document one page at a time. Also, pressing your arrow keys moves your insertion cursor one line or one character in the four compass directions.

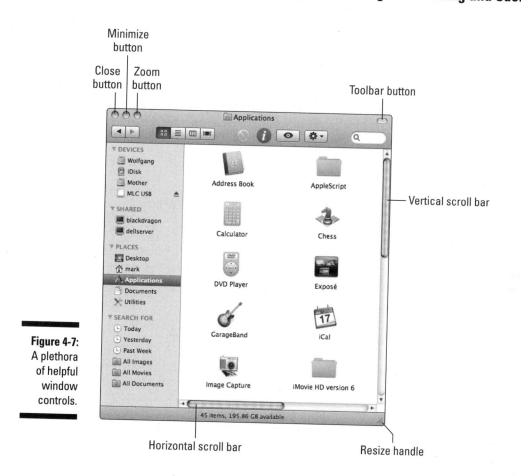

Figure 4-7: A plethora of helpful window controls.

You can also resize most Finder and application windows by enlarging or reducing the window frame itself. Move your mouse pointer over the Resize handle in the lower-right corner of the window (which smartly bears a number of slashed lines to help it stand out) and then drag the handle in any direction until the window is the precise size you need.

Minimizing and restoring windows

Resizing a window is indeed helpful, but maybe you simply want to banish the doggone thing until you need it again. That's a situation for the Minimize button, which also appears in Figure 4-7. A *minimized* window disappears from the Desktop but isn't closed: It simply reappears in the Dock as a miniature icon. Minimizing a window is easy: Move your mouse pointer over the Minimize button at the top-left corner of the window — a minus sign appears in the button to tell you that you're on target — and then click. Here's a good shortcut: double-clicking the window's *title bar* (that's the top frame of the window, which usually includes a document or application name) minimizes the window.

Hold down the Shift key whilst you minimize, and prepare to be amazed when the window shrinks in slow motion like Alice in Wonderland!

To restore the window to its full size again (and its original position on the Desktop), just click its window icon on the Dock.

Moving and zooming windows

Perhaps you want to move a window to another location on the Desktop so you can see the contents of multiple windows at the same time. Click the window's title bar and drag the window anywhere you like. Then release the button. (Don't click the icon in the center of the title bar, though. You won't move the window, just the icon itself.)

Many applications can automatically arrange multiple windows for you. Choose Window⇨Arrange All menu item (if it appears).

To see all that a window can show you, use the Zoom feature to expand any Finder or application window to its maximum practical size. (This is different from zooming with the Multi-Touch feature because you're expanding only the window — and not an image or a document.) Note that a zoomed window can fill the entire screen, or (if that extra space isn't applicable for the application) the window might expand only to a larger part of the Desktop. To zoom a window, move your mouse pointer over the button (as shown in Figure 4-7) at the top-left corner of the window. When the plus sign appears in the Zoom button, click to claim the additional territory on your Desktop. (You can click the Zoom button again to automatically return the same window to its original dimensions.)

Only one can be active at once™

Yes, here's a very special Mark's Maxim in the Mac OS X universe.

> **Only one application window can be active in Leopard at any time.™**

You can always tell which window is active:

✔ **The active window is on top of other windows.**

Tip: You can still use a window's Close, Minimize, and Zoom buttons when it's inactive.

✔ Any input you make by typing or by moving your finger on the trackpad appears in the active window.

✔ Mac OS X *dims* inactive windows that you haven't minimized.

Toggling toolbars the Leopard way

Time to define a window control that's actually *inside* the window for a change. A *toolbar* is a strip of icons that appears under the window's title bar. These icons typically perform the most common actions within an application; the effect is the same as if you use a menu or press a keyboard shortcut. Toolbars are very popular these days. You see 'em within everything from the Finder window to most application windows.

You can banish a window's toolbar to make extra room for icons, documents, or whatever it happens to be holding. Just click the little lozenge-shaped button at the right corner of the window. (You guessed it — the Toolbar button is also shown in Figure 4-7.) *Note:* If you toggle the Finder toolbar off, you also lose the Finder window Sidebar.

Closing windows

When you're finished with an application or no longer need a window open, move your mouse pointer over the Close button at the top-left corner of the window. When the X appears in the button, click it. (And yes, I can get one more reference out of Figure 4-7, which I'm thinking of nominating as Figure of the Year.)

TIP

If you have more than one window open in the same application and you want to close 'em all in one swoop, hold down the Option key whilst you click the Close button on any of the windows.

REMEMBER

If you haven't saved a document and you try to close that application's window, Leopard gets downright surly and prompts you for confirmation. "Hey, human, you don't really want to do this, do you?" If you answer in the affirmative — "Why, yes, machine. Yes, indeed, I do want to throw this away and not save it." — the application discards the document that you were working on. If you decide to keep your document (thereby saving your posterior from harm), you can either save the document under the same filename or under a new name.

Chapter 5

Getting to the Heart of the Leopard

. . . .

In This Chapter

▶ Making the most of your Home folder

▶ Arranging your Desktop for greater efficiency

▶ Adding timesavers to the Dock

▶ Using the Trash (and rescuing precious stuff from it)

▶ Using Exposé, Spaces, and Dashboard to perform Desktop magic

▶ Printing documents

. . . .

*W*hen you're no longer a novice to Leopard and the basics of the Finder, turn your attention to a number of more advanced topics 'n tricks to turn you into a MacBook power user — which, after all, is the goal of every civilized consciousness on Planet Earth.

Consider this chapter a grab bag of Leopard knowledge. Sure, I jump around a little, but these topics are indeed connected by a common thread: They're all surefire problem-solvers and speeder-uppers. (I can't believe the latter is really a word, but evidently it is. My editors told me so.)

Home, Sweet Home Folder

Each user account that you create within Leopard is actually a self-contained universe. For example, each user has a number of unique characteristics and folders devoted just to that person, and Leopard keeps track of everything that user changes or creates. (In Chapter 16, I describe the innate loveliness of multiple users living in peace and harmony on your laptop.)

This unique universe includes a different system of folders for each user account on your system. The top-level folder uses the short name that Leopard assigns when that user account is created; don't necessarily look for a folder named "Home." Naturally, the actual folder name is different for each person, and Mac techno-types typically refer to this folder as your *Home folder.* (On the sidebar, look for the teeny house icon under the Places heading, marked with your account name.)

Each account's Home folder contains a set of subfolders, including

- ✔ Movies
- ✔ Music
- ✔ Pictures
- ✔ Downloads (for files you download by using Safari)
- ✔ Sites (for Web pages created by the user)
- ✔ Documents (created by the user)

Although you can store your stuff at the *root* (top level) of your hard drive, that gaggle of files, folders, and aliases can get very crowded and confusing very quickly. Here's a Mark's Maxim to live by:

Your Home folder is where you hang out and where you store your stuff. Use it to make your computing life *much* easier!™

Create subfolders within your Documents folder to organize your files and folders even further. For example, I always create a subfolder in my Documents folder for every book that I write so that I can quickly and easily locate all the documents and files associated with that book project.

I discuss security within your Home folder and what gets stored where in Chapter 16. For now, Figure 5-1 shows how convenient your Home folder is to reach because it appears in the Finder window Sidebar. One click of your Home folder, and all your stuff is in easy reach.

In addition to the Finder window Sidebar, you can also reach your Home folder in other convenient ways:

- ✔ **From the Go menu:** Choose Go⇨Home to display your Home folder immediately from the Finder window. Alternatively, you can press ⌘+Shift+H to accomplish the same thing.

- ✔ **From within Open and Save dialogs:** Leopard's standard File Open and File Save dialogs also include the same Home folder (and subfolder) icons as the Finder window Sidebar.

- ✔ **Within any new Finder window you open:** If you like, you can set every Finder window that you open to automatically display your Home folder.

    a. Choose Finder⇨Preferences to display the dialog that you see in Figure 5-2.

Sidebar

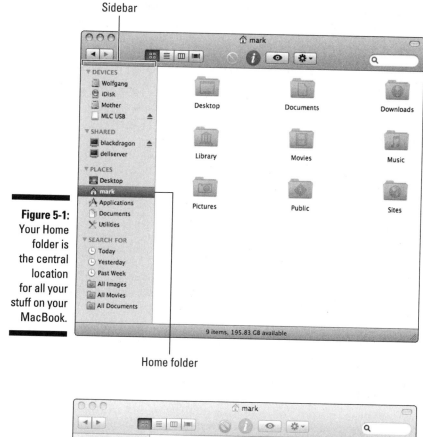

Figure 5-1:
Your Home
folder is
the central
location
for all your
stuff on your
MacBook.

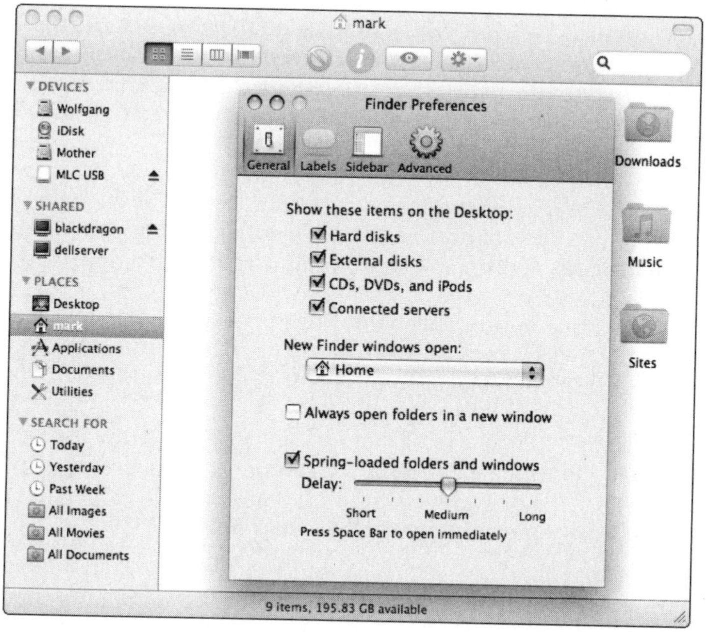

Home folder

Figure 5-2:
Set Leopard
to open
your Home
folder within
new Finder
windows.

    *b. Click the arrow button at the right side of the New Finder Windows
Open pop-up menu.*

    A menu pops up (hence, the name).

    c. Click the Home entry in the menu.

    d. Click the Close button at the top-left corner of the dialog.

    You're set to go. From now on, every Finder window you open displays your Home folder as the starting location!

Here's another reason to use your Home folder to store your stuff: Leopard expects your stuff to be there when you migrate your files from an older Mac to a new Mac.

Personalizing Your Desktop

Most folks put all their documents, pictures, and videos on their Leopard Desktop because the file icons are easy to locate! Your computing stuff is right in front of you . . . or *is* it?

Call me a finicky, stubborn fussbudget — go ahead, I don't mind — but I prefer a clean Leopard Desktop without all the iconic clutter. In fact, my Desktop usually has just three or four icons even though I use my MacBook Pro several hours every day. It's an organizational thing; I work with literally hundreds of applications, documents, and assorted knickknacks daily. Sooner or later, you'll find that you're using that many, too. When you keep your stuff crammed on your Desktop, you end up having to scan your screen for one particular file, an alias, or a particular type of icon, which ends up taking you more time to locate it on your Desktop than in your Documents folder!

Plus, you'll likely find yourself looking at old icons that no longer mean anything to you or stuff that's covered in cobwebs that you haven't used in years. Stale icons . . . *yuck.*

I recommend that you arrange your Desktop so you see only a couple of icons for the files or documents that you use the most. Leave the rest of the Desktop for that cool image of your favorite actor or actress.

Besides keeping things clean, I can recommend a number of other favorite tweaks that you can make to your Desktop:

   ✔ **Keep Desktop icons arranged as you like.**

    a. From the Finder menu, choose View⊅Show View Options.

    b. Select the Arrange By check box.

    c. From the pop-up menu, choose the criteria that Leopard uses to auto-matically arrange your Desktop icons, including the item name, the last modification date, or the size of the items.

    I personally like things organized by name.

✓ **Choose a favorite background.**

    a. Hold down the Control key while you click any open spot on your Desktop. (Or, if you use a pointing thing with a right mouse button, click that instead.)

    b. From the right-click menu that appears, choose Change Desktop Background.

    You see the Desktop & Screen Saver pane appear, as shown in Figure 5-3. Browse through the various folders of background images that Apple provides or use an image from your iPhoto library.

✓ **Display all the peripherals and network connections on your system.**

    a. Choose Finder⇨Preferences.

    b. Make sure that all four of the top checkboxes (Hard Disks; External Disks; CDs, DVDs, and iPods; and Connected Servers) are enabled.

    If you're connected to an external network or you've loaded an external hard drive or device, that shows up on your Desktop. You can double-click that Desktop icon to view your external stuff.

Figure 5-3:
Choose a
Desktop
background
of more
interest.

Customizing the Dock Just So

If the Dock seems like a nifty contraption to you, you're right again — it's like one of those big control rooms that NASA uses. From the *Dock* — that icon toolbar at the bottom of Leopard's Desktop — you can launch an application, monitor what's running, and even use the pop-up menu commands to control the applications that you launch. (Hey, that NASA analogy is even better than I thought!)

By default, the Dock hangs out at the bottom of your screen, but you can move it to another edge, change the size of the icons, or even hide it until it's necessary. (You can find more details on customizing your Dock in Chapter 6.)

When you launch an application — either by clicking an icon on the Dock or by double-clicking an icon in a Finder window or the Desktop — the icon begins to bounce hilariously on the Dock to indicate that the application is loading. (So much for my Mission Control analogy.) After an application is running, the application icon appears on the Dock with a shiny blue dot underneath. Thusly, you can easily see what's running at any time just by glancing at the Dock.

You can hide most applications by pressing ⌘+H.

Adding Dock icons

Ah, but there's more: The Dock can offer more than just a set of default icons! You can add your own MIS (or *Most Important Stuff*) to the Dock, making it the most convenient method of taking care of business without cluttering up your Desktop. You can add

✔ **Applications:** Add any application to your Dock by dragging the application icon into the area to the left of the *separator line* (the vertical dotted line on the Dock which appears between applications and folders or documents). The existing Dock icons move aside so that you can place the new neighbor in a choice location.

Do not try to add an application anywhere to the right of the separator line. You can't put applications there — and Leopard might even think that you want the application dumped in the Trash!

✔ **Folders:** Here's where you want to add things to the area to the right of the separator line. A folder or volume icon that you drag to the Dock is called a *Stack* in Leopard, and you can display the contents with a single click. (The contents of the folder "fan out" into a half-circle or grid arrangement, depending on the number of items in the folder.) To open or launch an item, just click it in the Stack display. Folders that include many items are displayed in a grid view.

Leopard already includes two Stacks in the Dock by default: your Documents folder and your Downloads folder.

✔ **Web URLs:** Sure, you can add your favorite Web site from Safari! Drag it right from the Safari Address bar into the area to the right of the separator line. When you click the URL icon, Safari opens the page automatically.

Removing Dock icons

You can remove an icon from the Dock at any time (as long as the application isn't running). In fact, I always recommend that every Leopard user remove the default icons that never get used to make more room available for your favorite icons. The only two icons you can't remove are the Finder and the Trash icons. To remove an icon from the Dock, just click and drag it off the Dock. You're rewarded with a ridiculous puff of smoke straight out of a Warner Brothers cartoon! (One of the Mac OS X developers was in a fun mood, I guess.)

When you delete an icon from the Dock, all you delete is the Dock icon: The original application, folder, or volume is not deleted.

Using Dock icon menus

From the Dock menu, you can open documents, open the location in a Finder window, set an application as a Login Item, control the features in some applications, and other assorted fun, depending on the item.

To display the right-click Dock menu for an icon

1. **Move your mouse over the icon.**

2. **Right-click.**

   Note that you can also press the Control key and click the icon, or even hold down the left mouse button for a second or two.

I cover the Dock settings that you can change within System Preferences in Chapter 6. You can also change the same settings from the Apple menu if you hover your mouse over the Dock menu item, which displays a submenu with the settings.

What's with the Trash?

Another sign of a Mac laptop power user is a well-maintained Trash can. It's a breeze to empty the discarded items you no longer need, and you can even rescue something that you suddenly discover you still need!

Previewing images and documents the Leopard way

Leopard's new Quick Look feature (available on the Finder window toolbar) has garnered a lot of attention within the technology press, and rightly so. Just select a file and click the Quick Look button (or just press the spacebar), and Leopard instantly displays the contents of the document or image, *without opening the application.* Heck, I've been waiting for such a magic lamp for two decades now!

However, don't forget that Mac OS X has always offered a Swiss Army knife application for viewing image files and documents: namely, Preview. You can use Preview to display digital photos in several popular image formats, including TIFF, GIF, PICT, PNG, JPEG, and Windows Bitmap.

I know, if that were the sum total of Preview's features, it wouldn't deserve coverage here. So, what else can it do? Here's a partial list (just my favorites, mind you):

✔ **Use Preview to add a bookmark at the current page within a PDF document by choosing Bookmarks⇨Add Bookmark.**

✔ **Fill out a form in a PDF document by choosing Tools⇨Text Tool.**

Click an area that's marked as an input field, and you can type text into that field. After you complete the form, you can fax or print it.

✔ **Take a *screen snapshot* (saving the contents of your screen as a digital photo) by choosing File⇨Grab⇨Timed Screen.**

Preview launches the Grab utility, which displays an onscreen timer and then snaps the image for you after ten seconds. (This gives you time to get things just right before saying, "Cheese!")

✔ **Convert an image into another format or into a PDF file by choosing File⇨Save As.**

If a PDF document can be edited, you can delete or insert pages at will.

✔ **Resize or rotate an image by using the commands on the Tools menu.**

Leopard automatically loads Preview when you double-click an image in a format that it recognizes or when you double-click a PDF file. It also acts as the Print Preview window, as you can read elsewhere in this chapter. However, if you want to launch Preview manually, open a Finder window, click the Applications folder in the Sidebar, and then double-click the Preview icon.

The Leopard Trash icon resides on the Dock, and it works just like the Trash has always worked in Mac OS X: Simply drag selected items to the Trash to delete them.

Note one very important exception: If you drag a Desktop icon for an external device or removable media drive to the Trash (such as an iPod, iPhone, DVD, or an external hard drive), the Trash icon automagically turns into a giant Eject icon, and the removable device or media is ejected or shut down — not erased. Repeat, *not erased.* (That's why the Trash icon changes to the Eject icon — to remind you that you're not doing anything destructive.)

Here are other methods of chunking items you select to go to the wastebasket:

✔ Choose File➪Move to Trash.

✔ Click the Action button on the Finder toolbar and choose Move to Trash from the list that appears.

✔ Press ⌘+Delete.

✔ Right-click the item and choose Move to Trash from the menu that appears.

You can always tell when the Trash contains at least one item because the basket icon is full of crumpled paper! However, you don't have to unfold a wad of paper to see what the Trash holds: Just click the Trash icon on the Dock to display the contents of the Trash. To rescue something from the Trash, drag the item(s) from the Trash folder to the Desktop or any other folder in a Finder window. (If you're doing this for someone else who's not familiar with Leopard, remember to act like it was a lot of work, and you'll earn big-time DRP, or *Data Rescue Points.*)

When you're sure that you want to permanently delete the contents of the Trash, use one of these methods to empty the Trash:

✔ **Choose Finder➪Empty Trash.**

✔ **Choose Finder➪Secure Empty Trash.**

   If security is an issue around your laptop and you want to make sure that no one can recover the files you've sent to the Trash, using the Secure Empty Trash command takes a little time but helps to ensure that no third-party hard drive repair or recovery program could resuscitate the items you discard.

✔ **Press ⌘+Shift+Delete.**

✔ **Right-click the Trash icon on the Dock and then choose Empty Trash from the menu that appears.**

Working Magic with Dashboard, Exposé, and Spaces

MacBook power users tend to wax enthusiastic over the convenience features built into Leopard. In fact, we show 'em off to our PC-saddled friends and family. Three of the features that I've demonstrated the most to others are Leopard's Dashboard display, the amazing convenience of Exposé, and the brand-new Spaces Desktop manager. In this section, I show 'em off to you as well. (Then you can become the Leopard evangelist on *your* block.)

Using Dashboard

The idea behind Dashboard is deceptively simple yet about as revolutionary as it gets for a mainstream personal computer operating system. *Dashboard* is an alternate Desktop that you can display at any time by using the keyboard or your mouse; the Dashboard desktop holds *widgets* (small applications that each provide a single function). Examples of default widgets that come with Leopard include a calculator, a world clock, weather display, and a dictionary/thesaurus.

Oh, did I mention that you're not limited to the widgets that come with Leopard? Simply click the plus button at the bottom of the Dashboard display and drag new widgets to your Dashboard from the menu at the bottom of the screen. To remove a widget while you're in this mode, click the X icon that appears next to each widget. When you're done with your widgets — that sounds a bit strange, but I mean no offense — press the Dashboard key again to return to your Desktop.

Widgets can also be rearranged any way you like by dragging them to a new location.

Simple applications like these are no big whoop — after all, Mac OS X has always had a calculator and a clock. What's revolutionary is how you access your widgets. You can display and use them anywhere in Leopard, at any time, by simply pressing the Dashboard key. The default key is F12 although you can change the Dashboard key via the Exposé & Spaces pane within System Preferences (or even turn it into a key sequence, such as Option+F12). You can also click the Dashboard icon on the Dock to summon your Dashboard widgets and then banish the Dashboard when you're done.

Click the scroll ball on your Mighty Mouse to display your Dashboard.

A WebClip widget is a portion of a Web page that can include text, graphics, and links, which Dashboard updates every time you display your widgets. Think about that for a second: Dynamic displays, such as weather maps, cartoons, and even the Free Music Download image from the iTunes Store are all good sources of WebClip widgets! (That last one is a real timesaver.)

Leopard even allows you to create your own Dashboard widgets! That's right, this new feature is sure to be a winner amongst the In Crowd. Follow these steps to create a new WebClip Dashboard widget from your favorite Web site:

1. **Run Safari and navigate to the site you want to view as a widget.**

2. **Click the Open This Page in Dashboard button on the Safari toolbar, which bears a pair of scissors and a dotted box.**

3. **Select the portion of the page you want to include in your widget.**

   Most Web pages use frames to organize and separate sections of a page, so this step allows you to choose the frame with the desired content.

4. **Drag the handles at the edges of the selection border to resize your widget frame to the right size and then click Add.**

   Bam! Leopard displays your new WebClip widget within Dashboard.

When you click a link in a WebClip widget, Dashboard loads the full Web page in Safari, so you can even use WebClips for surfing chores with sites you visit often.

Switching between apps with Exposé

Most MacBook owners are comfortable using the ⌘+Tab keyboard shortcut to switch between open applications. If you've moved to the Mac from a PC running Windows, you might think this simple shortcut is all there is to it. Ah, dear reader, you're in Leopard territory now!

Exposé is a rather racy-sounding feature, but (like Dashboard) it's really all about convenience. If you typically run a large number of applications at the same time, Exposé can be a real timesaver, allowing you to quickly switch between a forest of different application windows (or display your Desktop instantly without those very same windows in the way). The feature works in three ways:

✔ **Press the All Windows key (or key sequence) to display all your application windows on a single screen, as shown in the truly cool Figure 5-4. (By default, F9 is the All Windows key.)**

   Then just click the window that you want to make active.

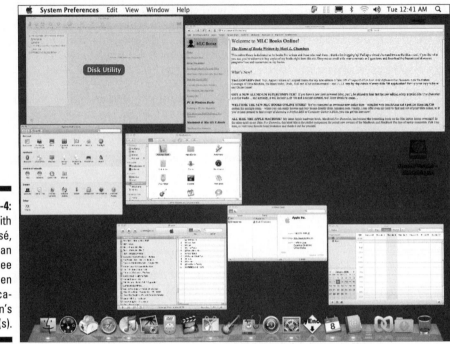

Figure 5-4:
With
Exposé,
you can
instantly see
every open
applica-
tion's
window(s).

✔ **Press the Application Windows key (or key sequence) to display all the windows that have been opened by the active application. (By default, F10 is the Application Windows key.)**

This comes in handy with those mega-applications like Photoshop Elements or FileMaker Pro, in which you often have three or four windows open at one time. Again, you can click the window that you want to make active.

✔ **Press the Desktop key (or key sequence) to move all your application and Finder windows to the sides of your Desktop so you can access your Desktop icons. (The default Desktop key is F11.)**

After you're done with your Desktop and you want to restore your windows to their original locations, press the Desktop key (F11) again to put things back.

Switching between desktops with Spaces

Ah, but what if you want to switch to an entirely different *set* of applications? For example, suppose that you're slaving away at your pixel-pushing job, designing a magazine cover with Pages. Your page design desktop also includes Photoshop and Aperture, which you switch between often by using one of the techniques I just described. Suddenly, however, you realize you need to schedule a meeting with others in your office by using iCal, and you also want to check your e-mail in Apple Mail. What to do?

Well, you could certainly launch those two applications on top of your graphics applications, and then minimize or close them. With Leopard's new *Spaces* feature, though, you can press the Control+← or Control+→ sequences to switch to a completely different "communications applications" desktop, with iCal and Apple Mail windows already open and in your favorite positions! Figure 5-5 illustrates the Spaces screen, showing two available desktops.

After you're done setting up your meeting and answering any important e-mail, simply press Control+← or Control+→ again to switch back to your "graphics" desktop, where all your work is exactly as you left it!

Now imagine that you've also created a custom "music" desktop for GarageBand and iTunes . . . or perhaps you joined iWeb, Safari, and iPhoto as a "Webmaster" desktop. See why everyone's so excited? (Let's see Windows Vista do *that* out of the box.)

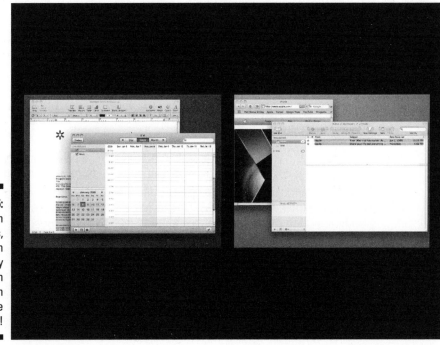

Figure 5-5: With Spaces, you can instantly switch between multiple desktops!

Unlike Exposé, Spaces has to be enabled and configured before you can use it. You can create new desktops, customize your desktops, and even choose a different set of key sequences to activate Spaces from within System Preferences. For the complete story on configuring Spaces, see Chapter 6.

You can activate Exposé, Spaces, and Dashboard by using your mouse rather than the keyboard:

1. **Click the System Preferences icon on the Dock.**

2. **Click the Exposé & Spaces icon to display the settings.**

3. **Click the desired Screen Corner pop-up menu to choose what function that screen corner will trigger.**

4. **Press ⌘+Q to save your changes and then exit System Preferences.**

   When you move your mouse pointer to that corner, the feature you've specified automatically kicks in.

Printing within Mac OS X

Leopard makes document printing a breeze. Because virtually all Mac printers use a Universal Serial Bus (USB) port, setting up printing couldn't be easier. Just turn on your printer and connect the USB cable between the printer and your MacBook; Leopard does the rest.

Printer manufacturers supply you with installation software that might add cool extra software or fonts to your system. Even if Leopard recognizes your USB printer immediately, I recommend that you still launch the manufacturer's Mac OS X installation disc. For example, my new Epson printer came with new fonts and a CD/DVD label application, but I wouldn't have 'em if I hadn't installed the Epson software package.

After your printer is connected and installed, you can use the same procedure to print from within just about every Mac OS X application on the planet! To print with the default page layout settings — standard 8½" x 11" paper, portrait mode, no scaling — follow these steps:

1. **Within the active application, choose File⇨Print or press the ⌘+P shortcut.**

   Mac OS X displays the Print sheet, as shown in Figure 5-6.

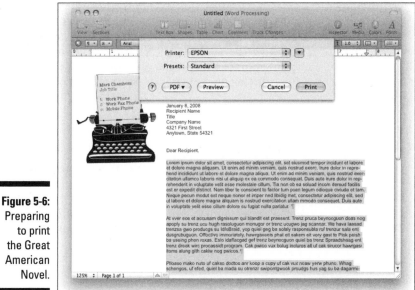

Figure 5-6:
Preparing
to print
the Great
American
Novel.

From this dialog, you can

- *Print from a different printer connected to your laptop or print over a network connection to a shared printer on another computer.*

 Click the Printer pop-up menu. In this pop-up menu, Leopard displays all the printers that you can access.

- *Check what the printed document will look like.*

 Click Preview to open it within the very same Preview application I discuss earlier in this chapter.

If you have to make changes to the document or you need to change the default print settings, click Cancel to return to your document. (You have to repeat Step 1 again to display the Print dialog again.)

If everything looks good at this point and you don't need to change any settings (like multiple copies or to print only a portion of the document), click Print — you're done! If not, click the Expand button next to the Printer pop-up menu. (It bears a downward-pointing arrow.) Now you can proceed with these steps:

1. **(Optional) For more than one copy, click in the Copies field and type the number of copies that you need.**

 Collation (separating copies) is also available, and it doesn't cost a thing!

2. **(Optional)** To print a range of selected pages, select the From radio button and then enter the starting and ending pages.

   To print the entire document, leave the default Pages option set to All.

3. **(Optional) If the application offers its own print settings, such as collating and grayscale printing, make any necessary changes to those settings.**

   To display these application-specific settings, click the pop-up menu in the Print dialog and choose the desired settings pane that you need to adjust. (You can blissfully ignore these settings and skip this step entirely if the defaults are fine.)

4. **When you're set to go, click Print.**

You can also save an electronic version of a document in the popular Adobe Acrobat PDF format from the Print dialog — without spending money on Adobe Acrobat. *(Slick.)*

1. **Click the PDF button to display the destination pop-up menu.**

2. **Click Save as PDF.**

   Leopard prompts you with a Save As dialog, where you can type a name for the PDF document and specify a location on your hard drive where the file should be saved.

Heck, if you like, you can even fax a PDF (with an external USB modem) or send it as an e-mail attachment! Just choose these options from the destination list rather than Save as PDF.

Chapter 6

A Nerd's Guide to System Preferences

In This Chapter

▶ Navigating System Preferences

▶ Searching for specific controls

▶ Customizing Leopard from System Preferences

Remember the old TV series *Voyage to the Bottom of the Sea?* You always knew you were on the bridge of the submarine Seaview because it had an entire wall made up of randomly blinking lights, crewmen darting about with clipboards, and all sorts of strange and exotic-looking controls on every available surface. You could fix just about anything by looking into the camera with grim determination and barking out an order. After all, you were On The Bridge. That's why virtually all the dialog and action inside the sub took place on that one (expensive) set: It was the nerve center of the ship, and a truly happenin' place to be.

In the same vein, I devote this entire chapter to the System Preferences window and all the settings within it. After all, if you want to change how Leopard works or customize the features within our favorite operating system, this one window is the nerve center of Mac OS X, and a truly happenin' place to be. (Sorry, no built-in wall of randomly blinking lights — but there are exotic controls just about everywhere.)

An Explanation (In English, No Less)

The System Preferences window (as shown in Figure 6-1) is a self-contained beast, and you can reach it in a number of ways:

✔ Click the Apple menu (🍎) and choose the System Preferences menu item.

✔ Click the System Preferences icon on the Dock — it's a collection of gears.

✔ Click the Apple menu (), choose Dock, and then choose the Dock Preferences menu item.

✔ Click the Time and Date display in the Finder menu and then choose the Open Date and Time menu item.

✔ Control-click (or right-click) any uninhabited area of your Desktop and then choose Change Desktop Background.

✔ Click most of the Finder menu status icons and then choose the Open Preferences menu item. (This includes the Bluetooth, AirPort, Display, Modem, and Clock icons.)

When the System Preferences window is open, you can click any of the group icons to switch to that group's *pane;* the entire window morphs to display the settings for the selected pane. For example, Figure 6-2 illustrates the Sound pane, which allows you to set a system alert sound, configure your MacBook's built-in microphone, and choose from several different output options.

Many panes also include a number of tabbed buttons at the top — in this case, Sound Effects, Output, and Input. You can click these tabs to switch to another *panel* within the same pane. Many panes within System Preferences have multiple panels. This design allows our friends at Apple to group a large number of related settings together in the same pane (without things getting too confusing).

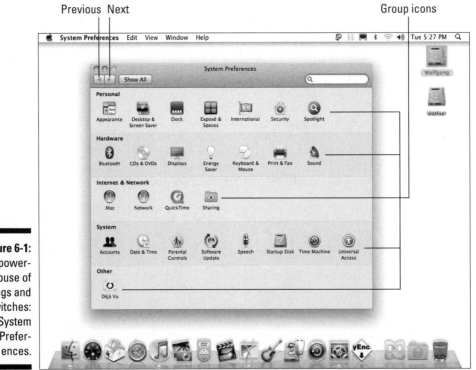

Previous Next   Group icons

Figure 6-1:
The power-house of settings and switches: System Prefer-ences.

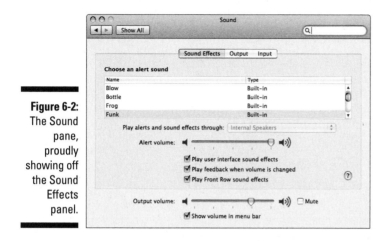

Figure 6-2:
The Sound
pane,
proudly
showing off
the Sound
Effects
panel.

To return to the top-level System Preferences panel from any pane, just click the Show All button (top left) or press ⌘+L. You can also click the familiar Previous and Next buttons to move backward through the panes you've already visited and then move forward again, in sequence. (Yep, these buttons work just like the browser controls in Safari. Sometimes life is funny that way.)

You won't find an OK button that you have to click to apply any System Preference changes — Apple's developers do things the right way. Your changes to the settings in a pane are automatically saved when you click Show All or when you click the Close button on the System Preferences window. You can also press ⌘+Q to exit the window and save all your changes automatically . . . a favorite shortcut of mine.

If you see an Apply button in a pane, you can click it to immediately apply any changes you made, without exiting the pane. This is perfect for some settings that you might want to try first before you accept them, like many of the controls on the Network pane. However, if you're sure about what you changed and how those changes will affect your system, you don't have to click Apply. Just exit the System Preferences window or click Show All as you normally would.

Locating That Certain Special Setting

Hey, wouldn't it be great if you could search through all the different panes in System Preferences — with all those countless radio buttons, check boxes, and slider controls — from one place, even when you're not quite sure exactly what you're looking for?

Figure 6-3 illustrates exactly that kind of activity taking place. Just click in the System Preferences Spotlight Search box (upper right, with the magnifying glass icon) and type in just about anything. For example, if you know part of the name of a particular setting you need to change, type that. Leopard highlights the System Preferences panes that might contain matching settings. And if you're a *Switcher* from the Windows world, you can even type in what you might have called the same setting in Windows XP or Vista!

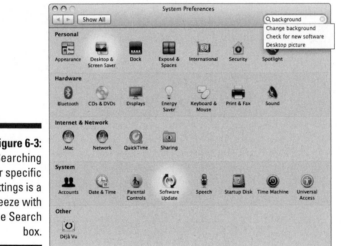

Figure 6-3:
Searching for specific settings is a breeze with the Search box.

The System Preferences window dims, and the group icons that might contain what you're looking for stay highlighted. *Slick.*

You can also search for System Preferences controls by using the Spotlight menu and Spotlight window. Find more on this cool feature in Chapter 7.

If you need to reset the Search box to try again, click the X icon that appears at the right side of the box to clear it.

Popular Preference Panes Explained

Time to get down to brass tacks. Open up the most often-used panes in System Preferences to see what magic you can perform! I won't discuss every pane because I cover many of them in other chapters. (In fact, you might never need to open some System Preferences panes at all, like the .Mac pane.) However, this chapter covers just about all the settings that you're likely to use on a regular basis.

The Displays pane

If you're a heavy-duty game player or you work with applications like Keynote or Final Cut Pro, you probably find yourself switching the characteristics of your monitor on a regular basis. To easily accomplish switching, visit the Displays pane (see Figure 6-4), which includes two panels:

✓ **Display:** Click a screen resolution to choose it from the Resolutions list on the left. Leopard displays the number of colors (or *color depth*) allowed at that resolution, and you can pick a color depth from the Colors pop-up menu. (Typically, it's a good idea to use the highest resolution and the highest number of colors.) If you have an external monitor connected to your laptop, click the Detect Displays button to scan for that monitor. Because MacBooks running Leopard have a flat-panel LCD, the refresh rate is disabled. If you're working with a projector, you can also use the Detect Displays button to configure external displays. Drag the Brightness slider to change the brightness level of your display.

When you enable (mark) the Show Displays in Menu Bar check box, you can switch resolutions and color levels right from the Finder menu!

✓ **Color:** Your MacBook can use a *color profile* file that controls the colors on your display. This setting comes in handy for graphic artists and illustrators who need color output from their printers that closely matches the colors displayed by the laptop. Click the Calibrate button to launch the Display Calibrator, which can create a custom ColorSync profile and calibrate the colors that you see on your monitor.

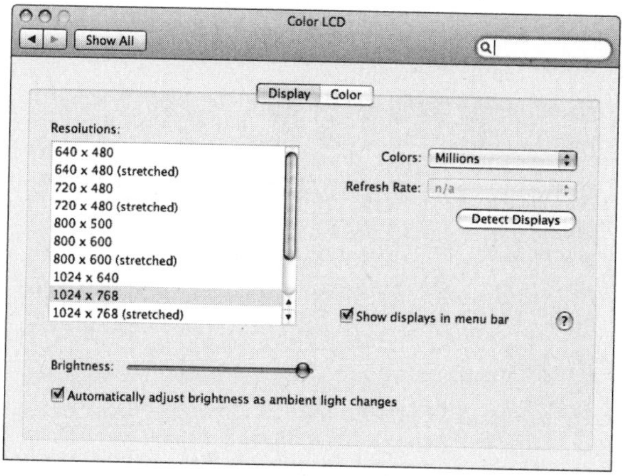

Figure 6-4:
The
Displays
pane also
comes in
a handy
Finder menu
bar size!

Color LCD

| ◀ ▶ | Show All | | | Q |

Display   Color

Resolutions:

640 x 480
640 x 480 (stretched)   Colors: [Millions ▼]
720 x 480
720 x 480 (stretched)   Refresh Rate: [n/a ▼]
800 x 500
800 x 600   (Detect Displays)
800 x 600 (stretched)
1024 x 640
1024 x 768
1024 x 768 (stretched)   ☑ Show displays in menu bar   ⑦

Brightness: ─────────────●──

☑ Automatically adjust brightness as ambient light changes

The Desktop & Screen Saver pane

Hey, no offense to the awesome Aurora background (new with Leopard), but who doesn't want to choose their own background? And what about that nifty screen saver you just downloaded from the Apple Web site? You can change both your background and your screen saver by using these options on the Desktop & Screen Saver pane.

The settings on the Desktop panel (as shown in Figure 6-5) include

- ✔ **Current Desktop picture:** To change your Desktop background, click a thumbnail. You can also drag a picture from a Finder window or the desktop and drop it into the *well* (the fancy Apple word for the square box with the sunken look). Leopard automatically updates your Desktop so you can see the results. To open another collection of images from Apple, click the desired collection folder in the list on the left of the panel. (I recommend the stunning images in the Nature folder.) If you want to open a different folder with your own images, click the Add button (which bears a plus sign) at the lower left of the panel and then navigate to that folder.

- ✔ **Arrangement:** You can automatically fit an image to your screen, *tile* your background image (repeat it across the Desktop), center it, or stretch it to fill the screen. Because the images from Apple are all sized correctly already, the Arrangement control appears only when you're using your own pictures.

The well

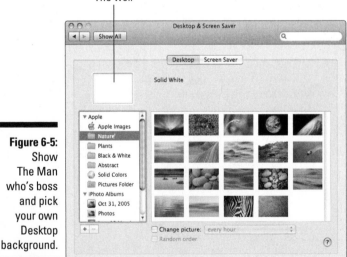

Figure 6-5:
Show
The Man
who's boss
and pick
your own
Desktop
background.

✔ **Change Picture:** If you like a bit of automatic variety on your Desktop, select the Change Picture check box. You can click the accompanying drop-down list box to set the delay period. The images in the current collection or folder are then displayed in the sequence in which they appear in the thumbnail list.

✔ **Random Order:** Select this check box to throw caution utterly to the wind and display random screens from the current collection or folder!

The settings on the Screen Saver tab include

✔ **Screen Savers:** Click the screen saver that you want to display from the Screen Savers list. Leopard displays an animated preview of the selected saver on the right. You can also click the Test button to try out the screen saver in full-screen mode. (Move your mouse a bit to end the test.)

If the selected screen saver has any settings you can change, the Options button displays them.

✔ **Start Screen Saver:** Drag this slider to choose the period of inactivity that triggers the screen saver. Choose Never to disable the screen saver entirely.

For additional security, check out the Security pane in System Preferences, where you'll find the Require password to wake this computer from sleep or screen saver check box. Enable the check box, and Leopard will require your user account password before allowing anyone to turn off the screen saver (a great idea when traveling, as you can imagine).

✔ **Use Random Screen Saver:** Another chance to rebel against conformity! Enable this check box, and Leopard picks a different screen saver each time.

✔ **Show With Clock:** Enable this check box, and Leopard adds a smart clock display to your screen saver. (A great help for those of us who spend many minutes on the phone.)

✔ **Hot Corners:** Click this button to display a drop-down sheet, and then click any of the four pop-up menus at the four corners of the screen to select that corner as an *activating hot corner.* (Moving your mouse pointer there immediately activates the screen saver.) You can also specify a corner as a *disabling hot corner* — as long as the mouse pointer stays in that corner, the screen saver is disabled. Note that you can also set the Dashboard, Spaces, and Exposé activation corners from here. (Read on for the entire lowdown.)

The Exposé & Spaces pane

The pane you see in Figure 6-6 illustrates the settings that control Leopard's Spaces, Dashboard, and Exposé features, which I discuss in more detail in Chapter 5. The settings on the Exposé tab include

✔ **Active Screen Corners:** The screen corners pop-up menus that I describe in the preceding section operate just like those in the Screen Savers panel. Click a corner's list box to set it as

- An Exposé *All Windows* corner (displays all windows on your Desktop).

- An Exposé *Application Windows* corner (displays only the windows from the active application).

- An Exposé *Desktop* corner (moves all windows to the outside of the screen to uncover your Desktop).

- A *Spaces* corner (activates the Spaces Desktop selection feature).

- A *Sleep Display* corner (immediately turns off your display, putting your screen in Sleep mode).

- A *Dashboard* corner (displays your Dashboard widgets). *Widgets* are small applications that each perform a single task; they appear when you invoke the awesome power of Dashboard.

These pop-up menus can also set the Screen Saver activate and disable hot corners.

✔ **Keyboard and mouse shortcuts:** Pretty straightforward stuff here. Click each pop-up menu to set the key sequences (and mouse button settings) for all three Exposé functions as well as Dashboard.

If you hold down a modifier key (Shift, Control, Option, or ⌘) while a shortcut pop-up menu is open, Leopard adds that modifier key to the selections you can choose! (Perfect for those folks who already have the F11 key in use by another application. Make your Desktop shortcut key the Shift+F11 key sequence instead.)

One of Leopard's hottest new features is *Spaces,* which is the system you use to configure and control multiple "prefabricated" desktops that you can switch between at will! The settings on the Spaces tab include

✔ **Enable Spaces:** Enable this check box to use Spaces. (Go figure.)

✔ **Show Spaces in Menu Bar:** When this check box is enabled, Leopard displays the Spaces desktop number you're currently using in the Finder menu bar. You can click the number in the menu bar to switch to another Spaces desktop or to open the Spaces Preferences pane.

✔ **Rows buttons:** To add a row of Spaces desktops to the Spaces grid, click the Add button with the plus sign. (By default, Spaces starts with two desktops enabled, so new rows and columns are numbered beginning with three.) To delete a row, click the Delete button (which bears a minus sign).

✔ **Columns buttons:** To add a column of Spaces desktops to the Spaces grid, click the Add (plus) button. Click the Delete (minus) button to remove a column from the grid.

If you choose to remove a column or row, Leopard alerts you that the *bindings* (the specific applications linked to the deleted columns or rows) will be reassigned.

✔ **Add/Remove Application:** Click the Add Application button (the button with the plus sign under the Application Assignments list) to add an application to one of your Spaces desktops. You can select which desktop should include an application by clicking the up/down arrows next to the Space column for that application's entry — just click the desired desktop from the pop-up menu that appears. To remove an application, click it in the Application Bindings list to select it and then click the Remove Application button (which sports a minus sign).

Spaces can even add an application to all your desktops; just choose Every Space from the pop-up menu.

✔ **Keyboard and mouse shortcuts:** Click each pop-up menu to set the key sequences (and mouse button settings) for all three Spaces functions.

Like with Dashboard and Exposé keyboard and mouse shortcuts, you can press Shift, Control, Option, and ⌘ keys (or even a combination of them) while the box is open to display modified choices.

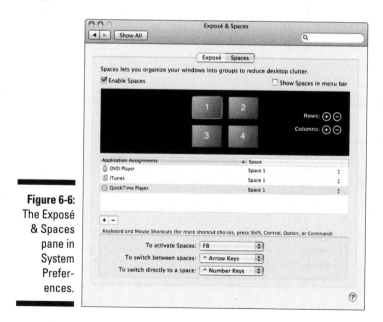

Figure 6-6:
The Exposé
& Spaces
pane in
System
Prefer-
ences.

The Appearance pane

The talented Appearance pane (as shown in Figure 6-7) determines the look and operation of the controls that appear in application windows and Finder windows. It looks complex, but I cover each option here.

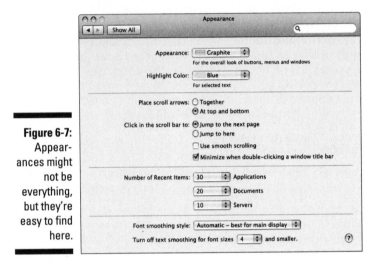

Figure 6-7: Appearances might not be everything, but they're easy to find here.

The settings include

- ✔ **Appearance:** Click this pop-up menu to specify the color Leopard uses for buttons, menus, and windows.

- ✔ **Highlight Color:** Click this pop-up menu to choose the color that highlights selected text in fields, pop-up menus, and drop-down list boxes.

- ✔ **Place Scroll Arrows:** Select a radio button here to determine whether the arrows that control the scroll bar in a window appear together at the bottom of the scroll bar, or separately at the top and bottom of the scroll bar.

- ✔ **Click in the Scroll Bar To:** By default, Leopard scrolls to the next or previous page when you click in an empty portion of the scroll bar. Select the Jump to Here radio button to scroll the document to the approximate position in relation to where you clicked. (Smooth scrolling slows down scrolling, which some people prefer.)

You can minimize a Finder or application window by simply double-clicking the window's title bar. To enable this feature, mark the Minimize When Double Clicking a Window Title Bar check box.

✔ **Number of Recent Items:** By default, Leopard displays ten recent applications, documents, and servers within Recent Items in the Apple menu.
Need more? Just click the corresponding pop-up menu and specify up to
50 items.

✔ **Font Smoothing Style:** This feature performs a little visual magic that
makes the text on your monitor or flat-panel look more like the text on
a printed page. Most MacBook owners should choose Automatic or
Medium (for a typical flat-panel LCD display).

✔ **Turn Off Text Smoothing for Font Sizes:** Below a certain point size, text
smoothing doesn't help fonts look any smoother onscreen. By default,
any font displayed at 8 point or smaller isn't smoothed, which is a good
choice for a MacBook with a flat-panel LCD screen.

The Energy Saver pane

I'm an environmentalist — it's surprising how many techno-types are colored green — so these two panels here are pretty doggone important. When
you use them correctly, you not only conserve battery power but also even
invoke the Power of Leopard to automatically start and shut down your
laptop whenever you like!

Laptop owners get special treatment within Leopard — notice the Settings
For and Optimization pop-up menus at the top of the pane, which don't
appear if you're using a mere desktop Mac. These menus allow you to quickly
switch between different settings for operation with a battery or AC adapter,
making it easy to fine-tune your power use wherever you may find yourself!
You can choose from two energy use settings (Battery or Power Adapter)
and three optimization modes (Better Battery Life, Normal, or Better
Performance). If you tweak the settings on this pane yourself, Leopard automatically assigns you a Custom optimization mode (perfect for those presentations where you need a longer screen saver delay).

Naturally, if you plug your MacBook into a convenient AC outlet, the Settings
menu automatically switches to Power Adapter. When you're running on battery power, System Preferences switches to Battery settings. (You can manually change at any time, however, if you need your laptop's best performance
on the road, or if you want to go green and conserve electricity while using
your power adapter.)

The panels (as shown in Figure 6-8) include

✔ **Sleep:** To save that precious battery power, drag the Put the Computer
to Sleep When It Is Inactive For slider to a delay period that triggers
sleep mode when you're away from the keyboard for a significant period

of time. (I prefer 30 minutes.) If your laptop must always remain alert and you want to disable sleep mode entirely, choose Never. You can set the delay period for blanking your monitor separately from the sleep setting with the Put the Display to Sleep When the Computer Is Inactive For slider. To conserve the maximum juice and cut down on wear, enable the Put the Hard Disk(s) to Sleep When Possible check box to power-down your hard drives when they're not needed. (This might cause a delay of a second or two while loading or saving files because the drives must spin back up.)

You can set Leopard to start or shut down your laptop at a scheduled time. Click the Schedule button and then select the desired schedule (the Start Up or Wake check box and the Shut Down/Sleep pop-up menu) to enable them. Set the trigger time by clicking the up and down arrows next to the time display for each schedule. Click OK to return to the Energy Saver pane.

✔ **Options:** By default, your laptop's display will dim to indicate that sleep mode is approaching, but you can disable the Automatically Reduce the Brightness of the Display check box to maintain full brightness until sleep mode actually kicks in. To reduce display power consumption, you can enable the Slightly Dim the Display When Using This Power Source check box. You can also enable or disable the Finder menu Battery meter from the Options panel.

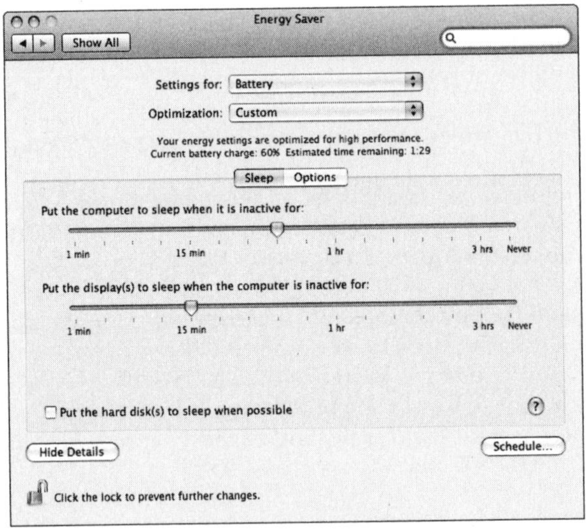

Figure 6-8:
Reduce your MacBook power consumption from the Energy Saver pane.

The Dock pane

I'll come clean: I think the Dock is the best thing since sliced bread! (I wonder what people referred to before sliced bread was invented?) You can use the settings, as shown in Figure 6-9, to configure the Dock's behavior until it fits your personality like a glove:

- ✔ **Size:** Pretty self-explanatory. Just drag the slider to change the scale of the Dock.

- ✔ **Magnification:** When you select this check box, each icon in your Dock swells like a puffer fish when you move your mouse cursor over it. (Just how much it magnifies is determined by the Magnification slider.) I really like this feature because I resize my Dock smaller, and I have a large number of Dock icons.

- ✔ **Position on Screen:** Select a radio button here to position the Dock on the left, bottom, or right edge of your Desktop.

- ✔ **Minimize Using:** Leopard includes two cool animations that you can choose from when shrinking a window to the Dock (and expanding it back to the Desktop). Click the Minimize Using pop-up menu to specify the genie-in-a-bottle effect or a scale-up-or-down-incrementally effect.

  If animation isn't your bag or you want to speed up the graphics performance of an older G4 iBook or PowerBook, you can turn off these mini- mizing effects.

- ✔ **Animate Opening Applications:** Are you into aerobics? How about punk rock and slam dancing? Active souls who like animation likely get a kick out of the bouncing application icons in the Dock. They indicate that you've launched an application and that it's loading. You can turn off this bouncing behavior by disabling this check box.

- ✔ **Automatically Hide and Show the Dock:** Select this check box, and the Dock disappears until you need it. (Depending on the size of your Dock, the Desktop that you gain can be significant.) To display a hidden Dock, move your mouse pointer over the corresponding edge of the Desktop.

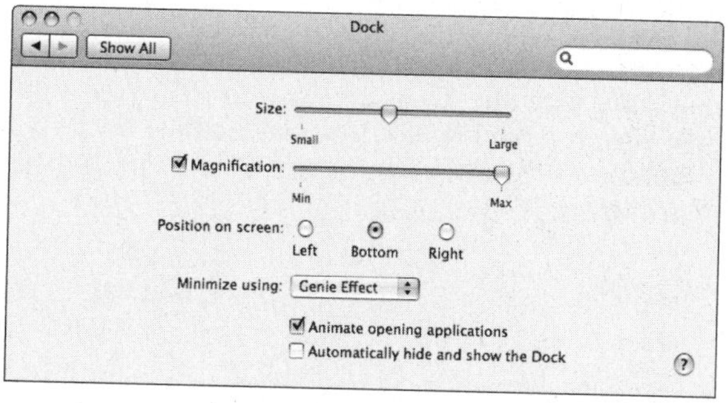

Figure 6-9:
Customize
your Dock
with these
controls.

The Sharing pane

So you're in a neighborly mood, and you want to share your toys with others on your local wired or wireless network. Perhaps you'd like to start your own Web site, or protect yourself against the Bad Guys on the Internet. All these fun diversions are available from the Sharing pane in System Preferences, as shown in Figure 6-10.

Click the Edit button to change the default network name assigned to your MacBook during the installation process. Your current network name is listed in the Computer Name text field.

Each entry in the Service list controls a specific type of sharing, including Screen Sharing, File Sharing (with other Macs and PCs running Windows), Printer Sharing, Web Sharing, Remote Login, Remote Management (using Apple Remote Desktop), Remote Apple Events, Xgrid Sharing, Internet Sharing, and Bluetooth Sharing. To turn on any of these services, enable the On check box for that service. To turn off a service, click the corresponding On check box to disable it.

From a security standpoint, I highly recommend that you enable only those services that you actually use because each service you enable automatically opens your Leopard firewall for that service. (Chapter 17 discusses your firewall in more detail.) A Mark's Maxim to remember:

Poking too many holes in your firewall is *not* A Good Thing.™

When you click one of the services in the list, the right side of the Sharing pane changes to display the settings you can specify for that particular service. To display all the details on these options, click the Help button (question mark) at the lower-right corner of the System Preferences dialog.

The Time Machine pane

Mac users are excited about the new Time Machine automatic backup feature that debuts with Leopard, and you can easily configure how Time Machine handles your backups from this pane (as shown in Figure 6-11). Chapter 21 covers how to use Time Machine. Of course, you need an external hard drive (or a Time Capsule wireless backup station) for the best backup security. Note that Time Machine won't work with your CD or DVD rewriteable drive: You must use a hard drive.

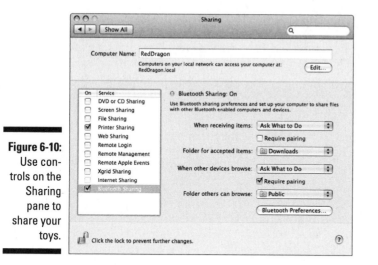

Figure 6-10:
Use controls on the Sharing pane to share your toys.

You can actually use a second partition on your existing internal hard drive to hold your Time Machine data, but guess what happens if your internal hard drive is hit with a hardware failure. You lose both your original data *and* your backup in one fell swoop! For this reason, I **strongly** recommend that you add an external hard drive to your MacBook for use with Time Machine. (I don't know why Apple even made this an option. Sigh.)

Figure 6-11:
Put Time Machine to work, and your data is always backed up.

To enable Time Machine, click the big On sliding switch and then select a disk (or partition) that will hold your Time Machine backup data. Click the desired backup location, and then click Use for Backup. It's really that simple!

Your Mac must be turned on to allow a Time Machine backup to run.

By default, Time Machine backs up all the hard drives on your system; however, you might not need to back up some hard drives or folders on your laptop. To save time and hard drive space, Time Machine allows you to exclude specific drives and folders from the backup process. Click the Options button; then click the Add button (with the plus sign) to select the drives or folders you want to exclude, and they'll appear in the Do Not Back Up list.

To remove an exclusion, select it in the list and click the Delete button (with the minus sign); note the Total Included figure increases, and Time Machine adds the item you deleted from the list to the next backup.

Chapter 7

Sifting through Your Stuff

In This Chapter

▶ Understanding how Spotlight works

▶ Searching for data, files, and folders via Spotlight

▶ Using the results you get from a Spotlight search

▶ Searching with the Find dialog and the Search box

▶ Searching for stuff on the Internet with Dashboard widgets

*W*hat would you say if I told you that you could search your entire system for every single piece of data connected with a person — and in only the short time it takes to type that person's name? And I'm not just talking about files and folders that might include that person's name. I mean every e-mail message and every iCal calendar event that references that person — and even that person's Address Book card to boot? Heck, how about if that search could dig up every occurrence of the person's name inside your electronic PDF documents?

You'd probably say, "That makes for good future tech — I'll bet I can do that in five or ten years. It'll take Apple at least that long to do it . . . and just in time for me to buy a new MacBook! (Harrumph.)"

Don't be so hasty: You can do all this, right now. The technology is the Mac OS X feature named *Spotlight,* built right into Leopard. In this chapter, I show you how to use it like a Mac power guru. I also show you how to take advantage of Internet search widgets you can display within Dashboard. (From what I hear, there's good stuff on the Internet, too.)

A Not-So-Confusing Introduction to Spotlight

Invoking the magic of Spotlight is a snap. As you can see in Figure 7-1, the Spotlight search field always hangs out on the right side of the Finder menu bar. You can either click once on the magnifying glass icon or just press ⌘+spacebar. Either way, Leopard displays the Spotlight search box.

Spotlight search box

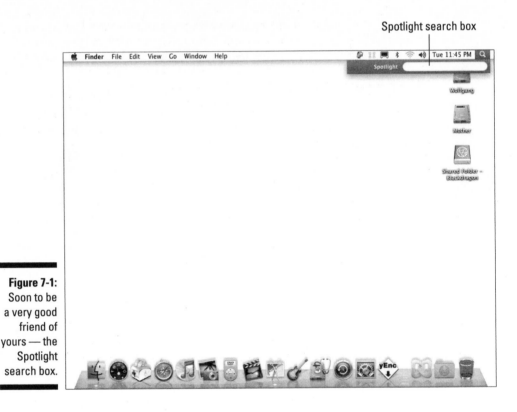

Figure 7-1:
Soon to be
a very good
friend of
yours — the
Spotlight
search box.

Spotlight works by *indexing* — in other words, searching for and keeping track of keywords within your files. (In case you've never heard the term before, a *keyword* is a word in the title or innards of a document that describes the contents, like *leopard, music,* or *soda.* That last one turns up a lot in my documents.)

In fact, Leopard indexes the contents of your MacBook's hard drives into one huge file, which it constantly maintains while you create new files and modify existing files. Leopard can search this index file in a fraction of a second after you enter your search criteria. Your index file contains all sorts of data, including quite a bit of information from inside various documents: hence, Spotlight's ability to present matching data inside your files and application records.

When you first boot Leopard, it spends anywhere from a few minutes to an hour or two creating the initial Spotlight index file. A blue dot appears in the middle of the magnifying glass icon while indexing is underway. Creating this full index happens only once, so it's no great burden to bear.

You can search for any string of text characters in Spotlight, and you'll be surprised at everything this plucky feature will search. For example, Spotlight searches through your Address Book contacts, Mail messages, iCal calendars, iChat transcripts, temporary Web page cache, and even System Preferences! Yep, you can even use it to find specific settings in all those System Preferences panes, such as *printer sharing* or *Dashboard.* Of course, Spotlight includes matching files and folders — like that other operating system — but it does it in the blink of an eye.

Spotlight matches all the items that include all your search text: Therefore, if you enter just the word *horse,* you're likely to get far more matches than if you enter a more-restrictive word string, such as *horse show ticket.*

If you add *metadata* to your documents — such as a Comment field in a Word document (which you can display in the Get Info dialog box) — Spotlight matches that information as well. Other recognized file formats include iWork documents, Excel spreadsheets, Keynote presentations, and third-party applications that offer a Spotlight plug-in.

Searching with Spotlight

To begin a Spotlight topic search, click within the Spotlight box and start typing. As soon as your finger presses the first key, you'll see matching items start to appear. Check out Figure 7-2, in which I typed only a single character (L). No need to press Return to start the process, by the way. When you type more characters, Spotlight's results are updated in real time to reflect those more-restrictive qualifiers. For example, if I had typed three characters — say, **Leo** — my results would be far more specific: everything from *Leopard* to *Leonard Bernstein.*

Spotlight displays what it considers the top 20 matching items within the Spotlight menu itself. These most relevant hits are arranged into categories, such as Documents, Images, and Folders. You can change the order in which categories appear (via the Spotlight pane within System Preferences, which I cover a bit later in this chapter).

With its internal magic, Spotlight presents the category Top Hit (with what it considers the single, most-relevant match) at the top of the search results, as also shown in Figure 7-2. You'll find that the Top Hit is often just what you're looking for. To open or launch the Top Hit item from the keyboard, click the entry or press the down-arrow key (↓) to select Top Hit; then press Return.

Didn't find what you were after? Click the X icon that appears at the right side of the Spotlight box to reset the search box and then start over.

If all you know about the item you're searching for is its file type, prefix a keyword with the text *kind:* in front of the file type in the Searchlight field. For example, say you're searching for a QuickTime movie, but you don't know the title. In this case, you'd type **kind:movies.** This trick also works with image files (kind:images), contacts (kind:contacts), applications (kind:applications), and audio files (kind:music), too.

Figure 7-2:
A Spotlight
menu
search
takes as
little as one
character.

Here's another trick that's built into Spotlight: You can type in a date a file was created or received, such as **modified:=>01/01/08,** to match all items modified on or after January 1, 2008. Heck, you can even combine appended criteria, such as **kind:music created:07/18/07.** *Note:* Be sure to include a space between the criteria. Spotlight then matches every audio file that was created on that date. One-hundred-percent *sassy!*

To allow even greater flexibility in your searches, Apple uses those helpful Boolean search friends that you might already be familiar with: AND, OR, and NOT (separated by spaces). For example, in Leopard, you can perform Spotlight searches, such as

- Horse AND cow: Collects all references to both those barnyard animals into one search

- Batman OR Robin: Returns all references to either Batman or Robin, but not both

- Apple NOT PC: Displays all references to Apple that don't include any information on dastardly PCs

WARNING!

How secure is Spotlight?

Say you're sharing your Mac as a multiuser computer, or accessing other Macs remotely. What about all those files, folders, contacts, and events that you *don't* want to appear in Spotlight? Can other folks search for and access your personal information through Spotlight?

Definitely not! The results displayed by Spotlight are controlled by file and folder permissions as well as your account login, just like the applications that create and display your personal data. For example, you can't access other users' calendars by using iCal, and they can't see your Mail messages. Only *you* have

access to *your* data, and only after you log in with your username and password. Spotlight works the same way. If a user doesn't normally have access to an item, it simply doesn't appear when that user performs a Spotlight search. (In other words, only you get to see your stuff.)

However, you can even hide certain folders and disks from your own Spotlight searches if necessary. Perhaps you'd prefer keeping your tax and financial records away from Spotlight's all-searching eye? Check out the last section of this chapter for details on setting private locations on your system.

Working with matching stuff

After you run a fruitful search, and Spotlight finds the proverbial needle in your system's haystack, what's next?

Just click the item — that's all it takes. Depending on the type of item, Leopard does one of four things:

- ✔ Launches an application
- ✔ Opens a specific pane in System Preferences (if the match is the name of a setting or contained in the text on a Preferences pane)
- ✔ Opens a document or data item, such as an Address Book card
- ✔ Displays a folder within a Finder window

To see all sorts of useful info about each Spotlight menu item — otherwise known as *filtering* — click the Show All item (above the Top Hit listing; refer to Figure 7-2) to expand your Spotlight menu into the Results window, as shown in Figure 7-3. From the keyboard, you can press the Results window shortcut key, which you can set from System Preferences (more on this in a page or two).

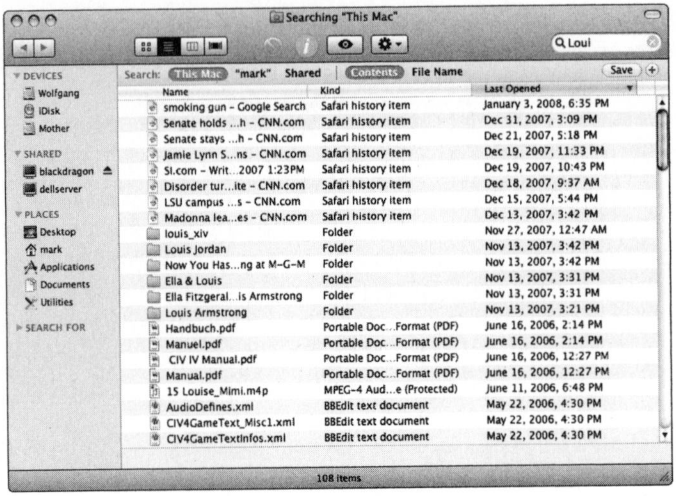

Figure 7-3:
The Spotlight Results window offers more ways to group and sort your matches.

To further filter the search, click one of the buttons on the Spotlight Results window toolbar or create your own custom filter. Click the button with the plus sign to display the search criteria bar and then click the pop-up menus to choose from criteria, such as the type of file, text content, or the location on your system (such as your hard drive, your Home folder, or a network server). You can also filter your results listing by the date when the items were created or last saved. To add or delete criteria, click the plus and minus buttons at the right side of the search criteria bar. To save a custom filter that you created, click Save.

After you locate the item you want, click it to open, launch, or display it, just like you would in the Spotlight menu.

Tweaking Spotlight in System Preferences

The System Preferences window boasts a Spotlight pane, which you can use to customize what search matches you see and how they are presented. To adjust these settings, click the System Preferences icon on the Dock (look for the Three Gears of Justice) and then click the Spotlight icon (under Personal).

Configuring the Search Results settings

Figure 7-4 illustrates the Search Results tab of the Spotlight Preferences pane. From here, you can

✔ **Pick your categories.** To disable a category (typically because you don't use those types of files), select the check box next to the unnecessary category to clear it.

✔ **Specify the order that categories appear within Spotlight.** Drag the categories into the order that you want them to appear in the Spotlight menu and Results window.

✔ **Select new Spotlight menu and Spotlight Results window keyboard shortcuts.** In fact, you can enable or disable either keyboard shortcut, as you like. Click the pop-up menu to choose a key combination.

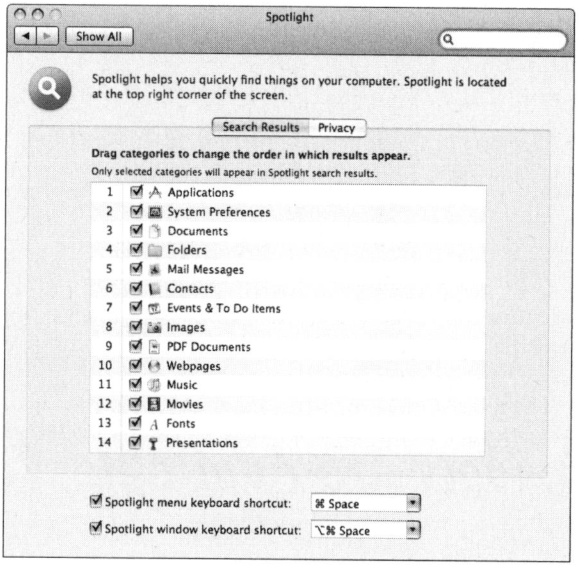

Figure 7-4:
These settings control how your matches are presented within Spotlight.

> Spotlight
>
> Show All | | Q
>
> Spotlight helps you quickly find things on your computer. Spotlight is located at the top right corner of the screen.
>
> Search Results | Privacy
>
> **Drag categories to change the order in which results appear.**
> Only selected categories will appear in Spotlight search results.
>
> 1 ☑ Applications
> 2 ☑ System Preferences
> 3 ☑ Documents
> 4 ☑ Folders
> 5 ☑ Mail Messages
> 6 ☑ Contacts
> 7 ☑ Events & To Do Items
> 8 ☑ Images
> 9 ☑ PDF Documents
> 10 ☑ Webpages
> 11 ☑ Music
> 12 ☑ Movies
> 13 ☑ Fonts
> 14 ☑ Presentations
>
> ☑ Spotlight menu keyboard shortcut: ⌘ Space
> ☑ Spotlight window keyboard shortcut: ⌥⌘ Space

Marking stuff off-limits

Click the Privacy tab (as shown in Figure 7-5) to add disks and folders that should never be listed as results in a Spotlight search. The disks and folders that you add to this list won't appear even if they actually match your search string. This safeguard can come in handy for organizations (such as hospitals) that are required by law to protect their patient or client data. However, you can select a removable hard drive here, which is often stored in a safe after business hours.

To add a private location, click the Add button (which bears a plus sign) and navigate to the desired location. Then click the location to select it and click Choose.

If you already have the location open in a Finder window, you also can drag folders or disks directly from the window and drop them into the list.

Add button

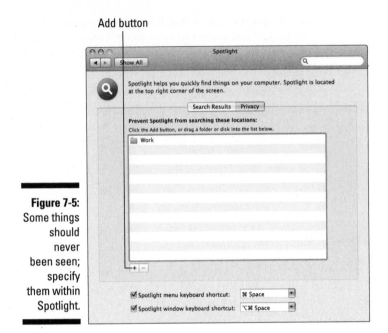

Figure 7-5:
Some things
should
never
been seen;
specify
them within
Spotlight.

Other Search Tools Are Available, Too

The Finder window toolbar has featured a Search box for a few years now
(and Leopard includes a Find dialog), but even the older Search features
within Leopard have been updated to take advantage of Spotlight technology.
Now you can even use file types (such as *image* or *movie*) and relative time
periods (such as *yesterday* and *last week*) in the Finder window Search box
and Find displays!

Typically, I use the Finder window Search box if I need to do a simple file or
folder name search: It works the same as using the Spotlight search field.
Just begin typing. To reset the field and start anew, click the X button in the
Search box. To choose a specific location for your search — say, your Home
folder or a hard drive volume — click the desired button along the top of the
Search results display. The Finder window automatically turns into a Results
display.

Leopard also includes the oldest Search method in the book: the Find display. (It used to be a dialog all by itself, but Find controls are now displayed
in the Finder window, so it's more of an extension to the Finder window.)
Choose File➪Find or press ⌘+F to display the Find controls. From here, you
can click pop-up menus to choose a specific filename or portion of a filename.
Other modifiers include the file type, content, file size, and the most recent
date when the file was opened. Again, click the location buttons at the top of
the window to choose where to search.

For a truly mind-blowing list of modifiers, click the Other item in the modifier menu. You'll find you can search for all photos where a certain shutter speed was used, or all files that are read-only. Heck, I sometimes use this expanded list to search for documents that use a certain font!

The Find display, however, is a little more sophisticated than the toolbar Search box. You can click the plus (+) button next to a search criterion field in the Find display to add another field, allowing for matches based on more than one condition. Click the minus (–) button next to a search criterion field to remove it.

After you find a match, both older Search methods work the same: Click the item once to display its location, or double-click it to launch or open it. Files can also be moved or copied, respectively, from the Results and Find displays with the standard drag or Option+drag methods. You can return to the more mundane Finder window display by clicking the Back button on the toolbar to erase the contents of the Spotlight box.

These older Search methods can also do one thing that Spotlight doesn't offer: You can use them to create a new *Smart Folder,* which is a folder with contents that Leopard automatically updates according to the criteria you set — the same modifiers I discuss earlier.

Click the Save button in either the Finder window Search Results or Find display. You're prompted to specify the name and location for the new Smart Folder and whether it should appear in the Finder window Sidebar.

After you create the folder, Leopard automatically updates the contents of the Smart Folder with whatever items match the criteria you saved. You never have to search using the same text or criteria again because the search is saved as part of the Smart Folder! (Each icon in a Smart Folder is a link to the actual file or folder — just like an alias — so nothing gets moved, and no extra space is wasted with multiple copies of the same items.) In other words, you can work with the files and folders inside a Smart Folder as if they were the actual items themselves.

With Widgets, the Internet Is Your Resource

No chapter on searching within Mac OS X would be complete without the Internet resources available through your Leopard Dashboard. (I describe widgets in illuminating detail in Chapter 5.) Figure 7-6 illustrates many of these widgets:

✔ **Dictionary:** This multipurpose widget can display the Oxford American dictionary or thesaurus entry for the word you enter.

✔ **Weather:** Check out the six-day forecast for a specific ZIP code or city/state combination at a glance.

To enter the location data, click the tiny *i* button that appears when you mouse over the right corner of the widget. This trick works with just about every widget, allowing you to set any options it offers.

✔ **Flight Tracker:** Keep tabs on the arrival and destination time for the flight you specify.

✔ **Google:** Yep, it's a shortcut to the King of all Internet search engines. Just type in the words you want to search for and then press Return. The widget automatically launches Safari with the results!

✔ **Business:** Put your local Yellow Pages to work by typing in a business name or category. This widget displays matching telephone numbers and addresses. Click an entry to get directions or a map from the Web.

Okay, I know you're going to roll your eyes, but I have to remind you that you need an Internet connection to use these widgets. Otherwise, Business and Flight Tracker are about as useful as a pair of swim fins in the Sahara Desert.

Naturally, you'll find countless other Internet-enabled widgets on the Apple Web site, in the Download area. For all the details on adding built-in widgets to your Dashboard, visit Chapter 5.

Figure 7-6:
These widgets use the Internet to help you search for answers to Life's Persistent Questions.

Part III
Connecting and Communicating

"I can be reached at home on my cell phone, I can be reached on the road with my pager and PDA. Soon I'll be reachable on a plane with e-mail. I'm beginning to think identity theft wouldn't be such a bad idea for a while."

In this part . . .

You want to do the Internet thing, don't you? Sure, you do! In this part, I describe and demonstrate your Safari Web browser. You also find out about Apple's .Mac Internet subscription service. Finally, this part fills you in on connecting important stuff, such as printers and scanners, as well as how you can use the cool-looking Apple Remote and your laptop's built-in iSight Web cam and Photo Booth.

Chapter 8

Taking Your Laptop on Safari!

In This Chapter

▶ Introducing the Safari window and controls

▶ Visiting Web sites with Safari

▶ Moving between sites

▶ Creating and using bookmarks

▶ Receiving files with Safari

▶ Surfing with your tabs showing

▶ Saving Web pages to disk

▶ Protecting your privacy on the Web

▶ Blocking those irritating pop-ups

*L*ooking for that massive Microsoft monster of a Web browser on your MacBook? You know, the one that practically everyone uses in the Windows world. What's it called? I forget the name.

You see, I use a MacBook Pro, and I proudly surf the Web via a lean, mean — and *very* fast — browser application. That's Safari, of course, and it just keeps getting better with each new version of Mac OS X. It doesn't matter whether you're working wirelessly from a hotel room or safely ensconced in your office: Safari delivers the Web the right way, without the wait.

If you need a guide to Safari, this is your chapter. Sure, you can start using it immediately, but wouldn't you rather read a few pages in order to surf like a power user?

It's Not Just Another Web Browser

Figure 8-1 illustrates the Safari window. You can launch Safari directly from the Dock, or you can click the Safari icon (which looks like a compass dial) within your Applications folder.

Bookmarks bar   Toolbar

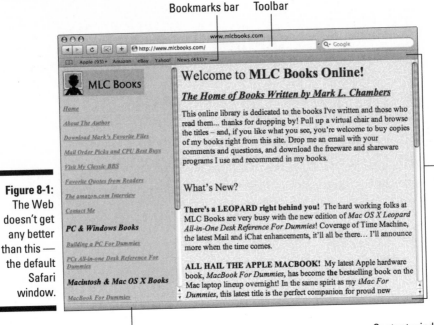

Figure 8-1:
The Web
doesn't get
any better
than this —
the default
Safari
window.

Status bar

Content window

Major sections of the Safari window include

✔ **The Toolbar:** You'll find the most often-used commands on this toolbar for everyday tasks, such as navigation, adding bookmarks, and searching Google. Plus, here, you can type or paste the address for Web sites that you'd like to visit. You can hide the Toolbar to open up more real estate in your browser window for Web content. To toggle hidden mode, press ⌘+| (the vertical bar right above the backslash) or choose View➪Hide/Show Toolbar.

✔ **The Bookmarks bar:** Consider this a toolbar that allows you to jump directly to your favorite Web sites with a single click. I show you later, in the section "Adding and Using Bookmarks," how to add and remove sites from your Bookmarks bar. For now, remember that you can toggle the display of the Bookmarks bar by choosing View➪Hide/Show Bookmarks Bar, or by pressing ⌘+Shift+B.

✔ **The Content window:** Congratulations! At last, you waded through all the pre-game show and reached the area where Web pages are actually displayed. Like any other window, the Content window can be scrolled; when you minimize Safari to the Dock, you get a *thumbnail* (minimized) image of the Content window.

The Content window often contains underlined text and graphical icons that transport you to other pages when you click them. These underlined words and icons are *links,* and they make it easy for you to move from one area of a site to another or to a completely different site.

✔ **The status bar:** The status bar displays information about what the mouse pointer is currently resting upon, like the address for a link or the name of an image; it also updates you on what's happening while a page is loading. To hide or display the status bar, press ⌘+/ (forward slash).

Visiting Web Sites

Sure, you're likely saying, "Mark, I already know this stuff. I can operate a Web browser blindfolded — while listening to *The Best of Air Supply,* even." I agree wholeheartedly, but I get paid by the word, and some folks might just not be aware of all the myriad ways of visiting a site. You can load a Web page from any of the following methods:

✔ **Type (or paste) a Web site address into the Toolbar and then press Return.**

If you're typing in an address and Safari recognizes the site as one that you already visited, it helps by completing the address for you. If this is a new site, just keep typing.

✔ **Click a Bookmarks entry within Safari.**

✔ **Click the Home button, which takes you to the home page that you specify.**

More on this in the section, "Putting Down Roots with a New Home Page," later in this chapter.

✔ **Click a page link in Apple Mail or another Internet-savvy application.**

✔ **Click a page link within another Web page.**

✔ **Use the Google box in the Toolbar.**

Click in the Google box, type the contents that you want to find, and then press Return. Safari presents you with the search results page on Google for the text that you entered. (In case you've been living under the Internet equivalent of a rock for the last couple of years, *Google. com* is the preeminent search site on the Web. People use Google to find everything from used auto parts to ex-spouses.)

✔ **Click a Safari page icon on the Dock or in a Finder window.**

For example, Mac OS X sports an icon in the default Dock that takes you to the Mac OS X page on the Apple Web site. Drag a site from your Bookmarks bar and drop it on the right side of the Dock. Clicking the icon that you add launches Safari and automatically loads that site.

This trick works only on the side of the Dock to the right of the vertical line.

If you minimize Safari to the Dock, you'll see a thumbnail of the page with the Safari logo. Click this thumbnail in the Dock to restore the page to its full glory.

Basic Navigation While on Safari

A typical Web surfing session is a linear experience — you bop from one page to the next, absorbing the information that you want and discarding the rest. However, after you visit a few sites, you might find that you need to return to where you've been or head to the familiar ground of your home page. Safari offers these navigational controls on the Toolbar:

- **Back:** Click the Back button (the left-facing arrow) on the toolbar to return to the last page that you visited. Additional clicks take you to previous pages, in reverse order. The Back button is disabled if you haven't visited at least two sites.

- **Forward:** If you've clicked the Back button at least once, clicking the Forward button (the right-facing arrow) takes you to the next page (or through the pages) where you were, in forward order. The Forward button is disabled if you haven't used the Back button.

- **Home:** Click this button (look for the little house) to return to your home page.

Not all these buttons and controls might appear on your Toolbar. To display or hide Toolbar controls, choose View➪Customize Toolbar. The sheet that appears works just like the Customize Toolbar sheet within a Finder window: Drag the control you want from the sheet to your Toolbar, or drag a control that you don't want from the Toolbar to the sheet.

- **AutoFill:** If you fill out a lot of forms online — when you're shopping at Web sites, for example — you can click the AutoFill button (which looks like a little text box and a pen) to complete these forms for you. You can set what information is used for AutoFill by choosing Safari➪Preferences and the clicking the AutoFill toolbar button.

To be honest, I'm not a big fan of releasing *any* personal information to *any* Web site, so I don't use AutoFill often. If you do decide to use this feature, make sure that the connection is secure (look for the padlock icon in the upper-right corner of the Safari window) and read the site's Privacy Agreement page first to see how your identity data will be treated.

- **Text Size:** Use this to shrink or expand the text on the page, offering smaller, space-saving characters (for the shrinking crowd) or larger, easier-to-read text (for the expanding crowd). Hence the button, which is labeled with a small and large letter A.

✔ **Stop/Reload:** Click Reload (which has a circular arrow) to *refresh* (reload) the contents of the current page. Although most pages remain static, some pages change their content at regular intervals or after you fill out a form or click a button. By clicking Reload (look for the curvy arrow), you can see what's changed on these pages. (I use Reload every hour or so with CNN.com, for example.) While a page is loading, the Reload button turns into the Stop button — with a little X mark — and you can click it to stop the loading of the content from the current page. This is a real boon when a download takes *foorrevverr,* which can happen when you're trying to visit a very popular or very slow Web site (especially if you're using a dialup modem connection to the Internet). Using Stop is also handy if a page has a number of very large graphics that are going to take a long time to load.

✔ **Open in Dashboard:** Click this button to create a Dashboard widget using the contents of the currently displayed Web page. Safari prompts you to choose which clickable section of the page to be included within the widget's borders (like the local radar map on your favorite weather Web site). Click Add, and Dashboard loads automatically with your new widget. (More on widgets in Chapter 5.)

✔ **Add Bookmark:** Click this Toolbar button (which carries a plus sign) to add a page to your Bookmarks bar or Bookmarks menu. (More on this in a tad.)

✔ **Google Search:** As I mention earlier, you can click in this box, type text that you want to find on the Web via the Google search engine, and then press Return to display the results. To repeat a recent search, click the down arrow in the Google Search box and select it from the pop-up menu.

✔ **Print:** Click this convenient button to print the contents of the Safari window. Dig that crazy printer icon!

✔ **Report Bug:** A rather strange creature, the Safari Bug button makes it easy to alert Apple when you encounter a page that doesn't display properly in Safari. (Software developers call such glitches *bugs:* hence, the name.) When you click the Bug button, you'll see a sheet with the settings shown in Figure 8-2; there, you can enter a short description of the problem that you're having. (I also enable the Send Screen Shot of Current Page and the Send Source of Current Page check boxes to give the Apple folks more to work with while they're debugging Safari.) Then click the Submit button to send the bug report to Apple.

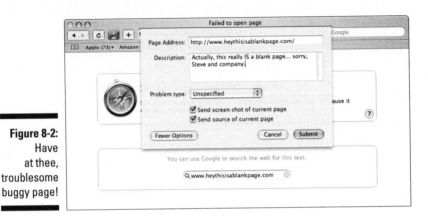

Figure 8-2:
Have
at thee,
troublesome
buggy page!

Putting Down Roots with a New Home Page

Choosing a *home page* (that's the page that initially appears when you launch Safari) is one of the easiest methods of speeding up your Web surfing, especially if you're using a dialup modem connection. However, a large percentage of the Mac owners with whom I've talked have never set their own home page, simply using the default home page provided by their browser. With Safari running, take a moment to follow these steps to declare your own freedom to choose your own home page:

1. **Display the Web page you want as your new home page, in Safari.**

   I recommend electing a page with few graphics or a fast-loading popular site.

2. **Choose Safari➪Preferences or press ⌘+, (comma).**

3. **Click the General button.**

   You see the settings shown in Figure 8-3.

4. **Click the Set to Current Page button.**

5. **Alternatively, click the New Windows Open With pop-up menu and choose Empty Page if you want Safari to open a new window with a blank page.**

   This is the fastest choice of all for a home page (and a good choice for those using a dialup modem connection because then Safari doesn't have to download anything upfront).

6. **Click the Close button to exit the Preferences dialog.**

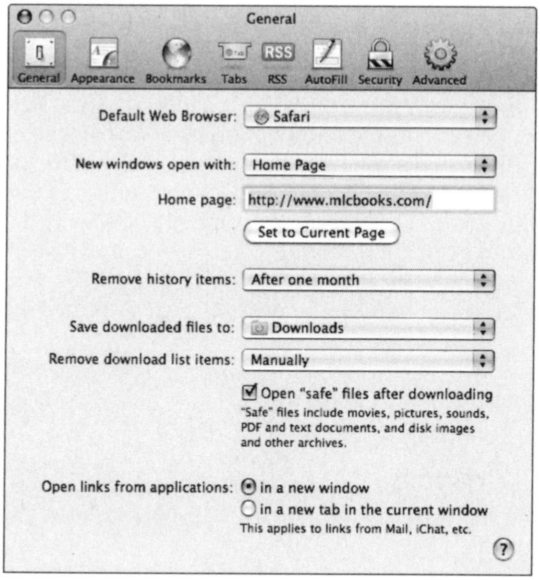

Figure 8-3:
Adding
your own
home page
is an easy
change you
can make.

TIP

Visit your home page at any time by pressing the Home button on the Toolbar.

Lean, fast, and mean — That's RSS

Well, maybe not *mean* — after all, I don't want you to be afraid of RSS (RDF Site Summary or really simple syndication) pages! RSS Web sites display updated information by using a shortened list format, rather like a newspaper headline, without unnecessary graphics or silly advertisements. You can tell when a Web site has RSS pages available because Safari displays an RSS icon at the right side of the Address box. (When you click the RSS icon, the Web address switches to a `feed://` prefix — another indication that you're not in Kansas reading HTML pages anymore.)

To display more information about a news item on an RSS page, click the item headline. Safari opens the corresponding Web page — yep, once again you're back in the world of

HTML — where you can read the full story. To return to the RSS feed, click the Back button on the Toolbar. Naturally, RSS feed pages can be bookmarked. In fact, Apple gives you a number of RSS sites that you can explore immediately.

To customize your RSS display, choose Safari⇨Preferences and then click the RSS tab. By default, Safari checks for updated RSS headlines on your bookmarked feeds every 30 minutes, but you can change this to an hourly or daily check. (Of course, you can also check for updates manually by reloading the RSS page, just like you would any other Web page.) New articles can be assigned any color you like, and you can specify the amount of time an item should remain on the RSS page after it's published.

Adding and Using Bookmarks

No doubt about it: Bookmarks make the Web a friendly place. When you set bookmarks in Safari, you can immediately jump from one site to another with a single click of the Bookmarks menu or the buttons on the Bookmarks bar. (The Bookmarks menu opens up in a separate pane on the left side of the Safari window, and the Bookmarks bar appears right below the Toolbar: your choice!)

To add a bookmark, first navigate to the desired page and then do any of the following:

 ✔ **Choose Bookmarks⇨Add Bookmark.**

 ✔ **Press the ⌘+D keyboard shortcut.**

  Safari displays a sheet where you can enter the name for the bookmark and also select where it appears (on the Bookmarks bar or the Bookmarks menu).

 ✔ **Drag the icon next to the Web address from the Toolbar to the Bookmarks bar.**

You can also drag a link on the current page to the Bookmarks bar, but note that doing this adds only a bookmark for the page corresponding to the link — not the current page.

To jump to a bookmark

 ✔ **Choose it from the Bookmarks menu.**

  If the bookmark is contained in a folder, which I discuss later in this section, move your mouse pointer over the folder name to show its contents and then click the bookmark.

 ✔ **Click the bookmark on the Bookmarks bar.**

  If you've added a large number of items to the Bookmarks bar, click the More icon on the edge of the Bookmarks bar to display the rest of the buttons.

 ✔ **Click the Show All Bookmarks button (which looks like a small, opened book) on the Bookmarks bar and then click the desired bookmark.**

  The Bookmarks window that you see in Figure 8-4 appears, where you can review each collection of bookmarks at leisure.

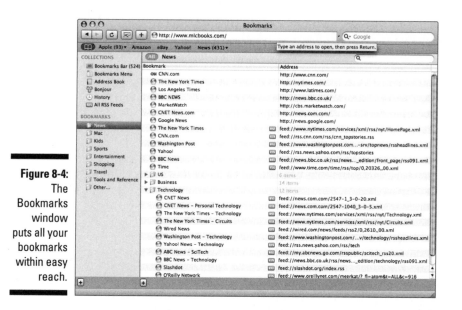

Figure 8-4:
The
Bookmarks
window
puts all your
bookmarks
within easy
reach.

The more bookmarks that you add, the more unwieldy the Bookmarks menu and the Bookmarks window become. To keep your bookmarks organized, choose Bookmarks➪Add Bookmark Folder and then type a name for the new folder. With folders, you can organize your bookmarks into *collections,* which appear in the column at the left of the Bookmarks window (or as separate submenus within the Bookmarks menu). You can drag bookmarks into the new folder to help reduce the clutter.

To delete a bookmark or a folder from the Bookmarks window, click it and then press Delete.

Downloading Files

A huge chunk of the fun that you'll find on the Web is the ability to download images and files. If you've visited a site that offers files for downloading, you typically just click the Download button or the download file link, and Safari takes care of the rest. You'll see the Downloads status window, which keeps you updated with the progress of the transfer. While the file is downloading, feel free to continue browsing or even download additional files; the status window helps you keep track of what's going on and when everything will be finished transferring. To display the Download status window from the keyboard, press ⌘+Option+L.

By default, Safari saves any downloaded files to your Mac OS X Downloads folder on the Dock, which I like and use. To specify the location where downloaded files are stored — for example, if you'd like to scan them automatically with an antivirus program — follow these steps:

1. **Choose Safari⇨Preferences or press ⌘+, (comma).**

2. **Click the General tab (refer to Figure 8-3) and then click the Save Downloaded Files To pop-up menu.**

3. **Choose Other.**

4. **Navigate to the location where you want the files stored.**

5. **Click the Select button.**

6. **Click the Close button to exit Preferences.**

To download a specific image that appears on a Web page, move your mouse pointer over the image and hold down Control while you click (or right-click, if you've got the button to spare). Then choose Save Image As from the pop-up menu that appears. Safari prompts you for the location where you want to store the file.

You can choose to automatically open files that Safari considers safe — things such as movies, text files, and PDF files that are **very** unlikely to store a virus or a damaging macro. By default, the Open "Safe" files After Downloading check box is enabled on the General pane. However, if you're interested in preventing anything you download from running until you manually check it with your antivirus application, you can disable the check box and breathe easy.

Luckily, Safari has matured to the point that it can seamlessly handle virtually any multimedia file type that it encounters. However, if you've downloaded a multimedia file and Safari doesn't seem to be able to play or display it, try loading the file within QuickTime. QuickTime is the Swiss Army knife of multimedia players, and it can recognize a huge number of audio, video, and image formats.

Using Subscriptions and History

To keep track of where you've been, you can display the History list by clicking the History menu. To return to a page in the list, just choose it from the History menu. Note that Safari also arranges older history items by the date you visited the site, so you can easily jump back a couple of days to that page you forgot to bookmark!

Searching for pointed sewing implements in a haystack

Looking for a certain word or phrase on a huge Web page that seems to be 47 screens long? Don't despair! You can always press ⌘+F (or choose Edit➪Find➪Find) to display the Find bar (which appears directly under the Safari Toolbar). Type the word or phrase that you're looking for in the Find box — no need to press Return — and Safari highlights any matches that it finds!

Click the Next button in the Find bar to advance to each spot within the page in order, all the way to the bottom of the page. To search upward to the top of the page, click Previous. When you're finished searching, click the Done button to banish the Find bar.

Convenient, indeed. Consider that needle found!

In fact, Safari also searches the History list automatically, when it fills in an address that you're typing. That's the feature I mention in the earlier section, "Visiting Web Sites."

If you're worried about security and you'd rather not keep track of where you've been online, I show you how to clear the contents of the History file in the upcoming section, "Handling ancient history."

Tabs Are Your Browsing Friends

Safari also offers *tabbed browsing*, which many folks use to display (and organize) multiple Web pages at one time. For example, if you're doing a bit of comparison shopping for a new piece of hardware between different online stores, tabs are ideal.

When you hold down the ⌘ key and click a link or bookmark using tabs, a tab representing the new page appears under the Bookmarks bar. (Choose File➪New Tab or press ⌘+T to work the same magic.) Just click the tab to switch to that page. (If you don't hold down ⌘, things revert to business as usual, and Safari replaces the contents of the window with the new page.) Figure 8-5 illustrates a number of pages that I opened in Safari, using tabs.

To turn on tabbed browsing, choose Safari➪Preferences to display the Preferences dialog; then click Tabs. From here, select the ⌘-Click Opens a Link in a New Tab check box to enable it. After you turn on tabs, your browsing experience will never be the same.

Done with a page? You can remove a tabbed page by clicking the X button next to the tab's title.

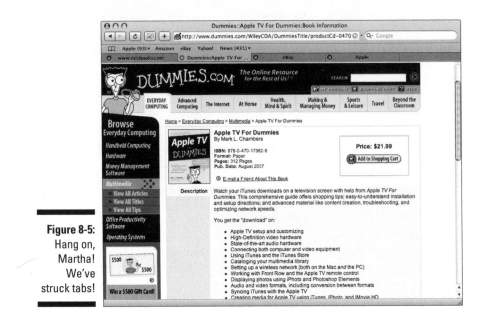

Figure 8-5:
Hang on,
Martha!
We've
struck tabs!

Saving Web Pages

If you encounter a page that you'd like to load later, you can save it to disk in its entirety as a Web archive (which stores all the page content, including the text and images). Follow these steps:

1. **Display the desired page.**

2. **Choose File⇨Save As, or press ⌘+S.**

3. **In the Export As text field, type a name for the saved page.**

4. **From the Where field, navigate to the location where you want to store the file on your system.**

    To expand the sheet to allow navigation to any location on your system, click the button with the down arrow.

5. **Click the Format pop-up menu to choose the format for the saved page.**

    Usually, you'll want to choose a Web Archive, which saves the entire page and can be displayed just as you see it (even if your MacBook no longer has an Internet connection). However, if you want to save just the HTML source code, choose Page Source.

6. Click Save to begin the download process.

After the Save file is created, double-click it to load it in Safari.

A quick word about printing a page within Safari: Some combinations of background and text colors might conspire together to render your printed copy practically worthless. In a case like that, use your printer's grayscale setting (if it has one). Alternatively, you can simply click and drag to select the text on the page, press ⌘+C to copy it, and then paste the text into Word or Pages, where you can print the page on a less offensive background (while still keeping the text formatting largely untouched).

If you'd rather mail the contents of a Web page to a friend — or just a link to the page, which is faster to send over a dialup Internet connection — choose File⇨Mail Contents of this Page/Mail Link to this Page. (From the keyboard, press ⌘+I to send the contents in an e-mail message, or press ⌘+Shift+I to send a link in e-mail.) Mail loads automatically, complete with a prepared e-mail message. Just address it to the recipients and then click Send!

Protecting Your Privacy

No chapter on Safari would be complete without a discussion of security, both against outside intrusion from the Internet and prying eyes around your MacBook. Hence, this last section, which covers protecting your privacy.

Although diminutive, the tiny padlock icon that appears in the top-right corner of the Safari window when you're connected to a secure Web site means a great deal! A *secure site* encrypts the information that you send and receive, making it much harder for those of unscrupulous ideals to obtain things like credit card numbers and personal information. Of course, the padlock doesn't ensure that you're on a "good" Web site — plenty of objectionable sites want your money as well — but at least you can be certain that your personal and financial information won't be intercepted in transit between your MacBook and the site.

Never — I mean *never* — enter any valuable personal or financial information on a Web page unless you see the secure connection padlock symbol.™

This type of information includes

- ✔ Obvious things, such as your credit card number, address, or telephone number
- ✔ Not-so-obvious things, such as your Social Security number or a login/password combination

If a site doesn't provide a secure connection and asks you for personal information, *find another spot in cyberspace to do your business.* Your identity should remain *yours.*

It's always a good idea to restrict your Web shopping to your home network. For example, I don't use airport or coffee shop wireless networks when I'm sending credit card or personal information across the Internet. Why? Because the "open" (as in *unencrypted*) architecture of these public networks can allow others to intercept the data that you send and receive. Therefore, I recommend that you use a public wireless network for simple Web surfing, but save the important stuff for your home or office. (You can find more information on wireless networking in Chapter 17.)

Yes, there are such things as bad cookies

First, a definition of this ridiculous term: A *cookie,* a small file that a Web site automatically saves on your hard drive, contains information that the site will use on your future visits. For example, a site might save a cookie to preserve your site preferences for the next time or — in the case of a site such as Amazon.com — to identify you automatically and help customize the offerings that you see.

In and of themselves, cookies aren't bad things. Unlike a virus, a cookie file isn't going to replicate itself or wreak havoc on your system, and only the original site can read the cookie that it creates. However, many folks don't appreciate acting as a gracious host for a slew of little snippets of personal information. Also, if you do a large amount of surfing, cookies can occupy a significant amount of your hard drive space over time. (Not to mention that some cookies have highly suggestive names, which could lead to all sorts of conclusions. End of story.)

You can choose to accept all cookies — the default — or you can opt to disable cookies altogether. You can also set Safari to accept cookies only from the sites you choose to visit. To change your *Cookie Acceptance Plan* (or CAP, for those who absolutely crave acronyms), follow these steps:

1. **Choose Safari⇨Preferences.**

2. **Click the Security button.**

   Safari displays the preference settings shown in Figure 8-6.

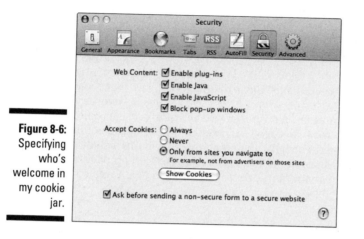

Figure 8-6:
Specifying
who's
welcome in
my cookie
jar.

3. Choose how to accept cookies via these radio button choices:

- *Never:* Block cookies entirely.

- *Always:* Accept all cookies.

- *Only from Sites You Navigate To:* Personally, I use this default option, which allows sites like Amazon.com to work correctly without allowing a barrage of illicit cookies.

4. To view the cookies currently on your system, click the Show Cookies button.

If a site's cookies are blocked, you might have to take care of things manually, such as providing a password on the site that used to be read automatically from the cookie.

5. Click the Close button to save your changes.

Cleaning your cache

Safari speeds up the loading of Web sites by storing often-used images and multimedia files in a temporary storage, or *cache,* folder. Naturally, the files in your cache folder can be displayed (hint), which could lead to assumptions (hint, hint) about the sites you've been visiting (hint, hint, hint). (Tactful, ain't I?)

Luckily, Safari makes it easy to dump the contents of your cache file. Just choose Safari⇨Empty Cache; then click Empty to confirm that you want to clean up your cache.

Handling ancient history

As you might imagine, your History file leaves a very clear set of footprints indicating where you've been on the Web. To delete the contents of the History menu, choose History⇨Clear History.

The latest version of Safari also allows you to specify an amount of time to retain entries in your History file. Open the Safari Preferences dialog, click the General tab, and then click the Remove History Items pop-up menu to specify the desired amount of time. Items can be rolled off daily, weekly, biweekly, monthly, or yearly.

Avoiding those @*!^%$ pop-up ads

I hate pop-up ads, and I'm sure you do, too. To block most of those pop-up windows with advertisements for everything from low-rate mortgages to "sure-thing" Internet casinos, click the Safari menu and verify that Block Pop-Up Windows is checked. (If it's not checked, click the menu item to toggle the menu item on.)

From time to time, you might run across a Web site that actually does something *constructive* with pop-up windows, like present a download or login prompt. If you need to temporarily deactivate pop-up blocking, press ⌘+Shift+K to toggle it off. Then press ⌘+Shift+K again to turn pop-up blocking back on after you've finished with the site.

Chapter 9

.Mac Is .Made for Mac Laptops

In This Chapter

▶ Understanding online storage

▶ Opening a new .Mac account

▶ Using your iDisk

▶ Backing up your hard drive with .Mac

*R*eaders often ask me to name my favorite reasons why they should switch — that is, why should a Windows user who thinks all is well move to the Apple universe? Of course, I always mention the superior hardware and how much of a better job Leopard does as an operating system. But here's my favorite selling point: "Apple simply does things right the first time, and everyone else plays catch-up."

And then I pose this question: "What if you could reach a hard drive with 5GB of your files over any Internet connection — anywhere in the world — and it just *showed up* on your Desktop automatically?" Usually, I get a thoughtful silence after that one, and another person decides to learn more — about Apple's .Mac online hosting service, that is. In this chapter, I save you the trouble of researching all the benefits of .Mac. Heck, that's one of the reasons why you bought this book, right?

Where Exactly Is My .Mac Stuff Stored?

Yep, that's the question everyone asks. Best that I answer this one first.

I'll begin with a definition. The online hard drive offered to .Mac subscribers (read about subscribing in the following section) is an *iDisk,* and it's well integrated into Mac OS X. In fact, if you didn't know the background, you might think that iDisk were simply another internal hard drive. Figure 9-1 illustrates my iDisk icon on my Desktop. The Finder window displays the contents; notice the folders visible there. (More on these folders later in the chapter.)

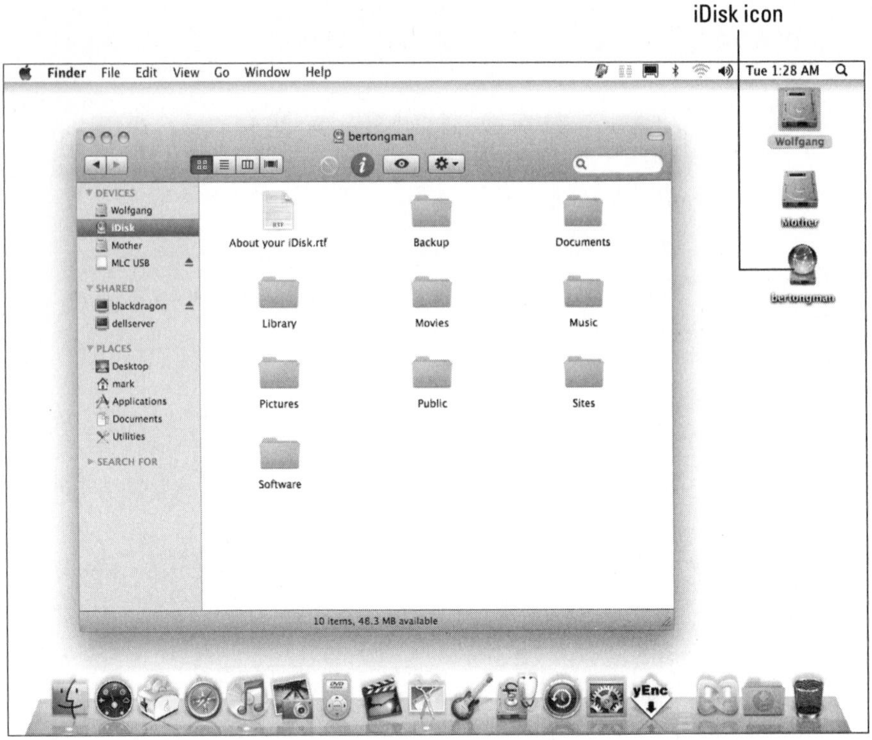

iDisk icon

Figure 9-1:
My iDisk
at work.
Looks like
a normal
hard drive,
doesn't it?

The files that I add to my iDisk are stored on an Apple server, location unknown. Literally. The physical storage (a massive file server that holds uncounted gigabytes of data) could be in Cupertino, or it might be in Timbuktu. There's a whole bunch of 'em, too. You and I don't need to care about the where part because

- ✔ **Your iDisk is always available.** Oh, yes. 24/7, your files are waiting for you.

- ✔ **Your iDisk is secure.** Apple goes to great lengths to guarantee the security of your data, encrypting the transfer of files and folders whenever you use your iDisk. You can also password-protect any data that you want to offer to others, just in case.

- ✔ **Your iDisk works even when you aren't on the Internet.** Yep, you read that right: You can create new documents and modify files to your heart's content while you're on a flight or relaxing on the beach. iDisk automatically updates whatever's changed the next time you connect to the Internet.

Now that I've piqued your interest (and answered the most common question about iDisk), return to the .Mac service for a moment so I can show you how to set up your account.

Opening a .Mac Account

If you haven't already opened your .Mac account, you get a chance to sign up when you turn on your laptop for the first time and also when you install (or upgrade to) Mac OS X. However, if you decided to pass on .Mac at that time, you can always join in the fun by following these steps:

1. Click the System Preferences icon on the Dock.

Read through Chapter 6 for the A–Z on System Preferences.

2. Click the .Mac icon.

3. Click the Learn More button.

This launches Safari (the Apple browser) and displays the Apple .Mac Welcome page (www.mac.com/dotmac). Click Free Trial and then follow the onscreen instructions to choose a member name and password.

When you're done with the clicking and you're rewarded with your login information, close Safari and then enter your name and password into the text boxes in the .Mac System Preferences pane.

Figure 9-2 illustrates an example login that I created.

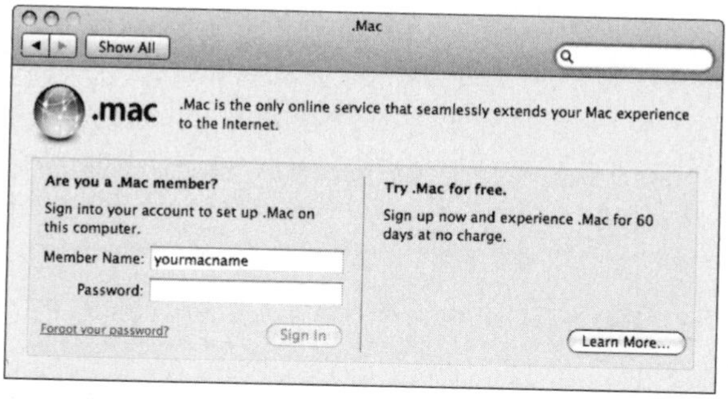

Figure 9-2:
The .Mac
pane within
System
Preferences
keeps track
of your login
information.

Like the convenient operating system that it is, Leopard handles all your .Mac login chores automatically from this point on.

If you're a dialup Internet user, you were likely dreading this moment, but here it is. I'm truly sorry, but in my opinion, a high-speed broadband connection is a real requirement in order to take full advantage of a .Mac subscription. You can certainly still use all the functionality of .Mac with any type of Internet connection, but you're going to spend from now until the next *Gone With the Wind* sequel waiting for files to copy and things to happen.

If you decide to sign up for a full year's .Mac membership, I salute you for your discerning taste in online services. However, you can opt for a 60-day trial subscription at this point, which is only fair because Apple wants you to check out things at your leisure. Table 9-1 shows the major differences between a free trial subscription and a full $100 yearly subscription to .Mac.

Table 9-1	What a Ben Franklin Buys with .Mac			
Status	*iDisk/ E-Mail Storage*	*Time Provided*	*Data Transfer*	*Backup Storage*
Trial, free	100MB total	60 days	3GB per month	100MB total
Member, $100 annually	10GB total	1 year	100GB per month	10GB total

A .Mac subscription also allows you to synchronize your e-mail, Address Book contact information, and your Safari bookmarks between multiple Macs. What a real boon if you spend time on the road with a member of the MacBook species!

Both trial and subscriber .Mac users can read .Mac e-mail through the Web-based browser offered on the .Mac Web site. That's neat, certainly, and you can use Web mail from any computer with an Internet connection. However, you can also send and receive .Mac e-mail seamlessly from Leopard's Mail application, which is the preferred method of checking your messages. In fact, Leopard automatically creates a matching Mail account for your trial .Mac account. Unadulterated *sweet!*

Is .Mac an ISP?

.Mac is many things, but it isn't an ISP (techno-nerd shorthand for *Internet service provider*). You need to join an ISP first because you need an existing Internet connection to use the services and features included in .Mac membership. This makes a lot of sense, considering that most of us already have Internet access. (Plus, Apple doesn't have to worry with all the support and hardware headaches that an ISP has to deal with.)

.Mac works with the ISP that you already have, so you don't have to worry about AOL or EarthLink conflicting with .Mac. (However, I can't guarantee that your system administrator at work will allow .Mac traffic across his or her pristine network. Perhaps a steak dinner would help your argument.)

If you decide that you want the extra functionality of a .Mac subscription, upgrading is easy. When you open the .Mac pane within System Preferences and click the Account button, Leopard displays a countdown reminder telling you how many days remain on your trial period. To upgrade, visit the .Mac Web site at any time and click the Join Now button.

Using Your iDisk on the iRoad

So how do you open your iDisk? Leopard gives you a number of different avenues:

- **Choose Go⇨iDisk from the Finder menu and then choose My iDisk from the submenu.**

  Keyboard types can press ⌘+Shift+I instead.

- **Click the iDisk icon in the Finder window Sidebar.**

- **Click the iDisk button on your Finder toolbar.**

  It's easy to add an iDisk button. Open a Finder window, click View, and then click Customize Toolbar. Drag the iDisk icon up to the toolbar and then click Done.

After you open your iDisk, an iDisk volume icon also pops up on your Desktop. You can open the little scamp later in your computing session by simply double-clicking the Desktop icon. The Desktop iDisk icon hangs around until you log out, restart, eject the iDisk, or shut down your MacBook.

It's all in the folders

Your iDisk contains a number of different folders. Some of them are similar to the subfolders in your Home folder, and others are unique to the structure of your iDisk. In this section, I provide the details on the iDisk folder family.

iDisk storage folders

Although you can store files and create folders in the *root* (or top level) of an iDisk, the same organizational tips apply as the root of your laptop's internal hard drive. In other words, most things that you copy to or create on your iDisk should be stored in one of these six storage folders. (Refer to Figure 9-1 to see them.)

✔ **Documents:** Store the documents that you create with your applications in this folder, which only you can access.

✔ **Movies:** This folder stores your QuickTime movies (including any that you might use in your .Mac Web pages).

✔ **Music:** iTunes music and playlists go here.

✔ **Pictures:** The digital images that you store in this folder can be used with other .Mac services (like your Web pages) or within iPhoto.

✔ **Public:** The files that you store in this folder are meant to be shared with other people (as well as offered on your .Mac Web pages). You can also allow others to copy and save files to your Public folder as well (more on this later in this section).

✔ **Sites:** You can use HomePage to create Web pages in this folder, or you can add Web pages that you've created with your own applications. You can read more about *HomePage,* the Apple Web page-creation application, in the upcoming section, "Publishing a Web Site with HomePage."

These folders can be opened in a Finder window just like any typical folder on your MacBook's internal hard drive, and you can open and save documents to your iDisk folders, using all your applications. In other words, these six iDisk folders act just like normal, everyday folders. Pretty doggone neat!

Funky specialized iDisk folders

Your iDisk contains three folders that you *can't* use to store stuff (directly, anyway):

✔ **Backup:** This is the storage vault for the backup files created with the .Mac Backup application. You can read more about Backup later in this chapter.

Because you have Read access to the Backup folder, you can copy the backup files from this folder to a CD, DVD, or removable drive on your MacBook. (I cover backing up later in this chapter.)

✔ **Library:** Like the Library folders that you find in the root of your hard drive (and in your Home folder), this folder stores all sorts of configuration settings for the .Mac features that you're using, like your Backup settings.

✔ **Software:** This read-only folder is a special case. Apple stuffs this folder full of a wide variety of the latest in freeware and shareware as well as commercial demo software. You can copy whatever you like from the Software folder to your MacBook's Desktop and then install your new toy from that local copy. (Oh, and the contents of the Software folder don't count against your total storage space limit.) Enjoy!

Mirror, mirror, on your drive . . .

You can use your iDisk even if you aren't connected to the Internet. This magic is accomplished through a *mirror,* or local copy of your iDisk, that's stored on your local hard drive. ("Hey, wasn't I supposed to be getting *away* from storing things locally?") If you choose to use a mirror — and you can enable this feature if you like — Leopard automatically synchronizes any files that you created or changed on your local iDisk copy the next time you connect to the Internet. This is a great feature if you have more than one Mac in different locations because you can update and synchronize your iDisk files from any of your computers — all automatically!

Without a mirror, you *must* have an active Internet connection to use your iDisk.

To enable (or disable) the mirror feature, open System Preferences, click the .Mac icon, and then click the iDisk tab to display the settings you see in Figure 9-3. Click the Start button, and — after a moment of preparation, complete with its own dialog — the text above the button reads iDisk Syncing On.

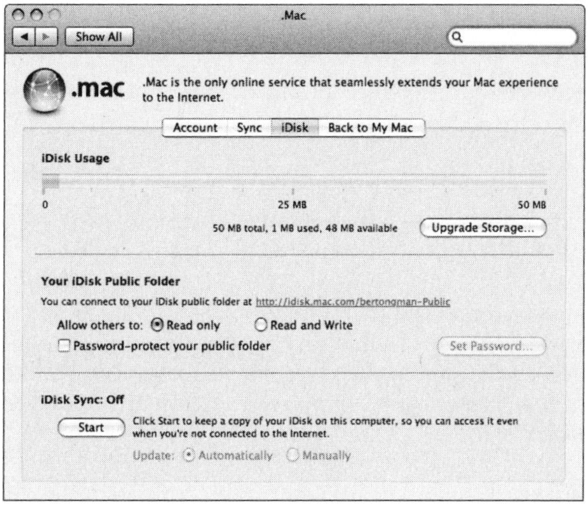

Figure 9-3:
Configure
iDisk within
System
Preferences.

If you use a local copy of your iDisk — and I recommend it — choose to synchronize automatically. This ensures that your files get updated even if you're somewhat forgetful, like I am.

A mirror makes things much faster when you browse your iDisk or when you save and load documents from your iDisk. Leopard actually uses your local copy from your hard drive, and then updates your remote iDisk files in the background while you work. (Leopard is updating your iDisk whenever you see that animated circular-yin-yang-thinglet rotating next to your iDisk icon in the Finder window. You'll know it when you see it.)

Monitoring and configuring your iDisk

The iDisk pane in System Preferences groups all the configuration settings that you can make to your iDisk and your .Mac account. In this section, I review the controls that you can find here.

Disk space

Concerned about how much of your 100MB (for trial users) or 10GB (for subscribers) remains? The iDisk panel (refer to Figure 9-3) includes the Disk Usage bar graph, which always displays how much of your iDisk space is free. (The bar actually totals only half of your storage because the other half of your iDisk is reserved for e-mail use.)

Public folder

The Finder Go menu includes a shortcut to access another .Mac member's Public folder.

Password

I strongly recommend that you set a password to protect the contents of your Public folder.

This password must be entered by anyone trying to open your Public folder. If you haven't supplied that person with the proper password, he can't open your Public folder. Just that simple. (There's nothing more embarrassing than discovering the bikini shots from your vacation are available for every .Mac user to peruse.)

Here's one drawback to this extra level of security: If you password-protect your Public folder, it can't be used to store anything that you offer on your .Mac Web pages.

Settings

While you're in the iDisk panel, you can configure your Public folder security settings. You can decide whether others should be able to

✔ **Only read the contents of your Public folder.**

By default, the Public folder is set to Read Only.

✔ **Copy documents to your Public folder.**

To give others the ability to save and copy, select the Read and Write radio button.

Backing Up Your Treasured Laptop Stuff

My editors have heard me drone on and on long enough about how important it is to back up your hard drive. They probably rub their eyes when they encounter yet another instance of my preaching about *the wages of backup sloth* and *losing everything but hindsight.*

Well, you're lucky, because I was just about to launch into another round of backup warnings. .Mac subscribers get a great utility application called *Backup* when they join the club. Backup is a great application that saves a copy of your treasured data on just about any media on the planet, including

✔ Your iDisk (using the Backup folder that I discuss earlier in this chapter)

✔ An external USB or a FireWire hard drive

✔ Recordable CD or DVD media

✔ Network servers

✔ Your iPod

Before you get too enthusiastic about backing up to your iPod, heed this: You can indeed back up to your iPod (or I wouldn't have listed it as an option), but your iPod's tiny hard drive isn't meant to handle the same serious thrashing as a full-size external hard drive. Personally, I've never used my iPod as a backup destination, and I don't recommend that you do, either, unless no other recording media is handy and you absolutely have to have a backup.

If you'd like an offline copy of your data that would survive a catastrophe like a fire or theft, consider using both Time Machine and Backup. That way, your stuff is covered in the WCS (short for *worst case scenario*). I cover Time Machine — Leopard's awesome new automatic backup system — in Chapter 21.

Installing Backup

Backup isn't built into Leopard; you have to download it from the .Mac site at www.apple.com/dotmac. After the image file is mounted on your Desktop, you see the Backup installation folder. Double-click the Backup.pkg file to begin the installation. After installation is complete, you can find Backup in your Applications folder.

Saving your stuff

Nothing is more important to a proud MacBook owner than a secure backup. In this section, I demonstrate how you can produce both *manual* backups (produced whenever you like) and *automated* backups (which are scheduled at regular intervals). **Do it!**

Remember that you're limited to 50MB of data storage with a trial .Mac membership! The other 50MB is dedicated to your .Mac e-mail account. (I'm still talking about several hundred JPEG images that can fit in 50MB, but that total isn't much when you consider digital video or your iTunes Library.)

Beginning a backup is as easy as marking the check boxes next to the items that you want to safeguard. These are the default Backup Plans available, and they're already scheduled to start automatically.

After you enable the check boxes for the items you want to back up, follow these steps to start a manual backup:

1. **Click Continue to display the Backup main window.**

   Notice that each backup plan you selected on the previous screen has a scheduled time assigned to it for automatic operation.

2. **Click the plan you want to select it; then click Back Up.**

The rest is cake as your irreplaceable stuff is saved to your iDisk.

If you ever need to restore from your backup, click the desired plan to select it, and then click the Restore button. Backup leads you through the restore process with the same aplomb.

The Backup application itself doesn't need to be running for the automated backup to kick off, but keep in mind that your laptop must remain awake! Make sure that

- ✔ You're logged in.
- ✔ Sleep mode is completely disabled on the Energy Saver pane within System Preferences.
- ✔ Your computer has an active Internet connection.

Publishing a Web Site with HomePage

HomePage is a very popular feature for .Mac members. Most MacBook owners aren't Web page designers, after all, and HomePage is extremely easy to use. Apple is smart enough to let trial .Mac members use HomePage; you can try it before you decide to invest in a .Mac subscription.

Follow these steps to create a new Web page on your .Mac site with HomePage:

1. **Launch Safari and visit** www.apple.com/dotmac.

2. **Click the Log In link.**

   Safari prompts you for your .Mac member name and password.

3. **Click the HomePage link at the top of the .Mac Welcome page.**

   The HomePage top-level page that you see in Figure 9-4 appears.

Figure 9-4:
Good call!
You're about
to create a
.Mac Web
page.

4. **Choose a theme for your page from the tabbed display at the left of the screen.**

   Some of the categories are specially designed for certain chores. For example, the Photo Album theme collection is perfect for showing off your digital photographs online, and the File Sharing category presents an easy downloading format for your visitors. Each of these different categories displays different onscreen instructions that are specific to their use.

   For an elegant site where you show off your best photography online, click the Formal frame in the Photo Album category.

5. **Choose the folder with the photos you want to include on the page.**

   This can be either your iDisk Pictures folder or a subfolder that you created within it.

6. **Click Choose.**

   HomePage loads all the images in the selected folder.

7. **Mark the Show check box for each image that you want to appear.**

8. **Drag the image thumbnails to the order that you want.**

9. **Select the text boxes to add**

   • The Web page title

   • An introductory sentence (or two)

   • The titles for each photo

You can display a *counter* (which tallies how many visitors came to your page) and an e-mail button (so your visitors can send a message to your .Mac e-mail account). To use either of these features, just mark the corresponding Show check box to enable it.

10. **Click Preview in the toolbar at the top of the page to see what your page will look like.**

If the page you see in Preview mode isn't up to snuff, click the Back button on the Safari Toolbar to edit it.

11. **If you like what you see, click the Publish button.**

   Huzzah! You're a Web page designer! (Insert sound of champagne cork popping here.)

   HomePage displays your new Web page address, which you can click to jump directly to your new work of art.

The steps to create a page vary by category. However, the only category that really requires any rocket science is the Advanced tab, which allows you to use your own HTML files that you copy to your iDisk Sites folder. Not to worry, though: Just follow the onscreen instructions for creating a Web site with your own HTML files, and you'll be fine.

Chapter 10

Spiffy Connections for the Road Warrior

....

In This Chapter

▶ Adding a printer or a scanner to your MacBook

▶ Using Photo Booth

▶ Putting Front Row to work

▶ Watching cable or satellite TV on your laptop

....

*T*his chapter is all about getting interesting things into — and out of — your MacBook. Some are more common (almost mundane these days) and pretty easy to take care of, such as scanners and printers. Then I might surprise you with something new to you, like your laptop's built-in video camera, which is built into your laptop and the perfect companion to Photo Booth.

I also show you how to turn your road warrior into a photo booth, and how to use an Apple Remote to control your MacBook or MacBook Pro wirelessly using Leopard's Front Row application. Heck, I'll even describe how you can pull that fancy satellite or cable TV signal into your laptop.

Sure, you can connect your MacBook Pro to a printer and do some serious work — but then again, you could also snap your photo and send it to your friends as an e-mail attachment or upload it to your blog. Decisions, decisions!

Connecting Printers

All hail the USB port! It's the primary connection point for all sorts of goodies. In this section, I concentrate on adding a local USB printer and the basics of adding a network printer to your system. (You find more on connecting a wireless Bluetooth printer in Chapter 18.)

USB printers

Connecting a USB printer to your MacBook is duck soup. Don't you wish all things in life were this easy? You might very well be able to skip most of the steps in this section entirely, depending on whether your printer came with an installation disc. (Virtually all do, of course, but you might have bought yours used, say from eBay.)

Your printer needs to be fully supported within Mac OS X:

- ✔ If the software is designed for earlier versions of Mac OS X (say, v. 10.3 or v. 10.4), it probably works with Leopard.

- ✔ I always recommend visiting the manufacturer's Web site to download the latest printer driver and support software *before* you install your printer. That way, you know that you're up to date. (Don't forget to check the Read Me file that accompanies your new software to make sure there are no new system requirements!)

Save and close open files and applications before installing your printer. You might have to restart your laptop to complete the installation.

The physical connections for your printer are pretty simple:

1. **Make sure that your printer's USB cable is plugged in to both your laptop and the printer itself.**

2. **After the USB connection is made, plug the printer in to an AC wall socket and turn it on.**

Don't forget to add the paper and check the cartridge(s)!

The finishing printer installation steps depend on whether you have a manufacturer's installation CD for your printer.

Sure, I've got the install disc

If your printer comes with its manufacturer's installation disc, follow these steps when everything is connected and powered on:

1. **Insert the installation disc in the laptop.**

   The disc contents usually appear in a Finder window. If they don't, double-click the installation disc icon on the Desktop to open the window.

   If you're using a MacBook Air, you need to use either the external SuperDrive or a computer with an optical drive on your local network.

2. **Double-click the installation application to start the ball rolling.**

3. **Follow the onscreen instructions.**

   Files get copied to your hard drive.

   You might have to restart your MacBook.

You're ready to print!

Don't forget to visit your printer manufacturer's Web site to check whether any driver updates are available for your particular model.

Whoops, I've got diddly-squat (Software-wise)

Didn't get an installation CD? Try installing the printer without software, or download the software from the manufacturer's Web site.

Installing without software

If you didn't get an installation CD with your printer, you might be lucky enough that your printer's driver was included in your installation of Mac OS X. First, press ⌘+P within an application to display the Print dialog, and see whether the printer you connected is already recognized.

If it's not displayed, here's how to check for that pesky driver after you connect the printer and switch it on:

1. **Open the System Preferences window.**

2. **Click the Print & Fax icon.**

3. **Click the Add button (which sports a plus sign).**

4. **Check the Printer list in the Printer Setup Utility window to see whether your printer has already been added automatically within Leopard.**

   If your printer appears here, dance a celebratory jig. You can close System Preferences and choose that printer from the Print dialog in your applications. You can set it as the default from the System Preferences Print & Fax pane; just click the Default Printer pop-up menu to select your new printer.

Downloading software

If you don't have installation software and your laptop doesn't automatically match your USB printer with a driver, it's time to check the Internet to locate a Leopard-compatible driver for your printer.

Check the manufacturer's Web site for your printer's software. Look for

✔ **Special software drivers that the printer might need**

Install any drivers you find *before* you run an installation application. Otherwise, the installation app might not be able to recognize or configure the printer if the driver hasn't been installed first.

✔ **Installation application**

If the manufacturer offers an installation application for your printer, download the application and run it.

Networked printers

Your wired or wireless Ethernet network provides a quick and easy way to share any printer that's connected to your MacBook. Follow these steps to share your printers across the network with others:

1. **Click the System Preferences icon on the Dock.**

2. **Click the Sharing icon.**

3. **Select the On check box next to the Printer Sharing service entry.**

4. **Click the Close button to exit System Preferences.**

In most cases, a printer that you share automatically appears in the Print dialog on other computers connected to your network. Therefore, if you want to access a printer being shared by another Mac across your network, open the Print dialog within your application and click the Printer pop-up menu to select it.

If the remote printer isn't listed automatically, you can dig a little further. To add a printer that another Mac on your network is sharing to your list of printers, follow these steps:

1. **Click System Preferences on the Dock.**

2. **Click the Print & Fax icon.**

3. **Click the Add button (which carries a plus sign).**

4. **Click the Default button on the toolbar.**

Leopard displays all the available local shared printers. Click the desired printer and then click Add.

Connecting Scanners

USB and FireWire scanners practically install themselves. As long as the model is listed as Mac OS X-compatible (check the system requirements on the scanner's box or on the manufacturer's Web site for compatible computers) and it supports the TWAIN device standard (just about all scanners do), things really *are* plug-and-play.

The MacBook Air doesn't have a FireWire port, so it's a USB-only ticket.

If you have the scanner manufacturer's installation disc, go ahead and use it. However, most scanners don't require specialized drivers, so even that orphan model that you picked up from Uncle Milton last year should work (if it's recognized by Mac OS X). It doesn't hurt to check the manufacturer's Web site to see whether any of the software has been updated since the disc was produced.

If Mac OS X doesn't support your older scanner, a third-party application might be able to help. Get thee hence to Hamrick Software at www.hamrick.com and download a copy of the latest version of VueScan. This great scanning application supports over 750 scanner models, including a number that don't work with Leopard otherwise. At $40, it's a world-class bargain to boot.

Ready to go? Make sure that your scanner is powered on and connected to your laptop (and that you load a page or photograph to scan). If your scanner's installation disc provided you with a proprietary scanning application, I recommend that you use that application to test your scanner. In fact, it's Mark's Maxim time!

If your printer or scanner includes bundled applications, *use them!*™

Sure, Mac OS X has the Print & Fax pane within System Preferences for printers and the Image Capture application for scanners and digital cameras, but these are bare-bones tools compared with the print manager and image acquisition software that comes bundled with your hardware. I turn to Leopard's built-in hardware handling stuff only when I don't have anything better.

Hey, I'm not saying that anything's wrong with Image Capture, which is in your Applications folder, if you need to use it. However, don't expect Image Capture to support any specialized features offered by your scanner (like one-button e-mail or Web publishing). You have to use the application especially designed for your manufacturer and model to take advantage of any extras that it offers.

Using Photo Booth and Front Row

Many Apple switchers and first-time owners quickly notice that tiny square lens and LED light at the top of the MacBook's svelte frame. You might also have received a device that looks like a stick of chewing gum with buttons. What gives?

First, allow me to identify these toys. The former is the lens of your laptop's built-in iSight camera, which allows you to capture video or snap a quick fun series of photos via Leopard's Photo Booth application. The latter is an Apple Remote, which you can use to control your MacBook from the comfort of your lounge chair or breakfast nook via Leopard's Front Row software.

If your MacBook didn't come with an Apple Remote, you can pick one up on Apple's Web site. Note, however, that the MacBook Air is not compatible with the Apple Remote because the Air model doesn't have an infrared sensor.

Capturing the moment with Photo Booth

What's that you say? You've never used a computer video camera? Well then, good reader, you've come to the right place!

The iSight camera's indicator light (see Figure 10-1) glows green whenever you're taking a snapshot or recording video . . . which, when you think about it, is A Good Thing (especially if you prefer chatting at home in Leisure Mode).

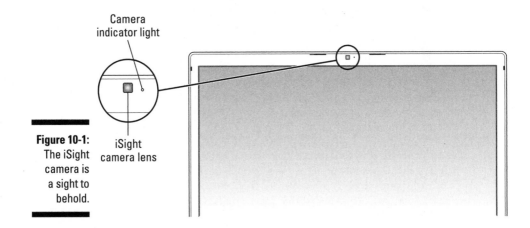

Camera
indicator light

iSight
camera lens

Figure 10-1:
The iSight
camera is
a sight to
behold.

TIP

If you need a quick picture of yourself for use on your Web page, or perhaps your iChat icon needs an update to show off your new haircut, use Photo Booth to capture images at 640 x 480 resolution and 32-bit color. Although today's digital cameras can produce a much higher-quality photo, you can't beat the built-in convenience of Photo Booth for that quick snapshot!

To snap an image in Photo Booth, follow these steps:

1. **Launch Photo Booth from the Dock or from the Applications folder.**

   Check out that glowing LED!

2. **(Optional) Click Effects button to choose an effect that you'd like to apply to your image.**

   Photo Booth displays four screens of thumbnail preview images. Each screen displays nine thumbnails (see Figure 10-2) so that you can see how each effect changes the photo. To move through the thumbnail screens, click the Previous and Next arrow buttons that appear around the Effects button.

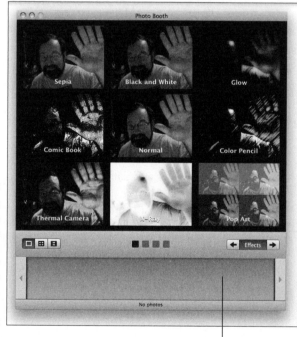

Figure 10-2:
Photo Booth does one thing particularly well — candid photography.

Film strip viewer

You can produce some of the simple effects you might be familiar with from Photoshop (such as a black-and-white image or a fancy, colored pencil filter), but it can also deliver some mind-blowing distortion effects, and even an Andy Warhol–style pop-art image!

Of course, you can always launch your favorite image editor afterward to use a filter or effect on a photo — for example, the effects available in iPhoto — but Photo Booth can apply these effects automatically as soon as you take the picture.

3. (Optional) Click a thumbnail to select the desired effect.

To return the display to normal, click the Normal thumbnail, which appears in the center. (Um, that would be Paul Lynde's spot, for those of you old enough to remember *Hollywood Squares.*)

4. Click the Camera button.

The image appears in the film strip at the bottom of the window.

Photo Booth keeps a copy of all the images you take in the film strip so that you can use them later. After you click a photo in the film strip, a series of buttons appear, inviting you take any one of a series of actions, including

- ✔ Sending the photo in an e-mail message
- ✔ Saving the photo directly to iPhoto
- ✔ Using the image as your Leopard user account icon
- ✔ Using the image as your iChat Buddy icon

To delete an image from the Photo Booth filmstrip, click the offending photo and then click the X button that appears underneath.

If you're itching to connect a USB digital camera for use with iPhoto, let me redirect you to Chapter 12, where I cover the iPhoto experience in depth.

To capture a video clip, click the Movie Clip button (which bears frames from an old-fashioned movie reel) at the lower left of the Photo Booth window. Click the Big Red Movie Button to start recording, and again to end the clip.

Controlling your laptop remotely with Front Row

Okay, you've seen some neat stuff so far, but things get *really* cool about now! With Apple's Front Row software, you can turn your MacBook into a multimedia presentation center that can show off all your digital media to your adoring public (and friends and family to boot). In fact, with the Apple Remote, you don't even have to leave the comfort of the couch to start the show.

The Front Row application performs four different functions:

✔ **Watching DVD movies with DVD Player:** If you already loaded a DVD into your optical drive, you can watch it. (Sorry, your MacBook doesn't load the DVD for you. I guess *some* things have to remain manually driven for a few years yet.) Naturally, MacBook Air owners need an external SuperDrive to watch movies from a disc.

✔ **Viewing photos and slide shows:** Front Row calls upon iPhoto so that you can see your albums, film rolls, and slideshows.

✔ **Displaying videos in QuickTime Player:** You can choose any video you download from the iTunes Music Store or save to your Movies folder.

✔ **Coaxing your favorite music, podcasts, and TV shows from your iTunes library:** Find your media and playlists available from Front Row.

All this is accomplished by using the awesome, infrared Apple Remote you see in Figure 10-3. If your last computer — the beige box — didn't *have* a remote control, don't panic. It's as simple to use as an iPod Shuffle!

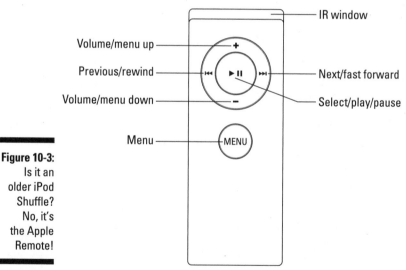

Volume/menu up

Previous/rewind

Volume/menu down

Menu

IR window

Next/fast forward

Select/play/pause

MENU

Figure 10-3:
Is it an older iPod Shuffle? No, it's the Apple Remote!

TIP

To launch the application, press the Menu button on the remote. As long as your laptop is on, Front Row runs automatically. To put your MacBook to sleep after a night of fun, press and hold the Select/Play/Pause button.

Table 10-1 includes the important functions of the Apple Remote in Front Row.

Table 10-1	Using the Apple Remote in Front Row
Action	*Purpose*
Menu	Press to launch Front Row or to return to the previous menu.
Volume/Menu Down	Press to navigate down through menu options or to lower the volume while media is playing.
Volume/Menu Up	Press to navigate up through menu options or to raise the volume while media is playing.
Select/Play/Pause	Press to select a menu item, or play or pause media from within iTunes, DVD Player, QuickTime, or iPhoto.
Next/Fast Forward	Press to skip to the next song or DVD chapter, or hold down to fast-forward through a song.
Previous/Rewind	Press to skip to the previous song or DVD chapter, or hold down to rewind a song.

You can also go the mundane route and use keyboard shortcuts to control Front Row (but it's nowhere near as cool). Table 10-2 explains the keyboard shortcuts.

Table 10-2	Using the Keyboard in Front Row
Action	*Keyboard Equivalent*
Menu	⌘+Esc to enter the menu; Esc to exit it
Volume/Menu Down	Down arrow (↓)
Volume/Menu Up	Up arrow (↑)
Select/Play/Pause	Spacebar or Return
Next/Fast Forward	Right arrow (→)
Previous/Rewind	Left arrow (←)

Note that Front Row has no complex configuration. Front Row is what designers call a *front-end application;* that is, it launches the Leopard applications necessary to display or play the media you select. (There is a simple Settings menu in Front Row, offering you the chance to toggle your screen saver and menu sound effects off or on. Both options are turned on by default.)

Your Apple Remote isn't designed to work with any other third-party applications at the time of this writing. For example, you can't use it as a presentation aid in PowerPoint. However, some Apple applications do recognize the Apple Remote (like Keynote), and it's a sure bet that Apple will continue to add functionality to the Apple Remote in the future. Check the Apple Remote section of Leopard's online Help system to keep tabs on what's happening!

Using iSight with iChat AV

Although your MacBook comes ready for videoconferencing, you should understand two caveats before embarking on the Voyage of Video Chat:

✔ **Speed is an issue.** To take advantage of video in iChat AV, you need a fast Internet connection — at least high-speed DSL or cable Internet, or even a connection between computers on the same network.

✔ **All participants need a video camera.** Plenty of folks online have suddenly realized that most of their iChat AV buddies didn't have video capability!

Even though your laptop has an iSight camera installed, you can still join text-based and audio chats. (Your Mac has a built-in microphone, so even if your online buddies aren't equipped with video hardware, you can enjoy an audio chat.) iChat AV displays audio and video buttons next to each person on your buddy list to help you keep track of who can communicate with you and how they can do it.

Starting a video chat is as simple as launching iChat AV from the Dock (or from your Application folder). Then in the buddy list, click any buddy entry with a Camera button next to it to connect. Wave hello for me!

Turning Your MacBook into a TV — And More

Your laptop's beautiful LCD screen would seem to be the perfect artist's canvas for watching live cable or satellite TV broadcasts, but there's no coaxial (coax) input on the back of your computer. Therefore, unless you invest in some additional hardware, you're restricted to watching DVD movies (using your optical drive) or watching movies and TV shows that you downloaded from the iTunes Store.

Such an obvious need is going to be filled quickly, and a number of different hardware manufacturers have produced external devices that can merge your MacBook and your TV signal. Most are USB or FireWire peripherals, and many have all the features of today's TiVo and digital video recorders.

My favorite example is the EyeTV Hybrid, from Elgato Systems (www.elgato.com), which uses a USB connection (so it's suitable for use with the MacBook Air). Check out what this superstar includes for your investment of $150.

✔ Built-in NTSC (analog) and ATSC (digital TV) tuners, cable-ready with a coaxial connector

✔ The ability to pause, fast-forward, record, or even edit the video you stored on your laptop's hard drive

✔ Capability to schedule recordings with an onscreen program guide

✔ Full-screen TV display or in a window anywhere on your Desktop

✔ No external power supply required

I really love the ability to fast-forward through commercials, and I can take anything that I record on my MacBook Pro and use it in iDVD and iMovie. The addition of TV under your control sorta finalizes the whole digital hub thing, now doesn't it?

Part IV
Living the iLife

The 5th Wave   By Rich Tennant

Okay, enlarge the chicken bone by 900 percent and attach it to an e-mail to the museum saying, "Getting close...send more money."

In this part . . .

Here they are, the applications that everyone craves. This part covers iTunes, iPhoto, iMovie, iDVD, and GarageBand like your Grandma's best quilt. You discover how to share your images, music, and video clips among the iLife '08 applications on your Mac laptop and how to create everything from your own DVDs to a truly awesome hardcover photo album!

Chapter 11

The Multimedia Joy of iTunes

In This Chapter

▶ Playing music with your laptop

▶ Arranging and organizing your music collection

▶ Tuning into the world with Internet radio

▶ Creating eye candy with the Visualizer

▶ Buying the good stuff from the iTunes Store

Sometimes, words just aren't enough. iTunes is that kind of perfection.

To envision how iTunes changes your relationship with your MacBook, you have to paint the picture with *music* — music that's easy to play, easy to search, and easy to transfer from place to place. Whether it be classical, alternative, jazz, rock, hip-hop, or folk, I can guarantee you that you won't find a better application than iTunes to fill your life with your music.

Whoops, I almost forgot: and podcasts. And video. And TV shows. And Internet radio. (See how hard it is to pin down this wonderful application? Along with your laptop, iTunes really does form the hub of your digital lifestyle.)

In this chapter, I lead you through all the features of my absolute favorite member of the iLife '08 suite . . . and it's going to be pretty doggone obvious how much I appreciate this one piece of software.

What Can I Play on iTunes?

Simply put, *iTunes* is a media player: It plays both audio and video files, which can come in many different formats. Some of the more common audio formats that iTunes supports are

✔ **MP3:** The small size of MP3 files has made them popular for file trading on the Internet. You can reduce MP3 files to a ridiculously small size (albeit at the expense of audio fidelity), but a typical CD-quality, three-minute pop song in MP3 format has a size of 3–5MB.

✔ **AAC:** *AAC* (short for Advanced Audio Coding) is an audio format that's very similar to MP3; in fact, AAC files offer better recording quality at the same file sizes. However, this format also supports a built-in, copy-protection scheme that prevents AAC music from being widely distributed on Macs. (Luckily, you can still burn AAC tracks to an audio CD, just like MP3 tracks.) The tracks that you download from the iTunes Store are in AAC format.

The iTunes Store's iTunes Plus tracks are also in AAC format, but these tracks are not copy-protected, and they're encoded at a higher-quality 256 Kbps rate. You can listen to your iTunes Plus tracks on as many Macs as you like.

✔ **Apple Lossless:** Another format directly from Apple, *Apple Lossless* format provides the best compromise between file size and sound quality. These tracks are encoded without loss of quality: hence the name, as opposed to "lossy" compression schemes, such as MP3. However, Apple Lossless tracks, which are somewhat larger than AAC files, are generally considered the favorite of the most discerning audiophile for their entire music library.

✔ **AIFF:** This standard Macintosh audio format produces sound of the absolute highest quality. This high quality, however, also means that the files are pretty doggone huge. A typical pop song in AIFF format has a size of 30–50MB.

✔ **WAV:** Not to be outdone, Microsoft created its own audio file format (WAV) that works much like AIFF. It can reproduce sound at higher quality than MP3, but the file sizes are very large, like AIFF.

✔ **CD audio:** iTunes can play audio CDs. Because you don't usually store CD audio anywhere but on an audio CD, file size is no big whoop.

✔ **Movies and video:** You can buy and download full-length movies, TV shows, music videos, and movie trailers from the iTunes Store. And, with an Apple TV unit connected to your home theater system, you can watch those movies and videos from the comfort of your sofa on the other side of your house.

✔ **Podcasts:** These relatively new programs are like radio programs for your iPod, but iTunes can play and organize them, too. Some podcasts also include video and photos, to boot.

✔ **Audiobooks:** No longer do you need cassettes or audio CDs to enjoy your spoken books. iTunes can play audiobooks for you, or you can send them to your iPod for listening on the go.

✔ **Streaming Internet radio:** You can listen to a continuous broadcast of songs from one of tens of thousands of Internet radio stations, with quality levels ranging from what you'd expect from FM radio to the full quality of an audio CD. You can't save the music in iTunes, but it's still great fun. (In fact, I run my own station . . . more on MLC Radio later in the chapter.)

Playing an Audio CD

Playing an audio CD in iTunes is simple. Just insert the CD in your laptop's optical drive, start iTunes by clicking its icon on the Dock, and then click the Play button. (Note that your MacBook might be set to automatically launch iTunes when you insert an audio CD.) The iTunes interface resembles that of a traditional cassette or CD player. The main playback controls of the iTunes display are Previous, Play, Next, and the volume slider, as shown in Figure 11-1.

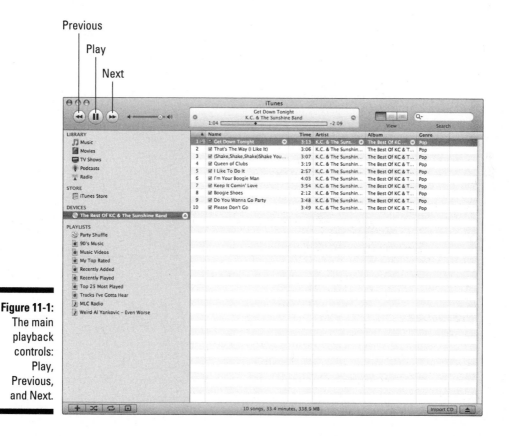

Figure 11-1:
The main playback controls: Play, Previous, and Next.

Click the Play button to begin listening to a song. While a song is playing, the Play button toggles to a Pause button. As you might imagine, clicking that button again pauses the music. If you don't feel like messing around with your trackpad, you can always use the keyboard. The spacebar acts as the Play and Pause buttons. Press the spacebar to begin playback; press it again to stop.

Click the Next button to advance to the next song on the CD. The Previous button works like the Next button but with a slight twist: If a song is playing and you click the Previous button, iTunes first returns to the beginning of the current song (just like an audio CD player). To advance to the previous song, double-click the Previous button. To change the volume of your music, click and drag the volume slider.

Like other Macintosh applications, you can control much of iTunes with the keyboard. Table 11-1 lists some of the more common iTunes keyboard shortcuts. (Note that iTunes must be the active application for these shortcuts to work.)

Table 11-1	Common iTunes Keyboard Shortcuts
Press This Key/Key Combination	*To Do This*
Spacebar	Play the selected song if iTunes is idle.
Spacebar	Pause the music if a song is playing.
Right-arrow key (→)	Advance to the next song.
Left-arrow key (←)	Go back to the beginning of a song. Press a second time to return to the previous song.
⌘+up-arrow key (↑)	Increase the volume.
⌘+down-arrow key (↓)	Decrease the volume.
⌘+Option+down-arrow key (↓)	Mute the audio, if any is playing. Press again to play the audio.

Playing Digital Audio and Video

In addition to playing audio CDs, iTunes can also play the digital audio files that you download from the Internet or obtain from other sources in the WAV, AAC, Apple Lossless, AIFF, and MP3 file formats. (You can read about these formats earlier in this chapter.)

Enjoying a digital audio file is just slightly more complicated than playing a CD. After downloading or saving your audio files to your laptop, open the Finder and navigate to wherever you stored the files. Then simply drag the music files (or an entire folder of music) from the Finder onto the Music entry in the iTunes Source list, on the left side of the iTunes window.

The added files appear in the iTunes Music Library. Think of the Music Library as a master list of your music. To view the Music Library, select the Music entry in the left-hand column of the iTunes player, as shown in Figure 11-2. Go figure.

Heck, you can also drag a song file from a Finder window and drop it on the iTunes icon in the Dock, which adds it to your Music Library as well.

If you drop the file on top of a playlist name in the Source list, iTunes adds it to that particular playlist as well as the main Library. (More about playlists in a bit.)

To play a song, just double-click it in the Music Library list. Alternatively, you can click the song once to select it and use the playback controls (Previous, Play, and Next) that I discuss earlier in this chapter. (Refer to Figure 11-1.)

The Source list of iTunes can list up to six possible sources for audio.

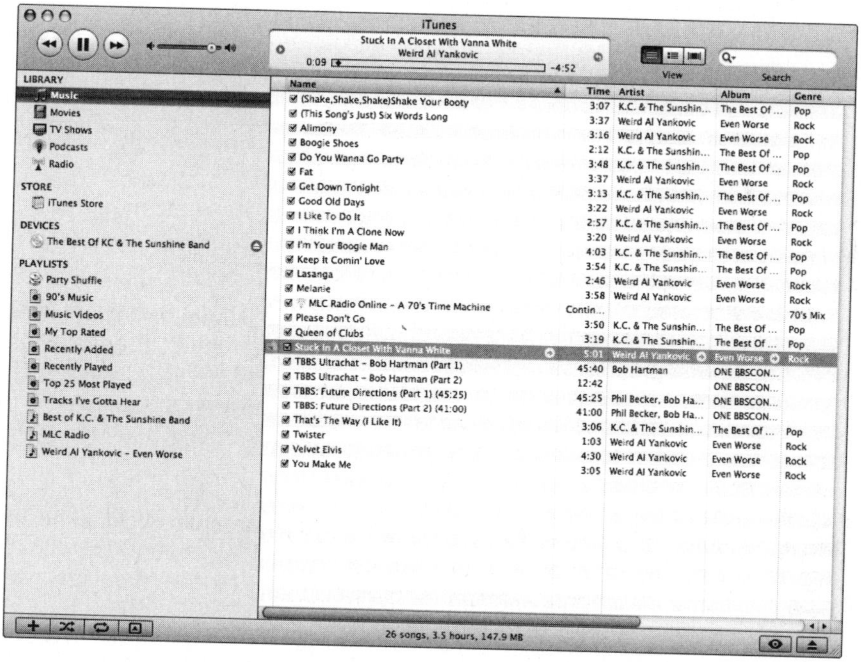

Figure 11-2:
The Music Library keeps track of all your audio files.

✔ **Library:** This section includes Music, Movies, TV Shows, Podcasts, Audiobooks, iPod Games, and Radio. (Think *Internet radio,* which I discuss further in the section, "iTunes Radio.") Discerning readers will note that Figure 11-2 doesn't show Audiobooks: That's because I don't have any loaded.

✔ **iPod:** If an iPod is connected, it appears in the list. (And yes, Virginia, other models of MP3 players from other companies also appear in the list if they support iTunes.)

✔ **iTunes Store:** I discuss this later in the section, "Buying Billie Holiday from the Apple Music Store."

✔ **Audio CD:** A standard audio CD . . . anything from the Bee Gees to Fall Out Boy.

✔ **Shared music:** If another Mac on your local network is running iTunes and is set to share part (or all) of its library, you can connect to the other computer for your music. (Shared music on another Mac appears as a separate named folder in the Source list.) Of course, you can elect to share your music with others as well.

✔ **Playlists:** Think of playlists as folders that you use to organize your music. (More on playlists later in this chapter.)

Notice also that the Library lists information for each song that you add to it, such as

✔ **Name:** The title of the song

✔ **Time:** The length of the song

✔ **Artist:** Who performs the song

✔ **Album:** The album on which the song appears

Most MP3 files have embedded data — title, album, or artist information, for example — that iTunes can read, but don't panic if those fields are blank or generic right now. If a song doesn't include any data, you can always add the information to these fields manually. I show you how later in the section, "Setting or changing the song information manually."

Clicking any of the column headings in the Library causes iTunes to reorder the Library according to that category. For example, clicking the Name column heading alphabetizes your Library by song title (and another click reverses the order). Oh, and you can drag column titles to reorder them any way you like.

iTunes can display your Music Library in three ways: By default, the application uses the list view that you see in Figure 11-1, where each song is one entry. Click the second View button (at the top of the iTunes window) to group tracks together by album. Click the third View button (Cover Flow), and you're browsing by album cover, complete with reflective surface!

In fact, you can even browse full-screen in Cover Flow mode. Click the Full-Screen button at the lower right of the cover pane — it looks like a box with arrows at each corner — and iTunes switches to full-screen mode, complete with those familiar play controls.

Browsing the Library

After you add a few dozen songs to iTunes, viewing the Library can become a task. Although a master list is nice for some purposes, it becomes as cumbersome as an elephant in a subway tunnel if the list is very long. To help out, iTunes can display your Library in another format, too: namely, browsing mode. To view the Library in browsing mode, click the Browse button at the lower-right corner of the iTunes window, which carries an eye icon.

The Browse mode of iTunes displays your library in a compact fashion, organizing your tunes into four sections:

- ✔ **Genre**
- ✔ **Artist**
- ✔ **Album**
- ✔ **Name**

Selecting an artist from the Artist list causes iTunes to display that artist's albums in the Album list. Select an album from the Album list, and iTunes displays that album's songs in the bottom section of the Browse window. (Those Apple software designers . . . always thinking of you and me.) Note that the Browse button is disabled in Cover Flow view mode.

Will I trash my Count Basie?

Novice iTunes users, take note: iTunes watches your back when you trash tracks.

To illustrate: Suppose you try to delete a song from the Library that's located only in the iTunes Music folder (which you didn't copy into iTunes from another location on your hard drive). That means you're about to delete the song entirely, with no copy remaining on your MacBook. Rest assured, though, that iTunes will prompt you to make sure that you really want to move the file to the Trash. (I get fearful e-mail messages all the time from readers who are loath to delete anything from iTunes because they're afraid they'll trash their digital music files completely.)

If you delete a song from the Library *that exists elsewhere on your hard drive* (outside the reach of the iTunes Music folder), it isn't deleted from your hard drive. In fact, if you mistakenly remove a song that you meant to keep, just drag it back into iTunes from the Finder, or even from the Trash. 'Nuff said.

Finding songs in your Music Library

After your collection of audio files grows large, you might have trouble locating that Swedish remix version of "I'm Your Boogie Man." To help you out, iTunes has a built-in Search function. To find a song, type some text into the search field of the main iTunes window. While you type, iTunes tries to find a selection that matches your search text. The search is quite thorough, showing any matching text from the artist, album, song title, and genre fields in the results.

For example, if you type **Electronic** into the field, iTunes might return results for the band named *Electronic* or other tunes that you classified as *electronic* in the Genre field. (The upcoming section, "Know Your Songs," tells you how to classify your songs by genre, among other options.) Click the magnifying glass at the left side of the Search field to restrict the search even more: by Artists, Albums, Composers, and Songs.

Removing old music from the Library

After you spend some time playing songs with iTunes, you might decide that you didn't really want to add 40 different versions of "Louie Louie" to your Library. (Personally, I prefer either the original or the cast from the movie *Animal House*.) To remove a song from the Library, click the song to select it and then press the Delete key on your keyboard. (If that sounds a bit daunting, check out the sidebar titled, "Will I trash my Count Basie?")

Watching video

Watching video in iTunes is similar to listening to your music. To view your video collection, click one of these entries in the Source list:

- ✔ **Movies**
- ✔ **Music Videos**
- ✔ **Video Podcasts**
- ✔ **TV Shows**

If you select Movies or TV Shows, iTunes displays your videos as thumbnails. Music Videos appear as a standard playlist.

From your collection, you can

- ✔ **Double-click a video thumbnail or an entry in the list.**
- ✔ **Drag any QuickTime-compatible video clip from the Finder window to the iTunes window.**

  These typically include video files ending in `.mov` or `.mp4`.

iTunes plays video full-screen, but when you move your finger across your trackpad, a control strip appears, sporting a standard slider bar that you can drag to move through the video (as well as a volume control and Fast Forward/Reverse buttons). You can also pause the video by clicking the Pause button.

Keeping Slim Whitman and Slim Shady Apart: Organizing with Playlists

Given time, your iTunes Music Library can quickly become a fearsomely huge beastie. Each Library can contain thousands upon thousands of songs: If your Library grows anywhere near that large, finding all the songs in your lifelong collection of Paul Simon albums is not a fun task. Furthermore, with the Library, if you just click Play you're stuck listening to songs in the order that iTunes lists them.

To help you organize your music into groups, use the iTunes playlist feature. A *playlist* is a collection of some of your favorite songs from the Library. You can create as many playlists as you want, and each playlist can contain any numbers of songs. Whereas the Library lists all available songs, a playlist displays only the songs that you add to it. Further, any changes — deleting a song, for example — that you make to a playlist affect only that playlist, leaving the Library intact.

For example, suppose that you want to plan a party for your polka-loving friends. Instead of running to your computer after each song to change the music, you could create a polka-only playlist. Select and start the playlist at the beginning of the party, and you won't have to worry about changing the music the whole night. (You can concentrate on the accordion.)

To create a playlist, you can do any of the following:

- ✔ **Choose File⇨New Playlist.**
- ✔ **Press ⌘+N.**

✔ **Choose File➪New Playlist from Selection.** This creates a new playlist and automatically adds any tracks that are currently selected in the Library. iTunes also attempts to name the playlist automatically for you.

✔ **Click the New Playlist button in the iTunes window** (the plus sign button in the lower-left corner). You get a newly created empty playlist (the toe-tappin' *untitled playlist*).

All playlists appear in the Source list. To help organize your playlists, it's a good idea to . . . well . . . *name* them. (Aren't you glad now that you have this book?) To load a playlist, select it in the Source list; iTunes displays the songs for that playlist. Click the playlist entry in the source list again to type a new name for the playlist.

To add a song from the library to your new playlist, click the Library and find the song you want to include, and then drag it to the desired playlist entry in the Source list.

The same song can appear in any number of playlists because the songs in a playlist are simply pointers to songs in your Music Library — not the songs themselves. Add and remove them at will to any playlist, secure in the knowledge that the songs remain safe in the Library. As for removing playlists themselves, that's simple, too. Just select the playlist in the Source list and then press Delete.

Removing a playlist doesn't actually delete any songs from your Library.

Some playlists are smarter than others

From the File menu, take a look at a menu command for creating a smart playlist. The contents of a *smart playlist* are automatically created from a specific condition or set of conditions that you specify via the Smart Playlist dialog: You can limit the track selection by mundane things, such as album, genre, or artist; or, you can get funky and specify songs that were played last, or by the date you added tracks, or even by the sampling rate or total length of the song. For example, iTunes can create a playlist packed with songs that are shorter than three minutes, so you can fill your iPod Shuffle with more stuff! Ah, but wait! You're not limited to a single criterion. If you want to add other criterion, click the plus sign at the right side of the dialog, and you get another condition field to refine your selection even further.

You can choose the maximum number of songs to add to the smart playlist; or limit the size of the playlist by the minutes or hours of play, or the number of megabytes or gigabytes the playlist will occupy. (Again, great for automatically gathering as much from your KISS collection that will fit into a specific amount of space on a CD or your iPod.) Mark the Live Updating check box for the ultimate in convenience. iTunes automatically maintains the contents of the smart playlist to keep it current with your conditions at all times in the future. (If you remove tracks manually from a smart playlist, iTunes adds other tracks that match your conditions.)

Click the Party Shuffle playlist, and you encounter a random selection of songs taken from your iTunes Music Library — perfect for your next party! You can change the order of the songs in the Party Shuffle playlist, add songs from your Library, or delete songs that don't fit the scintillating ambience of your gathering. Enjoy!

Know Your Songs

Besides organizing your music into Elvis and non-Elvis playlists, iTunes gives you the option to track your music at the song level. Each song that you add to the Music Library has a complete set of information associated with it. iTunes displays this information in the Info dialog, including

- **Name:** The name of the song
- **Artist:** The name of the artist who performed the song
- **Composer:** The name of the astute individual who actually wrote the song
- **Album Artist:** The name of the artist responsible for a compilation or tribute album
- **Album:** The album where the song appears
- **Grouping:** A group type that you assign
- **Year:** The year when the artist recorded the song
- **BPM:** The beats per minute (which indicates the song's tempo)
- **Track Number:** The position of the song on the original album
- **Disc Number:** The original disc number in a multi-CD set
- **Comments:** A text field that can contain any comments on the song
- **Genre:** The classification of the song (such as rock, jazz, or pop)

You can display this information by clicking a song name and pressing ⌘+I to make the fields appear on the Info tab. Alternatively, you can choose File⇨Get Info.

Setting the song information automatically

Each song that you add to the iTunes Music Library might have song information included with it. If you add music from a commercial audio CD, iTunes connects to a server on the Internet and attempts to find the information for each song on the CD. If you download a song from the Internet, it often comes with some information embedded in the file already; the amount of included information depends on what the creator supplied. (And believe me, it's often misspelled as well — think *Leenard Skeenard*.) If you don't have an Internet connection, iTunes can't access the information and displays generic titles instead.

Internet connection restored? You can download the information on a CD at any time by choosing Advanced⇨Get CD Track Names.

Setting or changing the song information manually

If iTunes can't find your CD in the online database or someone gives you an MP3 with incomplete or inaccurate information, you can change the information yourself — believe me, you want at least the artist and song name! To view and change the information for a song, perform the following steps:

1. **Select the song in either the Music Library list or a playlist.**

2. **Press ⌘+I or choose File⇨Get Info.**

3. **Edit the song's information on the Info tab, as shown in Figure 11-3.**

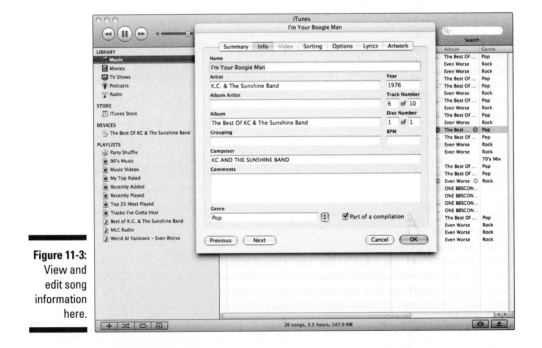

Figure 11-3: View and edit song information here.

Keep in mind that the more work you put into setting the information of the songs in your Music Library, the easier it is to browse and use iTunes. Incomplete song information can make it more difficult to find your songs in a hurry. If you prefer, you don't have to change all information about a song. (It just makes life easier later if you do.) Normally, you can get away with setting only a song's title, artist, and genre. The more information you put in, however, the faster you can locate songs and the easier they are to arrange. iTunes tries to help by automatically retrieving known song information, but sometimes you have to roll up your sleeves and do a little work. (Sorry, but the Data Elves are out to lunch.)

"What about cover art, Mark?" Well, I'm overjoyed that you asked! iTunes displays the artwork in a number of different places (including Album view and Cover Flow view), and the application can try to locate artwork automatically for the tracks you select. (Note that adding large images can significantly increase the size of the song file.) Follow these steps:

1. **Select the desired songs from the track list.**

2. **Choose Advanced⇨Get Album Artwork.**

You can set iTunes to automatically attempt the addition of album artwork every time you rip tracks from an audio CD, or when you add songs without artwork to your Music Library. Click iTunes and choose Preferences. Click the General button and then select the Automatically Download Missing Album Artwork check box to enable it.

Unfortunately, the Get Album Artwork feature often doesn't pull in any artwork for little-known artists. Luckily, you can always add album covers to your song info manually! Select one (or all) of the songs from a single album in the track list, display the Info dialog, and click the Artwork tab. Now launch Safari, visit Amazon.com, and do a search on the same album. Drag the cover image from the Web page right into the Info dialog and then drop it on top of the image well. When you click OK, the image appears in the Summary pane, and you can display it while your music is playing by pressing ⌘+G, or by pressing the Show or Hide Song Artwork button at the lower left of the iTunes window! (Again, adding large images can significantly increase the size of the song file.)

Ripping Audio Files

You don't have to rely on Internet downloads to get audio files: You can create your own MP3, AAC, Apple Lossless, AIFF, and WAV files from your audio CDs with iTunes. (If you have a MacBook Air, you need the external SuperDrive to read audio CDs. Go figure.) The process of converting audio files to different formats is *ripping.* (Audiophiles with technical teeth also call this process *digital extraction,* but they're usually ignored at parties by the popular crowd.)

Depending on what hardware or software you use, you're likely to encounter differences in formats. For example, most iPod owners prefer MP3 or AAC files, but your audio CDs aren't in that format. Being able to convert files from one format to another is like having a personal translator in the digital world. You don't need to worry if you have the wrong format: You can simply convert it to the format that you need.

The most common type of ripping involves converting CD audio to MP3 format. To rip MP3s from an audio CD, follow these simple steps:

1. **Launch iTunes by clicking its icon on the Dock.**

   Alternatively, you can locate it in your Applications folder.

2. **Choose iTunes⇨Preferences.**

3. **In the Preferences window that appears, click the Advanced toolbar button.**

4. **Click the Importing tab.**

5. **Choose MP3 Encoder from the Import Using pop-up menu.**

6. **Choose High Quality (160 Kbps) from the Setting pop-up menu and then click OK.**

   This bit rate setting provides the best compromise between quality (better than CD quality, which is 128 Kbps) and file size. (Tracks that you rip will be significantly smaller than "audiophile" bit rates, such as 192 Kbps or higher.)

7. **Load an audio CD into your MacBook.**

   The CD title shows up in the iTunes Source list, which is on the left side of the iTunes interface. The CD track listing appears on the right side of the interface.

   If iTunes asks you whether you want to import the contents of the CD into your Music Library, you can click Yes and skip the rest of the steps. However, if you disabled this prompt, just continue with the remaining two steps.

8. **Clear the check box of any song that you don't want to import from the CD.**

   All songs on the CD have a check box next to their title by default. Unmarked songs aren't imported.

   Notice that the Browse button changes to Import CD.

9. **After you select the songs that you want added to the Library, click the Import CD button.**

Tweaking the Audio for Your Ears

Besides the standard volume controls that I mention earlier in this chapter, iTunes offers a full equalizer. An *equalizer* permits you to alter the volume of various frequencies in your music, allowing you to boost low sounds, lower high sounds, or anything in between. Now you can customize how your music sounds and adjust it to your liking.

To open the Equalizer, do one of the following.

 ✔ **Choose Window⇨Equalizer.**

 ✔ **Press ⌘+Option+2.**

 ✔ **Choose View⇨Show Equalizer.**

The Equalizer window has an impressive array of 11 sliders. Use the leftmost slider (Preamp) to set the overall level of the Equalizer. The remaining sliders represent various frequencies that the human ear can perceive. Setting a slider to a position in the middle of its travel causes that frequency to play back with no change. Move the slider above the midpoint to boost that frequency; conversely, move the slider below the midpoint to reduce the volume of that frequency.

Continue adjusting the sliders until your music sounds how you like it. When you close the Equalizer window, iTunes remembers your settings until you change them again. If you prefer to leave frequencies to the experts, the iTunes Equalizer has several predefined settings to match most musical styles. Click the pop-up menu at the top of the Equalizer window to select a genre.

A New Kind of Radio Station

Besides playing back your favorite audio files, iTunes can also tune in Internet radio stations from around the globe. You can listen to any of a large number of preset stations, seek out lesser-known stations not recognized by iTunes, or even add your favorite stations to your Playlists. This section shows you how to do it all.

What's with the numbers next to the station names?

When choosing an Internet radio station, keep your Internet connection speed in mind. If you're using a broadband DSL or cable connection — or if you're listening at work over your company's high-speed network — you can listen to stations broadcasting at 128 Kbps (or even higher). The higher the bit rate, the better the music sounds. At 128 Kbps, for example, you're listening to sound that's as good as an audio CD.

However, if you're listening over a dialup modem connection, iTunes can't keep up with audio streaming at higher bit rates, so you're limited to stations broadcasting at 56 Kbps or lower.

iTunes Radio

Although it's not a radio tuner in the strictest sense, iTunes Radio can locate virtual radio stations all over the world that send audio over the Internet — a process usually dubbed *streaming* amongst the "In" Internet crowd. iTunes can track down hundreds of Internet radio stations in a variety of styles with only a few clicks.

To begin listening to Internet radio with iTunes, click the Radio icon located beneath the Library icon in the Source list. The result is a list of more than 20 types of radio stations, organized by genre.

When you expand a Radio category by clicking its triangle, iTunes queries a tuning server and locates the name and address of dozens of radio stations for that category. Whether you like Elvis (or those passing fads, like new wave, classical, or alternative), something's here for everyone. The Radio also offers news, sports, and talk radio.

After iTunes fetches the names and descriptions of radio stations, double-click one that you want to hear. iTunes immediately jumps into action, loads the station, and begins to play it.

Tuning in your own stations

Although iTunes offers you a large list of popular radio stations on the Web, it's by no means comprehensive. Eventually, you might run across a radio station that you'd like to hear, but it's not listed in iTunes. Luckily, iTunes permits you to listen to other stations, too. To listen to a radio station that iTunes doesn't list, you need the station's Web address.

I have an itch to hear "Kung Fu Fighting!"

This particular technology author has a preference for a certain hot Net jam spot: *MLC Radio,* the Internet radio station I've been running for several years now. I call my station a '70s Time Machine because it includes hundreds of classic hits from 1970–1979, inclusive. You hear everything from "Rock and Roll Hoochie Koo" by Rick Derringer to "Moonlight Feels Right" by Starbuck. (Hey, I'm summing up a decade here, so be prepared for both Rush and the Captain and Tennille, too.) The station broadcasts at 128 Kbps (audio CD quality), so you need a broadband connection to listen. For the radio's Internet address or help connecting to MLC Radio, visit my Web site at www.mlcbooks. om — then follow the steps in the next section to add MLC Radio to your playlists!

In iTunes, choose Advanced⇨Open Stream (or press ⌘+U). In the Open Stream dialog that appears, enter the URL of your desired radio station and then click OK. Within seconds, iTunes tunes in your station, and the station name is added as an entry in your Library.

Radio stations in your Playlists

If you find yourself visiting an online radio station more than once, you'll be glad to know that iTunes supports radio stations in its Playlists. To add a radio station to a Playlist, do the following:

1. **Open the category that contains the station that you want to add to your Playlist.**

2. **Locate the station that you want to add to your Playlist and drag it from the Radio list to the desired Playlist on the left.**

   If you haven't created any Playlists yet, see the section, "Keeping Slim Whitman and Slim Shady Apart: Organizing with Playlists," earlier in this chapter to find out how.

Adding a radio station that doesn't appear in the Radio list is a bit trickier but possible nonetheless. Even though iTunes allows you to load a radio station URL manually by using the Open Stream command in the Advanced menu, it doesn't give you an easy way to add it to the Playlist. Follow these steps to add a specific radio station to a Playlist:

1. **Add any radio station from the Radio list to your desired Playlist.**

   Any station in the list will do because you'll immediately change both the station's URL and name to create your new station entry in the Playlist.

2. **Press ⌘+I or choose File➪Get Info to bring up the information dialog for that station.**

3. **Click the Summary section and change the URL by clicking the Edit URL button.**

4. **Enter the desired URL and then click OK.**

5. **Click the Info tab, type the new station name, and then click OK.**

Burning Like a True Techno

Besides being a great audio player, iTunes is adept at creating CDs, too. iTunes makes recording songs to a CD as simple as a few clicks — now, putting together the modern version of a compilation (or *mix*) tape is easier than getting a kid to eat ice cream. iTunes lets you burn CDs in one of three formats:

- ✔ **Audio CD:** This is the typical kind of commercial music CD that you buy at a store. Most typical music audio CDs store 700MB of data, which translates into about 80 minutes of music.

- ✔ **Data CD or DVD:** A standard CD-ROM or DVD-ROM is recorded with the audio files. This disc can't be played in any standard audio CD player (even if it supports MP3 CDs, which I discuss next). Therefore, you can listen to these songs only by using your MacBook and an audio player, like iTunes or a PC running Windows.

Yes, Virginia, you can broadcast your music

If your MacBook has built-in AirPort Extreme wireless hardware (all recent models do) and you're using an AirPort Express portable wireless Base Station, you can ship your songs right to your Base Station from within iTunes — and from there to your home stereo or boom box! (I get into some serious discussion of AirPort Express in Chapter 17.)

After your AirPort Express Base Station is plugged in and you connect your home stereo (or a boom box, or a pair of powered stereo speakers) to the stereo mini-jack on the Base Station, you see a Speakers pop-up list button appear at the bottom of the iTunes window. (If the Speakers button doesn't appear, choose iTunes➪Preferences to open the Preferences dialog and click the Advanced tab. Make sure that the Look for Remote Speakers Connected with AirTunes check box is enabled.)

Click the Speakers button, and you can choose to broadcast the music you're playing in iTunes across your wireless network. Ain't technology truly *grand?*

✔ **MP3 CD:** Like the ordinary computer CD-ROM that I describe, an MP3 CD holds MP3 files in data format. However, the files are arranged in such a way that they can be recognized by audio CD players that support the MP3 CD format (especially boom boxes, personal CD players, and car stereos). Because MP3 files are so much smaller than the digital audio tracks found on traditional audio CDs, you can fit as many as 160 typical, four-minute songs on one disc. These discs can also be played on your laptop via iTunes.

MP3 CDs aren't the same as the standard audio CDs that you buy at the store, and you can't play them in older audio CD players that don't support the MP3 CD format. Rather, this is the kind of archival disc that you burn at home for your own collection.

First things first: Before you burn, you need to set the recording format. Open the iTunes Preferences dialog by choosing iTunes⇨Preferences. Click the Advanced button, click the Burning tab, and select the desired disc format by enabling the corresponding radio button. Click OK to close the Preferences window when you're finished.

The next step in the CD creation process is to build a playlist (or select an existing playlist that you want to record). If necessary, create a new playlist and add to it whatever songs you would like to have on the CD. (See the earlier section, "Keeping Slim Whitman and Slim Shady Apart: Organizing with Playlists," if you need a refresher.) With the songs in the correct order, select the playlist. Click the Burn Disc button at the bottom of the iTunes window to commence the disc burning process. iTunes lets you know when the recording is complete.

Backing up within iTunes

iTunes offers a built-in backup feature for your media library. (I told you this was the best media player ever designed!) Choose File⇨Back Up to Disc to start the process. You can choose to back up your entire iTunes library and all your playlists (which I recommend) or just the content you purchased from the iTunes Store. Personally, if I lost everything in my collection except for what I've bought from the iTunes Store, I'd be just as crushed. Back it all up, and you won't be sorry.

Click Back Up, and iTunes will prompt you for blank CDs or DVDs. If you need to restore from your completed backup, just launch iTunes and load the first backup disc into your drive.

How often is often enough when it comes to backing up your content? That depends completely on how often your media library changes. The idea is to back up often enough so that you always have a recent copy of your media files close by.

Visualization: Music for your eyes

By now, you know that iTunes is a feast for the ears, but did you know that it can provide you with eye candy as well? With just a click or two, you can view mind-bending graphics that stretch, move, and pulse with your music.

To begin viewing iTunes visuals, choose View⇨Turn On Visualizer (or press ⌘+T). Immediately, most of your iTunes interface disappears and begins displaying groovy lava lamp-style animations (like, *sassy,* man). To stop the visuals, choose View⇨Turn Off Visualizer (or press ⌘+T again). The usual sunny aluminum face of iTunes returns.

You can also change the viewing size of the iTunes visuals in the View menu. From the View menu item, choose Full Screen (or press ⌘+F). To escape from the Full Screen mode, click the trackpad button or press Esc.

You can still control iTunes with the keyboard while the visuals are zooming around your screen. See Table 11-1, earlier in this chapter, for a rundown on common keyboard shortcuts.

Buying Billie Holiday from the Apple Music Store

Before we wave goodbye to the happy residents of iTunes iSland, I won't forget to mention the hottest spot on the Internet for buying music and video: the iTunes Store, which you can reach from the cozy confines of iTunes. (That is, as long as you have an Internet connection. If you don't, it's time to turn the page to a different chapter.)

Figure 11-4 illustrates the lobby of this online audio/video store. Click the iTunes Store item in the Source list, and after a few moments, you're presented with the latest offerings. Click a link in the Store list to browse according to media type; or, click the Power Search link to search by song title, artist, album, or composer. The Back/Forward buttons at the top of the iTunes Store window operate much like those in Safari, moving you backward or forward in sequence through pages that you've already seen. Clicking the Home button (which, through no great coincidence, looks like a miniature house) takes you back to the Store's main page.

Figure 11-4:
Hmm....
Now
where's that
Liberace
section?

To display the details on a specific album or track, just click it. If you're interested in buying just certain tracks (for that perfect road warrior mix), you get to listen to 30 seconds of any track — for free, no less, and at full sound quality. To add an item to your iTunes Store shopping cart, click the Add Song/Movie/Album/Video/Podcast button (sheesh!). When you're ready to buy, click the Shopping Cart item in the Source list and then click the Buy Now button. (At the time of this writing, tracks are 99 cents a pop, and an entire album is typically $9.99 . . . what a bargain! As I mention earlier in the chapter, Apple now offers iTunes Plus tracks, which are higher in quality and aren't hobbled with copy protection. These tracks are also 99 cents each.)

The iTunes Store creates an account for you based on your e-mail address, and it also keeps secure track of your credit card information for future purchases. After you use the iTunes Store once, you never have to log in or retype your credit card information again — iTunes identifies you by your user account, and saves your buying method and information for future purchases.

The tracks and files that you download are saved to a separate playlist called Purchased. After the download is finished, you can play 'em, move 'em to other playlists, burn 'em to CD or DVD, share 'em over your network, or ship 'em to your iPod, just like any other item in your iTunes Library. If you rent a movie, though, you have a limited amount of time to view the film on your MacBook before it's automatically erased — this is the new millennium, so there's no need to be kind by rewinding.

Remember all those skeptics who claimed that buying digital audio and video could never work over the Internet because of piracy issues and high costs? Well, bunkie, hats off to Apple: Once again, our favorite technology leader has done something the *right* way!

Chapter 12

That Masterpiece That Is iPhoto

In This Chapter

▶ Importing pictures from your hard drive or digital camera

▶ Organizing images with iPhoto

▶ Tweaking the appearance of photographs

▶ Sharing photos with your friends

*V*irtually every Mac owner is likely to have a digital camera or a scanner. Digital video (DV) camcorders have certainly grown more plentiful over the past three or four years, and the iPod is the hottest piece of music hardware on the planet at the time of this writing. The digital camera, however, has reached what those funny (strange) marketing people refer to as saturation, and iPhoto was written to address the needs of every person with a digital camera and a Mac laptop!

With iPhoto '08, you organize, edit, and even publish your photographs. (It sports more features than a handful of Swiss Army knives.) After you shoot your photos with a digital camera, you can import them into iPhoto, edit them, and publish them. You're not limited to photos that you take yourself, either; you can edit, publish, and organize all kinds of digital image files. You can even create a photo album and use the iPhoto interface to order a handsome hard-bound copy shipped to you.

To sum it all up, I'm willing to bet that iPhoto is either the first or the second iLife application that you fall in love with (running neck and neck with iTunes). In this chapter, I show you how you can work digital image magic with true Apple panache!

Delving into iPhoto

In Figure 12-1, you can see most of the major controls offered in iPhoto. Other controls automatically appear when you enter different modes, I cover them in upcoming sections of this chapter.

Source list   Viewer

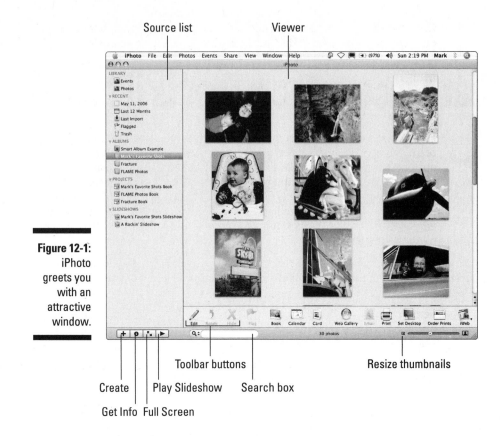

Figure 12-1:
iPhoto
greets you
with an
attractive
window.

Toolbar buttons   Resize thumbnails

Create   Play Slideshow   Search box

Get Info Full Screen

Although I cover these controls as well as the various parts of the window in more detail in the following sections, here's a quick rundown of what you're looking at:

✔ **Source list:** This list of image locations determines which photos iPhoto displays.

    • You can choose to display either your entire image library or just the last "roll" of digital images that you downloaded from your camera.

    • You can display photos grouped by *events* — for example, a birthday party or family vacation. Each event covers a specific period of time.

    • You can create new *albums* of your own that appear in the source list; albums make it much easier to organize your photos.

    • You can create books, calendars, cards, and slideshows as well.

✔ **Viewer:** This pane displays the images from the selected photo source.

    You can drag or click to select photos in the Viewer for further tricks, such as assigning keywords and image editing.

- **Create button:** Click this button to add a new blank album, book, cal-endar, Web Gallery (for .Mac subscribers), greeting card, postcard, or slideshow to your source list.

  Read all about .Mac in Chapter 9.

- **Get Info button:** Click this button to display information on selected photos.

- **Full Screen button:** Click this button to switch to a full-screen display of your photos. In full-screen mode, the images in the selected album appear in a film strip across the top of the screen, and you can click one to view that image, using your MacBook's entire screen real estate. You can also use the same controls that I discuss later in this chapter for editing and adjusting images. Just move the mouse cursor to the top edge of the full-screen display to show the menu or to the bottom edge to show the toolbar.

- **Play Slideshow button:** Select an event, album, book, or slideshow in the Source list and then click this button to start a full-screen slideshow using those images.

- **Search box:** Click the button next to the Search text box to locate photos by specific criteria, or just click in the box and start typing to search by description and title.

- **Toolbar buttons:** This group of buttons selects an operation that you want to perform on the images you select in the Viewer.

- **Thumbnail Resize slider:** Drag this slider to the left to reduce the size of the thumbnails in the Viewer. This allows you to see more thumbnails at once, which is a great boon for quick visual searches. Drag the slider to the right to expand the size of the thumbnails, making it easier to differ-entiate details between similar photos in the Viewer.

Working with Images in iPhoto

Even a superbly designed image display and editing application (like iPhoto) would look overwhelming if everything were jammed into one window. Thus, Apple developers provide different operation *modes* (such as editing and book creation) that you can use in the one iPhoto window. Each mode allows you to perform different tasks, and you can switch modes at just about any time by clicking the corresponding toolbar button.

In this section, I discuss three of these modes — import, organize, and edit — and what you can do when you're in them. Then I conclude the chapter with sections on publishing and sharing your images.

Import Images 101

In *import* mode, you're ready to download images directly from your digital camera — that is, as long as your specific camera model is supported in iPhoto. You can find out which cameras are supported by visiting the Apple iPhoto support section at

`www.apple.com`

Follow these steps to import images:

1. **Connect your digital camera to your MacBook.**

   Plug one end of a USB cable into your camera and the other end into your laptop's USB port, and then prepare your camera to download images. (Turn on your camera and switch it to a Transfer mode if necessary.)

2. **Launch iPhoto.**

   Launch iPhoto by clicking its icon on the Dock (or in your Applications folder). Note that iPhoto will automatically launch by itself if your camera or media card reader is recognized. Thumbnails of the images on your camera or card reader appear in the iPhoto window, and the bottom of the window displays the Import text fields and buttons.

   The first time that you launch iPhoto, you have the option of setting its auto-launch feature. I recommend this feature, which starts iPhoto automatically whenever you connect a camera to your laptop.

3. **Click in the Event Name field at the bottom of the window and type an event name for the imported photos, like** Birthday Party **or** Godzilla Ravages Tokyo.

   Keep in mind that the images you're seeing on your screen haven't actually been copied over to your MacBook yet — the photos are still on your camera or card reader.

4. **Click in the Description box and type a description for the event.**

5. **To allow iPhoto to automatically separate images into events based on the date they were taken, select the Autosplit Events After Importing check box to enable it.**

   If you want to keep all these photos in a single event — even though the event spans multiple days — leave the Autosplit Events After Importing check box disabled.

6. **Click the Import button to import your photographs from the camera.**

   The images are added to your Photo Library, where you can organize them into individual albums or Events.

   To select specific images to import, hold down the ⌘ key and click each desired photo. Then click Import Selected rather than Import All.

Importing images from your hard drive

If you have a folder of images that you collected on your hard drive, a CD, a DVD, an external drive, or a USB Flash drive, adding them to your library is easy. Just drag the folder from a Finder window and drop it into the source list in the iPhoto window. iPhoto automatically creates a new album using the folder name, and you can sit back while the images are imported into that new album. iPhoto recognizes images in several formats: JPEG, GIF, RAW, PNG, PICT, and TIFF.

You can drag individual images as well. Select the images in a Finder window and then drag them into the desired album in the source list. To add them to the album displayed in the Viewer, drag the selected photos and drop them in the Viewer instead.

If you'd rather import images via a standard Mac Open dialog, choose File⇨Import to Library. Simplicity strikes again!

7. **Specify whether the images you're importing should be deleted from the camera afterward.**

    If you don't expect to download these images to another computer or another device, you can choose to delete the photos from your camera automatically by clicking Delete Originals. This saves you a step and helps eliminate the guilt that can crop up when you nix your pix. (Sorry, but I couldn't resist.)

    If you prefer to keep your images on your camera as a safeguard, click the Keep Originals button. Nothing's deleted, and you can delete the photos later by using your camera's built-in delete feature.

"What's that about an Event, Mark?" After you download the contents of your digital camera, those contents count as a virtual *Event* in iPhoto, based on the date they were taken. For example, you can always display the last images you imported by clicking Last Import. If you want to see photos from your son's graduation, they appear as a separate Event. (Both of these organizational tools will appear in the source list.) Think about that . . . it's pretty tough to arrange old-fashioned film prints by the moment in time that they document, but iPhoto makes it easy for you to see just which photos are part of the same group! I explain more about Events in the next section.

Organize mode: Organizing and sorting your images

In the days of film prints, you could always stuff another shoebox with your latest photos or buy another sticky album to expand your library. Your digital camera, though, stores images as files instead, and many folks don't print their digital photographs. Instead, you can keep your entire collection of digital photographs and scanned images well ordered and easily retrieved in iPhoto organize mode. Then you can display them as a slideshow, print them to your system printer, use them as Desktop backgrounds, or burn them to an archive disc.

The two methods of organizing photos are

✔ An *album*, which you might be familiar with from older versions of iPhoto

✔ *Events*, which are new in iPhoto '08

A new kind of photo album

The key to organizing images in iPhoto is the album. Each album can represent any division you like, be it a year, a vacation, your daughter, or your daughter's ex-boyfriends. Follow these steps:

1. **Create a new album.**

   Choose File⇨New Album or click the plus (+) button at the bottom of the source list. The New Album sheet appears, as shown in Figure 12-2.

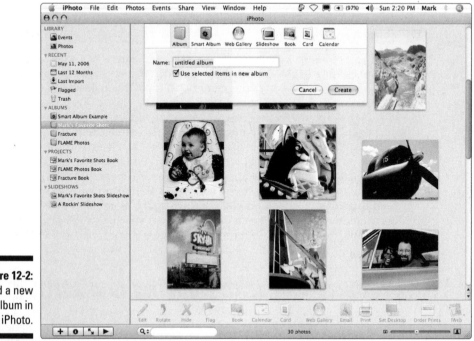

Figure 12-2:
Add a new album in iPhoto.

2. Type the name for your new photo album.

If you want to create an empty album (without using any images that might be selected), make sure you deselect the Use Selected Items in New Album check box to disable it.

3. Click Create.

iPhoto also offers a special type of album — a *Smart Album* — which you can create from the File menu. A Smart Album contains only photos that match certain criteria that you choose, using the keywords and rating that you assign to your images. Other criteria include recent film rolls, text within photo filenames, dates when the images were added to iPhoto, and any comments you might have added. Now here's the really nifty angle: iPhoto automatically builds and maintains Smart Albums for you, adding new photos that match the criteria (and deleting those that you remove from your Photo Library)! Smart Albums carry a gear icon in the source list.

You can display information about the selected item in the information panel under the source list. Just click the Show Information button at the bottom of the iPhoto window, which sports the familiar *i*-in-a-circle logo. You can also type a short note or description in the Description box that appears in the Information pane. For more in-depth information, select the desired item and then press ⌘+I.

You can also change information on an image by selecting it in the Viewer and clicking the Show Information button. Click on any of the headings in the pane (Title, Date and Time) to display a text edit box. Then simply click in the box to make your edits: Type in a new name, for example, or alter the photo's date stamp.

You can drag images from the Viewer into any album you choose. For example, you can copy an image to another album by dragging it from the Viewer to the desired album in the Source list.

To remove an album photo that has fallen out of favor, follow these steps:

1. In the Source list, select the desired album.

2. In the Viewer, select the photo (click it) that you want to remove.

3. Press Delete.

When you remove a photo from an album, you don't actually remove the photo from your collection (which is represented by the Photos entry under the Library heading in the source list). That's because an album is just a group of links to the images in your collection. To completely remove the offending photo, click the Photos entry under the Library heading to display your entire collection of images and delete the picture there, too.

To remove an entire album from the source list, just click it in the source list to select it — in the Viewer, you can see the images that it contains — and then press Delete.

To rename an album, click the entry under the Albums heading in the Source list to select it, and then click again to display a text box. Type the new album name and then press Return.

Change your mind? Daughter's ex is back in the picture, so to speak? iPhoto comes complete with a handy-dandy Undo feature. Just press ⌘+Z, and it's like your last action never happened. (A great trick for those moments when you realize you just deleted your only image of your first car from your Library.)

Arranging stuff by Events

As I mention earlier, *Events* are essentially a group of images that you shot at the same time. iPhoto figures that those images belong together (which is usually a pretty safe assumption). Figure 12-3 illustrates the Events I created in my iPhoto collection.

Like an album, an Event can be renamed just by using a different procedure. Click the Events entry under the Library heading in the Source list to display your Events in the Viewer, and then click the existing Event name in the caption underneath the thumbnail. A text box appears in which you can type a new name. Then press Return to update the Event.

Try moving your mouse cursor over an Event thumbnail in the Viewer, and you'll see that iPhoto displays the date range when the images were taken as well as the total number of images in the Event. Ah, but things get *really* cool when you move your mouse cursor back and forth over an Event with many images. The thumbnail animates and displays all the images in the Event, without using old-fashioned scroll bars or silly arrows! (Why can't I think of this stuff? This is the future, dear readers.)

To display the contents of an Event in the Viewer, just double-click the Event thumbnail. To return to the Events thumbnails, click the All Events button at the top of the Viewer.

Decided to merge those Prom Event pictures with your daughter's Graduation Event? No problem! You could drag one Event thumbnail on top of another, but that's the easy way. Alternatively, click the Events entry under the Library heading in the Source list to display your Events and then hold down ⌘ while you click the Events that you want to merge. Click the Merge button in the toolbar at the bottom of the window, or choose Events⇨Merge Events. (Forgot about that menu bar, didn't you?) Click Merge in the confirmation dialog that appears.

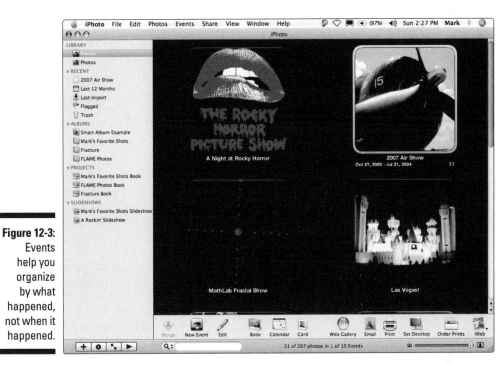

Figure 12-3:
Events
help you
organize
by what
happened,
not when it
happened.

While you're organizing, you can create a brand-new empty Event by choosing Events⇨Create Event. Feel free to drag photos from albums, other Events, or your Photo library into your new Event.

Organizing with keywords

"Okay, Mark, iPhoto albums and Events are great ideas, but do you really expect me to look through 20 albums just to locate pictures with specific people or places?" Never fear, good MacBook owner. You can also assign descriptive *keywords* to images to help you organize your collection and locate certain pictures fast. iPhoto comes with a number of standard keywords, and you can create your own as well.

To illustrate, suppose you'd like to identify your images according to special events in your family. Birthday photos should have their own keyword, and anniversaries deserve another. By assigning keywords, you can search for Elsie's sixth birthday or your silver wedding anniversary (no matter what Event or album they're in), and all related photos with those keywords appear like magic! (Well, *almost* like magic. You need to choose View⇨Keywords, which toggles the Keyword display on and off in the Viewer.)

iPhoto includes a number of keywords that are already available:

- ✔ **Favorite**
- ✔ **Family**
- ✔ **Kids**
- ✔ **Vacation**
- ✔ **Birthday**
- ✔ **Checkmark**

What's the Checkmark all about, you ask? It's a special case. Adding this keyword displays a tiny check mark icon in the bottom-right corner of the image. The Checkmark keyword comes in handy for temporarily identifying specific images because you can search for just your check-marked photos.

To assign keywords to images (or remove keywords that have already been assigned), select one or more photos in the Viewer. Choose Window➪Show Keywords or press ⌘+K to display the Keywords window, as shown in Figure 12-4.

Figure 12-4:
Time to add keywords to these selected images.

You're gonna need your own keywords

I'll bet you take photos of other things besides just kids and vacations — and that's why iPhoto allows you to create your own keywords. Display the iPhoto Keywords window by pressing ⌘+K, click the Edit Keywords button in the toolbar, and then click Add (the button with the plus sign). iPhoto adds a new unnamed keyword to the list as an edit box, ready for you to type its name.

You can rename an existing keyword from this same window, too. Click a keyword to select it and then click Rename. Remember, however, that renaming a keyword affects *all the images that were tagged with that keyword.* That might be confusing when, for example, photos originally tagged as Family suddenly appear with the keyword Foodstuffs. To remove an existing keyword from the list, click the keyword to select it and then click the Delete button, which bears a minus sign.

Click the keyword buttons that you want to attach to the selected images to mark them. Or, click the highlighted keyword buttons that you want to remove from the selected images to disable them.

Digging through your library with keywords

Behold the power of keywords! To sift through your entire collection of images by keywords, click the magnifying glass button next to the Search box at the bottom of the iPhoto window and then choose Keyword from the pop-up menu. iPhoto displays a pop-up Keywords panel, and you can click one or more keyword buttons to display just the photos that carry those keywords.

The images that remain in the Viewer after a search must have *all* the keywords that you specified. For example, if an image is identified by only three of four keywords you chose, it isn't a match and won't appear in the Viewer.

To search for a photo by title, or by words in its description (which you can add by clicking the Info button at the lower-left corner of the window), just click in the Search box and start typing. You can also click that same magnifying glass by the Search box to search through your images by date and rating as well. (And speaking of ratings. . . .)

Playing favorites by assigning ratings

Be your own critic! iPhoto allows you to assign any photo a rating of anywhere from zero to five stars. I use this system to help me keep track of the images that I feel are the best in my library. Select one (or more) image and then assign a rating by using one of the following methods.

✔ Choose Photos➪My Rating and then choose the desired rating from the pop-up submenu.

✔ Use the ⌘+0 (for your average snapshot) through ⌘+5 (front-page material) shortcuts.

Sorting your images just so

The View menu provides an easy way to arrange your images in the Viewer by a number of different criteria. Choose View➪Sort Photos and then click the desired sort criteria from the pop-up submenu. You can arrange the display by date, keyword, title, or rating. If you select an album in the source list, you can also choose to arrange photos manually, which means that you can drag and drop thumbnails in the Viewer to place them in the precise order you want them.

Naturally, iPhoto allows you to print selected images, but you can also send photos directly to iWeb for use on your .Mac Web site. Click the iWeb button in the toolbar and choose either a Photo page or a Blog page. iPhoto automatically sends the selected images or album to iWeb and launches the application! You can also use the iPhoto Web Gallery feature to get your photos on the Web. (Find more on the Web Gallery at the end of this chapter.)

Edit mode: Removing and fixing stuff the right way

Not every digital image is perfect. Just look at my collection if you need proof. For those shots that need a pixel massage, iPhoto includes a number of editing tools that you can use to correct common problems.

The first step in any editing job is to select the image you want to fix in the Viewer. Then click the Edit button on the iPhoto toolbar to switch to the Edit panel controls, as shown in Figure 12-5. Now you're ready to fix problems, using the tools that I discuss in the rest of this section. (If you're editing a photo that's part of an Event or an album, note the spiffy scrolling photo strip at the top, which allows you to switch to another image to edit just by clicking.)

Rotating tipped-over shots

If an image is in the wrong orientation and needs to be turned to display correctly, click the Rotate button to turn it once in a counterclockwise direction. Hold down the Option key while you click the Rotate button to rotate in a clockwise direction.

Figure 12-5:
iPhoto is
now in
edit mode.
Watch
out, image
problems!

Crop 'til you drop

Does that photo have an intruder hovering around the edges of the subject? You can remove some of the border by *cropping* an image, just like folks once did with film prints and a pair of scissors. (We've come a long way.) With iPhoto, you can remove unwanted portions of an image, which is a great way to get Uncle Milton's stray head (complete with toupee) out of an otherwise perfect holiday snapshot.

Follow these steps to crop an image:

1. **Click the Crop button in the Edit panel.**

2. **Select the portion of the image that you want to keep.**

   In the Viewer, click and drag the handles on the square to outline the part of the image that you want. Remember, whatever's outside this rectangle disappears after the crop is completed.

When you drag a corner or edge of the outline, a semi-opaque grid (familiar to amateur and professional photographers as the nine squares from the Rule of Three) appears to help you visualize what you're claiming. (Check it out in Figure 12-6.)

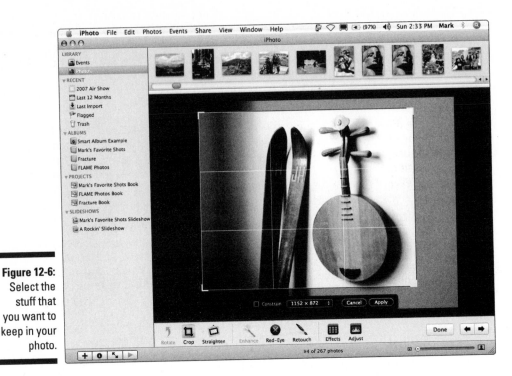

3. (Optional) Choose a preset aspect ratio.

If you want to force your cropped selection to a specific aspect ratio —
such as 4:3 for an iDVD project — select the Constrain check box and
then select the size from the Constrain pop-up menu.

4. Click the Apply button.

Oh, and don't forget that you can use iPhoto's Undo feature if you mess
up and need to try again — just press ⌘+Z.

iPhoto features multiple Undo levels, so you can press ⌘+Z several times to
travel back through your last several changes.

Enhancing images to add pizzazz

If a photo looks washed out, click the Enhance button to increase (or
decrease) the color saturation and improve the contrast. Enhance is automatic, so you don't have to set anything.

Removing rampant red-eye

Unfortunately, today's digital cameras can still produce the same "zombies
with red eyeballs" as traditional film cameras. *Red-eye* is caused by a camera's flash reflecting off the retinas of a subject's eyes, and it can occur with
both humans and pets.

iPhoto can remove that red-eye to turn frightening zombies back into your family and friends. Click the Red-Eye button and then select a demonized eyeball by clicking in the center of it. To complete the process, click the X in the button that appears in the image.

Retouching like the stars

The iPhoto Retouch feature is perfect for removing minor flecks or lines in an image (especially those images from scanned prints). Click Retouch, and the mouse cursor turns into a crosshair. Just drag the cursor across the imperfection. (Actually, you're matching the pixels in the selected area with the pixels surrounding it, which "smooths" out the imperfection.)

Switching to black-and-white or sepia

Ever wonder whether a particular photo in your library would look better as a black-and-white *(grayscale)* print? Or perhaps an old-fashioned sepia tone in shades of copper and brown? Just click the Effects button to convert an image from color to shades of gray or shades of brown, respectively. (To return to the original image, just click in the center square of the effects window.)

Adjusting brightness and contrast manually

Click Adjust to perform manual adjustments on brightness and contrast (the light levels in your image). To adjust the brightness and contrast, make sure that nothing's selected in the image and then drag the Brightness/Contrast sliders until the image looks the way that you want.

While you're editing, you can use the Next button to move to the next image in the current album (and the Previous button to revert to the previous image).

Producing Your Own Coffee-Table Masterpiece

Book mode unleashes what I think is probably the coolest feature of iPhoto: the chance to design and print a high-quality, bound photo book! After you complete an album — all the images have been edited just the way you want, and the album contains all the photos you want to include in your book — iPhoto can send your images as data over the Internet to a company that prints and binds your finished book for you. (No, they don't publish *For Dummies* titles, but then again, I don't get high-resolution color plates in most of my books, either.)

At the time of this writing, you can order many different sizes and bindings, including an 8.5 x 11" softcover book with 20 double-sided pages for about $20 and a hardbound 8.5 x 11" keepsake album with 10 double-sided pages for about $30 (shipping included for both). Extra pages can be added for 70 cents and $1 a pop, respectively.

iPhoto '08 can also produce and automatically order calendars and greeting cards, using a process similar to the one I describe in this section for producing a book. Who needs that stationery store in the mall anymore?

If you're going to create a photo book, make sure that the images have the highest quality and highest resolution. The higher the resolution, the better the photos look in the finished book. I personally always try to use images with more than 1,000 pixels in both the vertical and horizontal dimensions. Check your camera's manual for instructions on how to choose the maximum quality and resolution settings.

To create a photo book, follow these steps:

1. **Click the desired album in the source list to select it.**

2. **Click the Book toolbar button.**

3. **Select the size of the book and a theme.**

   Your choices determine the number of pages and layout scheme, as well as the background graphics for each page.

4. **Click Choose.**

   iPhoto displays a dialog box indicating that you can lay out your photos manually or allow iPhoto to do everything automatically (by clicking the Autoflow button on the toolbar). Automatic mode is fine, but I'm a thorough guy, so I'll lay out this book manually. You'll see the controls shown in Figure 12-7.

   In Book mode, the Viewer changes in subtle ways. It displays the current page at the bottom of the display and adds a scrolling row of thumbnail images above it. This row of images represents the remaining images from the selected album that you can add to your book. You can drag any image thumbnail into one of the photo placeholders to add it to the page. You can also click the Page button at the left of the thumbnail strip — it looks like a page with a turned-down corner — to display thumbnails of each page in your book. (To return to the album image strip, click the Photos button under the Page button.)

Figure 12-7:
Preparing
to publish
my own
coffee-table
master-
piece.

5. **Rearrange the page order to suit you by dragging the thumbnail of any page from one location to another in the strip.**

6. **In the Book toolbar below the page view, you can adjust a variety of settings for the final book, including the book's theme, background, page numbers, and text fonts.**

   At this point, you can also add captions and short descriptions (about a dozen words) to the pages of your photo album. Click any one of the text boxes in the page display and begin typing to add text to that page.

7. **When you're ready to publish your book, click the Buy Book button.**

8. **In a series of dialog boxes that appear, iPhoto guides you through the final steps to order a bound book.**

   Note that you're asked for credit card information.

I wouldn't attempt to order a book through a dialup modem connection. The images are likely far too large to be sent successfully. If possible, use a broadband or network connection to the Internet while you're ordering. If your only connection to the Internet is through a dialup modem, I recommend saving your book in PDF format and having it printed at a copy shop or printing service instead. (Choose File➪Print and then click the Save as PDF button.)

Introducing Web Gallery!

iPhoto '08 introduces a new feature — *Web Gallery* — that does for images what podcasting does for audio: You can share your photos with friends, family, business clients, and anyone else with an Internet connection! (Your adoring public doesn't even require a Mac; they can use That Other Kind of Computer.) iPhoto automatically uploads the selected images and leads you through the process of creating a new Web page to proudly display your photos. However, you *must* be a .Mac subscriber to use the Web Gallery feature. If you haven't heard the news on the Apple .Mac service yet, see Chapter 9 for the details.

To create a Web Gallery, you designate one or more albums to share by selecting them in the source list and then clicking the Add button at the bottom left of the iPhoto window. (Hold down ⌘ while you click to select multiple albums.) Click the Web Gallery toolbar button in the sheet that appears to display the Web Gallery settings, as shown in Figure 12-8.

Type a name for your new Web Gallery. You can elect to show the title of each photo, allow your visitors to download your images or upload their own, and even allow photos to be uploaded by other Mac owners using Apple Mail!

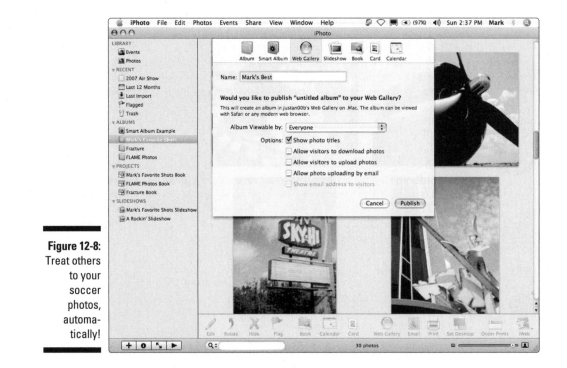

Figure 12-8:
Treat others
to your
soccer
photos,
automa-
tically!

By default, any visitor to your .Mac Web site can see your gallery. But what if you prefer a little security for those images? In that case, click the Album Viewable By pop-up menu, where you can limit your viewing audience. (You can even require that your visitors enter a login name and password before they can receive your photos.)

Click Publish, and you'll see that iPhoto indicates your images are being uploaded with a cool twirling progress icon to the right of the album in the source list. When the process is complete, iPhoto indicates that the album is being "photocasted" with a special networky-looking icon to the right of the album, and even a new Web Gallery heading in the Source list. You're on the air!

Now for the other side of the coin: By selecting your Web Gallery in the Source list and clicking Tell a Friend on the iPhoto toolbar, iPhoto automatically prepares an e-mail message in Apple Mail that announces your new Web Gallery! Just add the recipient names and click Send. This spiffy message includes instructions for

- ✔ **Folks using iPhoto '08 on a Mac:** As you can imagine, this is the easiest Receive option to configure. After these folks are subscribed, they get an automatically updated album of the same name that appears in their source list, and they can use those images in their own iPhoto projects. From within iPhoto, your visitors can subscribe to your Web Gallery by choosing File➪Subscribe to Photo Feed and entering the subscription URL from the e-mail message.

- ✔ **Folks using Windows or an older version of iPhoto:** These subscribers can use any Web browser with really simple syndication (RSS) support (like the Safari browser that comes with Leopard) or any RSS reader. (In effect, your Web Gallery becomes an RSS feed for those without iPhoto '08.)

By default, any changes you make to the contents of the albums in your Web Gallery are updated automatically on your .Mac account, and in turn, are updated automatically to everyone who receives your images. You can turn this feature off, however, if you have a large number of images and you update often (which can result in your sister's computer downloading a lot of data). To display the Check for New Photos setting for Web Gallery, choose iPhoto➪Preferences and then click the Web Gallery button on the Preferences window toolbar. (You can also change the title for your Gallery and monitor your iDisk usage from this pane.)

Chapter 13

Making Film History with iMovie

In This Chapter

▶ Taking stock of the iMovie window

▶ Importing and adding media content

▶ Using transitions in your movie

▶ Putting text titles to work

▶ Sharing your movie with others

Remember those home movies that you used to make in high school? They were entertaining and fun to create, and your friends were impressed. In fact, some kids are so downright inspired that you're not surprised when you discover at your high school reunion that they turned out to be graphic artists, or they're involved in video or TV production.

iMovie, part of the iLife '08 suite, makes movie making as easy as those home-made movies. Apple simplified all the technical stuff, such as importing video and adding audio, leaving you free to concentrate on your creative ideas. In fact, you won't find techy terms such as *codecs* or *keyframes* in this chapter at all. I guarantee that you'll understand what's going on at all times. (How often do you get a promise like that with video editing software?)

With iMovie, your digital video (DV) camcorder, and the other parts of the iLife suite, you can soon produce and share professional-looking movies, with some of the same creative transitions and titles used by Those Hollywood Types every single day.

If you turn out to be a world-famous Hollywood Type Director in a decade or so, don't forget the little people along the way!

Shaking Hands with the iMovie Window

If you've ever tried a professional-level, video editing application, you probably felt like you were suddenly dropped in the cockpit of a jumbo jet. In iMovie, though, all the controls you need are easy to use and logically placed.

Video editing takes up quite a bit of desktop space. In fact, you can't run iMovie at resolutions less than 1024 x 768, nor would you want to.

To launch iMovie, click the iMovie icon on the Dock. (It looks like a star from Hollywood's Walk of Fame, which I find very fitting.) You can also click the Application folder in any Finder window Sidebar and then double-click the iMovie icon.

To follow the examples that I show you here, follow these strenuous steps and create a new movie project:

1. **Click the Create a New Project button — located under the Project Library list — which bears a plus sign.**

   iMovie displays the window that you see in Figure 13-1.

Figure 13-1:
Creating a new movie project within iMovie.

2. **Type a name for your project.**

3. **Select the aspect ratio (or screen dimensions) for your movie.**

   You can select a widescreen display (16:9), a standard display (4:3), or a display especially suited for an iPhone (3:2). If compatibility with the familiar SDTV format is important, I always recommend that you choose the standard (4:3) ratio.

4. **Click Create.**

   You're on your way! Check out Figure 13-2: This is the whole enchilada, in one window.

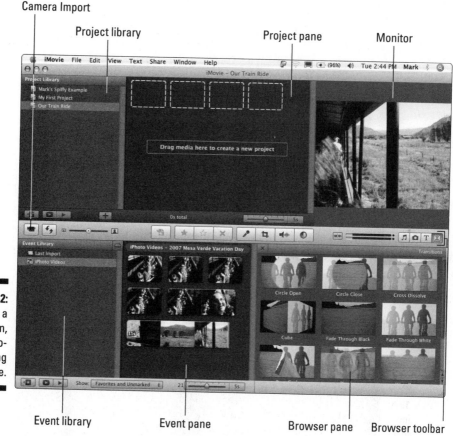

Camera Import

Project library

Project pane

Monitor

Figure 13-2: iMovie is a lean, mean, video-producing machine.

Event library

Event pane

Browser pane

Browser toolbar

Here are the controls and displays that you'll use most often.

- **Monitor:** Think of this as being just like your TV or computer monitor. Your video clips, still images, and finished movie play here.

- **Browser toolbar:** This row of buttons allows you to switch between your media clips (video clips, photos, and audio) and the various tools that you use to make your film. The selected items fill the browser pane below the toolbar. For example, Figure 13-2 illustrates the Transitions pane, which appears when you click the Transitions Browser button (go figure).

- **Event pane:** All the video clips that you use to create your movie are stored in the Event pane.

- **Project pane:** In this pane, iMovie displays the elements that you add to your movie project.

- **Playhead:** The red vertical line that you see in the Event and the Project panes is the *playhead,* which indicates the current editing point while you're creating your movie. When you're playing your movie, the playhead moves to follow your progress through the movie.

- **Editing toolbar:** This strip of buttons allows you to control editing functions such as cropping, audio and video adjustments, voiceovers, and selecting items.

- **Camera Import button:** Click this switch to import DV clips from your DV camcorder or iSight camera.

Those are the major highlights of the iMovie window. A director's chair and megaphone are optional, of course, but they do add to the mood.

A Bird's-Eye View of Moviemaking

I don't want to box in your creative skills here — after all, you can attack the moviemaking process from a number of angles. (Pun unfortunately intended.) However, I've found that my movies turn out the best when I follow a linear process, so before I dive into specifics, allow me to provide you with an overview of moviemaking with iMovie.

Here's my take on the process, reduced to seven steps:

1. Import your video clips into iMovie, directly from your DV camcorder, your iSight camera, or your hard drive.

2. Drag your new selection of clips from the Event pane to the Project pane and arrange them in the desired order.

3. Import or record audio clips (from iTunes; GarageBand; or external sources, such as audio CDs or audio files you recorded) and add them to your movie.

4. Import your photos (directly from iPhoto or from your hard drive) and place them where needed in your movie.

5. Add professional niceties — such as audio, transitions, effects, and text — to the project.

6. Preview your film and edit it further if necessary.

7. Share your finished film with others through the Web, e-mail, or a DVD that you create and burn with iDVD.

That's the first step-by-step procedure in this chapter. I doubt that you'll even need to refer to it, however, because you'll soon see just how easy it is to use iMovie.

Importing the Building Blocks

Sure, you need video clips to create a movie of your own, but don't panic if you have but a short supply. You can certainly turn to the other iLife '08 applications for additional raw material. (See, I told you that integration thing would come in handy.)

Along with video clips you import from your DV camcorder, iSight camera, and hard drive, you can also call on iPhoto for still images (think credits) and iTunes for background audio and effects. In this section, I show you how.

Pulling in video clips

Your MacBook or MacBook Pro is equipped already with the two extras that come in handy for video editing: namely, a large hard drive and a FireWire port. Because virtually all DV camcorders today use a FireWire connection to transfer clips, you're all set. (The MacBook Air can connect to any DV camcorder that uses a USB 2.0 connection.) Oh, and, of course: Your MacBook has an iSight camera onboard, so you're a self-contained movie studio!

Here's the drill if your clips are on your DV camcorder:

1. **Plug the proper cable into your MacBook.**

2. **Set the DV camcorder to VTR (or VCR) mode.**

   Some camcorders call this Play mode.

3. **Click the Camera Import button (labeled in Figure 13-2).**

   iMovie opens a new window.

4. **Click the Camera pop-up menu and select your DV camcorder or iSight camera.**

Playback controls appear under the Camera Import window, mirroring the controls on your DV camcorder. This allows you to control the unit from iMovie. *Keen!* You also get Import All and Import Checked buttons as a bonus.

5. **To import selected clips, set the Automatic/Manual switch to Manual.**

   To import all clips, set the Automatic/Manual switch to Automatic, and click Import All.

6. **Select the check boxes next to the clips that you don't want to import to disable them.**

7. **Click the Import Checked button.**

8. **Click the Save To pop-up menu and choose the drive that should store your clips.**

   You can choose to add the new clips to an existing Event, or create a new Event. Heck, if the Event spanned more than one day, you can create a new Event for each day. (How do they think up these things?)

9. **Click OK and admire your handiwork.**

   iMovie begins transferring the footage to your Mac and automatically adds the imported clips to your Event Library. Note that the footage remains pristine on your camera, and is **not** deleted.

If your clips are already on your hard drive, rest assured that iMovie can import them, including those in high-definition video (HDV) format. iMovie also recognizes a number of other video formats, as shown in Table 13-1.

Table 13-1	Video Formats Supported by iMovie
File Type	*Description*
DV	Standard digital video
MOV	QuickTime movies
HDV	High-definition (popularly called *widescreen*) digital video
MPEG-4	A popular format for streaming Internet and wireless digital video

To import a movie file, follow this bouncing ball:

1. **Choose File⇨Import Movies.**

2. **If you're importing 1080i video clips, choose the quality setting.**

   The Large setting (960 x 540 resolution) will save you a significant amount of hard drive space. (If you're not importing 1080i video, use the default Large setting and click OK.)

   If you are indeed importing 1080i (HD, or high definition) video and you want to take advantage of the whopping 1920 x 1080 resolution it provides, choose the Full setting. (And prepare to lose a nice-sized patch of free space on your hard drive!)

3. **Click the Save To pop-up menu and choose the drive that should store your clips.**

4. **Specify whether you want to add the imported video to an existing Event, or whether you'd like to create a new Event.**

   If you want to add the video to an existing Event, click the pop-up menu and choose an Event.

5. **Specify whether you want to copy the video (leaving the original movie intact), or whether the original movie should be deleted after a successful import.**

6. **Click Import.**

   Alternatively, you can also drag a video clip from a Finder window and drop it in the Project pane.

Making use of still images

Still images come in handy as impressive-looking titles or as ending credits to your movie. (Make sure you list a gaffer and a best boy to be truly professional.) However, you can also use still images to introduce scenes or to separate clips according to your whim. For example, I use stills when delineating the days of a vacation within a movie or different Christmas celebrations over time.

Here are two methods of adding stills to your movie:

✔ **Adding images from iPhoto:** Click the Photo Browser button on the Browser toolbar (or press ⌘+2), and you'll experience the thrill that is your iPhoto library, right from iMovie (as shown in Figure 13-3). You can elect to display your entire iPhoto library or more selective picks, such as specific albums or Events. When you find the image you want to add, just drag it to the right spot in the Project pane.

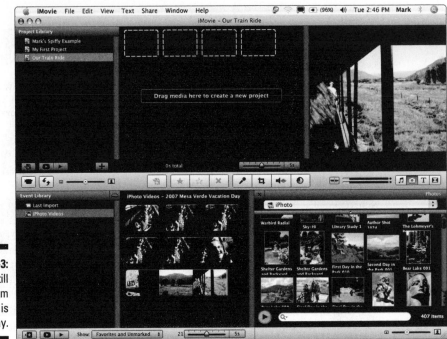

Figure 13-3:
Pulling still
images from
iPhoto is
child's play.

✓ **Importing images from your hard drive:** If you're a member of the
International Drag-and-Drop society, you can drag TIFF, JPEG, GIF, PICT,
PNG, and PSD images directly from a Finder window and drop them into
the Project pane as well.

Importing and adding audio from all sorts of places

You can pull in everything from Wagner to Weezer as both background music
and sound effects for your movie. In this section, I focus on how to get those
notes into iMovie and then how to add them to your movie by dragging them
to the Project pane.

You can add audio from a number of sources:

✓ **Adding songs from iTunes:** Click the Show Music and Sound Effects
button on the Browser toolbar (or press ⌘+1) to display the contents of
your iTunes library. Click the desired playlist in the scrolling list, like the
Dinah Washington playlist I selected in Figure 13-4. (If you've exported
any original music you composed in GarageBand to your iTunes Library,
you can use those songs in your own movie!) You can add a track to
your movie by dragging the song entry from the Music and Sound Effects
browser to the desired spot in the Project pane.

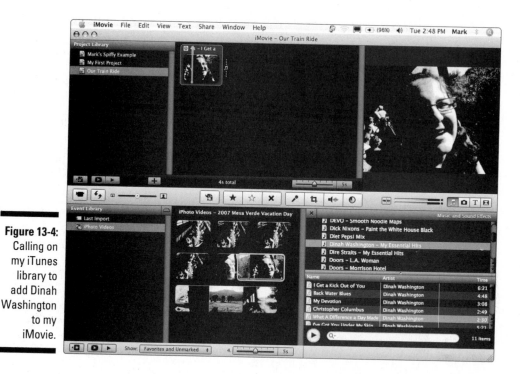

Figure 13-4:
Calling on my iTunes library to add Dinah Washington to my iMovie.

✔ **Adding sound effects:** Yep, if you need the sound of a horse galloping for your Rocky Mountain vacation clips, click the Show Music and Sound Effects button and then click either the iMovie '08 Sound Effects or iLife Sound Effects folders at the top of the scrolling list. To add a sound effect, drag it to the perfect spot in the Project pane.

If you have several gigabytes of music in your iTunes library, it might be more of a challenge to locate "Me and Bobby McGee" by Janis Joplin, especially if she's included in a compilation. Let your MacBook do the digging for you! Click in the Search box below the track list and begin typing a song name. iMovie narrows down the song titles displayed to those that match the characters you type. To reset the search box and display all your songs in the library or selected playlist, click the X icon that appears to the right of the box.

✔ **Ripping songs from an audio CD:** Load an audio CD and then choose Audio CD from the scrolling list. iMovie displays the tracks from the CD, and you can add them at the current playhead position the same way that you would an iTunes songs.

✔ **Recording directly from a microphone:** Yep, if you're thinking voiceover narration, you've hit the nail on the head. Check out the sidebar, "Narration the easy way," for the scoop.

Narration the easy way

Ready to create that award-winning nature documentary? You can add voiceover narration to your iMovie project that would make Jacques Cousteau proud. In fact, you can record your voice while you watch your movie playing, allowing perfect synchronization with the action! To add narration, follow these steps:

1. **Click the Voiceover button on the Editing toolbar — it sports a microphone icon — to open the Voiceover window.**

2. **Click the Record From pop-up menu and select the input device.**

   Your MacBook sports a decent internal microphone, but you can always add a USB microphone to your system.

3. **Drag the input volume slider to a comfortable level.**

   You can monitor the volume level of your voice with the left and right input meters. Try to keep the meters at 50% or so for the proper volume level.

4. **To block out ambient noise levels around you, drag the Noise Reduction slider to the right if necessary.**

If you'd like iMovie to enhance your voice electronically for a more professional sound, select the Voice Enhancement check box. If you need to hear the audio from your movie project while you speak, select the Play Project Audio While Recording check box. Note, however, that you need to listen to the audio while using a set of headphones (plugged into your laptop's headphone jack) to avoid feedback problems.

5. **Click in the desired spot within the Project pane where the narration should begin.**

6. **Begin speaking when prompted by iMovie.**

7. **Watch the video while you narrate so that you can coordinate your narration track with the action.**

8. **Click anywhere in the iMovie window to stop recording.**

   iMovie adds a purple icon to the Project pane underneath the video with the voiceover.

9. **Click the Close button in the Voiceover window.**

You can fine-tune both the audio within a video clip or the audio clips that you add to your project. With the desired clip selected, click the Adjust Audio button on the Editing toolbar. The Audio Adjustments window that appears includes an array of audio controls that allow you to change the volume of the selected clip, or give that audio priority over other audio playing simultaneously (such as a sound effect that needs to be clearly heard over background music and the video clip).

If your clips dramatically vary in volume, follow along:

1. **Click the Normalize Clip Volume button.**

2. **Select each clip that you want to set to the same volume.**

3. **Click Normalize Clip Volume again for each clip.**

4. **When you're done tweaking, click Done.**

You can always return the clip to its original volume. Just open this window again and click Revert to Original.

Building the Cinematic Basics

Time to dive in and add the building blocks to create your movie. Along with video clips, audio tracks, and still images, you can add Hollywood-quality transitions, optical effects, and animated text titles. In this section, I demonstrate how to elevate your collection of video clips into a real-life furshlugginer movie.

Adding clips to your movie

You can add clips to your movie by using the Project pane and the Event pane. The Dynamic Duo work like this:

- ✔ **Project pane:** This pane displays the media you added to your project, allowing you to rearrange the clips, titles, transitions, and still images in your movie.

- ✔ **Event pane:** This pane displays your video clips arranged by *Event* (the date they were shot), acting as the source repository for all your clips. Movies pulled into iMovie, imported to iPhoto, or added manually from the Finder appear here.

To add a clip to your movie

1. **Move your mouse pointer across clips in the Event pane to watch a preview of the video.**

   The clip's thumbnail actually displays the video in real time as you move your pointer across it. *Nice.*

2. **When you decide what to add to your project, you can add the entire clip or a selection.**

- *To select an entire clip:* Right-click the clip thumbnail and choose Select Entire Clip from the menu that appears.

- *To select a portion of a clip:* Drag your mouse cursor across the thumbnail. A yellow frame appears around your selection.

- *To change the length of the selected video:* Drag the handles that appear on either side. If you make a mistake while selecting video, just click any empty space within the Event pane to remove the selection frame, and then try again.

3. **Drag the selection from the Event pane to the spot where it belongs in the Project pane.**

   Alternatively, you can press the E key, or click the Add to Project button (the first button on the Editing toolbar).

Do this several times, and you have a movie, just like the editors of old used to do with actual film clips. This is a good point to mention a moviemaking Mark's Maxim:

Preview your work — and do it often.™

iMovie offers two Play Full Screen buttons: one under the Event Library, and one under the Project Library. Select the project or Event you want to play, and then click the corresponding button. You can also choose View⇨Play Full Screen to watch the selection. Press the spacebar to pause, and press Esc to return to iMovie. You can also move your mouse to display a filmstrip that you can click to skip forward or backward in the project or Event.

To play a selection from the Playhead position, press ⌘+G. (If you've ever watched directors at work on today's movie sets, they're constantly watching a monitor to see what things will look like for the audience. You have the same option in iMovie!)

While you're moving through clips in the Event pane, you might decide that a certain clip has a favorite scene . . . or that another clip has material you don't want, like Uncle Ed's shadow puppets. (Shudder.) iMovie '08 introduces *Favorite* and *Rejected* scenes, allowing you to view and use your best camera work (and ignore the worst stuff). To mark video, select a range of frames or an entire clip; then click the Mark as Favorite button on the Editing toolbar. Click the Reject button to hide the selected video or frames from view. (You can always unmark a Favorite scene by using the Unmark button on the Editing toolbar.)

Removing clips from your movie

Don't like a clip? Be gone! To banish a clip from your movie project

1. **Click the offending clip in the Project pane to select it.**

2. **Press Delete.**

   Alternatively, you can right-click the clip (or a selection you made by dragging) and choose either Delete Entire Clip or Delete Selection from the menu that appears.

The clip disappears — only from the project, *not* from your hard drive — and iMovie automatically rearranges the remaining clips and still images in your movie.

If you remove the wrong clip, don't panic. Instead, use the iMovie Undo feature (press ⌘+Z) to restore it.

Reordering clips in your movie

If Day One of your vacation appears after Day Two in your movie, you can easily reorder your clips and stills by dragging them to the proper space in the Project pane. When you release the mouse, iMovie automatically moves the rest of your movie aside with a minimum of fuss and bother.

Editing clips in iMovie

If a clip has extra seconds of footage at the beginning or end, you don't want that superfluous stuff in your masterpiece. Our favorite video editor gives you the following functions:

- ✔ **Crop:** Removes unwanted material from a video clip or still image, allowing you to change the aspect ratio of the media
- ✔ **Rotate:** Rotates a clip or image on its center axis
- ✔ **Trim:** Trims frames from a video clip

Before you can edit, however, you have to select a section of a clip:

1. **Click a clip or image in either the Project pane or the Event pane to display it in the Monitor (refer to Figure 13-2).**

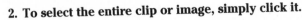

2. **To select the entire clip or image, simply click it.**

3. **Drag your mouse cursor across the thumbnail to select the section of the media you want to edit.**

Some editing functions automatically apply to the entire clip, such as Crop and Rotate.

The selected region is surrounded by a yellow frame. You're ready to edit that selected part of the clip.

Note the handles that appear at the beginning or ending of the selection. You can make fine changes to the selected section by dragging them.

✔ **To crop:** Click the Crop button on the Editing toolbar to display the frame in the Monitor pane, and then click Crop at the top of the Monitor pane. Drag the edges of the frame and the handles to select the section you want to keep. To preview your selection, click the Play button at the top of the monitor. When you're ready, click Done, and everything but the selected region is removed.

✔ **To rotate:** Click the Crop button on the Editing toolbar, and then click one of the two rotation buttons (which carry a curved arrow icon). Each click rotates the media 90 degrees in that direction. Click Done when the clip or image is properly oriented.

✔ **To trim:** Choose Edit⇨Trim to Selection. iMovie removes the frames from around the selected video.

Edits that you make to one clip or still image can actually be copied to multiple items! Select the edited clip and choose Edit⇨Copy from the iMovie menu. Then you can select one or more clips and use the Edit⇨Paste Adjustments menu to apply Video, Audio, or Crop edits. (To apply all three types of edits, just choose All.)

Transitions for the masses

Many iMovie owners approach transitions as *visual bookends:* They merely act as placeholders that appear between video clips. Nothing could be farther from the truth, though, because judicious use of transitions can make or break a scene. For example, which would you prefer after a wedding ceremony — an abrupt, jarring cut to the reception or a gradual fadeout to the reception?

Today's audiences are sensitive to transitions between scenes. Try not to overuse the same transition. Also weigh the visual impact of a transition carefully.

iMovie includes a surprising array of transitions. To display your transition collection, click the Show Transitions button on the Browser toolbar (or press ⌘+4).

To see what a particular transition looks like, move your mouse pointer over the thumbnail to display the transition in miniature.

Adding a transition couldn't be easier: Drag the transition from the list in the Transitions Browser pane and drop it between clips or between a clip and a still image in the Project pane. In iMovie '08, transitions are applied in real time — you don't end up checking your mail or tapping your fingers on your desk waiting for a transition to *render* (a fancy word for *calculate*, which means that older versions of iMovie required you to wait while a transition was generated).

Even Gone with the Wind had titles

The last stop on our iMovie Hollywood Features Tour is the Titles Browser. You find it by clicking the Title button on the Browser toolbar (which bears a big capital T), or by pressing ⌘+3. You can add a title with a still image, but iMovie also includes everything you need to add basic animated text to your movie.

Most of the controls you can adjust are the same for each animation style. You can change the font, size, and color of the text.

To add a title

1. **Select an animation thumbnail from the browser pane and drag it to the desired spot in the Project pane.**

2. **Click the Show Fonts button to make any changes to the fonts or text attributes.**

3. **Click in a text box to type your own line of text.**

4. **Click the Play button to preview your title.**

   iMovie displays a preview of the effect in the monitor with the settings that you choose.

5. **Click Done.**

   The title appears in the Project pane.

Sharing Your Finished Classic with Others

Your movie is complete, you saved it to your hard drive, and now you're wondering where to go from here. Click Share on the application menu bar, and you'll see that iMovie can unleash your movie upon your unsuspecting family and friends (and even the entire world) in a number of ways:

- ✔ **iTunes:** Send your movie to your iTunes library as a movie. iMovie offers recommended settings for your iPod, iPhone, Apple TV, and for viewing on your MacBook.

- ✔ **.Mac Web Gallery:** Share your movie with the world at large by posting it within a Web Gallery on your .Mac Web site. (I provide more .Mac details to chew on in Chapter 9.)

- ✔ **Media Browser:** Make your iMovie project available within other iLife '08 applications, in four different sizes suited to different display devices.

- ✔ **Export Movie:** Create a copy of your movie on your hard drive, in one of four different sizes.

- ✔ **Export via QuickTime:** You can create a QuickTime movie with your project by using the QuickTime encoding engine, which allows you greater control over the export process and the attributes of the finished movie file.

  If you use this option, any computer with an installed copy of QuickTime can display your movies, and you can use QuickTime movies in presentations you create with Apple's Keynote application as well.

- ✔ **YouTube:** Yep, you read right, you can send your iMovie directly to the YouTube Web site! Can it get more convenient than that? (I think not.)

- ✔ **Export to Final Cut XML:** If you'd like to transfer your iMovie '08 project to Final Cut Pro, use this option to create a compatible XML file.

When you choose a sharing option, iMovie displays the video quality for the option, and makes automatic changes to the movie attributes. For example, choosing Tiny will reduce the finished movie as far as possible in file size, and the audio is reduced to mono instead of stereo.

After you adjust any settings specific to the desired sharing option, click Publish (or Save) to start the ball rolling.

Chapter 14

Creating DVDs on the Road with iDVD

In This Chapter

▶ Traversing the iDVD window

▶ Starting a new iDVD project

▶ Tweaking and adjusting your DVD Menu

▶ Previewing your (nearly) finished DVD

▶ Doing things automatically with OneStep DVD and Magic iDVD

▶ Burning a DVD for your friends and family

*H*ow does the old adage go? Oh, yes, it's like this:

> Any DVD movie must be a pain to create. You'll need a ton of money for software, too. And you'll have to take hours of training that will cause your brain to explode.

Funny thing is, *DVD authoring* — designing and creating a DVD movie — really was like that for many years. Only video professionals could afford the software and tackle the training needed to master all the intricacies of DVD Menu design.

Take one guess as to the company that changed all that. (No, it wasn't Coca-Cola.) Apple's introduction of iDVD was (quite literally) a revolution in DVD authoring. Suddenly you, your kids, and Aunt Harriet could all design and burn DVD movies and picture slideshows. Dear reader, this iDVD thing is *huge*.

Plus, you'll quickly find out that iDVD '08 is tightly connected to all the other slices of your digital hub. In plain English, you can pull content from iTunes, iPhoto, and iMovie as easily as a politician makes promises. You'll be creating DVDs for those special occasions on the fly, on the road. And that, friends and neighbors, is the quintessential definition of *cool*.

In this chapter, I show you how your MacBook can take on Hollywood as well as how you can produce a DVD movie with content that's as good as any you'd rent at the video store!

Hey, Where's the Complex Window?

Figure 14-1 shows iDVD in all its glory. The iDVD '08 window was designed by the same smart people who brought you the iMovie window. You have to supply your own digital video clips, background audio, and digital photographs, of course.

Menu display

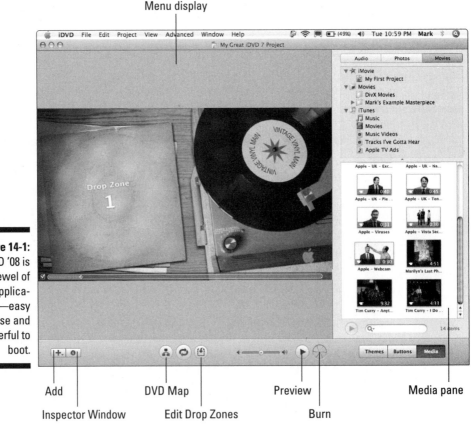

Figure 14-1:
iDVD '08 is a jewel of an application—easy to use and powerful to boot.

Add

Inspector Window

DVD Map

Edit Drop Zones

Preview

Burn

Media pane

Take a moment to appreciate iDVD — no half-a-dozen secondary windows to fiddle with or silly palettes strung out everywhere. (Can you tell that I've had my fill of old-style DVD authoring applications?) Allow me to list the highlights of the iDVD window:

- **Menu display:** This section takes up the largest part of the iDVD window, with good reason. You create your project here. In this case, *Menu* refers to your DVD Menu, **not** the menu at the top of your Mac's display.

- **Media pane:** You add video, still images, and audio to your project from here, as well as tweak and fine-tune things. The Media pane actually comprises three separate panes. To choose a new pane, click one of these buttons at the bottom right of the screen:

  - *Themes:* You apply themes (such as Travel Cards, Wedding White, and Baby Mobile) to your DVD Menu to give it a certain look and feel.

  - *Buttons:* These options apply to the selected item, such as drop shadows on your text titles or the appearance of your menu buttons.

  - *Media:* From here, you can add media items, such as video clips and photos, to your menu.

- **Add:** Clicking this button opens a pop-up menu (which sports a dapper plus sign) from which you can choose one of three types of buttons to add to a project. The choices are

  - *Add Submenu:* Choose this item to add a new submenu button to your DVD Menu. The person using your DVD Menu can click a button to display a new submenu that can include additional movies or slideshows. (If that sounds like ancient Greek, hang on. All becomes clearer later in the chapter in the section, "Adding movies.")

    In iDVD '08, a Menu can hold up to 12 buttons, so submenus let you pack more content on your DVD. (Older versions of the application only allowed six buttons, so don't feel too cheated.) Anyway, each submenu you create can hold another 12 buttons.

  - *Add Movie:* Yep, this is the most popular button in the whole shooting match. Click this menu item to add a new movie clip to your menu.

  - *Add Slideshow:* If you want to add a slideshow to your DVD — say, using photos from your hard drive or pictures from your iPhoto library — click this menu item. (Read all about iPhoto in Chapter 12.)

✔ **Inspector Window:** Click this button to display the Inspector window for the current menu or a highlighted object. From this window, you can change the look of an individual submenu button or an entire menu.

✔ **Motion:** Click this button (which bears two arrows in a circular shape) to start or stop the animation cycle used with the current iDVD theme. The animation repeats (just like it will on your finished DVD) until you click the Motion button again.

Need a visual indicator of the length of your menu's animation cycle? Just follow the animation *playhead,* which moves below the Menu display to indicate where you are in the animation cycle. Like other playheads in the iLife suite, you can click and drag the diamond-shaped playhead button to move anywhere in the animation cycle. Choose View➪Hide Motion Playhead to turn off the playhead display.

✔ **DVD Map:** Click the DVD Map button to display the organizational chart for your DVD Menu. Each button and submenu that you add to your top-level DVD Menu is displayed here, and you can jump directly to a particular item by double-clicking it. Use this road map to help design the layout of your DVD Menu system or to get to a particular item quickly. To return to the Menu display, click the DVD Map button again.

✔ **Edit Drop Zones:** Clicking this button allows you to edit the look and contents of a drop zone on your menu. Don't worry; I explain more about drop zones in the sidebar titled, "Taking advantage of drop zones," later in this chapter.

✔ **Preview:** To see how your DVD Menu project looks when burned to a DVD, click Preview. You get a truly nifty onscreen remote control that you can use to navigate your DVD Menu, just as if you were watching your DVD on a standard DVD player. To exit Preview mode, click the Stop button on the remote control. Read more about this control in the upcoming section, "Previewing Your Masterpiece."

✔ **Burn:** Oh, yeah, you know what this one is for — recording your completed DVD movie to a blank disc.

That's the lot! Time to get down to the step-by-step business of making movies.

Starting a New DVD Project

When you launch iDVD '08 for the first time (or if you close all iDVD windows), you get the sporty menu shown in Figure 14-2. Take a moment to discover more about these four choices.

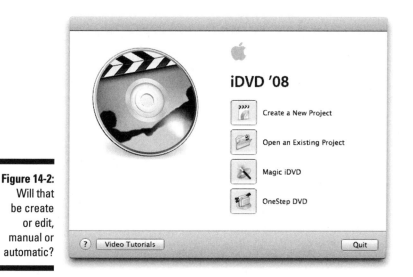

Figure 14-2:
Will that
be create
or edit,
manual or
automatic?

Creating a new project

If you choose Create a New Project, iDVD prompts you to type a name for
your new DVD project and to set a location where the project files should
be saved. By default, the very reasonable choice is your Documents folder.
You also get to choose whether your project will display in a Standard (full-
screen) aspect ratio of 4:3, or a Widescreen aspect ratio of 16:9. If you've
been watching DVD movies for some time, you recognize these two terms.

You'll probably crave Widescreen format if you have a widescreen TV — go
figure — but both formats will display on both types of televisions.

Click Create, and the iDVD window appears in all its glory.

Opening an existing project

If you've used iDVD and had a DVD project open the last time you quit the
application, iDVD automatically loads the DVD project you were working on.
However, you can open any DVD you created by clicking Open an Existing
Project. (To choose a different existing project from the iDVD window, press
⌘+O, or choose File⇨Open Recent.)

Automating the whole darn process

If you're a fan of click-it-and-forget-it (or are in a hurry), you can throw cau-tion to the wind and allow iDVD to create your latest epic for you! iDVD offers two automated methods of creating a DVD movie disc.

Using OneStep DVD

With OneStep, iDVD does most of the work automatically by using the media clips and photos that you specify. To allow iDVD to help you create a movie, click the OneStep DVD button on the top-level menu (refer to Figure 14-2). If you already opened a project, choose File⇨OneStep DVD from the applica-tion menu bar (to import clips directly from your camera) or File⇨OneStep DVD from Movie (to select a clip to import from your hard drive). I tell you more about the OneStep DVD feature later in the section, "A Word about Automation."

Using Magic iDVD

Magic iDVD is the newcomer on the block, and it falls neatly between total automation (with OneStep DVD) and total manual control. Click the Magic iDVD button on the top-level menu (as shown in Figure 14-2). If you already opened a project, you can choose File⇨Magic iDVD from the menu bar to choose a theme, drop specific movies and specific photos into filmstrips, and choose an audio track.

Unlike OneStep DVD, you get to preview the finished product. If it's to your liking, you can choose to either burn the disc directly or save a full-blown iDVD project to your hard drive with the results. *Sweet.*

You can find out more about the new Magic iDVD feature later in the section, "A Word about Automation."

Creating a DVD from Scratch

Doing things the old-fashioned, creative, and manual way (following the examples in this section) involves four basic steps:

1. Design the DVD Menu.

   Choose a theme and any necessary buttons or links.

2. Add media.

   You can drag movie files from iMovie HD, still images from iPhoto, and music from iTunes.

3. Tweak.

   Adjust and fine-tune your DVD Menu settings.

4. Finish things up.

   Preview and burn your DVD, or save it to your hard drive.

Choosing just the right theme

The first step to take when manually designing a new DVD Menu system is to add a theme. In the iDVD world, a *theme* is a preset package that helps determine the appearance and visual appeal of your DVD Menu, including a background image, menu animation, an audio track, and a group of settings for text fonts and button styles.

iDVD helps those of us who are graphically challenged by including a wide range of professionally designed themes for all sorts of occasions, as well as more generic themes with the accent on action, friendship, and technology. To view the included themes, click the Themes button in the lower-right corner of the iDVD window (see Figure 14-3).

Figure 14-3: Select a new theme from the Themes pane.

Taking advantage of drop zones

Most of Apple's animated themes include special bordered areas marked as drop zones. These locations have nothing to do with skydiving; rather, a *drop zone* is a placeholder in the Menu that can hold a single video clip or photograph. When you drag a video clip or an image to a drop zone, that clip or picture is added to the animation in Apple's theme! Think about that for a moment; I know I did. You can actually personalize a Hollywood-quality animated DVD menu with *your own photos and video!*

To add a video clip or image to a drop zone, simply drag the clip or photo from a Finder window and drop it on the desired drop zone. You can also drag clips or photos from other sources, including the Movie and iPhoto panes in iDVD, the iMovie window, or the iPhoto window. Drop zones don't act as links or buttons to other content; the stuff you add to a menu's drop zones appears only as part of the theme's animation cycle. You can even drag an iPhoto event or album to a drop zone, and it will continuously cycle through the images. *Wowsers!*

To choose a theme for your project — or to see what a theme looks like on your menu — click any thumbnail and watch iDVD update the Menu display.

If you decide while creating your DVD Menu that you need a different theme, you can change themes at any time. iDVD won't lose a single button or video clip that you add to your DVD Menu. You'll be amazed at how the look and sound of your DVD Menu completely changes with just the click of a theme thumbnail.

Adding movies

Drop zones and themes are cool, but most folks want to add video to their DVD. To accomplish this, iDVD uses buttons as links to your video clips. In fact, some iDVD Movie buttons display a preview of the video they'll display! To play the video on a DVD player, you select the Movie button with the remote control, just like you do for a commercial DVD.

To add a Movie button, drag a QuickTime movie file from the Finder and drop it onto your DVD Menu display. (Note that only MPEG-4 QuickTime movies are supported. MPEG-1 and MPEG-2 movie clips might be rejected, or converted when possible.) Alternatively, drag a clip from the iDVD media pane into the iDVD window, or click the Add button and choose Add Movie from the pop-up menu.

iDVD and iMovie are soul mates, so you can also display the iDVD Media pane and then click Movies from the pop-up menu. Now you can drag clips from your Movies folder.

No matter the source of the clip, when you drop it onto your DVD menu, iDVD adds a Movie button, as you can see in Figure 14-4. Note that some buttons appear as text links rather than actual buttons. The appearance of a Movie button in your DVD menu is determined by the theme you choose.

A Movie button doesn't have to stay where iDVD places it! By default, iDVD aligns buttons and text objects on an invisible grid. However, if you don't want such order imposed on your creativity, just drag the object wherever you'd like to turn on Free Positioning. (You can also right-click the object and choose the Free Positioning item from the menu that appears.) iDVD '08 even provides cool new automatic guides that help you align objects when you're using Free Positioning. You'll see them as yellow lines that appear when objects are aligned along a vertical or horizontal plane.

As I mention earlier, you can have up to 12 buttons on your iDVD Menu. To add more content than 12 buttons allow, add a submenu by clicking the Add button and choosing Add Submenu from the pop-up menu. Now you can click the submenu button to jump to that screen and drag up to another 12 movie files into it.

Figure 14-4:
A new
Movie
button
appears on
your pristine
DVD Menu.

A word on image dimensions

For best playback results on a standard TV, make sure that your background image has the same dimensions as standard digital video — 640 x 480 pixels. If the dimensions of your image don't match the dimensions of digital video, iDVD will stretch or shrink the image to fit, which might have undesirable effects. When your image is stretched and skewed to fit the DVD Menu, Aunt Harriet might end up looking like Shrek (or perhaps Fiona).

Keep in mind your target audience while you create your DVD. Standard TV sets have a different *aspect ratio* (height to width) and *resolution* (number of pixels on the screen) than a digital video clip, and a standard TV isn't as precise in focusing that image on the tube. If you select the Standard aspect ratio when you create the project, you can make sure that your DVD content looks great on a standard TV screen by following these steps:

1. **Click View on the old-fashioned iDVD menu (the one at the top of the screen).**

2. **Choose the Show TV Safe Area command.**

   You can also press the convenient ⌘+T shortcut.

   iDVD adds a smaller rectangle within the iDVD window to mark the screen dimensions of a standard TV.

3. **Place your content within the safe area.**

   If you take care that your menu buttons and (most of) your background image fit within this smaller rectangle, you're assured that folks with a standard television can enjoy your work.

To toggle off the TV Safe Area rectangle, press ⌘+T again.

If your entire family is blessed with a fleet of HD TVs (or you chose the Widescreen aspect ratio for this project), leave the Show TV Safe Area option off. Today's widescreen displays can handle just about any orientation.

Great! Now my audience demands a slideshow!

Many Mac owners don't realize that iDVD can use not only video clips but also digital photos as content. In fact, you can add a group of images to your DVD Menu via the Slideshow buttons, which allow the viewer to play back a series of digital photographs. iDVD handles everything for you, so there's no tricky timing to figure out or weird scripts to write. Just click the Add button at the bottom of the iDVD window and choose Add Slideshow. iDVD places a Slideshow button on your DVD Menu.

After the Slideshow button is on tap, add the content — in this case, by choosing the images that iDVD adds to your DVD Menu. Follow these steps to select your slideshow images:

1. **Double-click the Slideshow Menu button — the one you just added to the menu — to open the Slideshow display (see Figure 14-5)**

2. **Click the Media button (bottom right of the screen).**

3. **Click the Photos button (top right of the screen) to display your iPhoto library and photo albums.**

4. **Drag your favorite image thumbnails from the Photos list and drop them into the My Slideshow window.**

   You can also drag images straight from a Finder window or the iPhoto window itself. (Those Apple folks are sooooo predictable.).

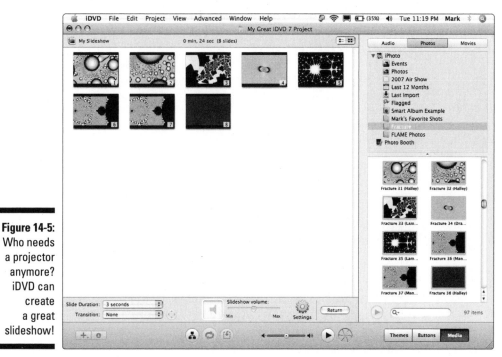

Figure 14-5:
Who needs a projector anymore? iDVD can create a great slideshow!

5. **Drag around the photos in the My Slideshow window to set their order of appearance in your slideshow.**

6. **To add audio to these pictures, drag your favorite audio file from the Finder and drop it in the Audio well in the My Slideshow window.**

   The *Audio well* is the box bearing the speaker icon, next to the volume control below the My Slideshow window.

   Alternatively, click the Audio button (top right of the screen) to select an audio track from your iTunes library, iTunes playlists, or GarageBand creations.

7. **Click the Return button on the Slideshow display to return to your DVD Menu.**

If you're using a menu with animated buttons that display an image (rather than text buttons), you can choose which image you want to appear on the Slideshow button. Click the Slideshow button that you added and see the slider that appears above the Slideshow button. Drag this slider to scroll through the images you added. When you find the image that you want to use for the Slideshow button in the DVD Menu, click the Slideshow button again to save your changes.

Now for the music . . .

Most of the Apple-supplied themes already have their own background music for your menu, so you might not even need to add music to your DVD Menu. However, if you want to change the existing background music (or if your menu currently doesn't have any music), adding your own audio to the current menu is child's play!

1. **Click the Media button.**

2. **Click the Audio button to reveal the musical Shangri-La, as shown in Figure 14-6.**

3. **Drag an audio file from the iTunes playlist or GarageBand folder display and drop it on the menu background.**

   iDVD '08 accepts every sound format that you can use for encoding in iTunes: AIFF, MP3, AAC, Apple Lossless, and WAV audio files.

4. **Click the Motion button (labeled in Figure 14-1) to watch your DVD Menu animation cycle set to the new background audio.**

5. **Click the Motion button again to stop the animation and return to serious work.**

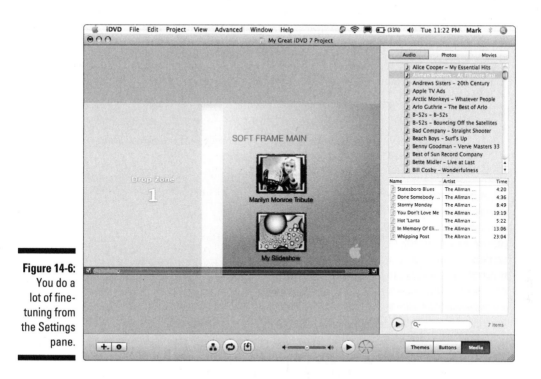

Giving Your DVD the Personal Touch

You can easily make changes to the default settings provided with the theme you choose. iDVD offers all sorts of controls that allow you to change the appearance and behavior of buttons, text, and the presentation of your content. In this section, I show you how to cast out iDVD's (perfectly good) defaults and then tweak things to perfection.

Using Uncle Morty for your DVD Menu background

Hey, Uncle Morty might not be a supermodel, but he has birthdays and anniversaries. Follow these steps to change the background of your DVD Menu:

1. **Click the Inspector button (refer to Figure 14-1).**

   iDVD displays the Menu Info dialog.

2. **Get an image, using one of the following methods:**

- *Drag an image from the Finder* and drop it into the Background well, which appears as a square with a white outline at the top of the Menu Info dialog.

- *Drag the image directly into the Menu display.*

- *Use an image from your iPhoto library* by clicking the Media button, choosing Photos, and then dragging the desired image into the Menu display.

iDVD updates the DVD menu to reflect your new background choice.

Adding your own titles

The one tweak you'll probably have to perform in every iDVD project is changing titles. Unfortunately, the default labels provided by iDVD are pretty lame, and they appear in two important places:

- **Menu title:** Your large main title usually appears at the top of the DVD Menu.

- **Button captions:** Each Submenu, Movie, and Slideshow button that you add to your menu has its own title.

To change the text in your Menu title or the titles below your buttons, follow these steps:

1. **Select the text by clicking it.**

2. **Click it again to edit it.**

A rectangle with a cursor appears to indicate that you can now edit the text.

3. **Type the new text and then press Return to save the change.**

Changing buttons like a highly paid professional

Customizing Movie buttons? You can do it with aplomb! Follow these steps:

1. **Click Buttons.**

2. **Click any Movie button from the DVD Menu to select it.**

A slider appears above the button, which you can drag to set the thumbnail picture for that button in your DVD Menu. (Naturally, this is only for animated buttons, not text buttons.)

Enable the Movie check box to animate the button.

3. To create a Movie button with a still image, drag a picture from a Finder window or the Media pane and drop it on top of the button.

4. To adjust the properties for the button, click the Inspector button.

Table 14-1 describes the button properties. Note that some properties won't appear for text buttons.

Table 14-1	Button Settings You Can Customize
Movie Button Property	*What It Does*
Label Font	Changes the label font, text size, color and attributes.
Label Attributes	Specifies the position of the label and whether it has a shadow.
Custom Thumbnail	Allows you to select the image that will appear on the button. Drag an image to the Custom Thumbnail well. For Slideshow buttons, drag the Thumbnail slider to select the image that will appear on the button.
Transition	Determines the transition that occurs when the button is clicked (before the action occurs).
Size	Adjusts the size of the button. Move the slider to the right to increase the button size.

Give my creation motion!

Earlier in this chapter, you can read how to use a different image for your background, but what about using an animated background? You can use any QuickTime movie from your iMovie library to animate your DVD Menu background! Didn't I tell you that this iDVD thing was *huge?*

Keep in mind that your background movie should be a short clip; 20–30 seconds is optimal. A clip with a fade-in at the beginning and a fade-out at the end is the best choice because iDVD loops your background clip continuously, and your animated background flows seamlessly behind your menu.

I'm not talking drop zones here. (See the sidebar, "Taking advantage of drop zones.") You can add a movie to a drop zone, of course, but by using a movie clip as a background, you're replacing the entire animation sequence rather than just a single area of the background.

Follow these steps to add a new animated background:

1. **Click your old friend, the Inspector Window button (refer to Figure 14-1).**

   Make sure that no individual objects are highlighted so that the Inspector window displays the Menu properties instead.

2. **Drag a movie from the Finder and drop it into the Background well.**

   You can click the Movies button in the Media pane to instantly display your iMovie collection.

3. **Click the Motion button in the iDVD window to try out your new background.**

4. **Click the Motion button again to stop the animation cycle.**

Previewing Your Masterpiece

Figure 14-7 captures the elusive Preview remote control — truly an awesome sight. When you click Preview, the Media pane disappears, and your DVD Menu appears exactly as it will on the finished DVD.

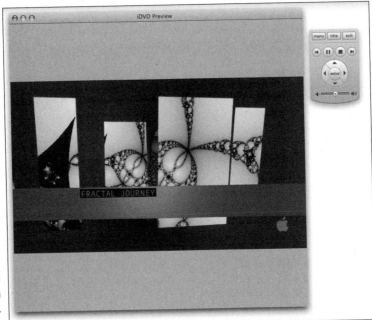

Figure 14-7: Preview mode — an incredible simulation indeed.

Ah, but appearances aren't everything: You can also use your DVD Menu! Click the buttons on the remote control to simulate the remote on your DVD player, or think outside the box and click a menu button directly with your mouse pointer. iDVD presents the video clip, runs the slideshow, or jumps to a submenu, just as it will with the completed disc.

This is a great time to test-drive a project before you burn it to disc. To make sure that you don't waste a blank DVD, make certain that everything you expect to happen actually happens. Nothing worse than discovering that Aunt Edna's slideshow from her Hong Kong trip actually displays your family's summer trip to the zoo (whoops). If you made a mistake or something needs tweaking, click the Exit button on the controller, and you're back to the iDVD window proper, where you can edit or fine-tune your project.

iDVD '08 allows you to save your project as a standard Mac OS X disc image rather than as a simple project file (or a physical DVD) — which a good idea if you're out of blank media because you can use the Apple Disk Utility to open and mount the disc image as if it were a burned disc. (If you're a MacBook Air Road Warrior without your external SuperDrive, this feature is just plain wonderful!) To save an iDVD project as a disc image, choose File⇨Save as Disc Image (or press ⌘+Shift+R).

Interested in tweaking settings across your entire project? Perhaps you'd like to improve the quality of your recorded video, or you'd like to switch video modes from NTSC to PAL for a DVD that's to be sent overseas. If you'd like to view or change the overall settings for your entire DVD, click Project⇨Project Info to display the Project Info dialog.

A Word about Automation

At the beginning of the chapter, I mention the easy way to produce an iDVD disc or project, using either OneStep DVD (for complete automation) or Magic iDVD (for partial automation). In this section, I provide you with the details.

One-click paradise with OneStep DVD

If you're in a hurry to create a DVD from clips on your DV camcorder and you don't mind losing your creative input, OneStep DVD is just the ticket. In short, iDVD '08 allows you to plug in your DV camcorder, answer a question or two, and then sit back while the application does all the work. iDVD '08 imports the DV clips, creates a basic menu design, and burns the disc automatically!

Using OneStep DVD will appeal to any laptop owner. Why not produce a DVD right after a wedding or birthday that you can give as a gift — in minutes after the event is over? Photographers who cover those same special events might consider selling a DVD made with OneStep DVD. If you happen to capture something incredibly unique — say, a UFO landing or an honest politician — you can use OneStep DVD to create an instant backup of the clips on your DV camcorder. You could even keep your friends and family up to date with the progress of your vacation by sending them a daily DVD of your exploits! (You gotta admit that even Grandma would consider that eminently *sassy!*)

Follow these steps to start the OneStep DVD process:

1. **Click the OneStep DVD button on the iDVD '08 top-level menu (refer to Figure 14-2).**

   Alternatively, choose File⇨OneStep DVD.

   iDVD displays the OneStep dialog.

   If you want to use OneStep DVD with an existing movie on your MacBook's hard drive, choose File⇨OneStep DVD from Movie instead. iDVD prompts you for the video clip to use.

2. **Following the prompts, connect the FireWire cable from your DV camcorder; then turn on the camcorder and set it to VCR mode.**

3. **Click OK.**

4. **Load a blank DVD when prompted.**

Exercising control with Magic iDVD

Got a little extra time? For those who prefer to make just a few choices and let iDVD do the rest, the new Magic iDVD feature just plain rocks! However, you can't import clips directly from your DV camcorder like you can with OneStep DVD. Instead, you select the following:

- ✔ **An iDVD theme**
- ✔ **Video clips** you created with iMovie HD or that you dragged from the Finder
- ✔ **Photos** from your iPhoto library or dragged from the Finder
- ✔ **Audio** from your iTunes playlist or dragged from the Finder

Follow these steps to start the OneStep DVD process:

1. **Click the Magic iDVD button on the iDVD '08 top-level menu (refer to Figure 14-2).**

   iDVD displays the Magic iDVD window.

2. **Click in the DVD Title box and type a name for your disc (or project).**

3. **Click to select a theme from the Theme strip.**

4. **Click the Movies button and drag the desired clips into the Drop Movies Here strip.**

5. **To add a slideshow, click the Photos button and drag the desired photos into the Drop Photos Here strip.**

6. **To add audio for your slideshow, click the Audio button and drag the desired song into the Drop Photos Here strip.**

   No, there is no Drop Audio Here strip, but a speaker icon does appear in the first cell of the Drop Photos Here strip to indicate that you added a soundtrack.

7. **Click Preview to see a preview of the finished project, complete with remote control. To exit Preview mode, click Exit.**

8. **To open the project in its current form in the main iDVD window, click Create Project.**

   Opening your Magic iDVD work as a full iDVD project gives you full creative control over what's been completed so far. (In effect, Magic iDVD has acted as an assistant and helped you to quickly build the foundation for an iDVD project.)

9. **To record your completed project directly to DVD, load a blank DVD, and then click Burn.**

To return to the iDVD main window at any time, just click the Close button on the Magic iDVD window.

Recording a Finished Project to a Shiny Disc

When you're ready to record your next Oscar-winning documentary on family behaviors during vacation, just follow these simple words.

1. **Click the Burn button at the bottom of the iDVD window.**

   I have to admit, the Burn button that appears has to be my favorite single control in all my 20+ years of computing! It looks powerful, it looks sexy . . . it wants to *burn.* (Sorry about that. Rather wanton of me.)

2. **After iDVD asks you to insert a blank DVD-R into the SuperDrive, load a blank DVD-R, DVD-RW, DVD+R, or DVD+RW (depending on the media your Mac can handle).**

Your SuperDrive might be able to burn and read a DVD+R, DVD-RW, or DVD+RW, but what about your DVD player? Keep in mind that only DVD-Rs are likely to work in older DVD players. The latest generation of DVD players are likely DVD+R compatible as well. Therefore, remember the destination for the discs you burn and choose your media accordingly.

After a short pause, iDVD begins burning the DVD. The application keeps you updated with a progress bar.

When the disc is finished, you're ready to load it into your favorite local DVD player, or you can load it back into your laptop and enjoy your work, using the Apple DVD Player.

Either way, it's all good!

Chapter 15

GarageBand on the Go

. . . .

In This Chapter

▶ Navigating the GarageBand window

▶ Adding tracks and loops to your song

▶ Repeating loops and extending your song

▶ Building arrangements

▶ Adding effects to instruments

▶ Exporting your work to iTunes and iWeb

▶ Burning your song to an audio CD

. . . .

Do you dream of making music? I've always wanted to join a band, but I never devoted the time nor learned to play the guitar. You know the drill: Those rock stars struggled for years to gain the upper hand over an instrument, practicing for untold hours, memorizing chords, and. . . . Wait a second. I almost forgot. You don't need to do any of that now!

Apple's GarageBand '08 lets a musical wanna-be (like yours truly) make music with any MacBook — complete with a driving bass line, funky horns, and a set of perfect drums that never miss a beat. In fact, the thousands of prerecorded loops on tap in this awesome application even allow you to design your music to match that melody running through your head, from techno to jazz to alternative rock.

Oh, and did I mention that you can also use GarageBand '08 to produce podcasts on your MacBook? That's right! You can record your voice and easily create your own show, and then share it with others from your iWeb site! Heck, add photos if you like. You'll be the talk of your family and friends and maybe even your Mac user group.

This chapter explains everything you need to know to create your first song, no matter where you are: a hotel room, a bus, an airplane, or even a record store! I also show you how to import your hit record into iTunes so you can listen to it on your iPod with a big silly grin on your face (like I do) or add it to your next iMovie or iDVD project as a royalty-free soundtrack.

Don't be too smug when you think of all that practicing and hard work you missed out on. What a shame!

Shaking Hands with Your Band

As you can see in Figure 15-1, the GarageBand window isn't complex at all, and that's good design. In this section, I list the most important controls so you know your Play button from your Loop Browser button.

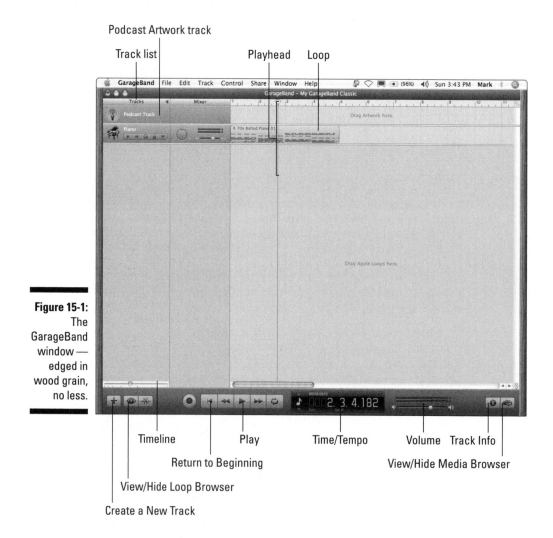

Podcast Artwork track

Track list   Playhead   Loop

Figure 15-1:
The
GarageBand
window —
edged in
wood grain,
no less.

Timeline   Play   Time/Tempo   Volume   Track Info

Return to Beginning   View/Hide Media Browser

View/Hide Loop Browser

Create a New Track

Your music-making machine includes

- **Track list:** In GarageBand, a *track* is a discrete instrument that you set up to play one part of your song. For example, a piece for a classical string quartet has four tracks — one each for violin, viola, cello, and bass. This list contains all the tracks in your song arranged so that you can easily see and modify them, like the rows in a spreadsheet. A track begins in the list, stretching out to the right all the way to the end of the song. As you can see in the upper left of Figure 15-1, I already have one track defined — a Grand Piano.

  If you're creating a podcast, a *Podcast artwork track* like the one you see at the very top of the list in Figure 15-1 can also appear.

- **Timeline:** This scrolling area holds the loops (see the following bullet) that you add or record, allowing you to move and edit them easily. When a song plays, the timeline scrolls to give you a visual look at your music. (Bear with me; you'll understand that cryptic statement in a page or two.)

- **Loop:** This is a prerecorded clip of an instrument being played in a specific style and tempo. *Loops* are the building blocks of your song. You can drag loops from the loop browser to a track and literally build a bass line or a guitar solo. (It's a little like adding video clips to the timeline in iMovie to build a film.)

- **Playhead:** This vertical line is a moving indicator that shows you the current position in your song while it scrolls by in the timeline. You can drag the playhead to a new location at any time. The playhead also acts like the insertion cursor in a word processing application: If you insert a section of a song or a loop from the Clipboard, it appears at the current location of the playhead. (More on copying and inserting loops later, so don't panic.)

- **Create a New Track button:** Click this button to add a new track to your song.

- **Track Info button:** If you need to display the instrument used in a track, click the track to select it and then click this button. You can also control settings, such as Echo and Reverb, from the dialog that's displayed.

- **View/Hide Loop Browser button:** Click the button with the striking eye icon to display the Loop Browser at the bottom of the window; click it again to close it. You can see more tracks at a time without scrolling by closing the Loop Browser.

- **View/Hide Media Browser button:** Click this button (which bears icons of a filmstrip, slide, and musical note) to display the Media Browser at the right side of the window; click it again to close it. When you close the media browser, you can see more of your tracks. If you're already familiar with iDVD or iMovie, you recognize this pane in the GarageBand window. Use it to add media (in this case, still images or video clips) to your GarageBand project for use in a podcast.

✔ **Return to Beginning button:** Clicking this button immediately moves the playhead back to the beginning of the timeline.

✔ **Play button:** Hey, old friend! At last, a control that you've probably used countless times before, and it works just like the same control on an audio CD player. Click Play, and GarageBand begins playing your entire song. Notice that the Play button turns blue. To stop the music, click Play again; the button loses that sexy blue sheen, and the playhead stops immediately. (If playback is paused, it begins again at the play-head position when you click Play.)

✔ **Time/Tempo display:** This cool-looking LCD display shows you the current playhead position in seconds. You can also click the time/tempo indicator (the blue LED numeric display at the bottom of the window) to change the tempo (speed) of your song.

GarageBand '08 expands the abilities of the default Time/Tempo display. Click the icon at the left of the display to choose other modes, such as Time (to show a more precise absolute time display) and Project (to show the key, tempo, and signature for the song).

✔ **Volume slider:** Here's another familiar face. Just drag the slider to raise or lower the volume.

Of course, more controls are scattered around the GarageBand window, but these are the main controls used to compose a song . . . which is the next stop!

Composing and Podcasting Made Easy

In this section, I cover the basics of composition in GarageBand, working from the very beginning. Follow along with this running example:

1. **Press ⌘+N.**

   GarageBand displays the Project Select dialog.

2. **Click Create New Music Project to create a new song, or click Create New Podcast Episode to create a new podcast.**

   GarageBand displays the New Project dialog, as shown in Figure 15-2. (The Tempo, Signature, and Key controls don't appear if you're creating a new podcast.)

3. **Type a name for your new song or podcast. If you're creating a new song, drag the Tempo slider to select the beats per minute (bpm).**

   A GarageBand song can have only one tempo (speed) throughout, expressed as beats per minute.

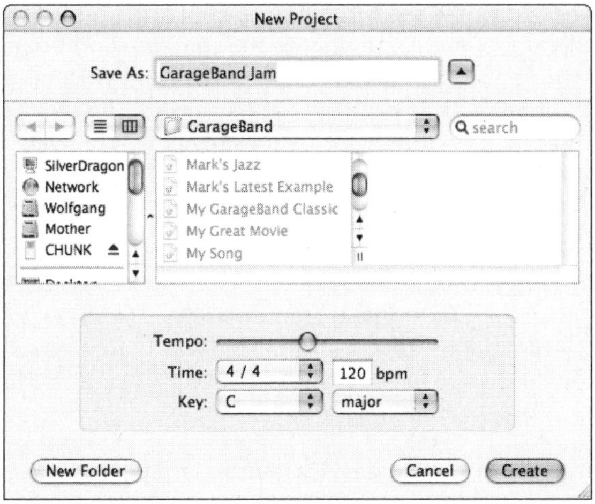

Figure 15-2:
Start
creating
your new
song here.

4. **If you want to adjust the settings for your song, you can select the**

   • *Time signature:* The Time pop-up

   • *Key:* The Key pop-ups

   If you're new to *music theory* (the rules/syntax by which music is created and written), just use the defaults. Most of the toe-tappin' tunes that you and I are familiar with fit right in with these settings.

5. **Click the Create button.**

   You see the window shown in Figure 15-1. The Ballad Piano 01 section in the middle of Figure 15-1 — which I show you how to add in the next section — is an example of a typical loop.

Adding tracks

Although I'm not a musician, I am a music lover, and I know that many classical composers approached a new work in the same way you approach a new song in GarageBand: by envisioning the instruments that you want to hear. (I imagine Mozart and Beethoven would've been thrilled to use GarageBand, but I think they did a decent job with pen (quill?) and paper, too.)

If you've followed along to this point, you've likely noticed two problems with your GarageBand window.

✓ **The tiny keyboard in the middle of your GarageBand window ain't the greatest.** You can record the contents of a software instrument track by "playing" the keyboard: that is, clicking the keys with your mouse. (As you might imagine, this isn't the best solution.) If you're a musician, the best method of recording your own notes is with a MIDI instrument, which you can connect to your laptop by using the USB port. For now, you can banish the keyboard window by clicking the window's Close button. To display it again at any time, press ⌘+K.

✓ **The example song has only one track.** If you want to write the next classical masterpiece for Grand Piano (the default track when you create a new song in GarageBand), that's fine. Otherwise, you could start with a clean slate by choosing Track⇨Delete Track on the GarageBand menu bar. It's up to you; you're the composer!

These are the four kinds of tracks you can use in GarageBand '08:

✓ **Software instrument tracks:** These tracks aren't audio recordings. Rather, they're mathematically precise algorithms that your laptop *renders* (builds) to fit your needs. If you have a MIDI instrument connected to your aluminum supercomputer, you can create your own software instrument tracks. Read more on MIDI instruments later in this chapter.

In this chapter, I focus on software instrument tracks, which are the easiest for a non-musician to use.

✓ **Real instrument tracks:** A real instrument track is an actual audio recording, such as your voice or a physical instrument without a MIDI connection. (Think microphone.)

✓ **Podcast artwork track:** You get only one of these, which holds photos that will appear on a video iPod (or a window on your iWeb site) when your podcast is playing. Apple's iWeb application makes it easy to create your own Web pages, complete with your podcasts. I discuss more on sending your podcast to an iWeb project, later in this chapter.

✓ **Video tracks:** The video sound track appears if you're *scoring* (adding music) to an iMovie movie. Along with the video sound track, you get a cool companion video track that shows the clips in your movie. (More on this in the sidebar, "Look! I'm John Williams!," later in this chapter.)

Time to add a software instrument track of your very own. Follow these steps:

1. **Click the Create a New Track button (which carries a plus sign, labeled in Figure 15-1).**

   GarageBand displays the New Track sheet.

2. **Select the Software Instrument Track radio button and then click Create.**

The New Track sheet disappears, and you're presented with all those great instruments in the Track Info pane on the right.

3. **Choose the general instrument category by clicking it.**

   I chose Drum Kits.

4. **From the right column, choose your specific style of weapon, such as Jazz Kit for a jazzy sound.**

   If you haven't installed the extra kits along with GarageBand, note that you might see disabled instruments appear in the list. Click the right arrow to install the complete set of instruments and loops.

   Figure 15-3 illustrates the new track that appears in your list when you follow these steps.

If you're creating a podcast and you want to add a series of still images that will appear on a video iPod's screen (or on your iWeb page), follow these steps:

1. **Click the View Media Browser button (labeled in Figure 15-1).**

2. **Click the Photos button.**

   GarageBand displays all the photos in your iPhoto library and film rolls.

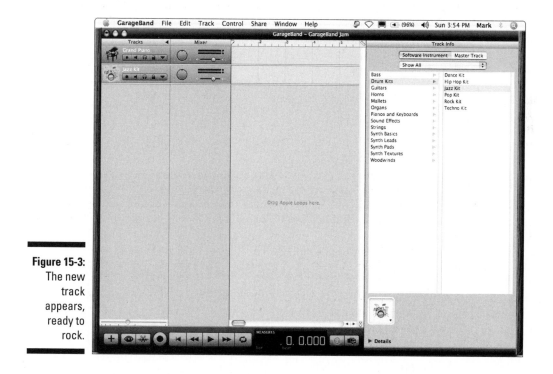

Figure 15-3:
The new track appears, ready to rock.

3. **Drag an image from your iPhoto library in the media browser to the Track list.**

   The Podcast track appears at the top of the Track list, and you can add and move images in the list at any time, just like the loops that you add to your instrument tracks. (More on adding and rearranging the contents of a track later in this section.)

Choosing loops

When you have a new, empty track, you can add something that you can hear. You do that by adding loops to your track from the Loop Browser — and Apple provides you with thousands of loops to choose from — as well as photos from your Media Browser. Click the Loop Browser button (which bears the all-seeing eye) to display your collection, as shown in Figure 15-4.

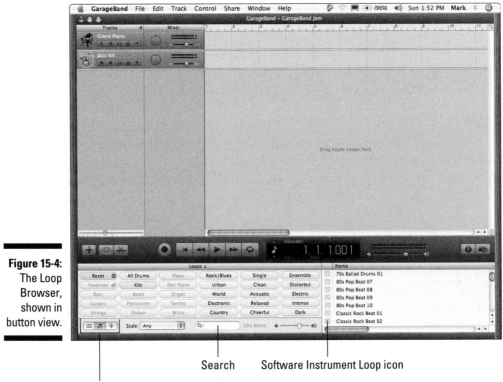

Figure 15-4:
The Loop Browser, shown in button view.

Search   Software Instrument Loop icon

View: Column/Button/Podcast sounds

If your browser looks different from what you see in Figure 15-4, that's because of the view mode you're using, just like the different view modes available for a Finder window. The three-icon button in the lower-left corner of the Loop Browser toggles the browser display between column, musical button, and podcast sounds views. Click the middle of the three buttons to switch to button mode.

Looking for just the right loop

The track in this running example uses a jazz drum kit, but I haven't added a loop yet. (Refer to Figure 15-3.) Follow these steps to search through your loop library for just the right rhythm:

1. **Click the button that corresponds to the instrument you're using.**

   In this example, use the Kits button (which appears as the second button in the second row within the Loop Browser). Click it, and a list of different beats appears in the pane to the right of the browser window. (Check out Figure 15-4 for a sneak peek.)

2. **Click one of the loops with a green, music note icon.**

   Go ahead; this is where things get fun! GarageBand begins playing the loop nonstop, allowing you to get a feel for how that particular loop sounds.

   Because I'm using only software instruments in this track (and in examples throughout this chapter), you should choose only software instrument loops, which are identified with a green, music note icon.

3. **Click another entry in the list, and the application switches immediately to that loop.**

   Now you're beginning to understand why GarageBand is so cool for both musicians and the note-impaired. It's like having your own band, with members that never get tired and play whatever you want while you're composing. (Mozart would've *loved* this.)

   If you want to search for a particular instrument, click in the Search field (labeled in Figure 15-4) and type the text you want to match. GarageBand returns the search results in the list. (Read all about searching in Chapter 7.)

4. **Scroll down the list and continue to sample the different loops until you find one that fits like a glove.**

   For this reporter, it's Lounge Jazz Drums 01.

5. **Drag the entry to your Jazz Kit track and drop it at the very beginning of the timeline (as indicated by the playhead).**

   Your window will look like Figure 15-5.

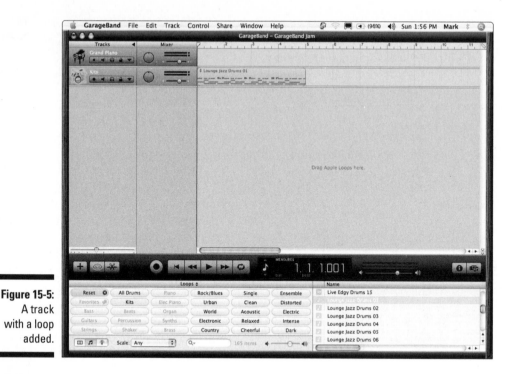

Figure 15-5:
A track
with a loop
added.

Whoops! Did you do something that you regret? Don't forget that you can undo most actions in GarageBand by pressing the old standby ⌘+Z immediately afterward.

Second verse, same as the first

When you compose, you can add additional tracks for each instrument that you want in your song:

- ✔ Each track can have more than one loop.
- ✔ Loops don't have to start at the beginning; you can drop a loop anywhere on the timeline.

For example, in Figure 15-6, you can see that my drum kit kicks in first, but my bass line doesn't begin until some time later (for a funkier opening).

You put loops on separate tracks so they can play simultaneously on different instruments. If all your loops in a song are added on the same track, you hear only one loop at any one time, and all the loops use the same software instrument. By creating multiple tracks, you give yourself the elbowroom to bring in the entire band at the same time. It's uber-convenient to compose your song when you can see each instrument's loops and where they fall in the song.

Figure 15-6:
My timeline
with a jazz
piano and
an upright
smooth bass
onboard.
Cool,
Daddy-o!

Click the Reset button in the loop browser to choose another instrument or genre category.

Resizing, repeating, and moving loops

If you haven't already tried listening to your entire song, try it now. You can click Play at any time without wreaking havoc on your carefully created tracks. Sounds pretty good, doesn't it?

But wait: I bet the song stopped after about five seconds, right? (You can watch the passing seconds by using either the Time/Tempo display or the second rule that appears at the very top of the timeline.) I'm sure that you want your song to last more than five seconds! After the playhead moves past the end of the last loop, your song is over. Click Play again to pause the playback; then click the Return to Beginning button (labeled in Figure 15-1) to move the playhead back to the beginning of the song.

The music stops so soon because your loops are only so long. Most are five seconds in length, and others are even shorter. To keep the groove going, you have to do one of three things.

✔ **Resize the loop.** Hover your mouse cursor over either the left or right edge of most loops, and an interesting thing happens: Your cursor changes to a vertical line with an arrow pointing away from the loop. That's your cue to click and drag — and while you drag, most loops expand to fill the space you're making, repeating the beats in perfect time. By resizing a loop, you can literally drag the loop's edge as long as you like.

✔ **Repeat the loop.** Depending on the loop that you chose, you might find that resizing it won't repeat the measure. Instead, the new part of the loop is simply dead air. In fact, the length of many loops is limited to anywhere from one to five seconds. However, if you move your cursor over the top-right corner of a loop that you want to extend, it turns into a vertical line with a circular arrow, which tells you that you can click and repeat the loop. GarageBand actually adds multiple copies of the same loop automatically, for as far as you drag the loop. In Figure 15-7, I repeat the bass loop in Figure 15-6.

✔ **Add a new loop.** You can switch to a different loop to change the flow of the music. Naturally, the instrument stays the same, but there's no reason why you can't use a horn riff loop in your violin track (as long as it sounds good played by a violin!). To GarageBand, a software instrument track is compatible with any software instrument loop that you add from the Loop Browser as long as that loop is marked with our old friend, the green music note.

Figure 15-7:
By re-
peating
the bass
loop, you
can keep
the thump
flowing.

You can also use the familiar cut (⌘+X), copy (⌘+C), and paste (⌘+V) short-cuts to um, cut, copy, and paste loops from place to place, both on the timeline and from track to track. Hold down Option and drag a loop to repeat it, and click a loop and drag it anywhere to move it. After all, you're working under Mac OS X — the Leopard breed of cat.

Each track can be adjusted so that you can listen to the interplay between two or more tracks or hear how your song sounds without a specific track:

✔ Click the tiny speaker button under the track name in the list, and the button turns blue to indicate that the track is muted. To turn off the mute, click the speaker icon again.

✔ You can change the volume or balance of each individual track by using the mixer that appears next to the track name. This comes in handy if you want an instrument to sound louder or confine that instrument to the left or right speaker.

A track doesn't have to be filled for every second with one loop or another. As you can see in Figure 15-8, my first big hit — I call it *Turbo Techno* — has a number of repeating loops with empty space between them as different instruments perform solo. Not bad for an air guitarist who can barely whistle. Listen for it soon at a rave near you!

Figure 15-8:
The author's upcoming techno-hit — produced on a Mac, naturally.

Using an Arrange track

GarageBand '08 adds another method you can use to monkey with your music: Use an *Arrange track* to define specific sections of a song, allowing you to reorganize things by selecting, moving, and copying entire sections. For example, you're probably familiar with the chorus (refrain) of a song, and how often it appears during the course of the tune. In an Arrange track, you can reposition the entire chorus within your song, carrying all the loops and settings within the chorus along with it! If you need another chorus, just copy that arrangement.

To use an Arrange track, display it by choosing Track⇨Show Arrange Track. It appears as a thin strip at the top of the track list. Click the Add Region button in the Arrange track (which carries a plus sign), and you see a new untitled region appear (as shown in Figure 15-9). You can drag the right side of the Arrange region to resize it, or drag it to move it anywhere in the song.

Who wants an arrangement full of regions named *untitled?* To rename an Arrangement region, click the word `untitled` to select it (the Arrange track turns blue), and then click the title again to display a text box. Type a new name for the region and then press Return.

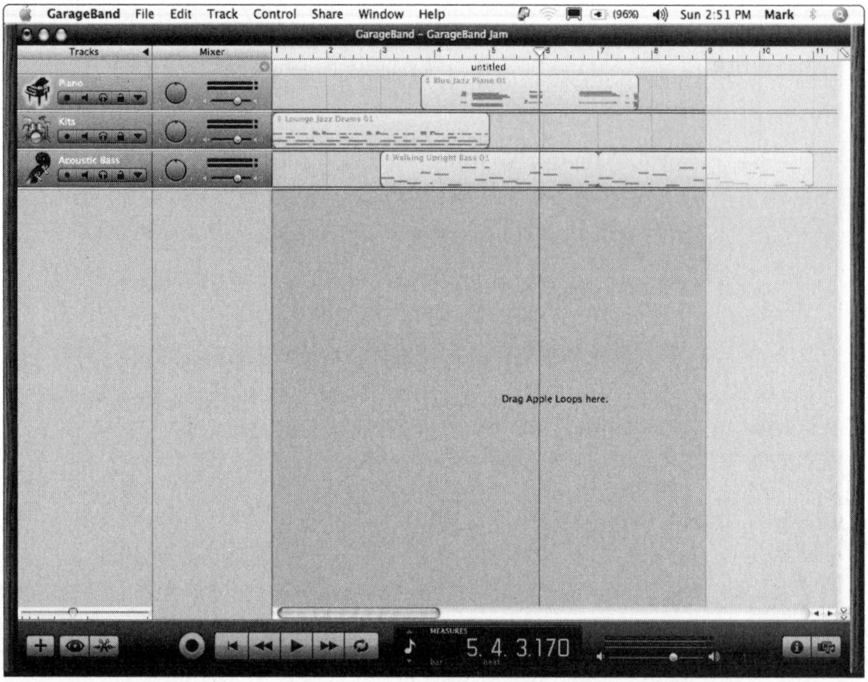

Figure 15-9:
I add a new region in my song's Arrange track.

Now, here's where arrangement regions get cool:

- **To move an entire arrangement region,** click the region's title in the Arrange track and then drag it anywhere you like within the song.

- **To copy an arrangement region,** hold down the Option key and drag the desired region's title to the spot where you want the copy to appear.

- **To delete an arrangement region,** select it and press ⌘+Option+Delete.

- **To replace the contents of an arrangement region with those of another arrangement region,** hold down the ⌘ key and drag the desired region's title on top of the offending region's title.

- **To switch two arrangement regions in your song** — swapping the contents completely — drag one of the arrangement region titles on top of the other and then release the mouse button.

Tweaking the settings for a track

You don't think that John Mayer or U2 just "play and walk away," do you? No, they spend hours after the recording session is over, tweaking their music in the studio and on the mixing board until every note sounds just like it should. You can adjust the settings for a track, too. The tweaks that you can perform include adding effects (pull a Hendrix, and add echo and reverb to your electric guitar track) and kicking in an equalizer (for fine-tuning the sound of your background horns).

To make adjustments to a track, follow these steps:

1. **Click the desired track in the track list to select it.**

2. **Click the Track Info button (labeled in Figure 15-1).**

3. **Click the Details triangle at the bottom to expand the pane and show the settings shown in Figure 15-10.**

4. **Select the check box of each effect you want to enable.**

   Each of the effects has a modifier setting. For example, you can adjust the amount of echo to add by dragging its slider.

   GarageBand '08 provides a new Visual Equalizer window that you can use to create a custom equalizer setting for each track. You can display the Visual EQ window by clicking the Edit button at the far right of the Visual EQ controls in the expanded Track Info pane. To change the Bass, Low Mid, High Mid, or Treble setting for a track, click and drag the equalizer waveform in the desired direction. And, yep, you can do this while your song is playing, so you can use both your eyes *and* ears to define the perfect settings!

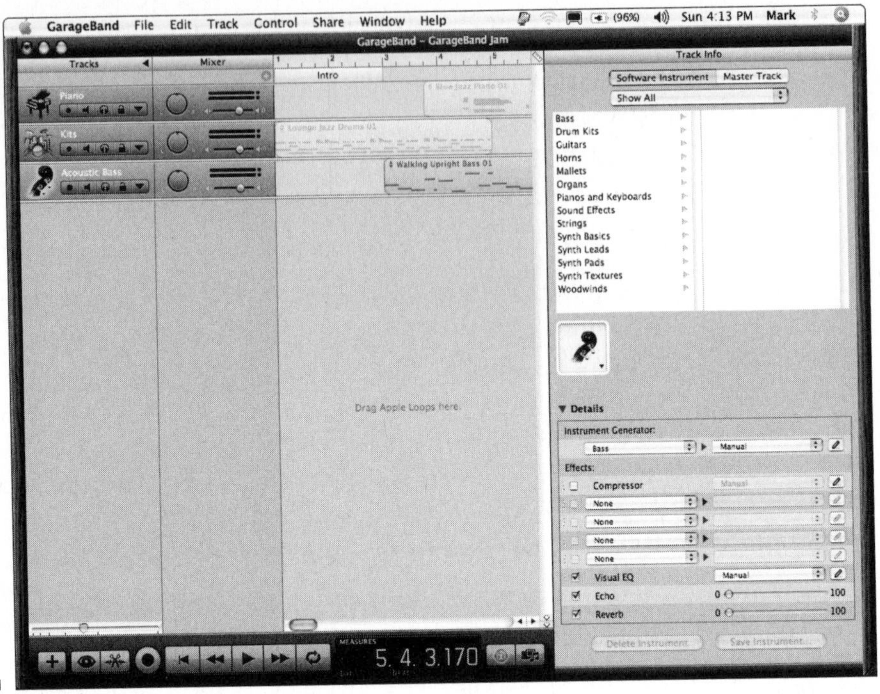

Figure 15-10:
Finesse your tune by tweaking the sound of a specific track.

5. **To save the instrument as a new custom instrument (so that you can choose it the next time you add a track), click the Save Instrument button.**

6. **Click the Track Info button again to return to GarageBand.**

Time for a Mark's Maxim:

Save your work often in GarageBand, just like in the other iLife applications. One power blackout, and you'll never forgive yourself. Press ⌘+S, and enjoy the peace of mind.™

Automatic Composition with Magic GarageBand

In a hurry? Too rushed to snag loops and tweak effects? Never fear, GarageBand '08 can even compose a song automatically! The new Magic GarageBand feature provides a wide range of eight different genres of music to choose from — everything from blues to reggae to funk and rock.

To create a new song automatically, follow these steps:

1. **Press ⌘+N to start a new project.**

   If you're working on a song, GarageBand prompts you to save it before closing the window.

2. **Click the Magic GarageBand button on the Project Select dialog.**

   You see an imposing curtain, with a button for each song genre.

3. **Click the desired genre button.**

4. **To hear the entire song with the default instruments, click Entire Song and the click the Play button.**

   Alternatively, to hear a short sample of the song, click Snippet and then click the Play button.

5. **Click Audition to switch instruments or use the default musical arrangement.**

   The curtains open, and you see each individual instrument on stage. To choose a different musical style for an instrument (or a different variation of the instrument), click it, and then select the desired sound from the menu below the stage.

   Click My Instrument (the empty space in the middle of the stage) to add your own voice or instrumental, using a microphone or MIDI instrument.

6. **After the song fits like a glove, click Create Project to open the song as a project in GarageBand.**

   Now you can edit and tweak the song to your heart's delight like any other GarageBand project, adding other software or real instrument tracks as necessary.

Sharing Your Songs and Podcasts

After you finish your song, you can play it whenever you like through GarageBand. But then again, that isn't really what you want, is it? You want to share your music with others with an audio CD or download it to your iPod so that you can enjoy it yourself while walking through the mall!

iTunes to the rescue! Just like the other iLife applications that I cover in this book, GarageBand can share the music you make through the digital hub that is your MacBook.

Creating MP3 and AAC files

You can create digital audio files in MP3 or AAC format from your song or podcast project. (MP3 and AAC are by far the most popular formats for digital audio because they offer excellent audio quality with far smaller file sizes than the older, uncompressed WAV and AIFF formats.) Follow these simple steps:

1. **Open the song that you want to share.**

2. **Choose Share⇨Send Song to iTunes.**

3. **Click in each of the four text boxes to type the playlist, artist name, composer name, and album name for the tracks you create.**

   You can leave the defaults as-is, if you prefer. Each track that you export is named after the song's name in GarageBand.

4. **From the Compress Using pop-up menu, choose the encoder that GarageBand should use to compress your song file.**

   The default is AAC, but you can also choose MP3 encoding for greater compatibility.

5. **From the Audio Settings pop-up menu, choose the proper audio quality for the finished file.**

   The higher the quality, the larger the file.

   GarageBand displays the approximate file size and finished file information in the description box.

6. **Click Share.**

After a second or two of hard work, your laptop opens the iTunes window and highlights the new (or existing) playlist that contains your new song.

Sending a podcast to iWeb or iTunes

If you've prepared a new podcast episode in GarageBand, you can send it automatically to iWeb or iTunes by following these steps:

1. **Open the podcast that you want to export to iWeb.**

   Make sure that the Podcast track is displayed. If necessary, choose Track⇨Show Podcast Track to display it.

2. **Choose Share⇨Send Podcast to iWeb (or Share⇨Send Podcast to iTunes).**

3. **From the Compress Using pop-up menu, choose the encoder GarageBand should use to compress your podcast file.**

   Your choices are AAC or MP3 format. AAC files are slightly smaller than MP3 files, but the MP3 format is supported by far more music players and audio applications.

4. **From the Audio Settings pop-up menu, choose the proper audio quality for the finished file.**

5. **Click Share.**

Burning an audio CD

Ready to create a demo CD with your latest GarageBand creation, using your MacBook's optical drive? Follow these steps to burn an audio disc from within GarageBand:

1. **Open the song that you want to record to disc.**

2. **Choose Share⇨Burn Song to CD.**

3. **Load a blank disc into your optical drive.**

Part V
Sharing Access and Information

"He saw your MacBook and wants to know if he can check out the new OS X features."

In this part . . .

Ready to share your Mac laptop among all the members of your family? If you want to synchronize your Bluetooth cell phone with your MacBook, or you decided to build a home network (wired or wireless), you've come to the right place. In this part, I show you how to provide others with access to your documents and data — securely, mind you, and with the least amount of hassle.

Chapter 16

Your Laptop Goes Multiuser

In This Chapter

▶ Enjoying the advantages of a multiuser MacBook

▶ Understanding access levels

▶ Adding, editing, and deleting user accounts

▶ Restricting access for managed accounts

▶ Configuring your login window

▶ Sharing files with other users

▶ Securing your stuff with FileVault

*E*verybody wants a piece. (Of your laptop, that is.)

Perhaps you live in a busy household with kids, significant others, grandparents, and a wide selection of friends — all of them clamoring for a chance to spend time on the Internet, take care of homework, or enjoy a good game.

On the other hand, your MacBook might occupy a college classroom or board room at your office — and suddenly your classmate or co-worker wants his own Private iDaho on the road warrior, complete with a reserved spot on the hard drive and his own hand-picked attractive Desktop background. (Even flying at 30,000 feet, your co-worker will be eyeing your MacBook.)

Before you throw your hands up in the air in defeat, read this chapter and take heart! Here you find all the step-by-step procedures, explanations, and tips to help you build a *safe* multiuser MacBook that's accessible to everyone with clean hands.

Oh, and you still get to use it, too. And, no, that's not being selfish.

Once Upon a Time (An Access Fairy Tale)

Okay, so you don't have Cinderella, Snow White, or that porridge-loving kid with the trespassing problem. Instead, you have your brother Bob.

Every time Bob visits your place, it seems he needs to do "something" on the Internet, or he needs a moment with your MacBook Air to bang out a quick message, using his Web-based e-mail application. Unfortunately, Bob's forays onto your laptop always result in stuff getting changed, like your Desktop settings, Address Book, and Safari bookmarks.

What you need, good reader, is a visit from the Account Fairy. Your problem is that you have but a single user account on your system, and Leopard thinks that Bob is *you*. By turning your MacBook into a multiuser system and giving Bob his own account, Leopard can tell the difference between the two of you, keeping your druthers separate!

With a unique user account, Leopard can track all sorts of things for Bob, leaving your computing environment blissfully pristine. A user account keeps track of stuff such as

- Address Book contacts
- Safari bookmarks and settings
- Desktop settings (including background images, screen resolutions, and Finder tweaks)
- iTunes libraries, just in case Bob brings his own music (sigh)
- Web sites that Bob might ask you to host on your computer (resigned sigh)

Plus, Bob gets his own reserved Home folder on your laptop's hard drive, so he'll quit complaining about how he can't find his files. Oh, and did I mention how user accounts keep others from accessing *your* stuff? And how you can lock Bob out of where-he-should-not-be, such as certain applications, iChat, Mail, and Web sites (including that offshore Internet casino site that he's hooked on)?

Naturally, this is only the tip of the iceberg. User accounts affect just about everything you can do in Leopard and on your laptop. The moral of my little tale? A Mark's Maxim to the rescue:

Assign others their own user accounts, and let Leopard keep track of everything. Then you can share your MacBook with others and still live happily ever after!™

Big-Shot Administrator Stuff

Get one thing straight right off the bat: *You* are the administrator of your MacBook. In network-speak, an *administrator* (or *admin* for short) is the one with the power to Do Unto Others — creating new accounts, deciding who gets access to what, and generally running the multiuser show. In other words, think of yourself as the Monarch of Mac OS X. (The ruler, not the butterfly.)

I always recommend that you have only one (or perhaps two) accounts with administrator-level access on any computer. This makes good sense because you can be assured that no one can monkey with your laptop while you're away from the keyboard. So why might you want a second admin account? Well, if you're away from your laptop — think "daughter takes it with her on trip to Europe" — you might need to assign a second administrator account to a *trusted* individual who knows as much about your road warrior as you do. (Tell 'em to buy a copy of this book.) That way, if something breaks or an account needs to be tweaked in some way, the other person can take care of it whilst you're absent (but without giving that person access to your personal data).

In this section, I explain the typical duties of a first-class MacBook administrator.

Deciding who needs what access

Leopard provides three levels of individual user accounts:

- ✔ **Admin (administrator):** See the beginning of this section.
- ✔ **Standard level:** Perfect for most users, these accounts allow access to just about everything but don't let the user make drastic changes to Leopard or create new accounts.
- ✔ **Managed with Parental Controls level:** These are standard accounts with specific limits that are assigned either by you or by another admin account.

Assign other folks standard-level accounts and then decide whether each new account needs to be modified to restrict access as a managed account. Another Mark's Maxim is in order:

Never assign an account admin-level access unless you deem it truly necessary.™

Standard accounts are quick and easy to set up, and I think they provide the perfect compromise between access and security. You'll find that standard access allows your users to do just about anything they need to do, with a minimum of hassle.

Managed accounts (with Parental Controls) are highly configurable so you can make sure that your kids don't end up trashing the hard drive, sending junk mail, or engaging in unmonitored chatting. (*Note:* Attention, all parents, teachers, and those folks designing a single public access account for a library or organization — this means *you.*)

Adding users

All right, Mark, enough pre-game jabbering — show this good reader how to set up new accounts! Your laptop already has one admin-level account set up for you (created during the initial Leopard set-up process), and you need to be logged in with that account to add a user. To add a new account, follow these steps:

1. **Click the System Preferences icon on the Dock and then click the Accounts icon to display the Accounts pane that you see in Figure 16-1.**

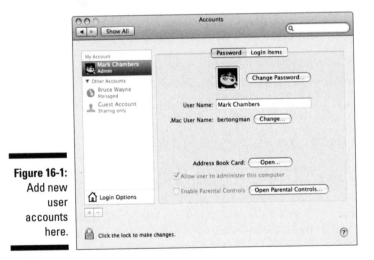

Figure 16-1:
Add new user accounts here.

2. **Click the New User button — the one with the plus sign at the bottom of the accounts list — to display the new user sheet shown in Figure 16-2.**

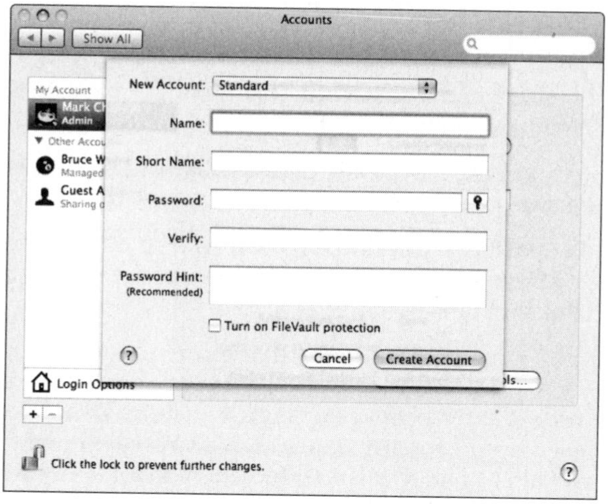

Figure 16-2:
Fill out those
fields, and
you have a
new user.

If your New User button is grayed out, your Accounts pane is locked. Remember that you can toggle the padlock icon at the lower-left corner of most of the panes in System Preferences to lock or allow changes. To gain access, do the following:

   a. Click the padlock icon to make changes to the Accounts pane.

   b. When Leopard prompts you for your admin account password (the account you're currently using), enter it. (This is the password you entered during Setup, when you create your personal user account.)

   c. Click OK.

   Now you can click the New User button.

3. **Click the New Account pop-up menu and specify the account level status.**

Choose from Administrator, Standard, or Managed with Parental Controls.

You should have only one or two administrator-level users, and your account is already an admin account.

4. **Type the name that you want to display for this account in the Name text box. Press Tab to move to the next field.**

Leopard displays this name on the Login screen, so behave! (For example, Bob has only one "o" the last time I checked.)

5. **(Optional) Although Leopard automatically generates the user's *short name* (for use in iChat, and for naming the user's Home folder), you can type a new one. (No spaces, please.) Press Tab again.**

6. **In the Password text box, type the password for the new account. Press Tab to move to the next field.**

   Generally, I recommend a password of at least six characters, using a mixture of alpha and numeric characters.

7. **In the Verify text box, retype the password you chose. Press Tab again to continue your quest.**

8. **(Optional) Leopard can provide a password hint after three unsuccessful login attempts. To offer a hint, type a short question in the Password Hint text box.**

   From a security standpoint, password hints are taboo. (Personally, I **never** use 'em. If someone is having a problem logging in to a computer I administer, you better believe I want to know *why*.) Therefore, despite the recommendation Leopard shows here, I strongly recommend that you skip this field — and if you *do* offer a hint, **keep it vague!** Avoid hints like, "Your password is the name of the Wookie in Star Wars." *Geez.*

9. **Click the Create Account button.**

   The new account shows up in the list at the left of the Accounts pane.

Each user's Home folder has the same default subfolders, including Movies, Music, Pictures, Sites, and such. A user can create new subfolders within his or her Home folder at any time.

Here's one more neat fact about a user's Home folder: No matter what the account level, most of the contents of a Home folder can't be viewed by other users. (Yes, that includes admin-level users. This way, everyone using your MacBook Pro gets her own little area of privacy.) Within the Home folder, only the Sites and Public folders can be accessed by other users — and only in a limited fashion. More on these folders later in this chapter. (And read all about Home folders in Chapter 5.)

Modifying user accounts

Next, consider the basic modifications that you can make to a user account, such as changing existing information or selecting a new picture to represent that user's unique personality.

To edit an existing account, log in with your admin account, display the System Preferences window, and click Accounts to display the account list. Then follow these steps:

1. **Click the account that you want to change.**

   Don't forget to unlock the Accounts pane if necessary. See the earlier section, "Adding users," to read how.

2. **Edit the settings that you need to change.**

   For example, you can reset the user's password, or (if absolutely necessary) upgrade the account to admin level.

3. **Click the picture well and then click a thumbnail image to represent this user (as shown in Figure 16-3).**

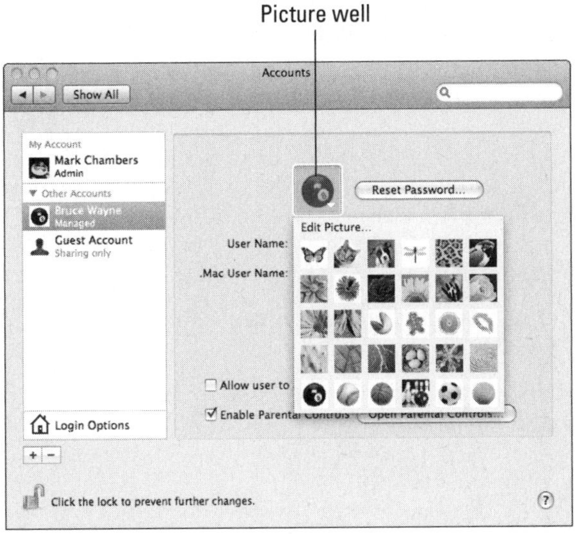

Picture well

Figure 16-3:
Pick the image that best represents a user.

An easy way to get an image is to use one from your hard drive. Click Edit Picture and then drag a new image from a Finder window into the picture well. (Alternatively, you could click Edit Picture and then click the Snapshot button — which bears a tiny camera — to grab a picture from your iSight video camera. When you've captured the essence of your subject as a photo, click Set to return to the Accounts pane.)

Leopard displays this image in the Login list next to the account name.

4. **When everything is correct, press ⌘+Q to close the System Preferences dialog.**

   No need to save your changes (as a separate step) within System Preferences because Leopard does that automatically when you close the System Preferences window.

Standard-level users have some control over their accounts — they're not helpless, after all. Standard users can log in, open System Preferences, and click Accounts to change the account password or picture, as well as the *My Card* assigned to them in Leopard Address Book. All standard users can also set up Login Items, which I cover later in this chapter. Note, however, that managed users might not have access to System Preferences at all, so they can't make changes. (Read about this in the upcoming section, "Managing access settings for an account."

I banish thee, Mischievous User!

Not all user accounts last forever. Students graduate, co-workers quit, kids move out of the house (at last!), and Bob might even find a significant other who has a faster cable modem. We can only hope.

Anyway, no matter what the reason, you can delete a user account at any time. Log in with your admin account, display the Accounts pane in System Preferences, and then follow these steps to eradicate an account:

1. **Click the account that you want to delete.**

2. **Click the Delete User button (which bears the Minus Sign of Doom). Refer to Figure 16-2.**

   Leopard displays a confirmation sheet, as shown in Figure 16-4. By default, the contents of the user's Home folder are saved in a disk image file, which you can restore with Disk Utility — in the Deleted Users folder.

Figure 16-4: This is your last chance to save the stuff from a deleted user account.

3. **To clean up completely, select the Delete the Home Folder radio button and then click OK.**

   Leopard wipes everything connected with the user account off your hard drive.

4. **Press ⌘+Q to close the System Preferences dialog.**

Time once again for a Mark's Maxim:

Always delete unnecessary user accounts. Otherwise, you're leaving holes in your laptop's security.™

Setting up Login Items and Parental Controls

Every account on your MacBook can be customized. Understandably, some settings are accessible only to admin-level accounts, and others can be adjusted by standard-level accounts. In this section, I introduce you to the things that can be enabled (or disabled) within a user account.

Automating with Login Items

Login Items are applications or documents that can be set to launch or load automatically as soon as a specific user logs in — for example, Apple Mail or Address Book. In fact, a user must be logged in to add or remove Login Items. Even an admin-level account can't change the Login Items for another user.

A user must have access to the Accounts pane within the System Preferences window in order to use Login Items. As you can read in the following section, a user can be locked out of System Preferences, which makes it more difficult for Login Items to be added or deleted for that account. (Go figure.)

To set Login Items for your account, follow these steps:

1. **Click the System Preferences icon on the Dock and then click the Accounts icon.**

2. **Click the Login Items tab to display the settings that you see in Figure 16-5.**

3. **Click the Add button (with the plus sign) to display a file selection sheet.**

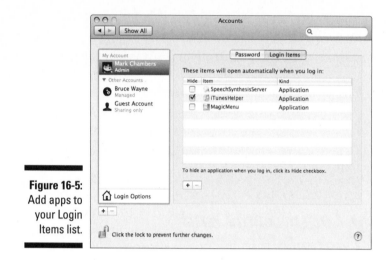

Figure 16-5:
Add apps to
your Login
Items list.

4. **Navigate to the application you want to launch each time you log in, click it to select it, and then click Add.**

   If you're in the mood to drag and drop, just drag the applications you want to add from a Finder window and drop them directly into the list.

5. **Press ⌘+Q to quit System Preferences and save your changes.**

Login Items are launched in the order that they appear in the list, so feel free to drag the items into any order you like.

Managing access settings for an account

A standard-level account with restrictions is a managed account. (You can read about these accounts earlier in this chapter.) With these accounts, you can restrict access to many different places within Leopard and your laptop's applications via *Parental Controls.* (Naturally, admin-level accounts don't need Parental Controls because an admin account has no restrictions.)

In short, Parental Controls come in handy in preventing users — family members, students, co-workers, friends, or the public at large — from damaging your computer, your software, or Leopard itself. If an account has been restricted with Parental Controls, the account description changes from Standard to Managed in the Accounts list.

To display the Parental Controls for a standard account, start here:

1. **Log in with an admin-level account.**

2. **Open System Preferences and then click Accounts.**

3. **Click the Standard account in the list and then select the Enable Parental Controls check box.**

Now click the Open Parental Controls button to display the specific categories (tabs) that you see in Figure 16-6:

✔ **System:** These settings (which I discuss in more detail in a second) affect what the user can do within Leopard as well as what the Finder itself looks like to that user.

✔ **Content:** These settings control the Dictionary and Safari applications. If you prefer that profane terms be hidden within the Dictionary for this user, select the Hide Profanity in Dictionary check box to enable it. Leopard also offers three levels of control for Web sites:

  • *Allow Unrestricted Access:* Select this radio button to allow unfettered access for this user.

  • *Try to Limit Access:* You can allow Safari to automatically block Web sites that it deems "adult." To specify particular sites that Safari should allow or deny, click the Customize button. On the Customize sheet, click the Add button under the Always Allow These Sites list box to enter the Web addresses that you approve; then click the Add button under the Never Allow These Sites list box to enter those Web addresses to be banned.

  • *Allow Access to Only These Websites:* Select this radio button to specify which Web sites that the user can view. To add a Web site, click the Add button (which bears a plus sign); Leopard then prompts you for a title and the Web site address.

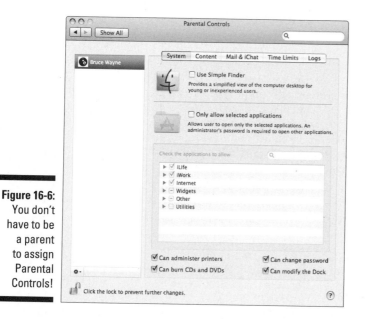

Figure 16-6:
You don't have to be a parent to assign Parental Controls!

✔ **Mail & iChat:** Select the Limit Mail and the Limit iChat check boxes to specify the e-mail and instant-messaging addresses that this user can communicate with. To add an address that the user can e-mail or chat with, click the Add button.

If you want a notification if the user is attempting to send an e-mail to someone not in the list, select the Send Permission Requests To check box to enable it and then type your e-mail address in the text box.

✔ **Time Limits:** Parents, click the Time Limits button, and you'll shout with pure joy! You can limit an account to a certain number of hours of usage per weekday (Weekday Time Limits), limit to a specified number of hours of usage per weekend day (Weekend Time Limits), and set a bed-time computer curfew time for both weekdays and weekend days.

✔ **Logs:** Leopard keeps a number of different types of *text log files* (which track where the user goes on the Internet, which applications are launched by the account, and the contents of any iChat conversations where the user was a participant). From this central pane, you can monitor all the logs for a particular account. Note that these logs are enabled or disabled from other locations within Leopard: For example, the log showing the Web sites visited and blocked is enabled from the Content panel that I describe a little earlier, whereas the applications log is enabled from the System panel. iChat logging is turned on from the Preferences dialog within the iChat application.

You can always tell whether an account has been assigned Parental Controls because the account description changes from Standard to Managed in the Accounts list.

Of particular importance are the System controls. Click the System tab to modify these settings:

✔ **Use Simple Finder:** The Simple Finder is a great idea for families and classrooms with smaller children. For the ultimate in restrictive Leopard environments — think public access or kiosk mode — you can assign the Simple Finder to an account. Even the Dock itself is restricted, sporting only the Finder icon, Trash, the Dashboard, and those folders that allow the user to access their documents and applications.

✔ **Only Allow Selected Applications:** When this option is enabled, you can select the specific applications that appear to the user. These restrictions are in effect whether the user has access to the full Finder or just the Simple Finder.

• *To allow access to all the applications of a specific type:* Select the check box next to the desired group heading to enable it. This includes iLife, iWork, Internet, Widgets, Other, and Utilities.

- *To restrict access to all applications within a group:* If a group heading check box is enabled and you want to deny access to all the applications in that group, clear the check box next to the heading to disable it.

- *To toggle restriction on and off for specific applications within these groups:* Click the triangle icon next to each group heading to expand its list and then either mark or clear the check box next to the desired applications. Leopard denotes partial access within a group — a mixture of full and restricted applications — with a dash mark in the group heading check box.

To locate a specific application, click in the Search box and type the application name.

- *To add a new application to the Allow list:* Drag its icon from the Finder and drop it in the list within the Other group. After you add an application, it appears in the Other group, and you can toggle access to it on and off like the applications in the named groups.

✔ **Can Administer Printers:** With this check box enabled, the user can modify the printers and printer queues within the Print & Fax pane in System Preferences. If disabled, the user can still print to the default printer and switch to other assigned printers, but can't add or delete printers.

✔ **Can Burn CDs and DVDs:** Disable this check box to prevent the user from recording CDs or DVDs via the built-in disc recording features in Mac OS X. (*Note:* If you load a third-party recording program, such as Toast, the user can still record discs with it.)

✔ **Can Change Password:** Enable this check box to allow the user to change the account password.

If you're creating a single standard-level account for an entire group of people to use — for example, if you want to leave the machine in kiosk mode in one corner of the office or if everyone in a classroom will use the same account on the machine — I recommend disabling the ability to change the account password. (Oh, and please do me a favor . . . *don't* create a system with just one admin-level account that everyone is supposed to use! Instead, keep your one admin-level account close to your bosom and create a standard-level account for the Unwashed Horde.)

✔ **Can Modify the Dock:** Enable this check box, and the user can add or remove applications, documents, and folders from the Dock in the full Finder. (If you don't want the contents of the Dock changing according to the whims of other users, it's a good idea to disable this check box.)

Mundane Chores for the Multiuser Laptop

After you're hip on user accounts and the changes you can make to them, turn to a number of topics that affect all users of your MacBook — things like how they log in, how a user can share information with everyone else on the computer, and how each user account can be protected from unscrupulous outsiders with state-of-the-art encryption. (Suddenly you're James Bond! I told you Leopard would open new doors for you.)

Logging on and off in Leopard For Dummies

Hey, how about the login screen itself? How do your users identify themselves? Time for another of my "Shortest books in the *For Dummies* series" special editions. (The title's practically longer than the entire book.)

Leopard offers four methods of logging folks in to your multiuser laptop:

✔ **The username and password login:** This is the most secure type of login screen you'll see in Leopard because you have to actually type your account username and your password. (A typical hacker isn't going to know all the usernames on your MacBook.) Press Return or click the Log In button to compete the process.

  When you enter your username and password, you see bullets rather than your password because Leopard displays bullet characters to ensure security. Otherwise, someone could simply look over your shoulder and see your password.

  Keep your laptop secure: Use a username and password login, and always choose a password that's tough to guess.™

✔ **The list login:** This login screen offers a good middle of the road between security and convenience. Click your account username in the list and type your password when the login screen displays the password prompt. Press Return or click the Log In button to continue.

✔ **Fast User Switching:** This feature allows another user to sit down and log in while the previous user's applications are still running in the background. This is perfect for a fast e-mail check or a scan of your eBay bids without forcing someone else completely off the MacBook. When you turn on Fast User Switching, Leopard displays the currently active user's name at the right side of the Finder menu bar.

To switch to another account

a. *Click the current user's name in the Finder menu (see Figure 16-7).*

b. *Click the name of the user who wants to log in.*

Leopard displays the login window, just as if the laptop had been rebooted.

The previous user's stuff is still running, so you definitely shouldn't reboot or shut down the computer!

To switch back to the previous user

a. *Click the username again on the Finder menu.*

b. *Click the previous user's name.*

For security, Leopard prompts you for that account's login password.

✔ **Auto login:** This is the most convenient method of logging in but offers no security whatsoever. Leopard automatically logs in the specified account when you start or reboot your MacBook.

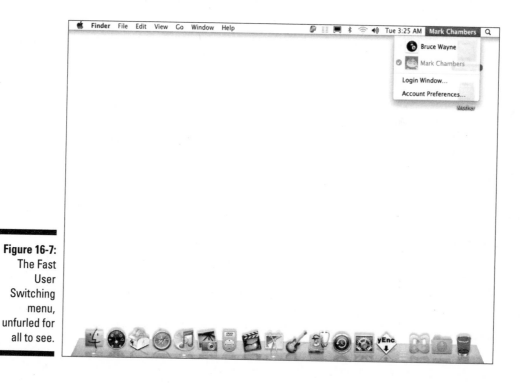

Figure 16-7:
The Fast
User
Switching
menu,
unfurled for
all to see.

I *strongly recommend* that you use auto login only if

- Your laptop is in a secure location — say, your home or a locked office. If you're on the road, you and your data need the protection of a username and password login!

- You are the only one using your laptop.

- You're setting up a public-access laptop kiosk, in which case you want your MacBook to immediately log in with the public account.

Working in a public environment? *Never* set an admin-level account as the auto login account. This is the very definition of ASDI, or *A Supremely Dumb Idea.*

To set up a username/password or list login, open System Preferences, click the Accounts icon, and then display the Login Options settings (see Figure 16-8). Select the List of Users radio button for a list login screen, or select the Name and Password radio button to require your users to type their full username and password.

To enable Fast User Switching, mark the Enable Fast User Switching check box (also shown in Figure 16-8).

To set Auto Login, click the Automatic Login pop-up menu and choose the account that Leopard should use (shown also by the now-legendary Figure 16-8).

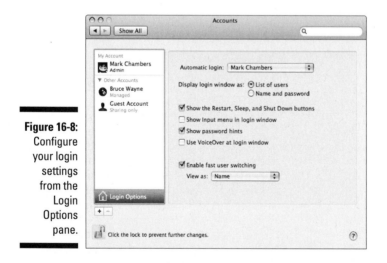

Figure 16-8:
Configure your login settings from the Login Options pane.

Logging out of Leopard all the way (without Fast User Switching) is a cinch. Just click the Apple menu (🍎) and then choose Log Out. (From the keyboard, press ⌘+Shift+Q.) A confirmation dialog appears that will automatically log you off in one minute. And that one minute is important because if someone walks up and clicks Cancel, he'll be using your laptop with your account! Your MacBook returns to the login screen, ready for its next victim. Heed this Mark's Maxim:

Always click the Log Out button on the logout confirmation dialog before you leave your MacBook.™

Interesting stuff about sharing stuff

You might wonder where shared documents and files reside on your MacBook. That's a good question. Like just about everything in Leopard, there's a simple answer. The Users folder on your laptop has a *Shared* folder within it. To share a file or folder, it should be placed in the Shared folder.

You don't have to turn on File Sharing in the Sharing pane of System Preferences to use Shared folders on your laptop. Personal File Sharing affects only network access to your machine by users of other computers.

Each user account on your MacBook also has a *Public* folder within that user's Home folder. This is a read-only folder that other users on your laptop (and across the network) can access: They can only open and copy the files that it contains. (Sorry, no changes to existing documents from other users, or new documents from other users.) Every user's Public folder contains a *Drop Box* folder, where other users can copy or save files but can't view the contents. Think of the Drop Box as a mailbox where you drop off stuff for the other user.

Encrypting your Home folder can be fun

Allowing others to use your Mac laptop always incurs a risk — especially if you store sensitive information and documents on your computer. Although your login password should ensure that your Home folder is off limits to everyone else, consider an extra level of security to prevent even a dedicated hacker from accessing your stuff. All it takes is a forgetful moment in an airport or classroom, and your personal and business data is suddenly within someone else's reach. Adequate security is A Supremely Good Thing!

To this end, Leopard includes *FileVault,* which automatically encrypts the contents of your Home folder. Without the proper key (in this case, either your login password or your admin's master password), the data contained in your Home folder is impossible for just about anyone to read. (I guess the FBI or NSA would be able to decrypt it, but they're not likely a worry at your place!)

The nice thing about FileVault is that it's completely transparent to you and your users. In other words, when you log in, Leopard automatically takes care of decrypting and encrypting the stuff in your Home folder for you. You literally won't know that FileVault is working for you (which is how computers are *supposed* to work).

To turn on FileVault protection for a specific account, follow these steps:

1. **Click the System Preferences icon on the Dock and then click the Security icon.**

2. **Click the FileVault button.**

3. **If necessary, click Set Master Password to create a master password.**

You need to be logged in with an admin-level account to set a master password. However, this needs to be done only once, no matter how many accounts you're hosting on your MacBook. When using this master password, any admin-level user can unlock any Home folder for any user.

Before you move to Step 4, note that you must be logged in using the account that requires the FileVault protection. (Therefore, if you had to log in using your admin-level account to set a master password, you have to log out and log in again using the account you want to protect. Arrgh.)

4. **Click the Turn on FileVault button.**

5. **Enter your account's login password when prompted and then click OK.**

6. **Click the Turn on FileVault button on the confirmation screen.**

7. **After Leopard encrypts your Home folder and logs you out, log in again normally.**

You're done!

Remember those passwords. Again, **do not forget** your account login password, and make doggone sure that your admin user never forgets the master password! If you forget these passwords, you can't read anything in your Home folder, and even the smartest Apple support technician will tell you that nothing can be done.

Chapter 17

Working Well with Networks

In This Chapter

▶ Considering the benefits of a network

▶ Choosing between wired and wireless networks

▶ Sharing an Internet connection

▶ Gathering the stuff you need to network

▶ Making the network connection

▶ Using your network

▶ Protecting your MacBook with a firewall

*I*n my book, network access ranks right up there with air conditioning and the microwave oven. Like other "I can't imagine life without them" kinds of technologies, it's hard to imagine sharing data from your laptop with others around you without a network. Sure, I've used a sneakernet (the old-fashioned term for running back and forth between computers with a floppy disk), but for a long time now, Apple computers don't even come with floppy drives. (Heck, the MacBook Air doesn't even come standard with an optical drive any more!)

Nope, networking is here to stay. Whether you use it to share an Internet connection, challenge your friends to a nice relaxing game of WWII battlefield action, or stream your MP3 collection to other computers that use iTunes, you'll wonder how you ever got along without one. In this chapter, I fill you in on all the details you need to know to get your road warrior hooked up to a new (or an existing) network.

What Exactly Is the Network Advantage?

If you have other family members with computers or if your MacBook is in an office with other computers (*including* those rascally PCs), here's just a sample of what you can do with a network connection.

✔ **Share an Internet connection.** This is *the* major reason why many families and most small businesses install a network. Everyone can simultaneously use the same digital subscriber line (DSL) or cable Internet connection on every computer on the network.

✔ **Share a printer.** You say your fellow employee — or even worse, your big sister — has a great printer connected to their computer? Luckily, that printer can be shared with anyone across your network.

✔ **Copy and move files of all sizes.** Need to get a large iDVD project from one Mac to another? With a network connection, you can accomplish this task in just minutes. Otherwise you'd have to burn that file to a DVD-R or use an external hard drive. A network connection makes copying as simple as dragging the project folder from one Finder window to another. (MacBook Air owners, take note!)

✔ **Share documents across your network.** Talk about a wonderful collaboration tool. For example, you can drop a Word document or Keynote presentation file in your Public folder and ask for comments and edits from others in your office (or around the planet).

✔ **Stream music and video.** With iTunes, you can share your audio and video media collection on your MacBook Pro with other Macs and PCs on your network. Your eyes and ears can't tell the difference!

✔ **Play multiplayer games.** Invite your friends over and tell 'em that you're hosting a *LAN party* (the techno-nerd term for a large gathering of game players, connected through the same network, all playing the same multiplayer game. (Suddenly you'll see firsthand just how devious a human opponent can be.) Each participant needs to buy a copy of the same game, naturally, but the fun you'll have is worth every cent you spend. Don't forget the chips!

If your laptop isn't within shouting distance of an existing network or you don't plan on buying any additional computers, stop right here because a lone MacBook hanging out in your home with no other computers around won't need a network.

If you have just your Mac laptop and an Internet connection (either through a dialup modem or a high-speed DSL/cable modem) and you have no plans to add another computer or a network printer, a network isn't necessary.

Should You Go Wired or Wireless?

After you decide that you indeed need a network for your home or office, you have another decision to make: Should you install a *wired* network (running cables between your computers) or a *wireless* network? Heck, should you throw caution completely to the wind and build a combination network with both wireless and wired hardware?

Grafting wireless access to a wired network

Maybe you're caught in the middle, choosing between wired and wireless networking? Or perhaps you're already using a wired network but would be absolutely thrilled by the idea of sitting on your deck in the sunshine whilst checking your e-mail on your laptop, untethered. By combining both technologies, you can get the faster transfers of a wired network between all the computers in your office and the freedom you crave.

That is the configuration I use in my home office. I use a wireless base station that also includes a built-in wired switch, which is a very common feature in today's wireless routers and base stations. My family gets all the convenience a wireless network offers, and everyone can connect to the Internet from anywhere in our house. On the other hand, my office computers have the faster performance and tighter security of a wired network. *Sassy* indeed!

Your first instinct is probably to choose a wireless network for convenience. After all, this option allows you to eliminate running cables behind furniture (or in the ceiling of your office building). Ah, but I must show you the advantages to a wired network as well. Table 17-1 shows the lowdown to help you make up your mind.

Table 17-1	Network Decision Making	
Factor	*Wireless Networks*	*Wired Networks*
Speed	Moderate	Much faster
Security	Moderate	Better
Convenience	Better	Worse
Compatibility	Confusing standards	Easier to understand
Cables	Few (or none)	Required

As I call it, here are the advantages of choosing a wired or a wireless network setup:

✔ **Wired:** Using a wired network offers two significant perks over a wireless network:

- *Faster speeds:* In general, wired networks that are compatible with your MacBook are many times faster than the fastest 802.11n wireless connections.

  The performance of a wireless connection can be compromised by interference (from impeding structures, such as concrete walls; and from household appliances, such as some wireless phones and microwave ovens) and by distance.

- *Better security:* A wired network doesn't broadcast a signal that can be picked up outside your home or office, so it's more secure.

  Hackers can attack through your Internet connection, though. Hence the section, "USE YOUR FIREWALL!," later in this chapter.

✓ **Wireless:** A wireless connection really has only one advantage, but it's a big one: *convenience* (which, in this case, is another word for *mobility* for all your networked devices). Laptop owners crave this independence — a freedom that desktop computers can only dream about.

  Accessing your network anywhere within your home or office — without cables — is so easy. You can also easily connect a wireless printer. And when using an AirPort Express mobile Base Station, even your home stereo can get connected to your MP3 collection on your MacBook. Read more about Base Stations later on.

Be a Pal — Share Your Internet!

Time to see what's necessary to share an Internet connection. In this section, I cover two methods of connecting your network to the Internet. (And before you open your wallet, keep in mind that you might be able to use your laptop to share your broadband connection across your network!)

Using your MacBook as a sharing device

You can use your MacBook to provide a shared Internet connection across a simple wireless network, using either

✓ **A broadband DSL or cable connection**

✓ **An external USB dialup modem**

  I recommend sharing a dialup modem Internet connection *only* if you have no other option. A dialup modem connection really can't handle the data transfer speeds for more than one computer to access the Internet comfortably at one time. (In plain English, an external USB modem that you add to your MacBook isn't fast enough for both you and your significant other to surf the Web at the same time.) Sharing a dialup connection just isn't practical.

In these configurations, the only hardware you need to buy for your wired network is an external USB modem and an Ethernet switch (more on this device in the next section).

Because your MacBook has built-in AirPort Extreme wireless hardware, it's easy to share your broadband connection wirelessly with other computers in your home or office.

In either configuration, your laptop uses the Mac OS X Leopard built-in Internet connection–sharing feature to get the job done, *but your Mac must remain turned on to allow Internet sharing.* I show you how to do this in the upcoming section, "Network Internet connections."

Using a dedicated Internet-sharing device

You can also choose to use a dedicated Internet-sharing device (often called an *Internet router*) to connect to your cable or DSL modem. You do have to buy this additional hardware, but here's the advantage: Your MacBook doesn't have to remain turned on just so everyone can get on the Internet.

Internet routers usually include either wired or wireless network connections, and many include both.

Setting up an Internet router is usually a pretty simple matter, but the configuration depends on the device manufacturer and usually involves a number of different settings in System Preferences that vary according to the model of router you're installing. Grab a diet cola, sit down with the router's manual, and follow the installation instructions you'll find there. (In many cases, you must set up your cable or DSL modem as a *bridge* between your ISP and your router, which should be covered in your modem and router manuals as well.)

Most Internet routers offer a DHCP server, which automatically assigns Internet protocol (IP) addresses, and I **strongly** recommend that you turn on this feature! (You can read more on DHCP later in the chapter, in the sidebar titled, "The little abbreviation that *definitely* could.")

What Do 1 Need to Connect?

Most *normal* folks — whom I define as those who have never met a network system administrator, and couldn't care less — think that connecting to a network probably involves all sorts of arcane chants and a mystical symbol or two. In this section, I provide you with the shopping list that you need to set up a network — or connect to a network that's already running.

Wireless connections

Today's Mac laptops come complete with a built-in AirPort Extreme wireless card, so if you already have an AirPort Extreme or Express Base Station, you're set to go. Otherwise, hold on tight while I lead you through the hardware requirements for wireless networking.

The maximum signal range — and effectiveness — of any wireless network can be impeded by intervening walls or by electrical devices, such as microwave ovens and some wireless phones, all of which can generate interference.

Connecting a MacBook to an existing wireless network

Connecting a MacBook to an existing wireless network requires no extra hardware because your hardware is already built in. (Whew. That was easy!)

Using a base station to go wireless

If you decide that you want to build your own wireless network, you eschew cables, or you want to add wireless support to your existing wired network, you need a *base station.* (If you do have an existing wired network, the base station can act as a bridge between computers using wireless hardware and your wired network, allowing both types of computers to talk to each other.) Such a wireless base station will either have

- ✔ A port that can connect to your existing wired network's switch
- ✔ A full built-in switch for wired connectivity (which means you can sell your old wired Ethernet switch to your sister in Tuscon)

And, of course, a base station can simply act as a central switch for your wireless network (with no support for a wired network at all).

You can use either a cool Apple Base Station or a boring 802.11n generic wireless base station; however, the Apple hardware requires less configuration and tweaking. (Sounds like a Mark's Maxim!)

If you don't want the hassle of tweaking PC hardware to accommodate your Mac laptop, buy Apple hardware and software.™

Apple Base Station models

As listed in upcoming Table 17-2, your MacBook can work with four different Apple Base Station models for wireless networking:

✔ **AirPort Extreme**

I recommend using AirPort Extreme if your network needs an enhanced antenna, which provides greater range. You can read about connectivity ranges in upcoming Table 17-2.

✔ **Time Capsule**

Apple's *Time Capsule* unit (an external wireless backup unit) isn't just a wireless remote hard drive: It can also act as a full AirPort Extreme Base Station. In fact, the wireless specifications for a Time Capsule unit and an AirPort Extreme Base Station are almost identical.

✔ **AirPort Express (as shown in Figure 17-1)**

I recommend using AirPort Express if you want to

- *Carry your wireless base station with you.* Express is much smaller than the other Apple Base Station models. (Think "party on the patio" or a LAN gaming get-together at a friend's house.)

- *Connect your home stereo for wireless music streaming.* You can use the AirTunes feature in iTunes.

✔ **AirPort (discontinued)**

You might find an original 802.11b or 802.11g AirPort Base Station on eBay or at a garage sale. Go ahead and pick it up if you want to save cash, unless you're considering multiplayer gaming or using high-speed file transfers over your wireless network.

The 802.11n standard used by the AirPort Extreme, Time Capsule, and AirPort Express Base Stations delivers a connection that's several times faster than the old AirPort Base Station's 802.11b/802.11g standards. 802.11n is also compatible with *all* the older standards — 802.11b/a/g — so I highly recommend that you stick with 802.11n in the future. It plays well with others, and at warp speed to boot!

Figure 17-1:
The AirPort Express portable Base Station.

Table 17-2	Apple Wireless Network Base Stations		
Feature	**AirPort Extreme/ Time Capsule**	**AirPort Express**	**AirPort**
Price	$180/$299	$99	$40 (used)
Users (maximum)	50	10	50
802.11n support	Yes	No	No
802.11g support	Yes	Yes	No
802.11b support	Yes	Yes	Yes
LAN Ethernet jack (high-speed Internet connection)	Yes	Yes	Yes
WAN Ethernet jack (wired computer network)	Yes	No	No
Stereo mini-jack	No	Yes	No
USB printer port	Yes	Yes	No
Maximum signal range (approximate)	150 feet (standard) 250 feet (with add-on antenna)	150 feet	100 feet
AC adapter	Separate on AirPort Extreme/ built in on Time Capsule	Built in	Separate

The names of the Apple Base Stations are irritatingly similar; Apple usually does a better job differentiating their product names. Jot down the name of your model on a Stickie on your laptop's Desktop just so you don't get confused.

Installing an Apple Base Station is simple:

1. **If you have a DSL or cable modem, connect it to the WAN (wide area network) port on the Base Station with an Ethernet cable.**

2. **If you have an existing wired Ethernet computer network using a switch or router, connect it to the Ethernet LAN port on the Base Station with an Ethernet cable.**

   Remember that only the AirPort Extreme and Time Capsule stations have a WAN port.

3. **If you have a USB printer, connect it to the USB port on the Base Station.**

As I mention in Table 17-2, older AirPort Base Stations didn't have USB ports.

I cover the steps to share a printer in the upcoming section, "Sharing a network printer."

4. **Connect the power cable from the AC power adapter.**

The AirPort Express and Time Capsule units have a built-in AC adapter, so if you're using one of these models, just plug the device itself into the wall.

5. **Switch on your Base Station.**

6. **Run the installation software provided by Apple on your laptop.**

Using non-Apple base stations

If any company other than Apple manufactured your wireless base station, the installation procedure is almost certainly the same. (Naturally, you should take a gander at the manufacturer's installation guide just to make sure, but I added many different brands of these devices and used the same steps for each one.)

However, I should note that Apple wireless hardware uses a slightly different security encryption standard than most PC wireless hardware, which results in an extra hurdle to connecting to a non-Apple base station or access point with your laptop. (More on this in the next section. For now, just remember that I recommend using Apple wireless hardware with your MacBook whenever possible. It's just a little easier!)

Joining a wireless network

As far as I'm concerned, the only two types of base stations on the planet are Apple and non-Apple (which includes all 802.11n and 802.11g Base Stations and access points). In these two sections, I relate what you need to know to get onboard using either type of hardware.

Apple AirPort Base Stations

To join a wireless network that's served by any flavor of Apple Base Station, follow these steps on each Mac with wireless support:

1. **Click the System Preferences icon on the Dock.**

2. **Click the Network icon.**

3. **From the Connection list on the left, click AirPort.**

4. **Mark the Show AirPort Status in Menu Bar check box.**

5. **Click the Apply button.**

6. **Press ⌘+Q to quit System Preferences and save your settings.**

7. **Click the AirPort status icon (which looks like a fan) on the Finder menu bar.**

8. **From the AirPort menu, choose an existing network connection that you'd like to join.**

   The network name is the same as the network name you chose when you set up your AirPort Base Station.

9. **If you set up a secure network, enter the password you assigned to the network during setup.**

By the way, security is always A Good Thing, and I strongly recommend that you enable the password encryption features of your Apple base station while installing it! (Luckily, the Apple Base Station setup application leads you through this very process.) In the words of an important Mark's Maxim:

Keep uninvited guests out of your network! Use your base station's security features and encrypt your data!™

Some wireless networks might not appear in your AirPort menu list. These are *closed networks*, which can be specified when you set up your AirPort Base Station. You can't join a closed network unless you know the exact network name (which is far more secure than simply broadcasting the network name). To join a closed network, follow these steps:

1. **Choose Join Other Network from the AirPort menu.**

   To open the menu, click the AirPort status icon (which looks like a fan) on the Finder menu bar.

2. **Type the name of the network.**

3. **If the network is secured with WEP or LEAP encryption — the two most popular security standards for protecting your data through encryption — click the Security pop-up menu and choose which type of encryption is being used.**

4. **Enter the network password, if required.**

To disconnect from an AirPort network, click the AirPort menu and either

✔ **Choose Turn AirPort Off.**

✔ **Connect to another AirPort network.**

   In other words, if you choose another available AirPort network from the AirPort menu, your MacBook will automatically drop the previous connection. (You can only be connected to one wireless network at a time, which makes Good Sense.)

Using non-Apple Base Stations

If you're using your MacBook to connect to a non-Apple Base Station at your office, you might need to follow a specific procedure that takes care of the slightly different password functionality used by standard 802.11b/g/n hardware.

Leopard can take care of many potential wireless "language barriers" caused by security encryption — the two most common forms are WEP and LEAP — so whether you need to massage your password to connect to your non-Apple base station depends on the specific hardware and encryption system that it uses.

To read or print the latest version of this procedure, fire up Safari and visit http://kbase.info.apple.com/index.html, searching for the number 106250. (This is the Apple Knowledge Base article number, which you can type in the first search field.) This article provides the details on how to convert a standard wireless encrypted password to a format that your AirPort Extreme hardware can understand.

Wired connections

If you're installing a wired network, your MacBook or MacBook Pro already comes with most of what you need for joining your new cabled world. You just connect the hardware and configure the connection. Don't forget that you also need cables and an inexpensive Ethernet switch. (If you're using an Internet router or other hardware sharing device, it almost certainly has a built-in 4- or 8-port switch.)

Another aside to owners of MacBook Air laptops: Your machine doesn't come from Apple with a wired Ethernet port onboard, but you can buy a USB-to-Ethernet connector that will allow you to use a wired network. After you add the connector to your system, you can follow along without any problem.

Connecting a MacBook or MacBook Pro to a wired network

Your Ethernet 10/100/1000 port (which looks like a slightly oversized modem port) is located on one of the sides of your MacBook or MacBook Pro, ready to accept a standard Ethernet Cat5/Cat5E/Cat6 cable with RJ-45 connectors. If you're connecting to an existing wired network, you need a standard Cat5/Cat5E/Cat6 Ethernet cable of the necessary length. I recommend a length of no more than 25 feet because cables longer than 25 feet are often subject to line interference (which can slow down or even cripple your connection). You'll also need a live Ethernet port from the network near your laptop. Plug the cable into your MacBook, and then plug the other end into the network port.

Wired network hardware

If you don't know your switch from your NIC, don't worry. Here, I provide you with a description of the hardware that you need for your wired network.

Wired network components

If you're building your own wired network, you need

- **A switch:** This gizmo's job is to provide more network ports for the other computers in your network. They typically come in 4- and 8-port configurations.

  As I mention earlier in this chapter, most Internet routers (sometimes called *Internet-sharing devices*) include a built-in switch, so if you've already invested in an Internet router, make doggone sure that it doesn't come equipped with the ports you need before you go shopping for a switch!

- **A number of Ethernet cables:** Exactly how many cables you need is determined by how many computers you're connecting. If you're working with a gigabit Ethernet system, you need Cat5E or Cat6 cables. Cat6 cables provide better performance, but they are more expensive.

Naturally, if you're using a broadband Internet connection, you'll also have a DSL or cable modem. These boxes always include a port for connecting to your wired Ethernet network. (If you have one of the new breed of *wireless* modems — which acts as a wireless base station — don't panic, for it should also have a wired port for connecting to your existing switch.)

Wired network connections

After you assemble your cables and your router or switch, connect the Ethernet cables from each of your computers to the router or switch, and then turn on the device. (Most need AC power to work.) Check the manual that comes with your device to make sure that the lights you're seeing on the front indicate normal operation. (Colors vary by manufacturer, but green is usually good.)

Next, connect your cable or DSL modem's Ethernet port to the WAN port on your switch with an Ethernet cable. If your modem isn't already on, turn it on now and check for normal operation.

When your router or switch is powered on and operating normally, you're ready to configure Mac OS X for network operation. Just hop to the upcoming section, "Connecting to the Network." (How about that? Now you can add network technician to your rapidly growing computer résumé!)

Joining a wired Ethernet network

After all the cables are connected and your central connection gizmo is plugged in and turned on, you've essentially created the hardware portion of your network. Congratulations! (Now you need a beard and suspenders.)

With the hardware in place, it's time to configure Leopard. In this section, I assume that you're connecting to a network with an Internet router or switch that includes a DHCP server. (Jump to the sidebar, "The little abbreviation that _definitely_ could," for more on DHCP.)

Follow these steps on each Mac running Mac OS X that you want to connect to the network:

1. **Click the System Preferences icon on the Dock.**

2. **Click the Network icon (under Internet & Network).**

3. **From the Connection list on the left, click Ethernet.**

4. **Click the Configure pop-up menu (see Figure 17-2) and choose Using DHCP.**

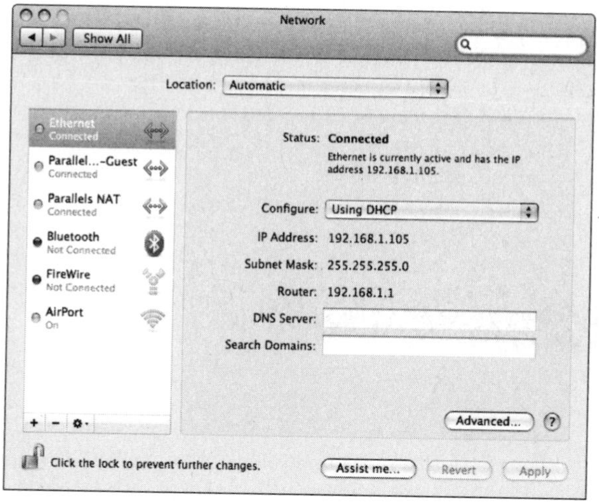

Figure 17-2: All hail DHCP, the magical networking fairy!

5. **Click the Apply button.**

The Apply button in the figure is grayed out because I'm already connected.

Enjoy the automatic goodness as Mac OS X connects to the DHCP server to obtain an IP address, a subnet mask, a gateway router IP address, and a Domain Name System (DNS) address. (Without a DHCP server, you'd have to add all this stuff manually. Ugh.)

A few seconds after clicking the Apply button, you should see the information come up. You might also notice that the DNS Server field is empty, but fear not because Mac OS X is really using DNS Server information provided by the DHCP server.

6. **Press ⌘+Q to quit System Preferences and save your settings.**

You're on!

Connecting to the Network

All right! The hardware is powered up, the cables (if any) are installed and connected, and you configured Leopard. You're ready to start (or join) the party. In this section, I show you how to verify that you're connected as well as how to share data and devices with others on your network.

The little abbreviation that *definitely* could

You know, some technologies are just *peachy.* (So much for my uber-tech image.) Anyway, these well-designed technologies work instantly, you don't have to fling settings around like wrapping paper on Christmas day, and every computer on the planet can use them: Mac, Windows, Linux, and even the laptops used by funny-looking folks from Roswell, New Mexico.

Dynamic Host Configuration Protocol, or DHCP for short, is about as peachy as it gets. This protocol enables a computer to automatically get all the technical information necessary to join a network. Let me hear you say, *"Oh yeah!"* Just about every network device on the planet can use DHCP these days, including Internet routers, hubs, switches, and (go figure) Mac OS X. Today's networking hardware and operating systems provide a *DHCP server,* which flings the proper settings at every computer on the network all by itself. Your Mac just accepts the settings and relaxes in a placid networking nirvana.

In this book, you can bet the farm that I assume you want to use DHCP and that your network hardware supports it as well. That way, I won't spend 30 pages of this book leading you through the twisting alleyways of manual network settings. (If you're really into such things, I spend those 30 pages and explain every single techno-wizard detail in my book *Mac OS X Leopard All-in-One Desk Reference For Dummies,* [Wiley]. It's about 800 pages long — hence the comprehensive angle.)

If you're connecting to an existing network, tell the network administrator that you're taking the easy route and using DHCP. One word of warning, however: Adding more than one DHCP server on a single network causes a civil war, and your system will lock up tight. Therefore, before adding hardware with a DHCP server to an existing network, ask that network administrator to make sure that you aren't making a mistake.

Verifying that the contraption works

After you have at least two computers on a wired or wireless network, test whether they're talking to each other over the network by *pinging* them. (No, I didn't make up the term, honest.) Essentially, pinging another computer is like yelling, "Are you there?" across a crevasse.

To ping another computer on the same network from any Mac running Leopard, follow these steps:

1. **Open a Finder window, click Applications, and then click Utilities.**

2. **Double-click the Network Utility icon to launch the application.**

3. **Click the Ping tab; see upcoming Figure 17-3.**

4. **In the Please Enter the Network Address to Ping text field, enter the IP address of the computer that you want to ping.**

   If you're pinging another Mac running Mac OS X, you can get the IP address of that machine by simply displaying its Network pane within System Preferences, which always displays the IP address.

   If you're trying to ping a PC running Windows and you don't know the IP address of that machine, follow these steps:

   a. *Click Start, right-click My Network Places (XP)/Network (Vista), and then choose Properties.*

   b. *From the Network Connections window, right-click your Local Area Network connection icon and then choose Status from the menu that appears.*

   c. *Click the Support tab.*

   The IP address of that PC is proudly displayed.

5. **Select the Send Only x Pings radio button and enter 5 in the text field.**

6. **Click the Ping button.**

   • *Yay!:* If everything is working, you should see results similar to those shown in Figure 17-3, in which I'm pinging my Windows server at IP address 192.168.1.103, across my wired Ethernet network.

   The address 192.168.1.*xxx* is a common series of local network IP addresses provided by Internet routers, hubs, and switches with DHCP servers, so don't freak if you have the same local IP address.

   • *Nay:* If you *don't* get a successful ping, check your cable connections, power cords, and Mac OS X settings. Folks using a wireless connection might have to move closer to the network base station to connect successfully, especially through walls.

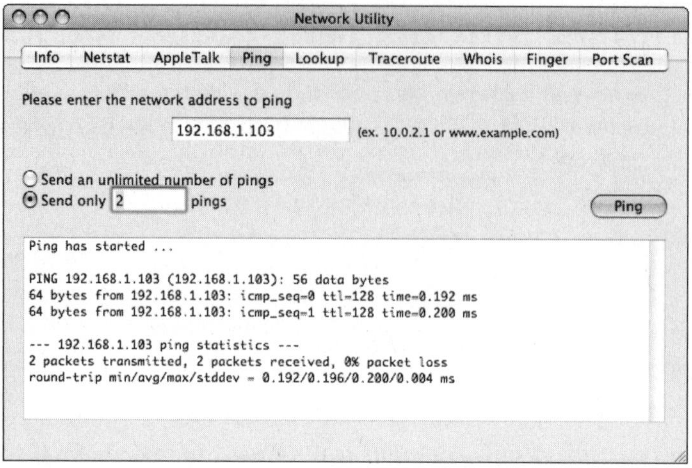

Figure 17-3:
Look, Ma,
I'm pinging!

Sharing stuff nicely with others

It works . . . by golly, it works! Okay, now what do you *do* with your all-new shining chrome network connection? Ah, my friend, let me be the first to congratulate you, and the first to show you around! In this section, I cover the most popular network perks. (And the good news is that these perks work with both wired and wireless connections.)

Network Internet connections

If your DSL or cable modem plugs directly into your MacBook (rather than a dedicated Internet sharing device or Internet router), you might ponder just how the other computers on your network can share that spiffy high-speed broadband connection. If you're running a wireless network, it comes to the rescue!

Follow these steps to share your connection wirelessly:

1. **Click the System Preferences icon on the Dock.**

2. **Click the Sharing icon (under Internet & Network).**

3. **Click the Internet Sharing entry in the Services list to the left of the pane.**

4. **From the Share Your Connection From pop-up menu, choose Ethernet.**

5. **Mark the AirPort check box (in the To Computers Using list).**

    Leopard displays a warning dialog stating that connection sharing could affect your Internet service provider (ISP) or violate your agreement with your ISP. I've never heard of this actually happening, but if you want to be sure, contact your ISP and ask the good folks there.

6. **Click Start in the warning dialog to continue.**

7. **Select the On check box next to the Internet Sharing entry in the Services list.**

8. **Click the Close button to exit System Preferences.**

Sharing an Internet connection (without an Internet router or dedicated hardware device) through Mac OS X requires your computer to remain on continuously. Remind others in your office or your home that the svelte laptop must remain on, or they'll lose their Internet connection! Naturally, when you take off on your next trip with your road warrior, the folks left at your home or office will be without an Internet connection until you return.

If your MacBook has an external USB modem, you can indeed share a dialup modem Internet connection. Just don't be too surprised if you quickly decide to shelve the idea. Those dinosaurs are s-l-o-w beyond belief.

Don't forget, you won't need to configure Internet sharing if your DSL or cable modem connects to a dedicated sharing device or router. That snazzy equipment automatically connects your entire network to the Internet.

Network file sharing

You can swap all sorts of interesting files with other Macintosh computers on your network. When you turn on Personal File Sharing, Leopard lets all Macs on the network connect to your MacBook and share the files in your Public folder. (Note that sharing across a network is different from sharing a single computer betwixt several people. I cover that environment in Chapter 16.)

Follow these steps to start sharing files and folders with others across your network:

1. **Click the System Preferences icon on the Dock.**

2. **Click the Sharing icon.**

3. **Select the On check box next to the File Sharing service entry to enable the connections for Mac and Windows sharing.**

   Other Mac users can connect to your computer by clicking Go in the Finder menu and choosing the Network menu item. The Network window appears, and your laptop is among the choices. If the other Macs are running Leopard, your MacBook's shared files and folders appear in a Finder window, and they're listed under the Shared heading in the Sidebar.

Windows XP users should be able to connect to your Mac from their My Network Places window, and Vista users can use the Network window. (Users of pre-XP versions of Windows, head to Network Neighborhood.) Those lucky Windows folks also get to print to any shared printers you've set up. (The following section covers shared printers.)

   4. **Click the Close button to exit System Preferences.**

Leopard conveniently reminds you of the network name for your MacBook at the bottom of the Sharing pane.

Sharing a network printer

Boy, howdy, do I love describing easy procedures, and sharing a printer on a Mac network ranks high on the list! You can share a printer that's connected to your laptop (or your AirPort Extreme, Time Capsule, or AirPort Express Base Station) by following these very simple steps:

   1. **Click the System Preferences icon on the Dock.**

   2. **Click the Sharing icon.**

   3. **Select the On check box next to the Printer Sharing service entry.**

   4. **Select the printer you want to share from the list at the right of the System Preferences window.**

   5. **Click the Close button to exit System Preferences.**

A printer that you share automatically appears in the Print dialog on other computers connected to your network.

USE YOUR FIREWALL!

Yep. That's the only heading in this entire book that's all uppercase. It's that important.

The following Mark's Maxim, good reader, isn't a request, a strong recommendation, or even a regular Maxim. Consider it an **absolute commandment** (right up there with *Get an antivirus application now*).

Turn on your firewall *now.*™

When you connect a network to the Internet, you open a door to the outside world. As a consultant to several businesses and organizations in my hometown, I can tell you that the outside world is chock-full of malicious individuals who would *dearly love* to inflict damage on your data or take control of your MacBook for their own purposes. Call 'em hackers, call 'em delinquents, or call 'em something I can't repeat, but *don't let them in!*

Leopard comes to the rescue again with the built-in firewall within Mac OS X. When you use this, you essentially build a virtual brick wall between you and the hackers out there (both on the Internet, and even within your local network). Follow these steps:

1. **Click the System Preferences icon on the Dock.**

2. **Click the Security icon.**

3. **Click the Firewall tab.**

4. **Select the Allow Only Essential Services radio button to activate your firewall.**

5. **Click the Advanced button.**

6. **Select the Enable Stealth Mode check box.**

   This is an important feature that prevents hackers from "trolling" for your MacBook on the Internet — or, in normal-speak, searching for an unprotected computer — so it's much harder for them to attack you.

7. **Click OK.**

8. **Click the Close button to exit System Preferences.**

Leopard even keeps track of the Internet traffic that you *do* want to reach your laptop, such as Web page requests and file sharing. When you activate one of the network features that I demonstrate in the preceding section, Leopard automatically opens a tiny hole (called a *port* by net-types) in your firewall to allow just that type of communication to your Mac.

For example, if you decide to turn on Web Sharing (as I demonstrate earlier), Leopard automatically allows incoming Web access.

You can also add ports for applications that aren't on the firewall's Allow list. This includes third-party Instant Messaging clients, multiplayer game servers, and the like. Depending on the type of connection, Leopard will often automatically display a dialog prompting you for confirmation before allowing certain traffic, so most folks won't need to do anything manually.

However, you *can* add a program manually to your list of allowed (or blocked) Firewall ports. Follow these steps:

1. **Click the System Preferences icon on the Dock.**

2. **Click the Security icon.**

3. **Click the Firewall tab.**

4. **Click the Add button.**

   Leopard displays a standard File browsing sheet.

5. **Browse to the application that requires access to the outside world — or the application that you want to block from outside communication — and click it to select it.**

6. **Click the Add button in the File sheet.**

   The application appears in the Firewall list. By default, it's set to Allow Incoming Connections.

7. **If you want to block any incoming communication to the application, click the Allow Incoming Connections pop-up menu and choose Block Incoming Connections instead.**

8. **Click the Close button to exit System Preferences.**

Chapter 18

Communicating with That Bluetooth Guy

In This Chapter

▶ Using Bluetooth for wireless connections

▶ Adding wireless keyboards and mice

▶ Moving data amongst devices with iSync

▶ Printing over a Bluetooth wireless connection

*T*ime to talk cordless. Your MacBook is already pretty doggone all-inclusive because everything that most other computers string together with cords has been integrated into the laptop's case, including the monitor and speakers. Depending on the connection options that you choose when you buy your laptop (or what you added since), the only cord that you absolutely need might be your AC power cord.

For most of us, this introduces an entirely new realm of possibilities . . . and that results in more questions. Exactly how do other wireless devices communicate with your MacBook? Can you really share the data on your laptop with your cellphone? Can you sit in the comfort of your overstuffed recliner and watch a DVD from 15 feet away?

In this chapter, I describe to you what's cooking in the world of wireless devices. I won't delve into wireless Ethernet networking between your MacBook and other computers; that's covered in depth in the confines of Chapter 17. I also don't discuss the Apple Remote in this chapter; that's covered in Chapter 10. However, I *do* cover the wireless Bluetooth connections that you can make with devices other than computers.

Bluetooth: What a Silly Name for Such Cool Technology

Originally, wireless computer connections were limited to IR (infrared) and 802.11b (the original Wi-Fi specification for wireless Ethernet networks). This was fine; after all, what were you gonna connect to your Mac besides other computers? Ah, but progress marches on.

A little Danish history

Enter the explosion in popularity of modern cellphones and personal digital assistants (PDAs). In 1998, a consortium of big-name cellphone, PDA, and computer laptop manufacturers decided that their products needed a method of communicating with each other. This new wireless standard needed to be inexpensive and consume as little battery power as possible, so designers decided to keep the operational distance limited to a maximum of about 30 feet. Plus, the idea was to keep this new wireless system as hassle-free as possible: Everyone agreed that you should simply be able to walk within range of another device, and the two would link up immediately and automatically. Thus, *Bluetooth* was born!

 Bluetooth has been incorporated into a range of peripherals and devices, including

- ✔ Cellphones
- ✔ Laptops
- ✔ Wireless computer peripherals, such as keyboards and mice
- ✔ Printers
- ✔ Headphones

Is your MacBook Bluetooth-ready?

Danish royalty aside, you still need to know whether your MacBook is ready for a Bluetooth connection. At the time of this writing, all Apple laptops come with internal Bluetooth hardware. If you're using an older Mac laptop without Bluetooth built in, though, you're currently out of the Bluetooth loop.

However, you don't need to pitch your faithful MacBook if it doesn't yet talk to the pirate! You can add Bluetooth capability to your computer with a simple USB Bluetooth adapter. The USB Bluetooth adapter from Belkin (www. belkin.com) sells online for about $30. It includes automatic data encryption, which is necessary only if there's a hacker within about 30 to 60 feet of your computer (although more security is always better in my book). The adaptor can link with up to seven other Bluetooth devices simultaneously. (Come to think of it, there were a lot of people within 30 feet of my MacBook Pro during my last LAN party bash. I guess this stuff really *is* important!)

Leopard and Bluetooth, together forever

You'd expect a modern, high-tech operating system like Mac OS X to come with Bluetooth drivers. You'd be right, but Apple goes a step further: Leopard comes with System Preferences and a utility application to help you get your laptop connected with the Bluetooth devices that are likely hanging out in your coat pockets.

Click the System Preferences icon in the Dock. From the Bluetooth pane, you can

- **Set up new Bluetooth devices.** Click the Set Up New Device button to run the Bluetooth Setup Assistant, which configures Bluetooth devices for use with Leopard.

  Follow the device-specific onscreen instructions to set up a number of common Bluetooth toys (including keyboards, mice, cellphones, and printers), or you can work with other types of devices by choosing Other. Setup Assistant searches for your Bluetooth device and makes sure that it's ready to party with your MacBook.

  Make sure that your Bluetooth device is in range and *discoverable* (available for connections with other Bluetooth devices) before you run the Bluetooth Setup Assistant. Check your user manual to determine how to set your Bluetooth device as "discoverable," and make sure that you're about 20 feet away (or less) from your MacBook.

- **Configure Bluetooth connections.** Click the Advanced button to create, remove, enable, or disable your Bluetooth connections, using them as virtual serial ports (for the simple transfer of data) or virtual modems (for bidirectional transfers, such as using an Internet connection through a Bluetooth cellphone).

  These openings to the outside world are presented as individual connections in the Serial Port list, and you can toggle them on and off individually. You can also specify whether a Bluetooth port is encrypted. Figure 18-1 shows an active Bluetooth virtual modem that's set up to allow my MacBook Pro to sync up with my Palm Pilot, using the Bluetooth-PDA-Sync service.

I recommend that you enable the Show Bluetooth Status in the Menu Bar check box. The Bluetooth menu lets you conserve power by turning off your Bluetooth hardware until you need it. You can also conveniently toggle your laptop's discovery status as well as set up a device or send and browse files. (You can even see what devices are connected to your Mac with the click of a menu icon. 'Nuff said.)

Figure 18-1:
You can add, delete, enable or disable Bluetooth ports from the Advanced sheet.

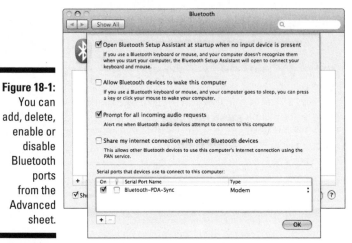

If you know you won't be using Bluetooth devices while you're on the road, disabling a Bluetooth service on a laptop can help conserve battery power.

The other Bluetooth resource that you can use is the standalone application *Bluetooth File Exchange.* (Yes, you can call it *BFE* if you like. I do whenever possible.) You have to launch BFE the old-fashioned way; it's located in your Utilities folder, inside your Applications folder. Much like a traditional FTP (File Transfer Protocol) application, double-clicking the Bluetooth File Exchange icon presents you with a file selection dialog, where you choose the file(s) you want to send to the connected Bluetooth device! You can also elect to browse the files on a networked Bluetooth device so that you can see what the owner of that device is offering.

You can also set up your defaults for file exchanges from the Sharing pane in System Preferences. Click the Sharing icon and then select the Bluetooth Sharing check box to display the settings shown in Figure 18-2. Here you can control what Leopard does when you receive files or Personal Information Manager (PIM) data with BFE. For instance, with these settings, Leopard can

✔ Prompt you for permission to receive each file or PIM item

✔ Accept all files and PIM items without restriction or prompting

✔ Save all incoming files and items to the folder that you specify

✔ Offer only the files and items in the folder that you specify when other Bluetooth items browse your MacBook

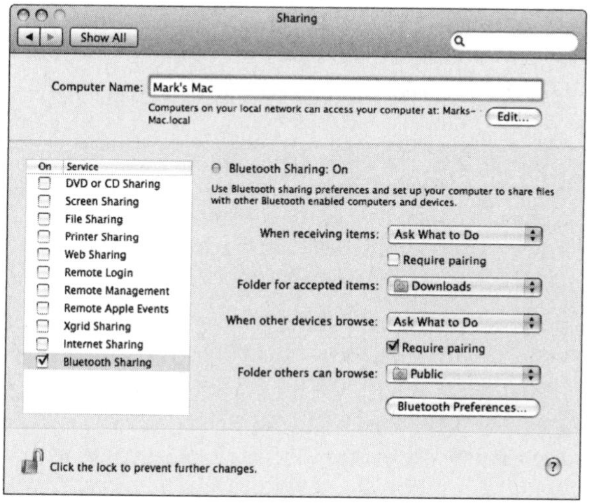

Figure 18-2: Configure file exchanges in System Preferences.

Personally, I'm all for the defaults in Leopard for file exchanges:

✔ I want to know when someone's sending me something.

✔ I want anything I receive to be saved in my Downloads folder.

✔ If I turn on File Transfer, I want to allow others to browse the contents of my Public folder.

However, feel free to adjust, enable, and disable to your heart's content.

Adding Wireless Keyboards and Mice to Your Laptop

The current crop of Mac laptops arrive at your doorstep in a fully wireless configuration: Apple throws in an internal Bluetooth adapter and an internal AirPort Extreme wireless card. Everything's already included for you.

Therefore, you can indeed work keyboard and mouse magic from across the room from your laptop, using a wireless keyboard and mouse that you can buy separately. (Or perhaps you just want a full-size keyboard and external mouse to use when you're working from your home or office.)

A number of wireless Bluetooth keyboard/mouse packages are on the market, and any one of 'em should work fine with your Mac. In fact, you can buy Apple's wireless Bluetooth keyboard and mouse separately, for a total of about $150. Other offerings from Logitech and our old buddy Microsoft run about the same amount.

When shopping for a Bluetooth keyboard/mouse desktop, keep these facts in mind:

✔ **Some keyboards are created more than equal.** Many of today's third-party keyboards are encrusted with extra function buttons that do everything from opening your e-mail application to searching your kitchen cabinets for another can of spray cheese.

I like these programmable function keys — they can bring up your favorite applications with a single keystroke while you're relaxing 20 feet away — so look for the keyboard that offers the most programmable keys in your price range.

✔ **Rodents crave energy.** Does the wireless mouse come with its own recharging stand? If so, that's a big plus. Depending on how much you use your laptop, a mouse that runs on standard batteries can go through a set in as little as a month's time! (Not surprisingly, many computer owners use rechargeable batteries in their wireless mice.) In fact, some wireless mice include an on/off switch to help conserve battery power.

✔ **Wireless doesn't always mean Bluetooth.** Just because a keyboard or mouse is wireless doesn't automatically make it a Bluetooth device. Plenty of wireless RF (radio frequency) devices are out there, too. These toys need their own transmitters, which are usually USB-based as well, so things can get confusing. Therefore, read the box or technical specifications carefully to make sure you're buying Bluetooth.

✔ **Bluetooth stuff isn't self-cleaning.** Sure, your new wireless keyboard and mouse can hang out with you on the sofa, but that doesn't mean they're happy sharing your nacho puffs and grape soda. Look for an optical mouse that doesn't use a ball, and check whether a prospective keyboard can be easily cleaned and maintained before you buy it.

Most Bluetooth devices are controlled through the Bluetooth pane in System Preferences. However, wireless keyboards and mice are a special case because they're monitored through the Bluetooth section of the Keyboard & Mouse pane. (You can even add a new wireless device from this tab. Geez, those Apple designers give you a dozen roads to the same spot on the map, don't they?)

Getting Everything in iSync

No jokes about boy bands, please. *iSync* is the data transfer and synchronizing utility application that ships with Leopard, and it works fine with both wired and wireless Bluetooth connections. The difference between Bluetooth File Exchange and iSync is a matter of intelligence:

- ✔ BFE merely transfers files and dumps them in the folders you specify.

- ✔ iSync copies and updates your Address Book, Safari, and iCal information between devices. iSync compares the information on both your laptop and your devices and makes sure they end up the same.

  iSync also allows you to synchronize data between multiple computers by using your .Mac membership so that the contacts, bookmarks, and calendar data on your MacBook match the data on your Mac Pro. You can control what gets sent from the .Mac pane in System Preferences. (For more on .Mac, visit Chapter 9.)

Just because your phone or PDA supports Bluetooth *doesn't* mean that iSync is guaranteed to work. I know a few Mac owners who are still seething over incompatible devices. For a complete list of the Bluetooth phones, PDAs, and other devices that work with iSync, visit `www.apple.com/isync/devices.html`.

After your supported Bluetooth device is linked to your Mac, follow these steps to add the new device to iSync and synchronize your data:

1. **Click the Finder icon on the Dock.**

2. **Click Applications in the Finder window Sidebar and double-click iSync.**

3. **Press ⌘+N.**

   iSync displays the Add Device dialog.

4. **Click Scan to display any Bluetooth devices in range.**

5. **Double-click the device that you want to use.**

   The window expands to allow you to specify what data is to be synchronized. (Other settings might appear as well, depending on the device.)

6. **Mark the check boxes for each data type that you want to exchange.**

7. **Click Sync Devices.**

Never disconnect a device while a synchronization is in progress. You risk corrupting the data being transferred, or your MacBook could lock up. Wait until iSync indicates that the synchronization is finished; the application displays a message when the process is complete.

Deleting a calendar event or a contact on either your laptop or the Bluetooth device deletes that same data from the other machine! For example, if you decide you no longer need your personal contacts on your Mac at work and you delete 'em, *they'll be deleted from your PDA when you synchronize.* When I say that iSync creates a mirror image on both sides of the connection, I'm not lying: Additions appear, and deletions disappear.

The Magic of Wireless Printing

To your Mac laptop, a wireless Bluetooth printer is just another Bluetooth connection — but to you, it's the very definition of convenience, especially if desk space is limited next to your Mac. Just set that paper-producing puppy up anywhere in the 30–40 foot range, plug it in, set up the printer in Leopard, and let 'er rip.

Not all printer manufacturers produce Bluetooth models that communicate properly with your Mac. Make sure that the Bluetooth printer you buy supports HCRP. (Another jawbreaker acronym. This time it stands for *Hardcopy Cable Replacement Protocol.*)

You have two options when installing a Bluetooth printer:

✔ Whenever possible, use the printer manufacturer's software. A printer might require a driver that a typical Bluetooth device doesn't need.

✔ You can usually successfully set up a printer via the Bluetooth Setup Assistant, which you can run from Bluetooth pane of System Preferences (as I discuss earlier in the chapter):

  a. *Make sure your printer is set as discoverable.*

     Check your printer manual to determine how to switch your printer to discoverable mode. This mode allows other Bluetooth devices within range (including your laptop) to recognize and make a connection to your printer.

  b. *Click the Set Up New Device button.*

  c. *Choose to install a printer.*

  d. *Follow the onscreen instructions.*

Luckily, after you successfully set up a Bluetooth printer, you can just press ⌘+P to open the Print dialog box and choose that printer from the Printer pop-up menu. No big whoop . . . and that's the way it *should* be.

Part VI

Necessary Evils: Troubleshooting, Upgrading, Maintaining

The 5th Wave   By Rich Tennant

Okay-you were right, I was wrong. F5 opens the garage door, and F6 backs the car out.

In this part . . .

No computer is completely trouble-free — and if your MacBook, MacBook Air, or MacBook Pro starts acting strangely, the troubleshooting tips you find in this part will help you get your favorite machine back to normal. I also provide you with all the guidance you need to maintain your MacBook properly as well as step-by-step instructions for upgrading your laptop with goodies such as additional RAM or external storage devices.

Chapter 19

When Good Mac Laptops Go Bad

In This Chapter

▶ Avoiding the blame (righteously)

▶ Putting basic troubleshooting precepts to work

▶ Using Mark's Troubleshooting Tree

▶ Getting help

1 wish you weren't reading this chapter.

Because you are, I can only surmise that you're having trouble with your MacBook, and that it needs fixing. (The other possibility — that you just like reading about solving computer problems — is more attractive, but much more problematic.)

Consider this chapter a crash course in the logical puzzle that is computer *troubleshooting:* namely, the art of finding out What Needs Fixing. You also see what you can do when you just plain can't fix the problem by yourself.

Oh, and you're going to encounter a lot of Tips and Mark's Maxims in this chapter — all of them learned the hard way, so I recommend committing them to memory on the spot!

Repeat After Me: Yes, 1 Am a Tech!

Anyone can troubleshoot. Put these common troubleshooting myths to rest:

✔ **It takes a college degree in computer science to troubleshoot.** Tell that to my troubleshooting kids in junior high. They'll think it's a hoot because they have Apple computers of their own in the classroom. You can follow all the steps in this chapter without any special training.

✔ **I'm to blame.** Ever heard of viruses? Failing hardware? Buggy software? Any of those things can be causing the problem. It's Mark's Maxim time.

Don't beat yourself up! Your laptop can be fixed.™

✔ **I need to buy expensive utility software.** Nope. You can certainly invest in a commercial testing and repair utility if you like. My favorite is TechTool Pro from Micromat (www.micromat.com), but a third-party utility isn't a requirement for troubleshooting. (I would, however, consider an antivirus application as a must-have, and you should have one already. Hint, hint.)

✔ **There's no hope if I can't fix it.** Sure, parts fail, and computers crash, but your Apple Service Center can repair just about any problem. And (ahem) if you backed up your laptop (like I preach throughout this book), you'll keep that important data (even if a new hard drive is in your future).

✔ **It takes forever.** Wait until you read the Number One Rule in the next section; the first step takes but 30 seconds and often solves the problem. Naturally, not all problems can be fixed so quickly, but if you follow the procedures in this chapter, you should fix your laptop (or at least know that the problem requires outside help) in a single afternoon.

With those myths banished for good, you can get down to business and start feeling better soon.

Step-by-Step Laptop Troubleshooting

In this section, I walk you through my Should-Be-Patented Troubleshooting Tree as well as the Leopard built-in troubleshooting application, Disk Utility. I also introduce you to a number of keystrokes that can make your MacBook jump through hoops.

The Number One Rule: Reboot!

Yep, it sounds silly, but the fact is that rebooting your MacBook can often solve a number of problems. If you're encountering these types of strange behavior with your laptop, a reboot might be all you need to heal

✔ Intermittent problems communicating over a network

✔ A garbled screen, strange colors, or screwed-up fonts

✔ The Swirling Beach Ball of Doom that won't go away after several minutes

Why is rebooting so darned effective?

Rebooting fixes problems because it resets *everything.* Your network connection, for example, might be acting up or have timed out, and rebooting restores it. Rebooting also fixes problems due to brownouts or those notorious AC power flickerings that we all notice from time to time, which can even affect a laptop running on an AC adapter. Such interruptions in constant juice might not bother you or me (or your less-intelligent toaster), but they can play tricks on your laptop that rebooting will fix.

✔ An application that locks up

✔ An external device that seems to disappear or can't be opened

To put it succinctly, here's a modest Mark's Maxim:

Always try a reboot before beginning to worry. Always.™

If you're in the middle of a document, try to save all your open documents before you reboot. That might not be possible, but try to save what you can.

If you need to force a *locked* application (one that's not responding) to quit so you can reboot, follow these steps to squash that locked application:

1. **Click the Apple (🍎) menu and choose Force Quit.**

   The dialog that you see in Figure 19-1 appears on your screen.

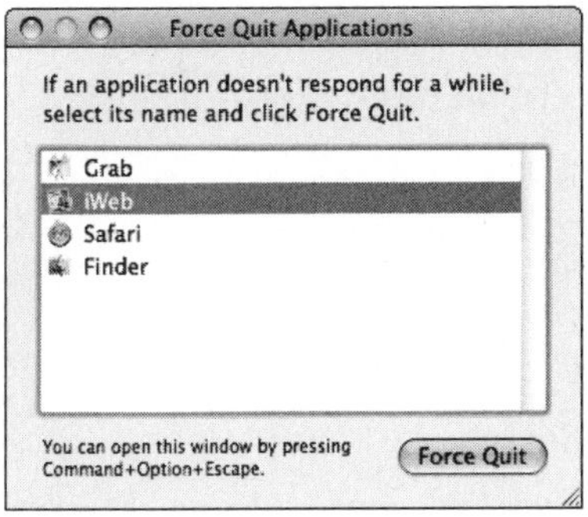

Figure 19-1: Force a recalcitrant application to take off.

2. **Click the offending application and then click the Force Quit button.**

When you get everything to quit, you should be able to click the Apple menu and choose Shut Down (not Restart) without a problem.

If your MacBook simply won't shut down (or you can't get the offending application to quit), then do what must be done:

1. **Press and hold your laptop's Power button until it shuts itself off.**

   You have to wait about five seconds for your MacBook to turn itself off.

2. **Wait about ten seconds.**

3. **Press the Power button again to restart the computer.**

After everything is back up, check whether the problem is still apparent. If you use your laptop for an hour or two and the problem doesn't reoccur, you likely fixed it!

Special keys that can come in handy

A number of keys have special powers over your MacBook. No, I'm not kidding! These keys affect how your road warrior starts up, and they can really come in handy whilst troubleshooting.

Using Safe Boot mode

You can use Safe Boot mode to force Leopard to run a directory check of your boot hard drive and disable any Login Items that might be interfering with Leopard. Use the Shut Down menu item from the Apple (🍎) menu to completely turn off your laptop, press the Power button to start the computer, and then press and hold down the Shift key immediately after you hear the startup tone. After Leopard completely boots, restart your MacBook again (this time without the Shift key) to return to normal operation.

Startup keys

Table 19-1 provides the lowdown on startup keys. Hold the indicated key down either *when you push your Power button* or *immediately after the screen blanks during a restart.* (As I just mentioned, the Shift key is the exception; it should be pressed and held down after you hear the startup tone.)

Table 19-1	Startup Keys and Their Tricks
Key	**Effect on Your MacBook**
C	Boots from the CD or DVD that's loaded in your optical drive (if you have one)
Media Eject	Ejects the CD or DVD in your optical drive (if you have one)
Option	Displays a system boot menu, allowing you to choose the operating system
Shift	Prevents your Login Items from running; runs a directory check
T	Starts your MacBook in FireWire Target Disk mode (except for the MacBook Air, which has no FireWire port)
⌘+V	Show Mac OS X Console messages
⌘+S	Starts your Mac in Single User mode
⌘+Option+P+R	Resets Parameter RAM (PRAM)

Some of the keys/combinations in Table 19-1 might never be necessary for your machine, but you might be instructed to use them by an Apple technician. I'll warrant that you'll use at least the C startup key fairly often.

All hail Disk Utility, the troubleshooter's friend

Leopard's *Disk Utility* is a handy tool for troubleshooting and repairing your hard drive. You can find it in the Utilities folder within your Applications folder.

Danger, Will Robinson!

Many Disk Utility functions can actually **wipe your hard drives clean of data** instead of repairing them! These advanced functions aren't likely to help you with troubleshooting a problem with your existing volumes anyway.

Remember: Don't use these Disk Utility functions unless an Apple technician *tells* you to use them:

✔ Partitioning and erasing drives

✔ Setting up RAID arrays

✔ Restoring files from disk images

Fire up Disk Utility and click the First Aid tab to bring up the rather powerful-looking window shown in Figure 19-2.

In the left column of the Disk Utility window, you can see

✔ **The *physical* hard drives in your system (the actual hardware)**

✔ **The *volumes* (the data stored on the hard drives)**

> You can always tell a volume because it's indented underneath the physical drive entry.

✔ **Any CD or DVD loaded on your MacBook**

✔ **USB or FireWire Flash drives**

For example, in Figure 19-2, I have one hard drive (the 298.1GB entry) and one USB Flash drive (the 3.7GB entry). The hard drive has two volumes (Wolfgang and Mother), and the USB drive has one volume (MLC USB).

The information at the bottom of the Disk Utility window contains the specifications of the selected drive or volume . . . things like capacity, free space, and the number of files and folders for a volume, or connection type and total capacity for a drive.

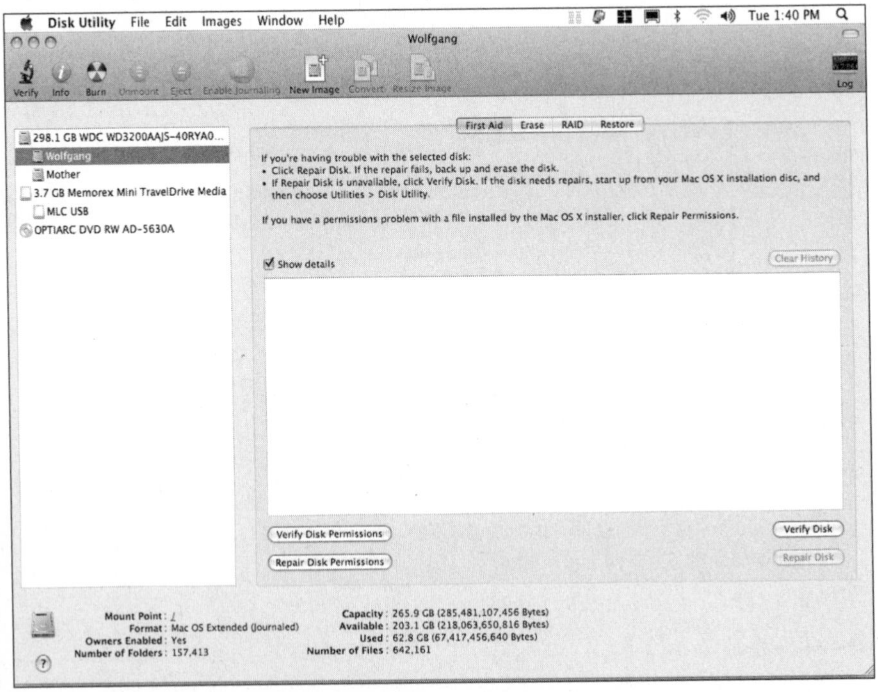

Figure 19-2:
The
physician
of hard
drives —
Leopard's
Disk Utility.

Repairing disk permissions

Because Leopard is built on a Unix base, lots of permissions can apply to the files on your drive — that is, who can open (or read or change) every application, folder, and document on your hard drive. Unfortunately, these permissions are often messed up by wayward applications or power glitches, or application installers that do a subpar job of cleaning up after themselves. And if the permissions on a file are changed, often applications lock up or refuse to run altogether.

I recommend repairing your disk permissions with Disk Utility once weekly. Figure 19-3 shows a permissions repair sweep on my internal hard drive's volume.

Use these steps to repair permissions on your MacBook's hard drive:

1. **Make sure that you're logged in with an admin account.**

   Chapter 16 shows you how to log in as an admin user.

2. **Save and close any open documents.**

3. **Double-click the Disk Utility icon in the Utilities folder.**

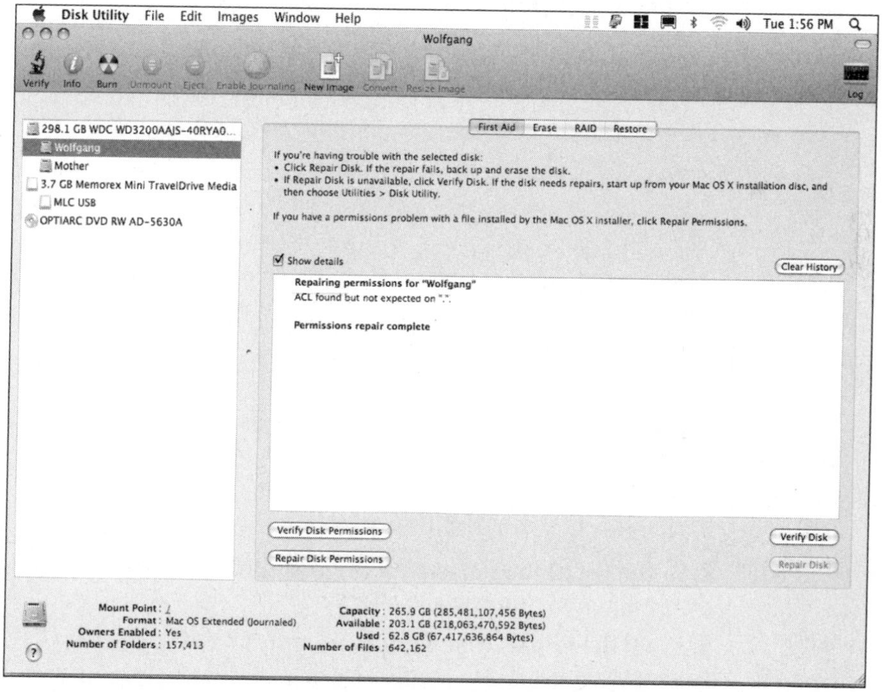

Figure 19-3:
A successful run, using Repair Disk Permissions.

4. **Click the volume that you want to check.**

5. **Click the Repair Disk Permissions button.**

   I don't worry about verifying. If something's wrong, you end up clicking Repair Disk Permissions, anyway. Just click Repair Disk Permissions; if nothing pops up, that's fine.

6. **To finish the process, always reboot after repairing permissions.**

   This shows you whether a problem has been corrected!

Repairing disks

Disk Utility can check the format and health of both hard drives and volumes with Verify Disk — and, if the problem can be corrected, fix any error by using Repair Disk.

Using Disk Utility to repair your hard drive carries a couple of caveats:

- ✔ **You can't repair the boot disk or the boot volume.** This actually makes sense because you're using that disk and volume right now.

  To verify or repair your boot hard drive, you need to boot from your Mac OS X installation disc by using the C startup key. (Refer to Table 19-1 for keys that come in handy.) After your laptop boots from the Mac OS X installation disc, choose the Utilities menu and click Disk Utility.

  You should be able to select your boot hard drive or volume, and the Verify Disk and Repair Disk buttons should be enabled.

- ✔ **You can't repair CDs and DVDs.** CDs and DVDs are read-only media and thus can't be repaired at all (at least by Disk Utility).

  If your MacBook is having trouble reading a CD or DVD, wipe the disc with a soft cloth to remove dust, oil, and fingerprints. Should that fail, invest in a disc-cleaning contrivance of some sort.

If you need to verify and repair a disk or volume, follow these steps:

1. **If you need to repair your *boot drive and volume,* save all your open documents and reboot from either *an external drive* or *your Mac OS X Installation disc.***

2. **Double-click the Disk Utility icon in the Utilities folder.**

3. **In the list at the left side of the Disk Utility window, click the disk or volume that you want to check.**

4. **Click the Repair Disk button.**

5. **If changes were made (or if you had to boot from a disc or external drive), reboot after repairing the disk or volume.**

Should I reinstall Mac OS X?

This question seems to get a lot of attention on Mac-related Internet discussion boards and Usenet newsgroups — and the answer is a definitive *perhaps*. (I know. That's really helpful.)

Here's the explanation. You *shouldn't* lose a single byte of data by reinstalling Mac OS X, so it's definitely okay to try it. However, reinstalling Mac OS X isn't a universal balm that fixes all software errors because the problem that you're encountering might be due to a buggy application, or a hard drive that's going critical,

or a video card with faulty memory modules. If the trouble you're having is because of a corrupted Mac OS X System folder, reinstalling Leopard might or might not fix the problem.

Therefore, the debate rages on. I would certainly follow the MacBook Troubleshooting Tree all the way to the end before I would even consider reinstalling Leopard, and I would recommend contacting an Apple support technician via the Apple Web site before you take this step.

Mark's MacBook Troubleshooting Tree

As the hip-hop artists say, "Alright, kick it." And that's just what my MacBook Troubleshooting Tree is here for. If rebooting your laptop hasn't solved the problem, follow these steps in order (until either the solution is found, or you run out of steps — more on that in the next section).

Step 1: Investigate recent changes

This is a simple step that many novice Mac owners forget. Simply retrace your steps and consider what changes you made recently to your system. Here are the most common culprits:

✔ **Did you just finish installing a new application?** Try uninstalling it by removing the application directory and any support files that it might have added to your system. (And keep your applications current with the most recent patches and updates from the developer's Web site.)

From time to time, an application's *preference file* — which stores all the custom settings you make — can become corrupted. Although the application itself is okay, it might act strangely or refuse to launch. To check your preference files for signs of corruption, try scanning your applications with Preferential Treatment, a freeware AppleScript utility by Jonathan Nathan, available from his Web site at www.jonn8.com/html/pt.html. (Preferential Treatment will flag any dicey preference files, setting them up for a quick trip to the Trash.)

✔ **Did you just apply an update or a patch to an application?** Uninstall the application and reinstall it without applying the patch. If your MacBook suddenly works again, check the developer's Web site or contact its technical support department to report the problem.

✔ **Did you just update Leopard by using Software Update?** Updating Leopard can introduce problems within your applications that depend on specific routines and system files. Contact the developer of the application and look for updated patches that bring your software in line with the Leopard updates. (And use Software Update in automatic mode to check for Mac OS X updates at least once weekly.)

✔ **Did you just make a change within System Preferences?** Return the options that you changed back to their original settings; then consult Chapter 6 for information on what might have gone wrong. (If the setting in question isn't in Chapter 6, consider searching Leopard's online Help or the Apple support Web site for more clues.)

✔ **Did you just connect (or reconnect) an external device?** Try unplugging the device and then rebooting to see whether the problem disappears. Remember that many peripherals need software drivers to run — and without those drivers installed, they won't work correctly. Check the device's manual or visit the company's Web site to search for software that you might need.

If you didn't make any significant changes to your system before you encountered the problem, proceed to the next step.

Step 2: Run Disk Utility

The preceding section shows how to repair disk permissions on your Leopard boot drive.

If you're experiencing hard drive problems, consider booting from your Mac OS X Installation CD or DVD to run a full-blown Repair Disk checkup on your boot volume.

Step 3: Check your cables

Cables work themselves loose, and they fail from time to time. Check all your cables to your external devices — make sure that they're snug — and verify that everything's plugged in and turned on. (Oh, and don't forget to check for crimps in your cables or even Fluffy's teeth marks.)

If a FireWire or USB device acts up, swap cables around to find whether you have a bad one. A faulty cable can leave you pulling your hair out in no time.

Step 4: Check your Trash

Check the contents of your Trash to see whether you recently deleted files or folders by accident. Click the Trash icon on the Dock once to display the contents. If something's been deleted by mistake, drag it back to its original folder, and try running the application again.

I know this one from personal experience. A slight miscalculation while selecting files to delete made an application freeze every time I launched it.

Step 5: Check your Internet and network connections

Now that always-on DSL and cable modem connections to the Internet are common, don't forget an obvious problem: Your laptop can't reach the Internet because your ISP is down, or your network is no longer working!

A quick visual check of your DSL or cable modem will usually indicate whether there's a connection problem between your modem and your ISP. For example, my modem has a very informative activity light that I always glance at first. However, if your laptop is connected to the Internet through a larger home or office network and you can't check the modem visually, you can check your Internet connection by pinging www.apple.com.

1. **Open your Utilities folder (inside your Applications folder).**

2. **Double-click Network Utility.**

3. **Click the Ping button.**

4. **Enter www.apple.com in the Address box.**

5. **Click Ping.**

   You should see successful ping messages. If you don't get a successful ping *and* you can still reach other computers on your network, your cable/DSL modem or your ISP are likely experiencing problems. If you can't reach your network at all, the problem lies in your network hardware or configuration.

Step 6: Think virus

If you made it to this point, it's time to run a full virus scan — and make sure that your antivirus application has the latest updated data files, too. My antivirus application of choice is Virus Barrier X from Intego (www.intego.com).

If a virus is detected and your antivirus application can't remove it, try *quarantining* it instead, which basically disables the virus-ridden application and prevents it from infecting other files.

Step 7: Disable your Login Items

Mac OS X might encounter problems with applications that you've marked as Login Items within System Preferences. In this step, I show you how to identify login problems and how to fix 'em.

Checking for problems

It's time to use another nifty startup key (refer to Table 19-1). This time, hold down Shift after you hear the startup tone.

This trick disables your account's Login Items, which are run automatically every time you log in to your MacBook. If one of these Login Items is to blame, your laptop will simply encounter trouble every time you log in.

Finding the Login Item that's causing trouble

If your laptop works fine with your Login Items disabled, follow this procedure for each item in the Login Items list:

1. **Open System Preferences, click Accounts, and then click the Login Items button.**

2. **Delete the item from the list; then reboot normally.**

   You can delete the selected item by clicking the Delete button, which bears a minus sign.

   When your MacBook starts up normally with Login Items enabled, you discovered the perpetrator. You'll likely need to delete that application and reinstall it. (Don't forget to add each of the *working* Login Items back to the Login Items list!)

Step 8: Turn off your screen saver

This is a long shot, but it isn't unheard of to discover that a faulty, bug-ridden screensaver has locked up your MacBook. (If you aren't running one of the Apple-supplied screensavers and your computer never wakes up from Sleep mode or hangs while displaying the screensaver, you found your prime suspect.)

Reboot your MacBook (if necessary), open System Preferences, and then click Desktop & Screen Saver, and click the Screen Saver button. Then do one of the following:

- ✔ Switch to an Apple screensaver.
- ✔ Drag the Start slider to Never.

If this fixes the problem, you can typically remove the screensaver completely by deleting the offending saver application in the Screen Savers folder inside your Mac OS X Library folder. If you can't find the screensaver application, try typing the saver name in the Spotlight search box.

Step 9: Run System Profiler

Ouch. You reached Step 9, and you still haven't uncovered the culprit. At this point, you narrowed the possibilities to a serious problem, like bad hardware or corrupted files in your Mac OS X System Folder. Fortunately, Leopard provides System Profiler, which displays real-time information on the hardware in your system. Click the Apple menu and choose About This Mac; then click More Info. Click each one of the Hardware categories in turn, double-checking to make sure that everything looks okay.

You don't have to understand all the technical hieroglyphics. If a Hardware category doesn't return what you expect or displays an error message, though, that's suspicious. (If your MacBook doesn't have a specific type of hardware onboard — including an optical drive or Fibre Channel hardware — you won't get information from those categories.)

Diagnostics shows whether your MacBook passed the Power On self-test.

Okay, I Kicked It, and It Still Won't Work

Don't worry, friendly reader. Just because you've reached the end of my MacBook tree doesn't mean you're out of luck. In this section, I discuss the online help available on the Apple Web site as well as local help in your own town.

Apple Help Online

If you haven't visited the Apple MacBook Support site yet, run — don't walk — to www.apple.com/support/macbook, where you can find

- ✔ **The latest patches, updates, and how-to tutorials** for the MacBook line
- ✔ **MacBook and Mac OS X discussion boards,** moderated by Apple
- ✔ **Tools** for ordering spare parts, checking on your remaining warranty coverage, and searching the Apple Knowledge Base
- ✔ **Do-it-yourself instructions** (PDF files) that you can follow to repair or upgrade your MacBook

Local service, at your service

In case you need to take in your MacBook for service, an Apple Store or Apple Authorized Service Provider is probably in your area. To find the closest service, launch Safari and visit

```
http://www.apple.com/buy/locator/service/
```

That's the Find Service page on the Apple Web site. You can search by city and state or ZIP code. The results are complete with the provider's mailing address, Web site address, telephone number, and even a map of the location!

Always call your Apple service provider before you lug your (albeit lightweight) laptop all the way to the shop. Make sure that you know your MacBook's serial number (which you can display in System Profiler) and which version of Mac OS X you're using.

Chapter 20

Adding New Stuff to Your Laptop

· ·

In This Chapter

▶ Adding memory

▶ Upgrading your hard drive

▶ Adding USB and FireWire devices

▶ Reviewing what add-ons are available

· ·

"*N*o laptop is an island." Somebody famous wrote that, I'm sure.

Without getting too philosophical — or invoking the all-powerful Internet yet again — the old saying really does make sense. All computer owners usually add at least one *peripheral* (external device), such as a printer, joystick, an iPod, a backup drive, or a scanner. I talk about the ports on your MacBook in Chapter 1. Those holes aren't there to just add visual interest to the sides of your treasured laptop. Therefore, I cover your USB and FireWire ports (and what you can plug into them) in detail in this chapter.

Ah, but what about the stuff *inside* your road warrior? That's where things get both interesting and scary at the same time. In this chapter, I describe what you can add to the innards of your computer as well as how to get inside there if you work up the courage to go exploring.

More Memory Will Help

Hey, wait a second. No *however* stuck on the end? You mean for once, there isn't an exception? Aren't all computers different? Hard as it is to believe, just keep in mind this Mark's Maxim:

More memory helps.™

Period. End of statement. No matter what type of computer you own, how old it is, or what operating system you use, adding more memory to your system (to the maximum it supports) significantly improves the performance of your operating system (and practically every application that you run).

Memory maximizes the power of your computer: The more memory you have, the less data your laptop has to temporarily store on its hard drive. Without getting into virtual memory and other techno-gunk, just consider that extra memory as extra elbowroom for your applications and your documents. (You can read how in Chapter 21.) Believe me, both Mac OS X and Windows XP/Vista efficiently make use of every kilobyte of memory that you can provide.

MacBook Air owners, I have good and bad news: The good news is that your laptop is already maxed out at 2GB of memory, and the bad news is that you can't add any more. Your ultrathin Air is a sealed unit — literally — and you must visit your local Apple hardware technician if your laptop's memory malfunctions and needs replacing. (The same is true for your Air's battery.) Therefore, you can skip the rest of this section!

Figuring out how much memory you have

To see how much memory you have in your computer, click the Apple menu (), choose About This Mac, click More Info, and click the Memory heading.

At the time of this writing, your MacBook or MacBook Pro has sockets for two DDR SDRAM memory modules. (Don't fret over what all the abbreviations mean. Rest assured that this memory type is fast.) These modules are available with up to 2GB of memory, so you can install as much as 4GB of memory in your Mac.

How you plan memory upgrades depends on how much memory you want. If your MacBook uses the single default 1GB module supplied by Apple, you have a couple of options:

> ✔ **Add up to 2GB of RAM** by inserting a 1GB or a 2GB memory module in the empty slot. At the time of this writing, a gigabyte memory module should set you back about $100 or so.
>
> 2GB of memory is plenty for running applications from the iLife and iWork suites as well as any of the applications bundled with Leopard.

> ✔ **Install up to 4GB of total memory** by removing the standard 1GB module and inserting high-capacity 2GB modules in both slots. (Naturally, if your laptop came with a single 2GB module installed, all you have to do is add another 2GB module to reach 4GB total Nirvana.)
>
> If your primary applications include video editing, game playing, or image editing, you can use all the memory your laptop can hold.

WARNING!

Climbing inside your Mac laptop

This section on laptop upgrades is short for a reason: Laptops simply aren't *meant* to be disassembled. As I mention several times in this book, internal expansion in your MacBook or MacBook Pro is severely limited. Basically, you can add extra memory and swap out your hard drive. Adding memory is easy, but swapping out your hard drive requires more work and considerable preparation. And, as I also mention earlier in this book, you can't make *any* internal modifications at all to your MacBook Air, which is a sealed unit. (Breaking in will very likely void your warranty.)

Therefore, I always recommend that you seek professional servicing when you need to repair your laptop. For example, if your laptop's LCD screen is cracked or broken, do *not* try to fix it yourself! Sure, you might see a number of used LCD panels on eBay, but these parts aren't designed to be easily swapped out, like a desktop computer's video card. Besides, if you make a mistake when trying to fix something deep in the bowels of your laptop, you might end up causing more damage than you repair.

The moral of the story? Let your local Apple dealer's service technicians perform major surgery on your laptop, and buy an AppleCare Protection Plan that will cover your laptop like a blanket for up to three years!

Read more about swapping out drives in the upcoming section, "Gotta have internal."

Although the MacBook Pro comes with a minimum of 2GB, the process is generally the same. The exception to the RAM upgrade circus is the MacBook Air, which is a sealed unit — you can't upgrade your RAM at all.

Unfortunately, Apple's prices for adding RAM are, well, *outrageous* (as in, "Boy, howdy, I can't afford that!") Therefore, I can heartily recommend any one of these online sources that cater to Mac owners:

- ✔ **MacMall:** `www.macmall.com`
- ✔ **CDW:** `www.cdw.com/content/brands/apple/default.aspx`
- ✔ **Newegg:** `www.newegg.com`

Installing memory modules

I'm happy to report that adding extra memory to your system is one of the easiest internal upgrades that you can perform. Therefore, I recommend that you add memory yourself unless you simply don't want to mess with your MacBook's internal organs. As I mention earlier, of course, your local Macintosh service specialist will be happy to install new RAM modules for you (for a price).

To add memory modules to a MacBook or MacBook Pro, follow these steps:

1. **Get ready to operate.**

   a. *Spread a clean towel on a stable work surface, such as your kitchen table.*

   The towel helps protect your screen from scratches.

   b. *Find a Phillips screwdriver.*

   c. *Shut down your laptop and wait at least ten minutes for it to cool down.*

   d. *Unplug all cables from the computer.*

2. **Close the computer and flip it over on top of the towel.**

3. **Ground thyself!**

   Check out the "Let's get grounded!" sidebar in this chapter.

4. **Remove the battery.**

   Slide both of the release latches up to pop out the battery (as shown in Figure 20-1), and then lift it out.

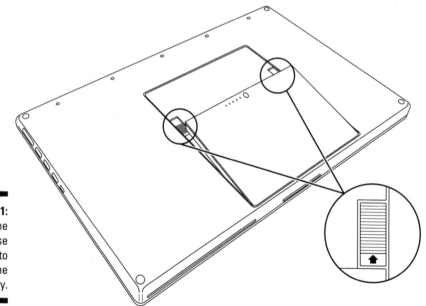

Figure 20-1:
Slide the release latches to access the battery.

5. **Remove the two screws holding the memory door closed.**

   Place the two screws in a handy plastic bowl for safekeeping. Tah-dah! That wasn't much of a challenge, was it? Here's your chance to gaze with rapt fascination at a portion of the bare innards of your favorite computer.

6. **Locate the memory modules in your Mac's svelte chassis.**

   Figure 20-2 illustrates their position.

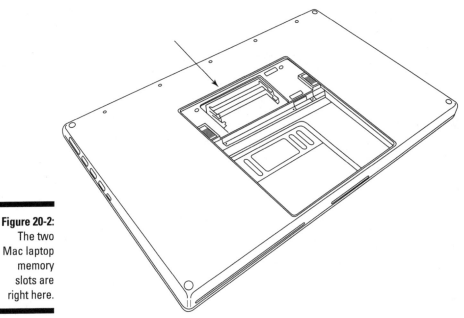

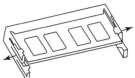

Figure 20-2:
The two
Mac laptop
memory
slots are
right here.

7. **If you're replacing an existing memory module, remove it.**

   To remove a memory module, gently spread the two tabs at the ends of the socket apart (as shown in Figure 20-3) and then lift and slide the module away from the socket.

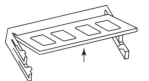

Figure 20-3:
Remove
a memory
module
like a pro.

Save the old module in the static-free packaging that held the new module. Your old RAM (which you can now sell on eBay) will be protected from static electricity.

8. Position the new module in the socket.

a. *Line up the module's gold connectors toward the socket, at a 25 degree angle.*

b. *Line up the notch in the module with the matching spacer in the socket.*

See what I mean in Figure 20-4.

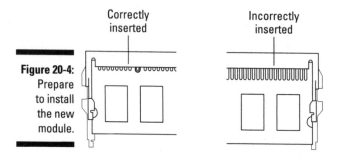

Correctly inserted   Incorrectly inserted

Figure 20-4: Prepare to install the new module.

9. Press gently (but firmly) on both ends of the module until the module's tabs click into place on both ends of the socket.

Figure 20-5 shows the direction you should press on the module.

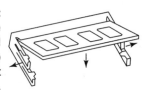

Figure 20-5: Press the new RAM module into place until it locks.

10. Replace the memory door and battery.

To replace the memory door and battery, just reverse the steps at the beginning of this list. (Rather like changing the oil on my Dad's 1970 Ford pickup truck.)

Congratulations! You've done it — you're now a MacBook memory guru! To verify that all is well with your road warrior, boot the computer, click the Apple menu, and choose About This Mac. Your laptop should report the additional memory.

Let's get grounded!

Follow one cardinal rule when the unguarded insides of any computer are in easy reach: *Always ground yourself before you touch anything!* Your body can carry enough static electricity to damage the circuitry and chips that make up the brains of your MacBook, and touching those parts without grounding yourself is an invitation for disaster.

Grounding yourself is easy to do: Just touch a metal surface for a few seconds before you dig in. After you ground yourself, you can then safely handle both the internal components of your laptop and any new hardware components that you might be installing (such as memory modules or a hard drive).

If you walk anywhere in the room — hunting for a screwdriver, perhaps, or taking a sip of liquid reinforcement that you've stashed a comfortable distance away — you *must* ground yourself again before you get back to work. *Remember:* You can pick up a static charge by simply walking. Go figure.

Considering a Hard Drive Upgrade?

Asking whether you can upgrade your hard drive is a trick question. Yes, you certainly can upgrade your hard drive. (**Note:** The 64GB solid-state drive available with the MacBook Air is not upgradeable.) But before you start cruisin' the Internet for a 500GB monster, though, I have two suggestions:

- ✔ Don't upgrade your internal hard drive yourself.
- ✔ Be sure you *really need* a hard drive upgrade.

And, all in all, Apple's pretty generous when configuring hard drive storage for its base systems — current models run with anywhere from an 80 to 300GB drive.

Most folks simply don't need more than 80GB of hard drive space (even with Windows loaded in a separate partition for use with Boot Camp, which I discuss in Chapter 2). You're likely to find that you still have plenty of elbow-room for a typical family's needs on your hard drive unless you're heavily into

- ✔ Digital video (DV)
- ✔ Cutting-edge video games
- ✔ Tons of digital audio

TIP

If you're short on hard drive space, clean up your existing hard drive by deleting all the crud you don't need, such as game and application demos, duplicate or "work" copies of images and documents, archived files you downloaded from the Internet, and the contents of your Trash. You can read how in Chapter 21.

If you decide that you *do* need to upgrade your MacBook's internal drive, I strongly recommend that you don't install your new hard drive yourself. Call on the services of an Apple technician to upgrade your drive!

Consider your external options

If you *do* need additional hard drive space, I recommend using an external drive! Use a high-speed FireWire or USB port to connect a second hard drive the quick and easy way. (MacBook Air owners can skip the stuff about FireWire because the Air doesn't have a FireWire port.)

Most of today's FireWire and USB peripherals don't even require the driver software that Mac old-timers remember with such hatred. You simply plug in a FireWire or USB device, and it works. You can move your external drive between different Macs with a minimum of fuss and bother.

An external hard drive can do anything that your internal hard drive can do. You can boot from it, for example, or install a different version of Mac OS X (great for beta testers like me). External optical drives work just the same as internal models; Apple sells an external USB SuperDrive optical drive for the MacBook Air for about $100.

Apple's Time Capsule unit is an external hard drive with a difference: It stores the huge Time Machine backup files created by the Macs running Leopard on your network, and it uses a wireless connection to transfer data! (In fact, if you're thinking of adding a wireless base station to your wired network, your Time Capsule actually acts as a full AirPort Extreme Base Station, complete with USB port for connecting a USB printer.) At the time of this writing, Time Capsule is available with either a 500GB ($299) or 1TB ($499) drive.

Here's one problem with external drives: Data transfers more slowly this way than via an internal drive (even with a FireWire 800 connection). That's why most Mac owners use their external drives for storing little-used documents and applications. Their favorite applications and often-used documents are housed on the internal drive.

Putting a port to work

A MacBook can carry up to three kinds of high-speed ports, any of which is a good match for connecting any external device.

USB 2.0

The USB standard is popular because it's just as common in the PC world as in the Mac world. (Most PCs don't have a FireWire port.) Your laptop carries at least one USB 2.0 port on the side of the case. Hardware manufacturers can make one USB device that works on both types of computers.

The MacBook Pro's Mystery Slot

If you're wondering what that slot is for on the left side of your MacBook Pro, you'll be pleased to hear that it's called an ExpressCard/34 slot. Why the glee? Well, some of the premium external devices for your laptop will use the ExpressCard/34 slot, which is like a drive-through window that allows the fastest possible data transfer rates to and from your computer. For example, the fastest external eSATA hard drives available these days can be connected to your MacBook Pro via an ExpressCard/34 adapter!

Although ExpressCard/34 hardware is generally more expensive than FireWire or USB hardware, the higher price may be justified by the speed increase — before you invest in an external device, do a little research and see whether the Mystery Slot can speed things up.

I heartily recommend that you avoid using any USB 1.1 devices (except, perhaps, a USB 1.1 keyboard or mouse). USB 1.1 is very slow compared with the USB 2.0 standard although you can connect a USB 1.1 device to a USB 2.0 port with no problem at all. You should buy only USB 2.0 external hard drives, CD/DVD recorders, or Flash drives. 'Nuff said.

FireWire 400

The original FireWire (also called *IEEE 1394*) is the best port for most digital video camcorders. Use your FireWire port for connecting external devices to your MacBook or MacBook Pro.

MacBook Air laptops don't have a FireWire port.

FireWire 800

A FireWire 800 drive offers much better performance than either a FireWire 400 or a USB 2.0 drive, and today's FireWire 800 drives are getting cheaper every day. MacBook Pro laptops proudly sport a FireWire 800 port on the side; MacBook and MacBook Air computers don't carry a FireWire 800 port.

The physical FireWire 800 connector is shaped differently than the FireWire 400 port, so don't try to force the wrong connector into the wrong port!

Connecting an external drive

With FireWire or USB, you can install an external hard drive without opening your laptop's case. With your MacBook turned on and the external drive disconnected from the AC outlet, follow these steps:

1. **Connect the FireWire or USB cable betwixt the drive and your computer.**

2. **Plug the external drive into a convenient surge protector or UPS (uninterruptible power supply).**

3. **Switch on the external drive.**

4. **If the drive is unformatted (or formatted for use under Windows), partition and format the external drive.**

   The drive comes with instructions or software for you to do this. (Don't worry, your external drive comes from the factory completely empty, and you won't damage anything by formatting it.) Partitioning divides the new drive into one (or more) volumes, each of which is displayed as a separate hard drive under Leopard.

   If the drive comes preformatted for use with a Windows PC, I strongly suggest reformatting it for use with Mac OS X — this will result in faster performance and more efficient use of space.

After the drive is formatted and partitioned, it immediately appears on the Desktop. Shazam!

Gotta have internal

If you decide that you have to upgrade your existing internal hard drive — or if your internal drive fails and needs to be replaced — you should always take your MacBook to an authorized Apple service center and allow the techs there to sell you a drive and make the swap. Here are four darned good reasons why:

- ✔ **Warranty:** You're very likely to void your laptop's warranty by attempting a drive upgrade yourself.

- ✔ **Selection:** If you're worried about choosing the proper drive, your friendly neighborhood Apple technician can order the right type and size of drive for you.

- ✔ **Difficulty:** Swapping a hard drive in your Mac laptop isn't anywhere as easy as adding RAM modules (although the hard drive is much easier to reach on the MacBook than it is on the MacBook Pro).

- ✔ **Backup:** That very same Apple service technician can back up all the data on your existing drive, format the new drive, and move all your data to its new mansion, so you won't lose a single document. That will save you time and possible angst.

To those who *truly* won't be satisfied with their lives until they upgrade an internal drive in a MacBook: Yes, I'm sure you can find a magazine article that purports to show you how. Even better, I've seen many how-to articles on the Web that will lead you down a rosy path to a hard drive upgrade. Here's my take on those savvy instructions: You're walking into a field of land mines with someone else's map, so you had better have *complete* faith in your tech skills. (And a darn good backup.)

A List of Dreamy Laptop Add-Ons

The USB and FireWire toys I cover in this section might add a cord or two to your collection at the side of your road warrior, but they're well worth the investment. And they can really revolutionize how you look at technologies, such as television, digital audio, and computer gaming.

Game controllers

If you're ready to take a shot at the enemy — whether they be Nazi soldiers, chittering aliens, or the latest jet fighters — you'll likely find your keyboard and mouse somewhat lacking. (And if that enemy happens to be a friend of yours playing across the Internet, you'll be ruthlessly mocked while you're fumbling for the right key combination.) Instead, either pick up a USB joystick (for flying games) or a gamepad (for arcade and first-person shooting games)!

Video controllers

For armchair directors, specialized USB digital video controllers make editing easier. The ShuttleXpress from Contour Design (www.contourdesign.com) provides a five-button jog control that can be configured to match any DV editor. For $60, you get the same type of editing controller as dedicated video-editing stations costing several thousand dollars.

Audio hardware

Ready to put GarageBand to the test with your favorite version of *Chopsticks?* You'll need a USB piano keyboard, and I recommend the KeyRig 49 from M-Audio (www.m-audio.com), which retails for a mere $130. It provides 49 keys and uses a USB connection.

Another neat audio favorite of mine is the USB-powered radio SHARK 2 from Griffin Technology (www.griffintechnology.com), which allows you to add AM/FM radio to your laptop, complete with recording capability, a pause feature, and scheduled recording, all for $50.

Chapter 21

Tackling the Housekeeping

In This Chapter

▶ Cleaning unnecessary stuff off your hard drive

▶ Backing up your data with Time Machine

▶ Fixing permission errors

▶ Automating tasks in Leopard

▶ Updating Mac OS X automatically

*N*othing runs better than a well-oiled machine, and your laptop is no exception. With a little Leopard maintenance, you can ensure that your MacBook is performing as efficiently as possible (which translates into longer battery life).

In this chapter, I demonstrate how you can make good use of every byte of storage space provided by your hard drive, as well as how to back up and restore that hard drive to an external drive, using Time Machine. Your hard drive also benefits from a periodic scan for permission errors.

Leopard's Automator application is a great housekeeping tool: It allows your laptop to perform tasks automatically that used to require your attention. I show you how you can create Automator applications and set them up to run by themselves. (It sounds a little spooky, but you'll have a ball!)

And it's important to never forget about updating Mac OS X itself. But then again, if you configure Software Update to run automatically, you can live life free and easy, watching your favorite soaps and eating ice cream (or yogurt — your pick).

Cleaning Unseemly Data Deposits

Criminy! Where does all this stuff *come* from? Suddenly that spacious 250GB hard drive has 19GB left, and you start feeling pinched.

Before you consider buying a new internal or external hard drive (which you can read about in Chapter 20), take the smart step: "Sweep" your hard drive clean of unnecessary and space-hogging software.

Getting dirty (Or, cleaning things the manual way)

If you're willing to dig into your data a little, there's no reason to buy additional software to help you clean up your hard drive. All you really need is the willpower to announce, "I simply don't need this application any longer." (And, sometimes, that's tougher than it might seem.)

Unnecessary files and unneeded folders

Consider all the stuff that you probably don't really need:

- Game demos and shareware that you no longer play (or even remember)
- Movie trailers and other QuickTime video files that have long since passed into obscurity
- Temporary files that you created and promptly forgot
- Log files that chronicle application installations and errors
- StuffIt archives that you downloaded and no longer covet
- iTunes music that no longer appeals to your ear

How hard is it to clean this stuff off your drive? Easier than you might think!

- You can easily delete files.
- You can get rid of at least the lion's share of any application (often the whole application) by deleting its application folder that was created during the installation process.

Removing an application or file from your hard drive is usually two simple steps:

1. **Display the file or application folder in a Finder window.**

2. **Delete the file or folder with one of these steps:**

    - Drag the icon to the Trash.
    - Press ⌘+Delete.
    - Right-click the icon and choose Move to Trash.
    - Select the icon and click the Delete button on the Finder toolbar (if you added one).

Truly, no big whoop.

Don't forget to actually *empty* the Trash, or you'll wonder why you aren't regaining any hard drive space. (Leopard works hard to store the contents of the Trash until you manually delete it, just in case you want to undelete something.) To get rid of that stuff permanently and reclaim the space

1. **Click the Trash icon on the Dock and hold down the mouse button — or right-click — until the pop-up menu appears.**

2. **Choose Empty Trash.**

Associated files in other folders

Some applications install files in different locations across your hard drive. (Applications in this category include Microsoft Office and Photoshop.) How can you clear out these "orphan" files after you delete the application folder?

The process is a little more involved than deleting a single folder, but it's still no big whoop. Here's the procedure:

1. **Click the Search text box in a Finder window.**

   You can read more about Search and Finder windows in Chapter 7.

2. **Type the name of the application in the Search text box.**

   Figure 21-1 shows this search. I want to remove Toast Titanium, so I search for every file with the word *toast* in its name.

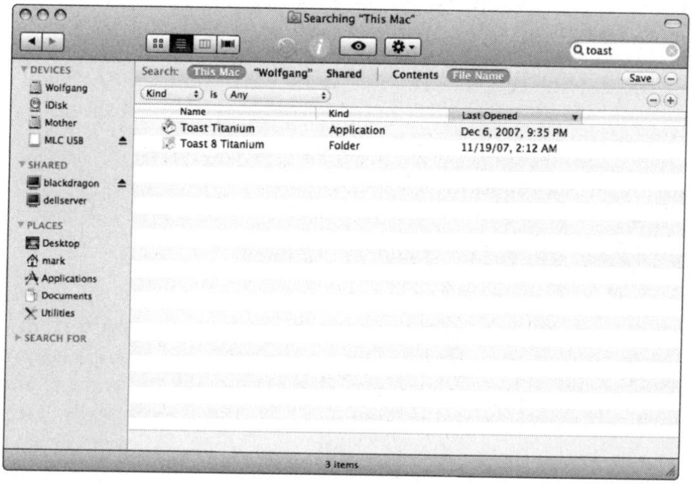

Figure 21-1: Mine your hard drive for additional files to delete.

3. **Decide which of these files belong to the to-be-deleted application.**

Be sure that the files you choose to delete are part of the deleted application. For example, a text file with the name *Instructions on Making a Perfect Piece of Toast* might not be part of Toast Titanium.

Many associated files either

- Have the same icon as the parent application
- Are in the Preferences, Caches, or Application Support folders

4. **In the Search Results window, click the associated file(s) that you want to delete and just drag them to the Trash.**

Don't empty the Trash immediately after you delete these files. Wait a few hours or a day. That way, if you realize that you deleted a file that you truly need, you can easily restore it from the Trash.

Using a commercial cleanup tool

If you'd rather use a commercial application to help you clean up your hard drive, a number of them are available, but most are shareware and perform only one task. For example, Tidy Up! from Hyperbolic Software (www.hyperbolicsoftware.com) finds only duplicate files on your hard drive, matching by criteria such as filename, size, and extension. It's a good tool at $30.

For a truly comprehensive cleanup utility, I recommend Spring Cleaning, from Smith Micro Software (my.smithmicro.com), the same company that produces the archiving utility StuffIt. Spring Cleaning is a bargain at $50, because not much crud squeaks by the application's search routines, including duplicates, orphan preference files, and log files. Spring Cleaning even includes a separate feature called MacUninstaller that can help automate the steps that I cover in the preceding section.

Backing Up Your Treasure

Do it. I'm not going to lecture you about backing up your hard drive . . . well, perhaps just for a moment. Imagine what it feels like to lose *everything* — names, numbers, letters, reports, presentations, saved games, photographs, and music. Then ask yourself, "Self, isn't all that irreplaceable stuff worth just a couple of hours every month?" Time for a Mark's Maxim:

Back up. On a regular basis. Then store those DVDs or that external backup device somewhere safe, away from calamities.™

You can back up your files either by saving them to external media or by using Leopard's awesome new Time Machine feature.

Saving files

The simplest method of backing up files is simply to copy the files and folders to an external hard drive or a CD or DVD. Nothing fancy, but it works.

Backing up to an external hard drive

If you use an external hard drive with your MacBook, you can easily drag backup files to it from your internal hard drive:

1. **Open separate Finder windows for**

   - The external hard drive

   - The internal hard drive

2. **Select the desired files that you want to back up from your internal drive.**

3. **Drag the selected files to the external drive window.**

Chapter 20 covers external hard drives.

Backing up to CD and DVD

You can burn backup files to a recordable CD or DVD. Owners of the MacBook Air will need to use an external SuperDrive, however.

Burning backups from the Finder

To use the Finder's Burn feature with a CD or DVD, follow these steps:

1. **Load a blank disc into your MacBook's optical drive.**

   If you're using the default settings in the CDs & DVDs pane in System Preferences, a dialog asks you for a disc name.

2. **Into the disc's Finder window, drag the files and folders that you want to back up.**

   They can be organized any way you like. Don't forget that the total amount of data shouldn't exceed 700MB on a CD. You should also stick within 4GB or so (on a standard recordable DVD) or 8GB (on a dual-layer recordable DVD). You can see how much free space remains on the disc at the bottom of the disc's Finder window.

3. **Click File and then choose Burn Disc from the menu.**

   You can also click the Burn button on the Recordable DVD bar — it appears at the top of the disc's Finder window.

4. **Choose the fastest recording speed possible.**

5. **Click Burn.**

Burning backups from other recording applications

If you've invested in Toast Titanium from Roxio (www.roxio.com) or another CD/DVD recording application, you can create a new disc layout to burn your backup disc. (Think of a layout as a "road map" indicating which files and folders Toast should store on the backup.)

Putting things right with Time Machine

If you enable backups via Leopard's new Time Machine feature, you can literally move backward through the contents of your MacBook's hard drive, selecting and restoring all sorts of data. Files and folders are ridiculously easy to restore — and I mean easier than *any* restore you've ever performed, no matter what the operating system or backup program. Time Machine can even handle such deleted items as Address Book entries or photos you sent to the Trash from iPhoto!

Because Time Machine should be an important and integral part of every Mac owner's existence, the Time Machine icon is included on the Dock. (Apple is not messing around!)

Apple's Time Capsule device is designed as a wireless storage drive for your Time Machine backup files. If you're interested in a single Time Machine backup location for multiple Macs across your wireless network, Time Capsule is a great addition to your home or office.

Before you can use Time Machine, it must be enabled within the Time Machine pane in System Preferences. I cover the Time Machine configuration settings (and how to turn the feature on) in more detail in Chapter 6.

Here's how you can turn back time, step by step, to restore a file that you deleted or replaced in a folder.

1. **Open the folder that contained the file you want to restore.**

2. **In a separate window, open your Applications folder and launch the Time Machine application, or click the Time Machine icon on the Dock (which bears a rather funky clock with a counterclockwise arrow).**

The oh-so-ultra-cool Time Machine background appears behind your folder, complete with its own set of buttons at the bottom of the screen (as shown in Figure 21-2). On the right, you see a timeline that corresponds to the different days and months included in the backups that Leopard has made.

3. **Click within the timeline to jump directly to a date (displaying the folder's contents on that date).**

   Alternatively, use the Forward and Back arrows at the right to move through the folder's contents through time. (You should see the faces of Windows users when you "riffle" through your folders to locate something you deleted several weeks ago!)

   The backup date of the items you're viewing appears in the button bar at the bottom of the screen.

4. **After you locate the file you want to restore, click it to select it.**

5. **Click the Restore button at the right side of the Time Machine button bar.**

   If you want to restore all the contents of the folder, click the Restore All button instead.

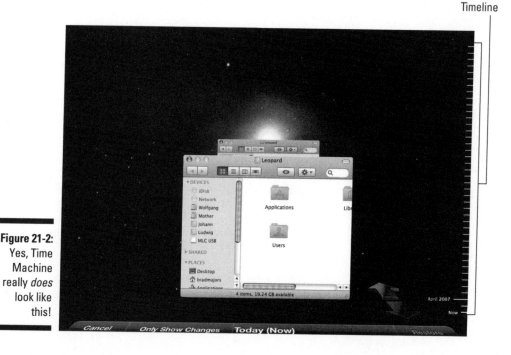

Timeline

Figure 21-2:
Yes, Time Machine really *does* look like this!

Time Machine returns you to the Finder, with the newly restored file now appearing in the folder. Out-*standing!*

For simple backup and restore protection, Time Machine has everything that a typical Mac owner at home is likely to ever need. Therefore, a very easy Mark's Maxim to predict:

Turn on Time Machine. *Do it now.* Don't make a humongous mistake.™

Maintaining Hard Drive Health

Shifty-eyed, sneaky, irritating little problems can bother your hard drive: *permissions errors.* Incorrect disk and file permissions can

- Make your MacBook lock up
- Make applications act screwy (or refuse to run at all)
- Cause weird behavior within a Finder window or System Preferences

To keep Leopard running at its best, I recommend that you fix permissions errors at least once per week.

To fix any permissions errors on your system, follow these steps:

1. **Open a Finder window, click Applications, and then click Utilities.**

2. **Double-click the Disk Utility icon.**

3. **Click the volume at the left (which in this case is a named partition, like Macintosh HD, which appears under your physical hard drive) that you want to check.**

4. **Click the Repair Disk Permissions button.**

   Disk Utility does the rest and then displays a message about whatever it has to fix. (When will someone invent a *car* with a Repair Me button?)

Automating Those Mundane Chores

One popular feature in Leopard — Automator — has generated a lot of excitement. You use Automator (as shown in Figure 21-3) to create applications with a compiled form of AppleScript. (In case you're not familiar with *AppleScript,* it's the simple programming language that you can use to automate tasks and applications within Leopard.)

Library list

Run button

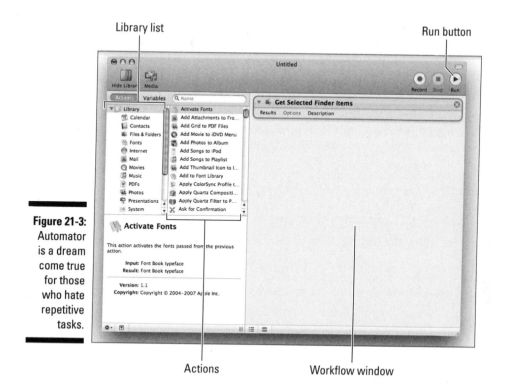

Figure 21-3:
Automator
is a dream
come true
for those
who hate
repetitive
tasks.

Actions

Workflow window

Of course, that might sound daunting — akin to building your own nuclear submarine single-handedly over a long weekend — but Automator is actually easy to use. Heck, you might find it downright *fun!*

You can also create *workflows,* which are sequential (and repeatable) operations that are performed on the same files or data, and then your Automator application can automatically launch whatever applications are necessary to get the job done.

Here's a great example: You work with a service bureau that sends you a CD every week with new product shots for your company's marketing department. Unfortunately, these images are flat-out *huge* — taken with a 12-megapixel camera — and they're always in the wrong orientation. Before you move them to the Marketing folder on your server, you have to laboriously resize each image and rotate it, and then save the smaller version.

With help from Automator, though, you can build a custom application that automatically reads each image in the folder, resizes it, rotates it, and even generates a thumbnail image or prints the image, and then moves the massaged images to the proper folder. You'd normally have to manually launch Preview to perform the image operations and then use a Finder window to move the new files to the right location. But now, with Automator, a single double-click of your custom application icon does the trick.

You'll find Automator in your Applications folder. Currently, Automator can handle specific tasks within about 30 or 40 applications (including the Finder), but both Apple and third-party developers are busy adding new Automator task support to all sorts of new and existing applications.

To create a simple application with Automator, launch the application and follow these steps:

1. **Select Custom and click Choose.**

2. **Click the desired item in the Library list.**

   Automator displays the actions available for the item you've selected. Some of these items are media files, while others include Address Book contacts, files and folders in the Finder, PDF documents, and even Apple Mail messages.

3. **Drag the desired action from the Library window to the workflow window.**

4. **Modify any specific settings provided for the action you chose.**

5. **Repeat Steps 1–3 to complete the workflow.**

6. **Click Run (upper right) to test your script.**

   Use sample files while you're fine-tuning your application lest you accidentally do something deleterious to an original (and irreplaceable) file!

7. **When the application is working as you like, press ⌘+Shift+S to save it.**

8. **In the Save dialog that appears, type a name for your new application.**

9. **Click the Where pop-up menu and specify a location where the file should be saved.**

10. **Click the File Format pop-up menu and choose Application.**

11. **Click Save.**

    Your new Automator application icon includes the Automator robot standing on a document. Why, most normal human beings would now call you a *programmer,* so make sure you're inscrutable from now on! If you're going to use your new Automator application often, don't forget that you can make it more convenient to use by dragging the application icon to your Dock or to your Desktop.

To find all the actions of a certain type within the Library list, click in the Search box at the bottom of the Library window and type in a keyword, such as **save** or **burn**. You don't even need to press Return!

If your Automator application should run every time you log in — for example, an application to track your time on a project — follow these steps to set it up as a Login Item:

1. **Open System Preferences.**

2. **Display the Accounts pane.**

3. **Click the Login Items button.**

4. **Click the plus button at the bottom of the list.**

5. **Navigate to the location of your new Automator application.**

6. **Click Add.**

   Now your Automator application is *really* automatic. Watch your significant other gape in amazement as your MacBook begins to work without you touching the keyboard! (If you've added the application icon to your Dock, you can also simply right-click on the icon and choose Open at Login from the right-click menu that appears. Either way, your MacBook gets the message.)

Updating Mac OS X Automatically

I prefer my MacBook to take care of cleaning up after itself, so updating Leopard should be automatic as well. In Mac OS X Leopard, operating system updates are performed by the Software Update application.

Software Update uses the Internet, so you need an Internet connection to shake hands with the Apple server and download any updates.

Software Update can be found in two convenient spots:

- ✔ **The Apple menu:** Click the Apple menu (🍎) and then choose Software Update, which displays the Update dialog and alerts you to anything new that's available.

- ✔ **System Preferences:** Click the Software Update icon to display the Software Update pane.

If you take the System Preferences route, you can set Software Update to check for updates automatically:

    a. Mark the Check for Updates check box to enable it.

    b. Choose the time period from the Check for Updates pop-up menu.

Software Update covers every Apple application, so I usually check once daily just to make sure that I don't miss anything.

If something needs to be updated, the program alerts you, either automatically downloading the update(s) or displaying a dialog letting you know what you can update (depending on the settings you choose in the System Preferences Software Update pane).

You can even check for updates immediately from System Preferences. That, dear reader, is just plain thoughtful design.

Part VII

The Part of Tens

In this part . . .

Ah, what book in the *For Dummies* series is truly complete without its Part of Tens? Here you find lots of this author's raw opinions: my best tips for Mac laptop Road Warriors as well as my infamous "Top Ten Things to Avoid Like the Plague."

Chapter 22

Top Ten Laptop Rules to Follow

In This Chapter

▶ Protect your laptop while you're in transit

▶ Pack that MacBook with RAM

▶ Track your Mac with a hidden beacon

▶ Encrypt your MacBook Home folder

▶ Engrave or tag your laptop

▶ Save energy by disabling wireless hardware

▶ Use a surge protector

▶ Control your power setting

▶ Use external input devices with your laptop

▶ Back up your laptop

*A*h, the sedentary life of a desktop Mac — it sits there, like a bump on a log, comfortable and immobile. As long as you have a stable surface and an uninterrupted power supply, your Mac Pro is a happy puppy.

But you, good reader, are *mobile!* Whether you're on campus or attending a convention, your Mac laptop is rarely running in the same spot, so it's susceptible to all sorts of road warrior pitfalls. In this chapter, I remind you of ten of the most important rules that every laptop owner should follow to prevent chaos and carnage while traveling.

Keep Your Laptop in a Bag

Sure, using a laptop case or bag *sounds* like common sense — but Mac laptops are so doggone sexy that you'd be surprised how many people carry them around without any protection at all. These Mac owners hear phrases like "rugged titanium" and "Sudden Motion Sensor hard drive protection" and figure that their laptop can tackle a construction site, a college campus, or a hotel room with impunity.

Part of that is indeed true. Mac laptops are some of the toughest laptops ever made, but they're not immune to bumps, scratches, and the (I hope) rare fall. But if you carry your MacBook from place to place without any protection, it'll soon look like a boxer after a bad fight.

If you're like me, you're proud that your computers remain in pristine condition, so use a laptop bag or case that offers ample padding and a convenient shoulder strap or carry handle. (My laptop bag even converts to a backpack, and it includes plenty of extra space for power supplies, discs, and all the assorted hoo-hah that you know you need to carry with you.) Spend an extra $30 on a laptop bag, and your $1,000 computer can weather the worst the world will dish out.

Many folks think that a traditional laptop bag draws too much attention — and to some extent, I agree. (That's one reason why no one totes an obvious 15 x 7 bag with a hardware manufacturer's logo emblazoned on the side these days.) If you're a member of this group, consider a *well-padded* laptop sleeve that will allow you to carry your MacBook in your backpack or briefcase — the laptop always goes in on top of those heavy books, of course. Remember, though, that the padding is the important thing — without that extra cushion, you might as well just toss your unprotected laptop in with the rest of your books and must-have equipment.

Maximize Your RAM

Like any other computer running Windows or Mac OS X, your laptop will benefit from all the system RAM (memory) that you can squeeze onto it. (Chapter 20 describes how to add memory and the benefits of extra RAM.) However, additional memory is even *more* effective with a laptop because your Mac laptop's internal hard drive runs more slowly than the corresponding internal hard drive in a full-size desktop Mac. Therefore, the virtual memory functionality built into Leopard (which I also describe in Chapter 20) will be even slower for your laptop, resulting in mediocre performance during memory-intensive tasks such as video and image editing.

With a full complement of RAM, your laptop's performance will rival the performance of a desktop computer with the same processor — and you'll be using it on the go!

As I also mention in Chapter 20, MacBook Air owners need not worry about upgrading their system RAM: The current Air models come from Apple already packed with the maximum amount of RAM they can carry (2GB), and you can't upgrade (or even reach) the memory modules in your Air.

Install a Tracker Application

The unthinkable happens: Your laptop is stolen while you're on vacation or on a business trip, and you know that the chances that it will be returned are next to nil. You've resigned yourself to replacing it (and all your data). But wait! What if I told you that you might just receive an e-mail message on your desktop computer that tells you the Internet (IP) address of the thief or perhaps even the telephone number he or she is using?

If this scenario sounds a little like a James Bond movie, you'll be surprised to discover that several *tracker applications* are available for Leopard that will run invisibly on your laptop. A tracker application can turn your MacBook into a transmitting beacon, broadcasting its current location and all the Internet information it can get to you — allowing you to alert police and apprehend the crook (who might be in the middle of creating an iPhoto library).

For example, XTool Laptop Tracker from XTool Mobile Security (www.xtool. com) invisibly sends a signal to the company's security center each time your laptop is connected to the Internet or a telephone line, as well as when the computer is rebooted or a user logs on. XTool Laptop Tracker costs about $70 per year, which is pocket change for a corporate Road Warrior or design professional who depends on both the laptop and the irreplaceable data it contains.

Keepest Thy Home Folder Encrypted

In Chapter 6, I discuss a number of System Preferences panes. The Security pane is particularly important to laptop users because it allows you to encrypt your Leopard Home folder. Encryption prevents just about anyone from accessing (or even *identifying*) any of the files you've stored in your Home folder. The robust encryption provided by Leopard will certainly stymie just about anyone but the NSA and FBI. (I won't even go there.)

In System Preferences, click Security, click the FileVault button, and then click Set Master Password to create a backup password that will unlock your Home folder, just in case. (Your login account password is your primary password.) Select Turn On FileVault, and Leopard takes care of automatically encrypting and unencrypting files as necessary.

To take full advantage of an encrypted Home folder, you need the proper login mode (as I discuss in Chapter 16). Think about this possible security back-door: From the Accounts pane, you've set your laptop to automatically log you in every time you boot your MacBook. This is the very definition of Not Secure because your login account password automatically bypasses the FileVault encryption! Therefore, make sure that you actually have to log in to access your account; for the full scoop, see Chapter 16.

Brand Your MacBook

Put your brand on your laptop! Whether with an engraving tool on the bottom of the machine (my personal favorite) or a permanent metal tag, your MacBook deserves some sort of identifying information. After all, most of the people in the world are honest, and you might not need that tracking software that I mention earlier in this chapter. You might have left your laptop by accident, and someone would like to return it to you. (Don't forget to offer a reward!)

Some laptop owners will want to include their name and address and other contact information, while other Road Warriors might feel more comfortable with just their name and e-mail address. Whatever you choose, branding your laptop is as important as backing it up.

Disable Your Wireless

Funny how we don't think about it, but wireless communications take juice, and that power comes straight from your laptop's battery! Because your Mac laptop comes with a built-in AirPort Express card and built-in Bluetooth hardware, you're constantly broadcasting — sending and receiving, or at least *trying* to exchange data with others.

And therein lies the rub: If you're not *connected* to a wireless network or a Bluetooth device, you're wasting your precious battery power. That's why Leopard gives you the ability to turn off your wireless Ethernet and Bluetooth hardware to save energy. And when you're sitting in a crowded auditorium without access to an AC socket or a wireless network, the energy savings you reap when you disable your wireless hardware can be significant.

In fact, you might **have** to disable your wireless connectivity in situations where cellphones are not allowed, such as on an airplane flight, or in certain areas of a hospital. And, because I'm a security-conscious kind of guy, I always disable my wireless hardware whenever I'm not using it (even if I am in range of a wireless network). Call me overly careful, but none of my shared files have ever been sucked out of my MacBook without my permission!

To turn off your wireless Ethernet from the Leopard Finder menu, click the AirPort status icon and choose Turn Airport Off from the menu. To turn off your Bluetooth hardware from the Finder menu, click the Bluetooth icon and choose Turn Bluetooth Off.

Bring a Surge Protector with You

I'll be honest: I usually am not a huge supporter of surge protectors because I think they do only half the job. That job is protecting both your hardware *and* your data . . . and, as you probably know, a surge protector doesn't provide backup power in case of a brownout or total loss of power like a UPS (uninterruptible power supply) can.

Of course, many locales around the world offer a less-than-perfect power grid, which translates into a sudden loss of power — usually at exactly the wrong moment. (Think Great American Novel Takes a Nosedive.) Your MacBook is smart enough to immediately switch from AC current to its battery in case of a power failure. So why am I suggesting a surge protector for your laptop, especially seeing as how it adds bulk and weight to your laptop bag or luggage?

- ✔ **The risk of a power spike:** A surge protector is good protection from a massive power spike, such as an overload or a lightning strike.

- ✔ **Extra sockets on tap:** Don't forget that you might need several more AC sockets for external devices, such as a hard drive, projector, and portable printer. A surge protector can provide the extra power, even when your host can't.

Naturally, if you're traveling to a country with different AC standards (and different socket configurations), invest in an AC plug adapter that's compatible with the standard used at your destination.

Use Leopard Power-Saving Features

Apple allows you considerable control over how fast your CPU will run, which is a real boon to power hungry laptop owners. In System Preferences, click Energy Saver to display the Settings For and Optimization list boxes.

If you're running your laptop while connected to an AC outlet, click the Settings For drop-down list box and click Power Adapter; then click the Optimization list box and choose the Better Performance setting. This setting provides the best performance your laptop's processor can provide — all your applications will run their fastest — but it also uses the most electricity.

If your laptop is running on battery power and you need to conserve as much power as possible, click the Settings For drop-down list box and click Battery; then choose Better Battery Life from the Optimization list box. Now you're squeezing the maximum amount of computing time out of your remaining battery power. (Your laptop will also run much cooler.)

Use an External Keyboard and Mouse

Does your laptop remain at your home, dorm room, or office for long periods of time? If so, I recommend that you invest in an external keyboard and an external mouse for two very good reasons:

- ✔ Adding external input devices helps lower the wear and tear on your laptop's keyboard and trackpad.
- ✔ External input devices are generally more comfortable and convenient to use than those offered by your Mac laptop, especially for gaming.

If price is no obstacle, a wireless keyboard and mouse will allow you far more freedom of movement, but a standard USB keyboard and mouse will do just as fine a job and will cost considerably less.

In fact, you can have two external keyboards if you like: one to work with your laptop while you're running Leopard (which will have all the keys unique to an Apple keyboard) and one to use when you're running Windows (with those gnarly Windows-specific keys). *Techno-suave.*

Not Again! What Is It with You and Backing Up?

Yes, it's one of the Top Ten Laptop Rules as well. I'm not kidding: If you think you don't need to back up on a regular basis, **you will eventually lose every byte of data you have.** Period. It's only a matter of time. Even if you have incredible luck and don't do something you regret with a Finder window, your MacBook is just a machine, and it will wear out in the long run. (Especially with the mobile life of a Road Warrior, with all the bumps and bruises of travel.) That's why hard drive manufacturers list MTBF — Mean Time Between *Failures* — figures for their hard drives.

Backing up your hard drive isn't difficult and doesn't take long. Chapter 21 explains everything you need to know. And after you finish your first full backup, drop me a line at `mark@mlcbooks.com` with the subject `I've Got Laptop Peace of Mind!` We can celebrate together.

Chapter 23

Ten Things to Avoid Like the Plague

In This Chapter

▶ Dodging USB 1.1 storage devices

▶ Shunning e-mail and Web phishing expeditions

▶ Skirting those strange-sized discs

▶ Keeping liquids at arm's length

▶ Banishing outdated disk utilities

▶ Eschewing pirated software

▶ Steering clear of the root/System Administrator account

▶ Sidestepping unsecured public wireless networks

▶ Spurning refurbished hardware

▶ Expelling dust and dirt

*I*f you've read other books that I've written in the *For Dummies* series, you might recognize the title of this chapter — it's a favorite Part of Tens subject of mine. I don't like to see any computer owner fall prey to pitfalls. Some are minor (such as not keeping your laptop clean), and others are downright catastrophic (such as providing valuable information over the Internet to persons unknown).

All these potential mistakes, however, share one thing in common: They're *easy to prevent* with a little common sense — that is, as long as you're aware of them. And that's my job. In this chapter, I fill in what you need to know. Consider these pages as experience gained easily!

USB 1.1 Storage Devices

Man, that is the very *definition* of sluggish. Let's see, what could I be talking about? Oh, yes . . . only a creaking USB 1.1 external device such as a hard drive or CD-ROM drive could be as slow as a turtle on narcotics.

Unfortunately, you still find countless examples of USB 1.1 storage hardware hanging around. eBay is stuffed to the gills with USB 1.1 hard drives, and your family and friends will certainly want to bestow that old 4x CD-RW drive to you as a gift. (This is one that you should politely refuse immediately, just like your Aunt Harriet's fruitcake.) These drives were considered cool in the early days of the colorful iMac G3, when USB was a new technology. Today, a USB 1.1 hard drive is simply a slow-as-maple-syrup-in-January *embarrassment*.

I do admit that plenty of great USB 1.1 devices are still around these days, such as joysticks, keyboards, mice, and other controllers, along with print-ers and scanners that work just fine with slower transfer rates. However, if a peripheral's job is to store or move data quickly — including hard drives, network connections, CD-ROM drives, and USB Flash drives — give a USB 1.1 connection a wide berth, opting instead for a USB 2.0 or FireWire device.

Phishing Operations

Phishing is no phun. No, that's not a misspelling. In Internet lingo, *phishing* refers to an attempt by unsavory characters to illegally obtain your personal information. If that sounds like an invitation to identity theft, it is — and thousands of sites have defrauded individuals like you and me (along with banks and credit card companies) out of billions of dollars. Unfortunately, the phishing industry has been growing like a weed, and more innocent folks are being ripped off every day. (The low-life running phishing operations are pond scum . . . and I'm being polite here because this will appear in print.)

A phishing scam works like this: You get an e-mail purporting to be from a major company or business, such as eBay, a government agency, or a major credit card company. The message warns you that you have to "update" your login or financial information to keep it current, or that you have to "validate" your information every so often — and even provides you with a convenient link to an official-looking Web page. After you enter your oh-so-personal information on that bogus page, it's piped directly to the bad guys, and they're off to the races.

Here's a Mark's Maxim that every Internet user should take to heart:

No *legitimate* company or agency will ever solicit your personal information through an e-mail message!™

Never respond to these messages. If you smell something phishy, open your Web browser and visit the company's site (the *real* one) directly. Then contact the company's customer support department. They'll certainly want to know about the phishing expedition, and you can help by providing them with the e-mail and Web addresses used in the scam.

In fact, sending any valuable financial information through unencrypted e-mail — even to those whom you know and trust — is a bad idea. E-mail messages can be intercepted or read from any e-mail server that stores your messages.

Oddly Shaped Optical Discs

Your Mac laptop's optical drive is a marvel of precision — and it's doggone svelte to boot. Every current Apple laptop model (including the external drive available for the MacBook Air) features the latest optical drives, which don't require silly trays. Just slide your CD or DVD inside the drive, and it smoothly disappears from sight. Press the Eject key, or drag the disc icon on your desktop to the trash, and the disc appears like magic. No need to give the loading and ejecting procedures a second thought, right?

Well, good reader, that's true — but *only* if you're loading a standard 1.2mm thick, 120mm *round* CD or DVD into your drive! Notice that I didn't say

- ✔ **An 80mm mini-disc:** Yes, they're cute. Yes, they're used by all sorts of devices these days, from DV camcorders to digital cameras. But, no, they're not supported by many slot-loading drives, so there's a good chance one will refuse to eject.

- ✔ **A credit-card or triangular-shaped disc:** Friends, these discs just aren't *natural!* Of course, that's part of their pizzazz for advertisers, who give them away in scads. A square disc will work in a tray-loading drive, but a slot drive will likely get indigestion and refuse to eject it.

- ✔ **A super-thick disc:** Sure, a tray DVD drive will likely be able to accept a disc with a thick printed paper label, but if that disc is more than 1.5mm thick, it can actually damage your laptop's slot-loading drive. Consider these words: "Marge, it's stuck in there!" Now imagine how you would feel if *you* were the one saying that.

All three of these oddly shaped discs share one thing in common: *The damage you may cause by attempting to use one in your MacBook is not covered under your Apple warranty.* A weighty statement indeed.

Submerged Keyboards

Do you really want a submerged keyboard? Your answer should be an unequivocal, "No!" And that's why everyone should make it a rule to keep all beverages well out of range of keyboards, trackpads, and external devices, such as speakers and mice. Especially when kids or cats are in close proximity to your laptop.

If a soda spill comes in contact with your MacBook, you're likely to be visited with intermittent keyboard problems (or, in the worst-case scenario, a short in your laptop's motherboard). Suffice it to say that 12 inches of open space can make the difference between a simple cleanup and an expensive replacement!

Antiquated Utility Software

It's the upgrade game, and everyone's gotta play. If you're using Mac OS X Leopard, you must upgrade your older utility programs — such as an older copy of TechTool Pro from Micromat (www.micromat.com) that supports only Mac OS X Tiger. I know that you spent good money on 'em, but these older disk utility applications can do more damage than good to a hard drive under Mac OS X Leopard. Of course, utility software designed for earlier versions of Mac OS X (such as Panther and Jaguar) should be strictly avoided!

A number of things change when Apple makes the leap to a new version of Mac OS X, including subtle changes to disk formats, memory management in applications, and the support provided for different types of hard drives. If you use an older utility application, you could find yourself with corrupted data. Sometimes a complete operating system reinstall is necessary.

Now that you're using Mac OS X Leopard, make sure that you diagnose and repair disk and file errors using only a utility application specifically designed to run in Leopard. Your laptop's hard drive will definitely thank you.

Software Piracy

This one's a no-brainer: Don't endorse software piracy. Remember, Apple's overall market share among worldwide computer users currently weighs in at around 10 percent. Software developers know this, and they have to expect (and *receive*) a return on their investment, or they're going to find something more lucrative to do with their time. As a shareware author, I can attest to this firsthand.

Pirated software seems attractive — the price is right, no doubt about it — but if you use an application without buying it, you're cheating the developer, who will eventually find Macintosh programming no longer worth the time and trouble. Believe me, a MacBook is a great machine, and Leopard is a great operating system, but the sexiest laptop and the best hardware won't make up for an absence of good applications.

Pay for what you use, and everyone benefits.

The Forbidden Account

You might never have encountered the *root,* or *System Administrator,* account in Mac OS X — and that's always A Good Thing. Note that I'm not talking about a standard Administrator (or Admin) account here. Every Mac needs at least one Admin account (in fact, it might be the only visible account on your computer), and any Standard user account can be toggled between Standard and Admin status with no trouble at all.

The root account, though, is a different beast altogether, and that's why it's disabled by default. All Unix systems have a root account. Leopard is based on a Unix foundation, so it has one, too. Anyone logging in with the root account can do *anything* on your system, including deleting or modifying files in the System folder (which no other account can access). Believe me, deliberately formatting your hard drive is about the only thing worse than screwing up the files in your System folder.

Luckily, no one can access the root/System Administrator account by accident. In fact, you can't assign the root account through System Preferences at all; you have to use the Directory Utility application located in your Utilities folder. Unless an Apple support technician tells you to enable and use it, you should promptly forget that the root account even exists.

Unsecured Wireless Connections

Okay, I like free Internet access as much as the next technology author — it's cool, it's convenient, and public access wireless networks are popping up all over the world. Heck, New Orleans is currently upgrading to citywide free wireless Internet access, which is perfect for checking your e-mail whilst you're catching beads or listening to jazz. More and more cities are certain to follow in the near future.

However, just because something is *free* doesn't mean that it's *safe.* (Impromptu bungee jumpers, take note.) Unfortunately, the free public wireless access you're likely to encounter is not secure: Anyone can join, and the information you send and receive can be intercepted by any hacker worthy of the name. A public network uses no WEP (Wired Equivalent Privacy) key, so no encryption is involved, and therefore no guarantee that your private e-mail, your company's financial spreadsheets, and your Great American Novel aren't being intercepted while you're uploading and downloading them in the airport.

If you *must* use your laptop on an unsecured public network, make sure that the connection itself is secure instead. For example, don't check your e-mail by using a Web browser unless your ISP or e-mail service offers an encrypted SSL (Secure Sockets Layer) connection. (Yep, I'm talking again about that little padlock that appears in Safari, which I discuss in Chapter 8. It's not just for ordering things online!) If you need to establish a secure connection with your home or office network, use an SSL-enabled Virtual Private Network (VPN) client, which allows you to transfer files and remotely operate a host computer with bulletproof security. (Visit www.gracion.com and download a trial copy of DigiTunnel for Mac OS X. The full version sells for about $60. You'll sleep better at night, Road Warrior.)

Refurbished Hardware

Boy, howdy, do I hate refurbished stuff. Like my single-minded quest to rid the world of floppy disks, I likewise make it a point to dispel the myth that you're actually saving money when you buy a refurbished (or "remanufactured") piece of hardware. To quote someone famous, "If the deal sounds too good to be true, it probably is."

Examine what you get when you buy a refurbished external hard drive. It's likely that the drive was returned as defective, of course, and was then sent back to the factory. There the manufacturer probably performed the most cursory of repairs (just enough to fix the known problem), perhaps tested the unit for a few seconds, and then packed it back up again. Legally, retailers can't resell the drive as a new item, so they have to cut the price so low that you're willing to take the chance.

Before you spend a dime on a bargain that's *remanufactured* — I can't get over that term — make sure that you find out how long a warranty you'll receive, if any. Consider that the hardware is likely to have crisscrossed the country at least once, and that it's likely to have picked up a few bumps and bruises during its travels. Also, you have no idea how well the repairs were tested or how thoroughly everything was inspected.

I don't buy refurbished computers or hardware, and most of the tales that I've heard of folks who do have ended badly. Take my advice: Spend the extra cash on trouble-free, new hardware that has a full warranty.

Dirty Laptops

Clean your machine. Every computer (and every piece of computer hardware) appreciates a weekly dusting.

Adding memory to your laptop? Seeing as how you have to open your Mac anyway, take advantage of the chance to use that trusty can of compressed air.

On the outside of your laptop, your screen should be cleaned at least once every two or three days — that is, unless you like peering through a layer of dust, fingerprints, and smudges. Never spray anything directly on your screen or your Mac's case. I highly recommend using premoistened LCD cleaning wipes typically used for notebook computers.

Your laptop's case really doesn't need a special cleaning agent — in fact, you shouldn't use any solvents — but a thorough wipe with a soft cloth should keep your case in spotless shape.

Index

• A •

AAC audio format, 164
active window, 74
Address Book application, 27
administrator accounts, 265
advanced hardware, 48–49
AIFF audio format, 164
AirPort, AirPort Extreme, or AirPort
    Express base stations. *See also*
    wireless networks
  adding cards to laptops, 16
  broadcasting music using, 180
  comparison of, 286–288
  connecting network printers, 152
  external hard drive, 332
  installing, 288–289
  joining wireless networks, 289–290
  sharing printers, 298
albums (iPhoto), 190–192
aliases, 65–66
Apple
  networking products, 286–288
  registering laptop with, 32
  Web-based support center, 51, 323
Apple Lossless audio format, 164, 232
Apple menu
  Force Quit command, 64, 313–314
  icon, identifying, 47
  Mac OS X Software command, 62
  overview, 56
  Recent Items, 63, 103
  Software Update command, 62, 320,
    347–348
  System Preferences command, 62
Apple Music Store, 182–184
Apple remote, 13, 19, 157–158
application menu, 47

applications. *See also specific applications*
  adding to dock, 82–83
  adding in Spaces, 10
  antiquated, avoiding, 360
  Automator for, 344–347
  cleanup utilities, 340
  Close button, 64
  frozen, forcing to quit, 64, 313–314
  icons for, 64
  imported by Migration Assistant, 38
  Internet tools, 26–27
  launching, 57, 61–63
  locked, 313–314
  in .Mac service Software folder, 142
  piracy, avoiding, 360–361
  preference file, corrupt, 319
  printer software, 150–152
  quitting, 63–64
  removing in Spaces, 101
  scanner software, 153
  shipped with laptops, 26
  switching between using Exposé, 87–88
  trackers, 353
  troubleshooting utilities, 360
  widgets, 11, 27, 100, 117–118
  Windows/Mac similarities, 50
arrow keys, 67
aspect ratio for iDVD video, 230
audio. *See also specific applications*
  books, 164
  built-in speakers and microphone
    for, 12
  connections for, 12, 15
  editing in iMovie, 213
  file formats supported by iTunes, 164–165
  hardware, 335
  iChat using, 159
  importing into iMovie, 212–215

audio *(continued)*
  sound effects for movies, 213
  special keys for, 70
Audio Mute key, 70
auto login, 277–279
Automator application, 344–347

• *B* •

background
  changing for desktop, 81, 94, 98
  changing for iDVD menu, 235–236
backing up
  CDs and DVDs, 341–342
  external hard drives, 341
  installing Backup application, 146
  with .Mac service, 145–146
  manually, 146
  media for, 142
  need for, 340–341, 356
  restoring from backup, 146, 342–343
  scheduling automatic backups, 106–108,
     340–344
  selecting files and folders for, 146
  Time Machine feature, 342–344
Backup application, 142, 146
bags for laptops, 351–352
battery
  calibrating, 34
  charging, 33
  compartment for, 13
  conserving power, 33–34, 355
  Energy Saver preferences, 103–104
  monitoring, 34–35
Belkin Bluetooth adapter, 303
BFE (Bluetooth File Exchange) application,
     304, 307
bindings, 101
bit rate, 176, 178
black-and-white photos, 199
Bluetooth
  adapter for, 303
  BFE application, 304, 307
  configuring connections, 303–304

described, 16
determining if supported, 302–303
file exchanges and transfers, 304–305
history of, 302
iSync utility with, 307–308
keyboard, 305–306
menu, 304
mouse, 305–306
printers, 308
security settings, 305
setting up new devices, 303
System Preferences, 303–305
wireless devices compared to, 305–306
bookmarks (Safari), 122, 125, 128–129
Boot Camp utility, 28, 41
boot disk, 318
branding your MacBook, 354
brightness
  adjustment for photos, 199
  display, 34, 97, 104
  keyboard backlighting, 70
browser. *See* Safari Web browser
Business widget, 118

• *C* •

cables
  checking, 320
  for Internet connection sharing, 284–285
  MacBook connections for, 24–25
  networking, 291–292
  power, 12–13
  set to have on hand, 29
  for USB printers, 90, 150–152
  wireless networks compared to, 282–284
cache, 135
calibrating battery, 34
camcorders (DV)
  importing clips from, 209–211
  Magic iDVD feature with, 226
  OneStep DVD feature with, 226
cameras, digital, 187–189. *See also* iSight
     camera
caring for laptop, 25

carpal tunnel syndrome, 29
cases for laptops, 351–352
CD & DVD Recording For Dummies (Chambers), 16
CDs
  avoiding non-standard discs, 359
  backing up, 341–342
  as backup media, 142
  for copying files from PC, 40–41
  displaying on desktop, 81
  importing images from, 189
  importing songs from, 175–176
  loading, 12
  Media Eject key for, 12
  music, playing with iTunes, 165–166
  opening in Finder, 56
  optical drives for, 16
  recording with iTunes, 180–181
  stopping from launching when loaded, 165–166
  types of, 29
CDW Web site, 327
charging battery, 33
chat, with iChat application, 27, 159, 274
Chess application, 27
cleaning laptop, 28, 363
cleaning up hard drive
  associated files in other folders, 339–340
  commercial tools for, 340
  emptying trash, 338–339
  need for, 337–338
  unnecessary files and folders, 338–339
closed wireless networks, 290
closing
  applications, 63–64
  frozen applications, 64, 313–314
  System Preferences window, 95
  windows, 75
color depth, 97
color profile, 97
connecting cables
  for Internet service, 24–25
  for networked printers, 152
  for networking, 291–292

power cord, 24
  for USB printers, 150–152
contextual menus, 48, 59–60, 83
Contour Design's ShuttleXpress, 335
contrast adjustment for photos, 198–199
Control key, 59, 81
cookies, 134–135
cooling pad, 22
copying items. *See also* importing
  Duplicate command for, 69
  iDisk mirror on local hard drive, 143–144
  loops (GarageBand), 250
  overview, 68–69
cordless connections
  adapter for Bluetooth, 303
  BFE application, 304, 307
  Bluetooth menu, 304
  configuring Bluetooth connections, 303–304
  determining Bluetooth support, 302–303
  file exchanges and transfers, 304–305
  history of Bluetooth, 16, 302
  iSync utility with, 307–308
  keyboard, 305–306
  mouse, 305–306
  printers, 308
  security settings, 305
  setting up new devices, 303
  System Preferences, 303–305
  wireless devices compared to Bluetooth, 305–306
CPU, 15, 19
cropping photos (iPhoto), 197–198

• D •

Dashboard application, 86–87
Dashboard widget, 27, 87
dead pixels, 32–33
deleting
  associated files in other folders, 339–340
  clips from movies, 217
  by dragging to trash, 84–85
  icons from dock, 83

deleting *(continued)*
  images from cameras, 189
  orphan files, 339–340
  photos in iPhoto, 191–192
  trash contents permanently, 339
  unnecessary files and folders, 338–339
  user accounts, 270–271
desktop. *See also* dock; Finder
  changing background for, 81, 94, 98
  cluttered, 80
  displaying connected items on, 81
  icons, 46, 80–81
  launching applications from, 62–63
  overview, 44–48
  switching between using Spaces, 88–90
  uncluttered, 80
  Windows/Mac similarities, 50
Detto Technologies' Move2Mac
  utility, 41
DHCP (Dynamic Host Configuration
  Protocol), 285, 294
Dictionary widget, 11, 117
digital cameras, 187–189. *See also* DV
  camcorders; iSight camera
DigiTunnel (Gracion), 362
disc image, saving iDVD project as, 237
discoverable Bluetooth port, 303
Disk Utility
  launching, 315–316
  repairing disk permissions with, 317–318,
    344
  repairing hard disks with, 318
  restoring from backup with, 342–344
  window, 316
displaying. *See also* finding; opening;
    playing
  connected items on desktop, 81
  contextual or right-click menus, 59–60
  photo information in iPhoto,
    187, 191, 195
  Preview application for, 84
  previewing movies, 236–237
  toolbars (toggling on and off), 75
  trash contents, 85

dock
  adding icons to, 82–83
  checking running applications on, 82
  hiding and showing, 105
  launching applications from, 57
  overview, 45–46, 57
  quitting applications from, 63
  removing icons from, 83
  right-click menu for icons, 83
  Systems Preferences, 105
documents
  icons for, 64
  moving, 41
Documents folder, 38, 41, 78, 83
DOS operating system, 49
.Mac service
  backing up using, 145–146
  configuring iDisk, 144–145
  described, 137
  folders on iDisk, 141–142
  iDisk location, 138
  Internet connection needed for, 139
  ISPs compared with, 140
  login, 139
  Mail application with, 140
  mirroring iDisk on hard drive, 143–144
  opening an account, 139–141
  opening iDisk, 141
  posting movies on, 220
  Public Folder, 144–145
  publishing Web sites with HomePage,
    147–148
  security, 144–145
  trial membership, 36, 139–140
  Web site hosting using, 137
drivers for printer, installing, 150
drives
  sharing CD/DVD, 21–22
  Windows/Mac similarities, 50
Drop Box folder, 279
duplicating items. *See also* importing
  Duplicate command for, 69
  iDisk mirror on local hard drive,
    143–144

loops (GarageBand), 250
overview, 68–69
DV camcorders
importing clips from, 209–211
Magic iDVD feature with, 226
OneStep DVD feature with, 226
DV video format, 210
DVD Player application, 27
DVDs. *See also* iDVD application
avoiding non-standard discs, 359
backing up, 341–342
as backup media, 142
for copying files from a PC, 40–41
discs for recording, 29
displaying on desktop, 81
importing images from, 189
loading, 12
Media Eject key for, 12
opening in Finder, 56
optical drives for, 16
widescreen aspect ratio for movies, 11
Dynamic Host Configuration Protocol
(DHCP), 285, 294

• **E** •

effects (iMovie), 213
Elgato Systems EyeTV Hybrid, 159
e-mail
configuring Mail application, 36
.Mac service integration with, 140
Mail application described, 27
parental controls for, 274
sending PDF documents, 92
encryption, Home folder, 279–280, 353
enhancing photos (iPhoto), 198
environment for laptop, 22–23
erasing
associated files in other folders, 339–340
clips from movies, 217
by dragging to trash, 84–85

icons from dock, 83
images from cameras, 189
trash contents permanently, 339
unnecessary files and folders, 338–339
user accounts, 270–271
Ethernet
port for, 14
wireless, 16
exporting
movies from iMovie, 220
songs from GarageBand, 257–258
switching using Exposé, 87–88
Exposé application, 87–88, 99–101
ExpressCard/34 slot, 14, 333
EyeTV Hybrid (Elgato Systems), 159

• **F** •

Fast User Switching feature, 276–277, 278
file formats supported
audio, 164–165
video, 210
files
adding to dock, 82–83
Bluetooth exchanges and transfers,
304–305
copying, 68–69
Disk Utility, 315–316
Exposé, 87
icons for, 64
imported by Migration Assistant,
37–42
moving, 69
orphan, removing, 339–340
Personal File Sharing, 297–298
removing unnecessary, 338–339
repairing permissions, 317–318, 344
Safari Web browser, 121
selecting for backup, 146
Windows/Mac similarities, 50
FileVault encryption, 279–280, 353

films and movies. *See* iMovie application
Finder. *See also* dock
  Apple menu, 56
  closing windows, 75
  desktop, 56
  icons, 56–57
  importance of mastering, 55
  keyboard shortcuts, 71–72
  launching applications from, 57, 63
  menu bar, 47–48, 56
  minimizing and restoring windows, 73–74
  monitoring battery level, 34, 35
  moving windows, 74
  opening CDs and DVDs in, 56
  opening iDisk in, 141
  opening windows in Home folder, 78–80
  parental controls for, 272–275
  playing songs on iTunes from, 166–167
  resizing windows, 72–73
  scrolling windows, 72–73
  search methods in, 117
  Sidebar, 58, 75, 78
  Spotlight feature, 109–117
  toggling toolbar on and off, 75
  window, 57
  zooming windows, 74
 finding
  creating Smart Folders for results, 117
  Find display for, 116–117
  Finder Search box for, 116
  photos using keywords, 195
  songs and artists in iTunes, 169–170
  Spotlight feature for, 109–112
  System Preferences settings, 95–96
  Web sites with Safari, 123–124
firewall, 298–300
FireWire, 14, 19, 333
Flash Drives, 20, 41, 63, 333, 358
Flight tracker widget, 118
folders
  adding to dock, 82–83
  Drop Box, 279
  duplicating, 69

Home, 77–80, 279–280, 353
  iDisk, 141–142
  Public, 144–145, 279
  removing unnecessary, 338–339
  selecting for backup, 146
  Shared, user account relationship to, 279
  Smart Folders, 117
  Windows/Mac locations, 41
  Windows/Mac similarities, 50
fonts, 103, 219
forcing applications to quit, 64, 313–314
Front Row application, 26, 156–158

• *G* •

game controllers, 335
GarageBand application
  adding new loops, 252
  adding tracks, 245–248
  adjusting song settings, 244–245
  adjusting tracks, 253, 254–256
  buttons and controls, 243–244
  choosing loops, 248–251
  composing songs automatically, 256–257
  creating AAC files from songs, 258
  creating MP3 files from songs, 258
  creating new project, 244–245
  cut, copy, and paste for loops, 253
  empty space between loops, 253
  MIDI instruments with, 246
  overview, 241–242
  placing loops on separate tracks, 250–251
  podcast creation using, 241, 244–245
  recording audio CDs, 259
  repeating loops, 252
  resizing loops, 252
  saving songs, 256
  sending podcasts to iWeb or iTunes, 258–259
  sharing songs and podcasts, 257–259
  tempo for songs, 244–245
  track types available, 246

Visual Equalizer window, 255–256
window, 242–244
Go menu, 78
Google search box (Safari), 125
Google widget, 118
Gracion's DigiTunnel, 362
graphical user interface (GUI), 50
graphics. *See* iPhoto application
grayed-out items on menus, 56
Griffin Technology's SHARK2, 335
grounding yourself, 331
GUI (graphical user interface), 50

● *H* ●

Hamrick Software's VueScan application,
153
handling laptop, 25
hard drives. *See also* backing up
comparisons between, 15
displaying on desktop, 81
external, 332–334
iDisk copy on, 143–144
importing images from, 189
importing songs to iTunes from, 175–176
internal, 334
opening in Finder, 56
refurbished, avoiding, 362–363
repairing disks, 318
repairing permissions, 317–318, 344
solid-state, 19–21
upgrading, 331–334
Hardcopy Cable Replacement Protocol
(HCRP), 308
hardware. *See also specific kinds*
advanced, 48–49
audio, 335
checking working status of, 23–24
icons for, 64
MacBook overview, 10–17
refurbished, avoiding, 362–363
HCRP (Hardcopy Cable Replacement
Protocol), 308

HDV video format, 210
headphone connector, 15
heat generated by MacBook, 35
help, 50–52, 323–324
hints for passwords, 268
Home folder
displaying, 78–80
FileVault encryption, 279–280, 353
opening Finder windows within,
78–80
organizing Documents folder in, 78
privacy of, 279–280
subfolders, 78
for user accounts, 279–280
HomePage, 147–148
housekeeping
automating tasks, 344–347
backing up, 340–344
cleaning up hard drive, 337–340
repairing permissions, 344
updating Mac OS X automatically,
347–348
hub, networking, 294
Hyperbolic Software's Tidy Up!, 340

● *I* ●

iBooks, 11
iCal application, 63, 89, 113, 307
iChat application, 27, 159, 274
icons
aliases, 65–66
for Apple menu, 47
desktop, 46, 80–81
dock, 46, 82–83
Finder, 56–57
guide to, 64–66
in margins of this book, 5–6
iDisk. *See also* .Mac service
backing up to, 145–146
configuring, 144–145
defined, 137
folders, 141–142

iDisk *(continued)*
  location of, 138
  mirroring copy on local hard drive,
    143–144
  opening, 141
  Public Folder, 144–145
  security, 144–145
  System Preferences, 143
iDVD application
  adding movies to DVDs, 223, 228–230
  adding music to DVDs, 232–233
  adding slideshows to DVDs, 223, 230–232
  adding submenus to DVDs, 223
  adding titles to DVDs, 234
  animated background for menu, 235–236
  animation cycle, 224
  aspect ratio for video, 230
  audio file formats supported, 232
  automating DVD creation, 226, 237–239
  button customization, 229, 234–235
  buttons, 223, 228–229
  changing menu background, 233–234
  creating DVDs from scratch, 226–233
  creating new projects, 224–225
  drop zones, 224, 228
  ease of use, 221–222
  iMovie integration with, 226, 228
  integration with other applications,
    221–222
  Magic iDVD feature, 226, 238–239
  media, 223
  OneStep DVD feature, 226, 237–238
  opening existing projects, 225
  organizational chart, 224
  previewing DVD, 224, 236–237
  recording projects to disc, 239–240
  resolution for video, 230
  saving projects as disc images, 237
  themes, 223, 227–228
  TV Safe Area command, 230
  window, 222–224
iLife '08 suite, 26. *See also specific programs*
Image Capture application, 153
images. *See iPhoto application*

iMovie application
  adding clips to movies, 215–216
  adding music with iTunes, 212–213
  basic steps for moviemaking, 208–209
  controls used most often, 207–208
  creating new projects, 206–207
  editing audio tracks, 213
  editing clips, 214–215, 217–218
  effects, 213
  iDVD integration with, 226, 228
  importing audio, 212–215
  importing video clips, 209–211
  iSight camera with, 209–210
  launching, 206
  marking clips, 216
  overview, 205
  previewing movies, 216
  recording narration, 213–214
  removing clips from movies, 217
  reordering clips in movies, 217
  sharing movies, 220
  sound effects for movies, 213
  stills for movies, 211–212
  titles for movies, 219
  transitions, 218–219
  trash, 217
  Undo feature, 217
  video formats supported, 210
  window, 206–208
importing
  from another Mac, 37–40
  audio into iMovie, 212–215
  images from digital cameras, 188–189
  images from disks, 189
  songs to iTunes, 175–176
  stills into iMovie, 211–212
  video clips into iMovie, 209–211
  video clips with OneStep DVD, 226
  from Windows, 40–42
information for Spotlight items, 113–114
installing
  Apple base stations, 288–289
  Backup application, 146
  Bluetooth printers, 308
  memory modules, 327–330

network printers, 150–152
reinstalling Mac OS X, 319
tracker applications, 353
USB printers, 90, 150–152
Intego's Virus Barrier X, 321
Intel CPU, 15, 18
Internet connection
  checking, 321
  Ethernet networking for, 25
  firewall for, 298–300
  iChat AV requirements, 159
  modem cables for, 24
  needed for .Mac service, 139
  for ordering photo books, 201
  sharing, 284–285, 296–298
  software for, 26–27
  streaming radio requirements, 178
Internet resources. *See also* .Mac service
  Apple Mac OS X page, 139
  Apple service locations, 324
  Apple support center, 33, 51, 323
  backup, 146
  Belkin, 303
  Bluetooth adapter, 303
  Boot Camp utility, 28
  cleanup utilities, 340
  Contour Design, 335
  Elgato Systems, 159
  finding with Safari, 123–124
  Griffin Technology, 335
  iPhoto support page, 188
  iSync support information, 307
  .Mac Welcome page, 139
  magazines, 51
  MLC Books, 179
  Move2Mac utility, 41
  newsgroups, 52
  passwords for networks, 289
  Preferential Treatment utility, 319
  printer software, 91, 298
  scanner software, 153
  streaming radio, 165
  support Web sites, 33
  TechTool Pro utility, 312, 360
  Toast recording software, 16
  Virus Barrier X, 321
  VueScan application, 153
  XTool Tracker utility, 353
Internet router, 285
invoice, saving, 24
IP address, 285, 293, 295
iPhoto application
  adding images to iMovie from, 211–212
  adding slideshows to DVDs, 230–232
  albums, 190–192
  Apple support page, 188
  arranging photos in viewer,
    191–192, 196
  calendars and greeting cards, 200
  controls, 185–187
  creating keywords, 195
  deleting images from cameras, 189
  editing photos, 196–199
  events, 190, 192–193
  finding photos using keywords, 195
  importing images, 188–189
  keywords for organizing photos, 193–195
  merging events, 192–193
  operation modes, 187
  organize mode, 189–196
  overview, 185
  photocasting feature, 203
  publishing photo books, 199–201
  rating photos, 195–196
  removing photos, 191–192
  renaming albums, 192
  renaming keywords, 195
  rolls of photos, 186
  standard keywords, 194
  Web Gallery feature, 202–203
iPod. *See also* podcasts
  backing up to, 136
  displaying on desktop, 81
  iTunes integration with, 164
iSight camera
  with iMovie, 209–210
  MacBook Air, 18
  overview, 13
  with Photo Booth, 154–156
iSight video format, 159

iSync utility, 307–308
iTunes application
  adding music to disks, 180–181
  adding or editing song information,
      173–175
  adding songs to iMovie, 212–213
  audio file formats supported, 164–165
  backup feature, 181
  broadcasting music using, 180
  browsing Library, 169–171
  buying songs from Music Store, 182–184
  defined, 163
  Equalizer, 177
  importing songs, 175–176
  keyboard shortcuts, 166
  playing audio CDs with, 165–166
  playing digital audio and video, 166–169
  playing songs with, 166–167
  playlist creation, 171–172
  preferences, 174–175
  recording CDs using, 180–181
  removing music from Library, 169, 170
  ripping audio files, 175–176
  searching for songs and artists, 169–170
  sending movies to, 220
  shuffle mode, 173
  streaming radio with, 177–180
  visualization mode, 182
  watching video with, 170–171
iWork application suite, 26

• K •

keyboard
  Bluetooth, 305–306
  caring for, 25, 360
  checking working status of, 33
  external, 23, 35, 356
  features of, 12, 18
  Front Row functions controlled by, 158
  special keys on, 70
  startup keys, 314–315
  wrist rest for, 29

Keyboard Illumination key, 70
keyboard shortcuts
  for Dashboard, 100
  for Exposé, 100
  in Finder (table), 71–72
  Front Row, 158
  for iTunes, 166
  for launching applications, 62
  for quitting applications, 63
  for Spaces, 101
  startup keys, 314–315
KeyRig49 (M-Audio), 335

• L •

laptop bags, 351–352
laptop stand, 35
launching. *See also* displaying
  aliases for, 66
  applications, 57, 61–63
  Automator applications, 346
  CDs and DVDs in Finder, 56
  Dashboard, 86
  existing iDVD projects, 225
  Finder windows in Home folder, 78–80
  iDisk, 141
  iMovie, 206
  Spotlight search box, 109–110
LCD screen
  calibrating, 97
  changing resolution and color depth, 97
  checking working status of, 32–33
  cleaning, 28
  color profile for, 97
  cracked or broken, 327
  overview, 10–11
  screen saver, 99, 322
Leopard Mac OS X
  actions controlled by, 44
  desktop, 44–48
  ease of use, 49
  firewall, 298–300
  Help system, 41, 51

Hints Web site, 51
MacBook Air on, 18
operating system defined, 44
performance, 48–49
reinstalling, 319
reliability, 48
setting up, 36–37
UNIX core of, 49
updating automatically, 347–348
Windows compared to, 49–50
lighting, 23
Linux operating system, 294
list login, 276
loading CDs or DVDs, 12
location for laptop, 22–23
locked applications, 313–314
login items
  defined, 63, 271
  disabling, 322
  launching applications from, 63
  setting for your account, 271–272
login to .Mac service, 139
login to user accounts
  auto, 277–279
  Fast User Switching, 276–277, 278
  list, 276
  username and password, 276
logs, 274

• M •

M-Audio's KeyRig49, 335
Mac OS X. *See also specific features*
  actions controlled by, 44
  desktop, 44–48
  ease of use, 49
  firewall, 298–300
  Help system, 41, 51
  Hints Web site, 51
  Leopard desktop, 44–48
  MacBook Air on, 18
  operating system defined, 44
  performance, 48–49
  reinstalling, 319
  reliability, 48
  setting up, 36–37
  UNIX core of, 49
  updating automatically, 347–348
  Windows compared to, 49–50
*Mac OS X Leopard All-in-One Desk
  Reference For Dummies*
  (Chambers), 49, 294
.Mac service
  backing up using, 145–146
  configuring iDisk, 144–145
  described, 137
  folders on iDisk, 141–142
  iDisk location, 138
  Internet connection, need for, 139
  ISPs compared with, 140
  login, 139
  Mail application with, 140
  mirroring iDisk on hard drive, 143–144
  opening an account, 139–141
  opening iDisk, 141
  posting movies on, 220
  Public Folder, 144–145
  publishing Web sites with HomePage,
    147–148
  security, 144–145
  trial membership, 36, 139–140
  Web site hosting using, 137
MacBook Air, 17–19
MacFixit Web site, 51
MacLife Web site, 51
MacMall Web site, 327

MacMinute Web site, 51
Macworld Web site, 51
Magic iDVD feature, 226, 238–239
MagSafe power connector, 12–13
Mail application
  configuring, 36
  described, 27
  .Mac service integration with, 140
  parental controls for, 274
  sending PDF documents, 92
managed user accounts, 265, 272–275
manual, need for reading, 11, 24
Media Eject key, 12
memory
  advantages of adding, 325–326, 352
  determining amount available, 326
  installing modules, 327–330
  MacBook Air, 19
  upgrade options, 326–327
menus. *See also* Apple menu
  adding to DVDs, 223
  animated background for iDVD, 235–236
  application, 47
  Bluetooth, 304
  changing background for iDVD, 235–236
  contextual or right-click, 48, 59–60, 83
  conventions in this book, 3
  Finder menu bar, 47–48, 56
  Go, 78
  grayed-out items on, 556
merging events (iPhoto), 192–193
Micromat's TechTool Pro, 312, 360
microphone, 18
Microsoft Windows
  Boot Camp utility for, 28, 41
  external keyboard for, 356
  importing items from, 40–41
  Mac OS X leopard compared to, 49–50
  running on Macs, 42
  switching from, 40–42, 49–50
MIDI (Musical Instrument Digital Interface), 246
Migration Assistant, 37–42
minimizing windows, 73–74
mirroring iDisk on hard drive, 143–144

MLC Books, 179
MLC Radio, 179
mouse. *See also* trackpad
  Bluetooth, 305–306
  external, 356
  replacing trackpad with, 58–59
Move2Mac utility (Detto Technologies), 41
movies. *See* iMovie application
moving items. *See also* importing
  to another location on same drive, 69
  arranging icons on desktop, 80–81
  arranging windows, 74
  media and documents, 41
  Movie buttons (iDVD), 229
  windows, 74
MP3 audio format
  overview, 164
  recording CDs with iTunes, 181
  saving GarageBand songs in, 258
MPEG-4 video format, 210, 228
Multi-Touch feature, 61, 74
multiplayer games, 282
music. *See* iTunes application
Music store (Apple), 182–184
Musical Instrument Digital Interface (MIDI), 246

• N •

naming
  albums (iPhoto), 192
  files linked to aliases, 65–66
  keywords (iPhoto), 195
narration, recording in iMovie, 213–214
Nathan, Jonathan (programmer), 319
networking. *See also* wireless networks
  benefits of, 281–282
  combining wired and wireless, 283
  components, 292
  connecting cables, 291–292
  connecting to networks, 286–291, 294–298
  connecting printers, 150–152

DHCP, 285, 294
displaying servers on desktop, 81
firewall for, 298–300
hub, 294
for Internet connection sharing,
284–291, 296–298
Internet service using, 24–25
joining a network, 289–290, 293–294
non-Apple hardware support, 289, 291
opening connections in Finder, 56
Personal File Sharing, 297–298
ports for, 14
for printer sharing, 298
printing over a network, 298
settings imported for, 38
testing networks (pinging),
295–296, 321
wired, 282–284
wireless, 282–284
Newegg Web site, 327
newsgroups, 52

• O •

OneStep DVD feature, 226, 237–238
opening. *See also* displaying
aliases for, 66
applications, 57, 61–63
Automator applications, 346
CDs and DVDs in Finder, 56
Dashboard, 86
existing iDVD projects, 225
Finder windows in Home folder, 78–80
iDisk, 141
iMovie, 206
Spotlight search box, 109–110
operating system (OS), 44. *See also*
Mac OS X
optical drives
avoiding non-standard discs, 359
hardware overview, 12, 16
MacBook Air, 19
sharing, 21–22
optical line in connector, 15
optical output connector, 15

OS (operating system), 44. *See also*
Mac OS X
OS X. *See* Mac OS X
outlets, needs for, 22

• P •

parental controls, 272–275
passwords
for FileVault encryption, 280
hints for, 268
importance of remembering, 280
for networks, 289
for user accounts, 266–268, 276
PDF format, 92
peripheral, 14
permissions, repairing, 317–318
Personal File Sharing, 297–298
phishing scams, 358–359
Photo Booth application, 26, 154–156
photocasting feature, 203
pictures or photos. *See* iPhoto application
pinging a network, 321
placement for laptop, 22–23
playing
music CDs with iTunes, 165–166
streaming radio with iTunes, 177–180
video with iTunes, 170–171
playlists, 168, 171–172. *See also* iTunes
application
podcasts
creating using GarageBand,
241, 244–245
defined, 164
sending to iWeb or iTunes, 258–259
sharing, 257–259
pop-up ads, 136
ports
audio and video, 15
Bluetooth discoverable setting for, 303
Ethernet, 14
ExpressCard/34, 14
firewall settings for, 300
FireWire, 14, 333

ports *(continued)*
  MacBook Air, 19
  USB, 14, 332–333
power button, 13, 31–32
power conservation, 20, 355
power cord (MagSafe), 12–13
power saving features, 355
PowerBooks, 11
preference files, 319
Preferential Treatment utility, 319
previewing. *See* displaying
printing
  Bluetooth printers for, 308
  connecting network printers, 152
  connecting USB printers, 90, 150–152
  driver installation, 150–151
  over a network, 91, 298
  to PDF format, 92
  steps for, 90–92
  Web pages from Safari, 125
privacy, 115, 133–136
processor (CPU), 15, 18
programs. *See also specific programs*
  adding to dock, 82–83
  adding in Spaces, 101
  antiquated, avoiding, 360
  Automator for, 344–347
  cleanup utilities, 340
  Close button, 64
  frozen, forcing to quit, 64, 313–314
  icons for, 64
  imported by Migration Assistant, 38
  Internet tools, 26–27
  launching, 57, 61–63
  locked, 313–314
  in .Mac service, 142
  piracy, avoiding, 360–361
  preference file, corrupt, 319
  printer software, 150–152
  quitting, 63–64
  removing in Spaces, 101
  scanner software, 153
  shipped with laptops, 26
  switching between using Exposé, 87–88

trackers, 353
troubleshooting utilities, 360
widgets, 11, 27, 100, 117–118
Windows/Mac similarities, 50
Public folder, 279
publishing photo books (iPhoto), 199–201

• *Q* •

Quick Look feature, 63, 84
QuickTime, 220
Quit command, 63
quitting
  applications, 63–64
  frozen applications, 64, 313–314
  System Preferences window, 95
  windows, 75

• *R* •

RAM. *See* memory
rating photos (iPhoto), 195–196
RDF Site Summary (RSS) feeds, 127
rebooting, problems solved by, 312–314
recent items, launching applications from, 63, 103
recording
  iDVD projects to disc, 239–240
  music or MP3 CDs, 175–176
  narration in iMovie, 213–214
red-eye removal for photos (iPhoto), 198–199
refresh rate, 97
refurbished hardware, 362–363
registering laptop, 35, 37
reinstalling Mac OS X, 319
reliability of Mac OS X, 48
Remember icon, 6
remote control, 13, 19, 157–158
removing
  associated files in other folders, 339–340
  clips from movies, 217

by dragging to trash, 84–85
icons from dock, 83
images from cameras, 189
orphan files, 339–340
photos in iPhoto, 191–192
trash contents permanently, 339
unnecessary files and folders, 338–339
user accounts, 270–271
renaming
albums (iPhoto), 192
files linked to aliases, 65–66
keywords (iPhoto), 195
repairing. *See also* troubleshooting
hard disks, 318
permissions, 317–318
resizing
loops (GarageBand), 252
minimizing and restoring windows, 73–74
windows, 72–73
zooming windows, 74
resolution for iDVD video, 230
restoring
from backup, 146, 342–343
items from trash, 85
minimized windows, 74
restraining cable, 29
retouching photos (iPhoto), 199
right-click menus, 48, 59–60, 83
root/System Administrator account, 361
rotating photos (iPhoto), 196–197
router (Internet), 285
Roxio Toast recording software, 16
RSS (RDF Site Summary) feeds, 127
running. *See* launching; opening

• S •

Safari Web browser
adding URLs to dock, 83
bookmarks, 122, 125, 128–129
buttons, 124–125
Content window, 122
described, 26–27
downloading files, 129–130
entering Web addresses, 123–124
Find bar, 131
Google search box, 125
History list, 130–131, 136
launching, 121
overview, 121–123
parental controls for, 272–275
preferences, 134–136
printing Web pages, 125
reading RSS feeds with, 127
saving Web pages, 132–133
searching for Web sites using, 123–124
secure connections in, 133–136
setting home page for, 126–127
status bar, 123
Tabbed browsing mode, 131–132
toolbar, 122
saving. *See also* backing up
document to PDF format, 92
GarageBand songs, 259
iDVD project as disc image, 237
scanners, 153
screen. *See* LCD screen
screen saver, 99, 322
searching
creating Smart Folders for results, 117
Find display for, 116–117
Finder Search box for, 116
photos using keywords, 195
songs and artists in iTunes, 169–170
Spotlight feature for, 109–112
System Preferences settings, 95–96
Web sites with Safari, 123–124
security. *See also* passwords
Bluetooth settings for, 305
closed wireless networks for, 290
deleting unneeded user accounts for,
270–271
FileVault encryption, 279–280, 353
firewall for, 298–300
iDisk, 144–145
phishing scams, 358–359

security *(continued)*
  Safari connections, 133–136
  Spotlight privacy settings, 113
  wired networks, 361–362
  wireless networks, 361–362
selecting
  files and folders for backup, 146
  movie clip sections (iMovie), 215–216
  overview, 66–68
sepia photos, 199
setting up system
  connecting cables, 24–25
  Mac OS X configuration, 36–37
  unpacking, 23–24
Shared folder, 279
sharing. *See also* networking; user accounts
  Internet connection, 284–285
  movies (iMovie), 220
  Personal File Sharing, 297–298
  podcasts (GarageBand), 257–259
  publishing photo books (iPhoto), 199–201
  songs (GarageBand), 258–259
SHARK2 (Griffin Technology), 335
shortcut keys. *See* keyboard shortcuts
shortcuts (aliases), 65–66
ShuttleXpress (Contour Design), 335
Sidebar (Finder), 58, 78
sleep mode preferences, 100, 103–104
slideshows, 223, 230–232
Smart Albums (iPhoto), 191
Smart Folders, 117
Smith Micro Software's Spring Cleaning, 340
sneakernet, 281
software. *See also* applications
  piracy of, 360–361
  upgrades to, 360
Software Update command, 62, 320, 347–348
solid-state drive, 19–21
sorting photos in iPhoto viewer,
    191–192, 196
sound. *See also specific applications*
  audio books, 164
  built-in speakers and microphone for, 12

connections for, 12, 15
editing in iMovie, 213
file formats supported by iTunes, 164–165
hardware, 335
iChat using, 159
importing into iMovie, 212–215
sound effects for movies, 213
special keys for, 70
Spaces application, 88–90, 99–101
speakers, 19
Spotlight feature
  clicking on found items, 113
  displaying information on items, 113–114
  displaying search box, 109–110
  filtering items by date or source, 113–114
  grouping results, 112
  overview, 109–111
  privacy settings, 113
  searching with, 111–112
  System Preferences, 114–116
Spring Cleaning (Smith Micro Software),
    340
stand for laptop, 35
standard user accounts, 265
starting. *See* launching
stopping. *See* closing
streaming music over a network, 180
streaming radio, 165
support
  Apple online support, 33, 323
  iPhoto support page, 188
  registration requirement for, 37
surge suppressor, 28, 355
switch, networking, 292
switching from Windows, 40–42
System Administrator/root account, 361
System Preferences
  Appearance pane, 102–103
  Apply button, 95
  Bluetooth pane, 303–305
  closing, 95
  Desktop pane, 98–99
  Displays pane, 97

Dock pane, 105
Energy Saver pane, 103–104
Exposé pane, 99–101
finding settings, 95–96
iDisk pane, 143
imported by Migration Assistant, 38
launching, 93–94
navigating in, 94–95
parental controls, 272–275
Screen Saver pane, 99
Sharing pane, 106
Software Update pane, 347–348
Spaces pane, 99–101
Spotlight pane, 114–115
Time Machine pane, 106–108
System Profiler, 323

● *T* ●

Technical stuff icon, 6
technical support
  Apple online support, 33, 323
  iPhoto support page, 188
  registration requirement for, 37
TechTool Pro (Micromat), 312, 360
themes (iDVD), 223, 227–228
Tidy Up! (Hyperbolic Software), 340
Time Capsule. *See* AirPort, AirPort
    Extreme, or AirPort Express base
    stations
time limits, 274
Time Machine feature, 342–344
Tip icon, 6
Toast recording software (Roxio), 16
toolbars, 75
trackball, 59
tracker applications, 353
trackpad
  checking working status of, 33
  clicking by tapping, 58
  launching applications using, 61–63
  MacBook Air, 18

mouse replacement by, 12
Multi-Touch feature, 61
objects other than finger on, 58
overview, 58–60
preferences for, 58–59, 61
quitting applications using, 63–64
replacing with mouse, 59
right button lacking on, 58
scrolling using, 60
transitions (iMovie), 218–219
trash
  checking for deleted files, 321
  deleting contents permanently,
      85, 339
  displaying contents, 84–85
  dragging devices or drives to, 85
  methods for removing items to, 84–85
  Quick Look feature, 84
  restoring items from, 85
troubleshooting
  Apple support site for, 323
  checking cables, 320
  checking trash for deleted files, 321
  defined, 311
  disabling login items, 322
  Disk Utility for, 315–318, 320
  investigating recent changes, 319–320
  Laptop Troubleshooting Tree, 319–323
  local service for, 324
  myths about, 311–312
  network testing (pinging), 321
  quitting frozen applications,
      64, 313–314
  rebooting to solve problems, 312–314
  reinstalling Mac OS X, 319
  repairing disk permissions,
      317–318, 344
  repairing hard disks, 318
  Safe Boot mode, 314
  startup keys for, 314–315
  submitting Bug reports for Safari, 125
  System Profiler for, 323
  turning off screen saver, 322

troubleshooting *(continued)*
  utility software for, 360
  viruses, 321
turning on laptop, 31–32
TV, 159–160

• *U* •

Undo feature, 192, 198, 217
Uniform Resource Locators (URLs). *See*
    also Internet resources
  adding to dock, 83
  conventions in this book, 3
  entering in Safari, 123–124
uninterruptible power supply (UPS), 28
Universal Serial Bus (USB)
  avoiding 1.1 storage devices, 358
  external, 21
  game controllers, 335
  hard drives, 332–333
  musing devices, 59
  ports for, 14
  printers, 90, 150–152
  scanners, 153
  video controllers, 335
UNIX as Mac OS X core, 49
unpacking system, 23–24
upgrades
  add-ons, 335
  grounding yourself before installing, 331
  hard drive, 331–334
  memory, 325–330, 352
  software, 360
UPS (uninterruptible power supply), 28
URLs (Uniform Resource Locators). *See*
    also Internet resources
  adding to dock, 83
  conventions in this book, 3
  entering in Safari, 123–124
USB (Universal Serial Bus)
  avoiding 1.1 storage devices, 358
  external, 21

  game controllers, 335
  hard drives, 332–333
  mousing devices, 59
  ports for, 14
  printers, 90, 150–152
  scanners, 153
  video controllers, 335
Usenet newsgroups, 52
user accounts
  adding new accounts, 266–268
  administrator, 265
  assigning access levels, 265–266
  auto login, 271
  deleting, 270–271
  editing existing accounts, 268–270
  Fast User Switching feature,
    276–278
  FileVault encryption for, 279–280
  Home folder, 78–80
  imported by Migration Assistant, 38
  list login, 276
  login items for, 271–272
  managed, 265, 272–275
  need for, 264
  parental controls for, 265–266, 272–275
  root/System Administrator, 361
  Shared and Public folders with, 279
  standard, 265
  username and password login, 276
user groups, 52

• *V* •

VGA/DVI connector, 15
video. *See also* iDVD application; iMovie
    application
  cards for, 17
  connections for, 15
  formats supported by iMovie, 210
  importing clips into iMovie, 209–211
  playing with iTunes, 170–171

video cameras. *See* DV camcorders
video cards, 17
video controllers, 335
videoconferencing, 13
viewing. *See also* finding; opening; playing
  connected items on desktop, 81
  contextual or right-click menus, 59–60
  photo information in iPhoto,
    187, 191, 195
  Preview application for, 84
  previewing movies, 236–237
  toolbars (toggling on and off), 75
  trash contents, 85
Virus Barrier X (Intego), 321
viruses, 321
visual effects (iMovie), 213
visualizing audio in iTunes, 182
Volume Down key, 70
Volume Up key, 70

• *W* •

Warning! icon, 6
WAV audio format, 164
Weather widget, 118
Web addresses. *See also* Internet resources
  adding to dock, 83
  conventions in this book, 3
  entering in Safari, 123–124
Web browser. *See* Safari Web browser
Web Gallery (iPhoto), 202–203
Web sites. *See also* .Mac service
  Apple Mac OS X page, 139
  Apple service locations, 324
  Apple support center, 33, 51, 323
  backup, 146
  Belkin, 303
  Bluetooth adapter, 303
  Boot Camp utility, 28
  cleanup utilities, 340
  Contour Design, 335
  Elgato Systems, 159
  finding with Safari, 123–124

  Griffin Technology, 335
  iPhoto support page, 188
  iSync support information, 307
  .Mac Welcome page, 139
  magazines, 51
  MLC Books, 179
  Move2Mac utility, 41
  newsgroups, 52
  passwords for networks, 289
  Preferential Treatment utility, 319
  printer software, 91, 298
  scanner software, 153
  streaming radio, 165
  support, 33
  TechTool Pro utility, 312, 360
  Toast recording software, 16
  Virus Barrier X, 321
  VueScan application, 153
  Web address convention in this book, 3
  XTool Tracker utility, 353
widescreen aspect ratio, 11, 18
widgets
  Business, 118
  Dashboard, 27
  Dictionary, 11, 117
  Flight Tracker, 118
  Google, 118
  preferences, 100
  Weather, 118
Windows (Microsoft)
  Boot Camp utility for, 28, 41
  external keyboard for, 356
  importing items from, 40–41
  Mac OS X Leopard compared to, 49–50
  running on Macs, 42
  switching from, 40–42, 49–50
windows (on-screen). *See also specific*
    applications
  active, determining, 74
  appearance preferences, 100
  opening within Home folder, 78–80
  toolbars, 75
  using and navigating, 72–75

wireless connections
  adapter for Bluetooth, 303
  BFE application, 304, 307
  Bluetooth menu, 304
  configuring Bluetooth connections,
    303–304
  determining Bluetooth support, 302–303
  file exchanges and transfers, 304–305
  history of Bluetooth, 16, 302
  iSync utility with, 307–308
  keyboard, 305–306
  mouse, 305–306
  printers, 308
  security settings, 305
  setting up new devices, 303
  System Preferences, 303–305
  wireless devices, 305–306
wireless networks. *See also* networking
  Apple base stations for, 286–291
  checking, 295–296, 321
  closed, 290
  combining with wired networks, 283
  connecting network printers, 152
  convenience as advantage of, 284
  described, 16
  disabling when not connected, 354
  interference with, 283
  for Internet connection sharing, 284–285,
    296–298
  joining, 289–290
  MacBook Air, 18
  non-Apple base station/hardware support
    for, 289, 291
  Personal File Sharing, 297–298
  for printer sharing, 298
  security, 361–362
  wired Ethernet compared to, 282–284
wrist rest, 29

● X ●

XTool Tracker (XTool Mobile Security),
  353

● Y ●

YouTube, 220

● Z ●

zooming windows, 74

BUSINESS, CAREERS & PERSONAL FINANCE

0-7645-9847-3   0-7645-2431-3

Also available:

- Business Plans Kit For Dummies
  0-7645-9794-9
- Economics For Dummies
  0-7645-5726-2
- Grant Writing For Dummies
  0-7645-8416-2
- Home Buying For Dummies
  0-7645-5331-3
- Managing For Dummies
  0-7645-1771-6
- Marketing For Dummies
  0-7645-5600-2

- Personal Finance For Dummies
  0-7645-2590-5*
- Resumes For Dummies
  0-7645-5471-9
- Selling For Dummies
  0-7645-5363-1
- Six Sigma For Dummies
  0-7645-6798-5
- Small Business Kit For Dummies
  0-7645-5984-2
- Starting an eBay Business For Dummies
  0-7645-6924-4
- Your Dream Career For Dummies
  0-7645-9795-7

HOME & BUSINESS COMPUTER BASICS

0-470-05432-8   0-471-75421-8

Also available:

- Cleaning Windows Vista For Dummies
  0-471-78293-9
- Excel 2007 For Dummies
  0-470-03737-7
- Mac OS X Tiger For Dummies
  0-7645-7675-5
- MacBook For Dummies
  0-470-04859-X
- Macs For Dummies
  0-470-04849-2
- Office 2007 For Dummies
  0-470-00923-3

- Outlook 2007 For Dummies
  0-470-03830-6
- PCs For Dummies
  0-7645-8958-X
- Salesforce.com For Dummies
  0-470-04893-X
- Upgrading & Fixing Laptops For Dummies
  0-7645-8959-8
- Word 2007 For Dummies
  0-470-03658-3
- Quicken 2007 For Dummies
  0-470-04600-7

FOOD, HOME, GARDEN, HOBBIES, MUSIC & PETS

0-7645-8404-9   0-7645-9904-6

Also available:

- Candy Making For Dummies
  0-7645-9734-5
- Card Games For Dummies
  0-7645-9910-0
- Crocheting For Dummies
  0-7645-4151-X
- Dog Training For Dummies
  0-7645-8418-9
- Healthy Carb Cookbook For Dummies
  0-7645-8476-6
- Home Maintenance For Dummies
  0-7645-5215-5

- Horses For Dummies
  0-7645-9797-3
- Jewelry Making & Beading For Dummies
  0-7645-2571-9
- Orchids For Dummies
  0-7645-6759-4
- Puppies For Dummies
  0-7645-5255-4
- Rock Guitar For Dummies
  0-7645-5356-9
- Sewing For Dummies
  0-7645-6847-7
- Singing For Dummies
  0-7645-2475-5

INTERNET & DIGITAL MEDIA

0-470-04529-9   0-470-04894-8

Also available:

- Blogging For Dummies
  0-471-77084-1
- Digital Photography For Dummies
  0-7645-9802-3
- Digital Photography All-in-One Desk Reference For Dummies
  0-470-03743-1
- Digital SLR Cameras and Photography For Dummies
  0-7645-9803-1
- eBay Business All-in-One Desk Reference For Dummies
  0-7645-8438-3
- HDTV For Dummies
  0-470-09673-X

- Home Entertainment PCs For Dummies
  0-470-05523-5
- MySpace For Dummies
  0-470-09529-6
- Search Engine Optimization For Dummies
  0-471-97998-8
- Skype For Dummies
  0-470-04891-3
- The Internet For Dummies
  0-7645-8996-2
- Wiring Your Digital Home For Dummies
  0-471-91830-X

Separate Canadian edition also available
Separate U.K. edition also available

Available wherever books are sold. For more information or to order direct: U.S. customers visit www.dummies.com or call 1-877-762-2974.
U.K. customers visit www.wileyeurope.com or call 0800 243407. Canadian customers visit www.wiley.ca or call 1-800-567-4797.

SPORTS, FITNESS, PARENTING, RELIGION & SPIRITUALITY

0-471-76871-5

0-7645-7841-3

Also available:
- Catholicism For Dummies
  0-7645-5391-7
- Exercise Balls For Dummies
  0-7645-5623-1
- Fitness For Dummies
  0-7645-7851-0
- Football For Dummies
  0-7645-3936-1
- Judaism For Dummies
  0-7645-5299-6
- Potty Training For Dummies
  0-7645-5417-4
- Buddhism For Dummies
  0-7645-5359-3

- Pregnancy For Dummies
  0-7645-4483-7 †
- Ten Minute Tone-Ups For Dummies
  0-7645-7207-5
- NASCAR For Dummies
  0-7645-7681-X
- Religion For Dummies
  0-7645-5264-3
- Soccer For Dummies
  0-7645-5229-5
- Women in the Bible For Dummies
  0-7645-8475-8

TRAVEL

0-7645-7749-2

0-7645-6945-7

Also available:
- Alaska For Dummies
  0-7645-7746-8
- Cruise Vacations For Dummies
  0-7645-6941-4
- England For Dummies
  0-7645-4276-1
- Europe For Dummies
  0-7645-7529-5
- Germany For Dummies
  0-7645-7823-5
- Hawaii For Dummies
  0-7645-7402-7

- Italy For Dummies
  0-7645-7386-1
- Las Vegas For Dummies
  0-7645-7382-9
- London For Dummies
  0-7645-4277-X
- Paris For Dummies
  0-7645-7630-5
- RV Vacations For Dummies
  0-7645-4442-X
- Walt Disney World & Orlando
  For Dummies
  0-7645-9660-8

GRAPHICS, DESIGN & WEB DEVELOPMENT

0-7645-8815-X

0-7645-9571-7

Also available:
- 3D Game Animation For Dummies
  0-7645-8789-7
- AutoCAD 2006 For Dummies
  0-7645-8925-3
- Building a Web Site For Dummies
  0-7645-7144-3
- Creating Web Pages For Dummies
  0-470-08030-2
- Creating Web Pages All-in-One Desk
  Reference For Dummies
  0-7645-4345-8
- Dreamweaver 8 For Dummies
  0-7645-9649-7

- InDesign CS2 For Dummies
  0-7645-9572-5
- Macromedia Flash 8 For Dummies
  0-7645-9691-8
- Photoshop CS2 and Digital
  Photography For Dummies
  0-7645-9580-6
- Photoshop Elements 4 For Dummies
  0-471-77483-9
- Syndicating Web Sites with RSS Feeds
  For Dummies
  0-7645-8848-6
- Yahoo! SiteBuilder For Dummies
  0-7645-9800-7

NETWORKING, SECURITY, PROGRAMMING & DATABASES

0-7645-7728-X

0-471-74940-0

Also available:
- Access 2007 For Dummies
  0-470-04612-0
- ASP.NET 2 For Dummies
  0-7645-7907-X
- C# 2005 For Dummies
  0-7645-9704-3
- Hacking For Dummies
  0-470-05235-X
- Hacking Wireless Networks
  For Dummies
  0-7645-9730-2
- Java For Dummies
  0-470-08716-1

- Microsoft SQL Server 2005 For Dummies
  0-7645-7755-7
- Networking All-in-One Desk Reference
  For Dummies
  0-7645-9939-9
- Preventing Identity Theft For Dummies
  0-7645-7336-5
- Telecom For Dummies
  0-471-77085-X
- Visual Studio 2005 All-in-One Desk
  Reference For Dummies
  0-7645-9775-2
- XML For Dummies
  0-7645-8845-1

HEALTH & SELF-HELP

0-7645-8450-2

0-7645-4149-8

Also available:
- Bipolar Disorder For Dummies
  0-7645-8451-0
- Chemotherapy and Radiation
  For Dummies
  0-7645-7832-4
- Controlling Cholesterol For Dummies
  0-7645-5440-9
- Diabetes For Dummies
  0-7645-6820-5* †
- Divorce For Dummies
  0-7645-8417-0 †

- Fibromyalgia For Dummies
  0-7645-5441-7
- Low-Calorie Dieting For Dummies
  0-7645-9905-4
- Meditation For Dummies
  0-471-77774-9
- Osteoporosis For Dummies
  0-7645-7621-6
- Overcoming Anxiety For Dummies
  0-7645-5447-6
- Reiki For Dummies
  0-7645-9907-0
- Stress Management For Dummies
  0-7645-5144-2

EDUCATION, HISTORY, REFERENCE & TEST PREPARATION

0-7645-8381-6

0-7645-9554-7

Also available:
- The ACT For Dummies
  0-7645-9652-7
- Algebra For Dummies
  0-7645-5325-9
- Algebra Workbook For Dummies
  0-7645-8467-7
- Astronomy For Dummies
  0-7645-8465-0
- Calculus For Dummies
  0-7645-2498-4
- Chemistry For Dummies
  0-7645-5430-1
- Forensics For Dummies
  0-7645-5580-4

- Freemasons For Dummies
  0-7645-9796-5
- French For Dummies
  0-7645-5193-0
- Geometry For Dummies
  0-7645-5324-0
- Organic Chemistry I For Dummies
  0-7645-6902-3
- The SAT I For Dummies
  0-7645-7193-1
- Spanish For Dummies
  0-7645-5194-9
- Statistics For Dummies
  0-7645-5423-9

Get smart @ dummies.com®

- **Find a full list of Dummies titles**
- **Look into loads of FREE on-site articles**
- **Sign up for FREE eTips e-mailed to you weekly**
- **See what other products carry the Dummies name**
- **Shop directly from the Dummies bookstore**
- **Enter to win new prizes every month!**

Separate Canadian edition also available
Separate U.K. edition also available

vailable wherever books are sold. For more information or to order direct: U.S. customers visit www.dummies.com or call 1-877-762-2974.
.K. customers visit www.wileyeurope.com or call 0800 243407. Canadian customers visit www.wiley.ca or call 1-800-567-4797.